How to Read a Japanese Poem

How to Read a Japanese Poem

Steven D. Carter

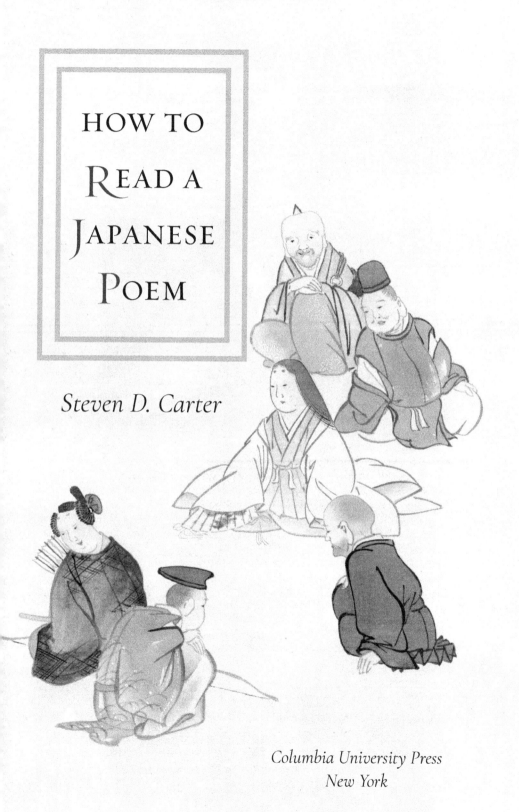

Columbia University Press
New York

COLUMBIA
UNIVERSITY
PRESS

Columbia University Press gratefully acknowledges the generous support for this book provided by Publisher's Circle member Bruno A. Quinson.

Columbia University Press wishes to express its appreciation for assistance given by the Pushkin Fund in the publication of this book.

Columbia University Press
Publishers Since 1893
New York   Chichester, West Sussex
cup.columbia.edu
Copyright © 2019 Columbia University Press
All rights reserved

Library of Congress Cataloging-in-Publication Data
Names: Carter, Steven D., author.
Title: How to read a Japanese poem / Steven D. Carter.
Description: New York : Columbia University Press, [2019] | Includes bibliographical references and index.
Identifiers: LCCN 2018032537 (print) | LCCN 2018052344 (ebook) | ISBN 9780231546850 (electronic) | ISBN 9780231186827 | ISBN 9780231186827 (cloth) | ISBN 9780231186834 (paperback) | ISBN 9780231546850 (electronic)
Subjects: LCSH: Japanese poetry—History and criticism. | Japanese poetry—Appreciation.
Classification: LCC PL727 (ebook) | LCC PL727 .C37 2019 (print) | DDC 895.6109—dc23
LC record available at https://lccn.loc.gov/2018032537

Cover design: Lisa Hamm

Cover image: © The Trustees of the British Museum. Art attributed to Suzuki Harunobu. 1765 to 1770, Meiwa Era. A portrait of the poetess, Ono no Komachi.

Title page image: Gift of Sebastian Izzard and Masaharu Nagano, in memory of T. Richard Fishbein, 2014. Metropolitan Museum of Art. *The Six Immortal Poets*, Kubo Shunman (Japanese, 1757-1820) , and others. Edo Period.

For Caroline and Mia

not coarse, hard
things last
longest, perhaps,

but fine, very fine:
if only the wind
could take letters

from "Tombstones" by A. R. Ammons

CONTENTS

Acknowledgments xi

Introduction 1

Chapter 1 Ancient Song and Poetry 17

Chapter 2 Long Poems and Short Poems 41

Chapter 3 Popular Songs 95

Chapter 4 Linked Verse 107

Chapter 5 Unorthodox Poems 135

Chapter 6 Comic Poems 175

Chapter 7 Poems in Chinese 189

Appendix 1: Technical Terms 203

Appendix 2: Aesthetic Ideals and Devices 215

Notes 273

Sources of Japanese Texts 279

Selected Bibliography 287

Index of Japanese Names, Titles, and Terms 305

Photo section follows page 172

ACKNOWLEDGMENTS

As always, I thank my wife, Mary, for her support and good advice, kindly given.

I would like to acknowledge the assistance and inspiration I have received from my many mentors in the study of Japanese poetry over the years, especially Professors Helen Craig McCullough, Kaneko Kinjirō, Robert H. Brower, Earl Miner, Edwin Cranston, and Iwasa Miyoko. Also due thanks are the participants in a reading group involving faculty, postdoctoral fellows, and students that I led at Stanford University over a number of years involving Christina Laffin, Rebecca Corbett, LeRon Harrison, Jeffrey Knott, Caroline Akiko Wake, Nancy Hamilton, and Lisa Wilcut. Many of the pages in this book got their first reading on those Friday afternoons, and I gained greatly from the comments and suggestions offered around our table. Any mistakes that remain in the book are of course mine alone.

Two anonymous readers for Columbia University Press made a number of helpful suggestions, for which I am duly grateful. I also thank Jack Stoneman for assistance with illustrations and Christine Dunbar, Leslie Kriesel, Christian Winting, and the whole staff at Columbia University Press for their tireless efforts to shepherd a very complex manuscript through the editing process.

Late Edo-period painting by Kubo Shunman of a woman at a writing desk.

Courtesy Metropolitan Museum of Art and Marjorie H. Holden Gift, 2012.

INTRODUCTION

Poets asked to define poetry, especially good poetry, often throw up their hands. "I can no more define poetry," said A. E. Housman, "than a terrier can define a rat."[1] The medieval Japanese poet Shōtetsu (1381-1459) says something similar, albeit less colorfully: "A truly excellent poem is beyond logic.... One cannot explain it in words; it can only be experienced of itself."[2] With that in mind, my title, *How to Read a Japanese Poem*, may seem a bit audacious. How does one dare to tell people how to read poetry if it is hard to even define what poetry is?

So perhaps my project would be better stated as, "How to *begin to* read a Japanese poem." My purpose is not to dictate a destination but to give a few signposts as readers walk the road. This book, then, offers my advice on how to approach Japanese poems in traditional forms, according largely to analytical methods established by Japanese poets, scholars, and critics over the centuries. Obviously there are other ways to approach such a task, but this one seems to me a wise one for beginners.

Each of my seven chapters focuses on separate genres of Japanese poetry and proceeds by analyzing examples in chronological order. In each case, I first give short notes about authorship, along with other details of context, including variously the time of composition, physical setting, social occasion, and textual setting—things to which particular attention has habitually been given by participants in Japanese poetic discourse from the earliest times. Then I move on to a short commentary. My decision to proceed from context to commentary is dictated by a central feature of Japanese poetic discourse—namely, that poems are so often occasional. In other words, Japanese poems were often written in specific situations—social, political, and historical situations, in the broad sense—that need to be described for them to be understood in their own milieu.

Throughout the book, I employ the technical vocabulary of Japanese poetic discourse to frame my comments. Thus readers not familiar with the subject will encounter new technical terms such as *kakekotoba* (pivot word) and *honkadori* (allusive variation), the meanings of which should become clear through usage. (For those who want more detail, I have included appendixes.) Beyond that, however, I have not been bashful about using other terms that are of broader scope, such as "metaphor," "symbol," and "prosody." While reducing Japanese poems to some Platonic notion of poetry writ large would be a mistake, not showing ways in which Japanese poetry is similar to poetry in other cultures would be equally foolish.

GENRES

Terminologies always do some harm to what they are meant to represent, and this is particularly true in the study of Japanese poetry. Throughout history, for instance, Japanese poets, critics, and scholars have often used the generic terms *waka* and *uta* almost interchangeably in reference to Japanese poetry in a general sense, while confusingly using those same terms to refer specifically to the highly canonical 5-7-5-7-7 genre that remained central to poetic discourse from the 700s to the 1800s. For the sake of clarity, in this book I use *uta* in reference to the general category of Japanese poetry and *waka* in the narrower sense of thirty-one-syllable poem—a defensible choice, I believe, however much it rankles the medievalist in me personally.[3] The first six of my chapters are in that sense devoted to what might be termed subgenres within *uta* as an overarching but untidy discourse, in the rough chronological order in which they emerge in history: *kodai kayō* (ancient song), *chōka* (long poem), *waka* (short poem), *kayō* (popular song), *renga* (linked verse), *haikai* (unorthodox poems), *kyōka* (comic *waka*), and *senryū* (comic *haikai*). I have also included a chapter on Chinese poems by Japanese poets (*kanshi*; also *karauta*, in contrast to *yamatouta*), a genre that was intertwined with Japanese-language poems throughout its long history. If this conception seems confusing I can only say that it is no more so than the reality I am trying to represent.

 Kodai kayō 古代歌謡 (ancient song) refers to our earliest Japanese poetic texts, usually called songs (the Japanese term used is, again, and frustratingly, *uta*) because they were often sung to instrumental accompaniment. The reader will notice, however, that on the page they often look no different from *chōka* or *waka* and use many of the same rhetorical techniques. By grouping all these forms—songs, *chōka*, and *waka*—together in a beginning chapter I am suggesting that in the earliest times the boundaries between them were not yet solid. However, as it is common practice to refer to these forms as they appear in early texts like *Kojiki* (*Record of Ancient Matters*, 712) as "songs" while referring to later examples in *Man'yōshū* (*Collection of*

Ten Thousand Leaves, ca. 759) and later texts as not songs but *chōka* or *waka*, I follow that practice here.

Chōka 長歌 (also read *nagauta*; literally, "long poem") are poems of indeterminate length, made up of alternating 5- and 7-syllable lines, concluding with a final 7-7-syllable couplet and often accompanied by a separate *hanka*, or "envoy," in 5-7-5-7-7 format. Poems of irregular prosody mostly predate the standardized form as employed in its heyday by Kakinomoto no Hitomaro (fl. ca. 680–700), Yamabe no Akahito (early eighth century), and others around the turn of the eighth century. At its zenith, the *chōka* allowed for more variety of subject matter than the *waka* form, but from the late ninth century on the *chōka* was employed primarily for elegies. Our primary sources for *chōka* are early histories and chronicles, the *Man'yōshū* and later imperial anthologies (*chokusenshū*), and the collections (*shū*) of individual poets. Poets writing in the form tend to employ parallelism and other kinds of repetitive syntax, formulaic phrasing such as fixed epithets or modifiers (*makurakotoba*, "pillow words"), and homophones and puns (*kakekotoba*) that function as syntactic pivots joining two predicates or clauses.

Waka 和歌 (also referred to as *tanka* 短歌, meaning literally "short poem") are poems of five lines, following the syllabic pattern 5-7-5-7-7, with a caesura appearing at the end of any line but most often at the end of the third line. Our earliest examples of *waka* come from the same time as our earliest *chōka*, and most of the writers of the latter wrote in both forms. The general topics of love and the four seasons dominate the *waka* canon from the eighth century onward, but other broad topics also appear, such as travel, Buddhism, and lamentation, and poems were also written in the context of correspondence and for ritual occasions. Our primary sources for *waka* are various kinds and sizes of collections, including those of individual poets, salons, or other kinds of groups, the largest being an entire "court" memorialized in an imperial anthology. Also important are poems inscribed on screen paintings, poems composed for poem contests, and poems contained in prose works (histories, tales, diaries, travel records, critical writings, etc.). Poets writing in the *waka* form employ parallelism only rarely but do use pillow words, pivot words, and other kinds of wordplay, while also using elliptical phrasing and other devices that allow for semantic expansion, such as borrowing phrases or lines from earlier poems.

Kayō 歌謡 (popular song): Throughout history, poems in Chinese or Japanese were often chanted. However, we also know that popular songs—i.e., lyrics written to be sung melodically or to instrumental accompaniment (*kayō*)—were a feature of Japanese culture from the earliest times. Four of the major subgenres are *saibara* (folk song), some of which may have had Chinese origins; *kagurauta* (sacred song), associated with Shinto rituals; *taueuta* (rice-planting song); and *imayō* (modern song) of the sort popular among the nobility from the mid-1100s onward. Later, beginning in the late medieval era, came *kouta*, or "little songs," a term that is also used to refer to songs to samisen accompaniment in the Edo period, which for reasons of length I have not included here. Songs often consist of alternating 5- and 7-syllable lines but are of varying length. That we rarely know their authorship hints that they evolved over time and changed greatly as they circulated. Topics are also various, but in a general way Japanese songs tend to express emotions of all sorts, from elation or passion to amazement or frustration. As is the case in other forms, love is a common subtheme, but all one can say beyond that is that songs tend to document the vicissitudes of human existence, often humorously and in dramatic terms.

Renga 連歌 (also read *tsuraneuta*; literally, "linked verse") are made up of alternating long (5-7-5) and short (7-7) stanzas, any two of which would make up a *waka*, in formal terms. At its zenith in the late fourteenth through the mid-sixteenth centuries, the standard form of *renga* was one hundred verses (a form known as the *hyakuin*). Generally speaking, *hyakuin* were composed by a group of poets at a sitting, although for practice and sometimes on social occasions poets often composed just *tsukeku* (linked "couplets" or simply "links"), which is in that sense the basic unit of *renga* composition. *Renga* collections, whether made up of works by one poet or many, generally offer only *tsukeku* and *hokku*, or "first verses." In a broad sense, the subject matter of the subgenre is the same as the subject matter for *waka*, although some variations in vocabulary and thematic material did occur over time. There were elaborate rules (*shikimoku*) involved in directing the composition of a sequence, the aesthetic and social purposes of which include thematic variety and highly regulated change. Many full *hyakuin* remain from the early 1400s onward, and the record also includes two imperially commissioned anthologies and the collections of the works by individual poets. Also important are *tsukeku* and *hokku* included in diaries and critical works. *Renga* poets use all the literary devices mentioned for *waka* and, as one might expect given the shortness of the form, go farther in the direction of enjambment and elliptical phrasing.

Haikai 俳諧 is a word used to refer to both "unorthodox" and "humorous" sequences and to the first verses (*hokku*) of such sequences. Links or first verses involving wordplay or bawdy subject matter were produced in *renga* meetings from the earliest days of that genre, but they began to be recorded and anthologized only around 1500, and then usually without their author's names being recorded. Not long after that, some *renga* masters became known for their *haikai* efforts and developed a new subgenre—*haikai renku*—"*haikai* linked verse"—that in time gained its own canons that departed from those for *waka* and *renga* and were in that sense unorthodox. The standard venue of composition was the *hyakuin*, although from around the time of Matsuo Bashō (1644-1694) the *kasen*, or thirty-six-verse form, gained acceptance. Composition of *tsukeku* for practice (*maekuzuke*) was common; later on, as first verses gained independent artistic status, *hokku* contests were also important. Our source for *haikai* is again collections of various kinds (although there are no imperial anthologies of the form), along with the collections of individual poets and poems appearing in prose works, especially travel journals and critical writings. Since compiling and publishing (in woodblock-print editions) collections including the work of one's disciples was a major practice of *haikai* masters, the written record for the genre dwarfs the written record for earlier forms. Ellipsis, enjambment, and punning and other kinds of wordplay are mainstays of *haikai*, as are various forms of (sometimes) outlandish metaphor, while allusive variations on lines from classical poems are less frequent. In the work of Bashō and many other *haikai* poets, the word "unorthodox" applies only in the way the genre allowed common vocabulary unacceptable in formal *waka* and *renga*.

Kyōka 狂歌 and *senryū* 川柳 (the latter also being called *zappai* 雑俳 and *kyōku* 狂句) are comic forms of *waka* and *haikai*. Humorous poems in Japanese appear from the earliest times, in all genres, but it is in the medieval era that various identifiable genres begin to appear in the historical record. *Kyōka* refers to comic *waka*, a subgenre of some prominence already in the 1500s that reached its heyday in the eighteenth and nineteenth centuries. *Senryū* is a genre that developed within the larger tradition of *haikai* and refers specifically to *haikai tsukeku* and *hokku* without the obligatory season words of their parent genre, composed from the early 1700s to the present. Elaborate punning, parody, and risqué humor are the mainstays of comic poetry, which comes down to us mostly in the form of large collections. Poets writing humorous poems tend to rely heavily on punning and other kinds of wordplay.

Kanshi 漢詩 is used in this book in reference to Chinese poems written by Japanese poets. From early times competence in written Chinese was a virtual requirement for most official service, and the Japanese imperial court (and later samurai governments) used Chinese in court documents. This was also true of Buddhist institutions. It should come as no surprise, then, that some of our earliest collections of poetry by Japanese authors are written not in Japanese but in Chinese or that many poets writing *waka* also wrote poems in Chinese. This tradition continued among government officials and clerics even during times when for political reasons contact with the continent was minimal. During the medieval period, Chinese poems by Zen monks were particularly prominent, while the same could be said for Chinese poems by Confucian scholars during the Edo period. As to subgenres, Japanese poets wrote in all forms, including the ancient *shi* (poems of indeterminate length made up of four-character lines), but favored mostly the *lüshi* ("regulated verse," containing four or eight lines of five, six, or seven characters) and the *jueju* (quatrains of two couplets of five or seven characters). Our sources for *kanshi* include large collections from all periods of Japanese history, as well as the collections of individual poets, poems quoted in prose works, inscriptions, etc. The devices of parallelism and repetition are major features of *kanshi*, but other devices basic to Japanese poetry—pillow words and pivot words, for example—do not appear.

The canon of Japanese poetry is immense and includes forms not introduced here, such as the poetic sections of Japanese Noh or *jōruri* plays or epic tales. But I have aimed for variety in every other way. Rather than concentrating only on canonical figures, I have also included lesser-known poets; and rather than only the most well-known genres—the thirty-one-syllable *waka* and the seventeen-syllable *hokku* (what we now call haiku)—I have also included poems in Chinese by Japanese poets (*kanshi*), long poems (*chōka*), linked verse (*renga*), comic poems, and a short book of popular songs. Though each of these subgenres has its own discourse, the resonances among them are numerous. My hope is that readers will come away with a sense of the great variety of the canon and the richness and diversity of Japanese poetic expression.

KEYWORDS

Readers will find an abundance of further introductory material in my analyses of specific poems. As an encouragement to those who want to begin with a greater sense of the broader characteristics of Japanese poetry, however, I offer the following seven musings, each illustrated by poems, as enticements to reflection. Basically, my thoughts concentrate on seven keywords that I find myself returning to again and again when reading Japanese poems: courtly elegance, ellipsis, context, intertextuality, Buddhist stoicism, natural icons, and rhetorical play.

Our earliest examples of Japanese poetry were collected by officers of the imperial court, and courtly ideals of rhetoric, decorum, diction, and proper subject matter would remain important throughout poetic history, just as the court would remain a potent cultural force long after it had lost much of its political power. Although the term *miyabi*, usually translated as "courtly elegance," does not appear as often as many other aesthetic terms in commentaries and critical writings, there can be no doubt that the ideals behind it—decorous language and subject matter and avoidance of anything smacking of vulgarity—were important in one way or another for nearly all poets writing well into the Edo period. Thus even the warrior-poet Kinoshita Chōshōshi (1569-1649), who is known for being somewhat unconventional, produced mostly poems like this one from his personal collection *Kyohakushū* (The Kyohaku collection, 1649; no. 1511):

"From among ten poems he composed at a hut named Toba View in the Eastern Hills"

Far and near	ochikochi no
the low slopes of the mountains	yamamoto shiroku
are white with rising mist,	tatsu kiri ni
but on the paddies at Toba	tobata no omo wa
the moon is shining clear.	tsuki zo sayakeki

Chōshōshi was known as an independent figure, but this poem shows that when presented with a famous landscape—the paddies at Toba, now Minami-ku, between Kyoto and Fushimi—he resorted automatically to established courtly rhetoric and imagery from the imperial anthologies. There, a half dozen poems include the phrase *tobata no omo* (on the surface of the Toba paddies). Furthermore, every phrase in his poem except for *yamamoto shiroku tatsu* (mountains / white with rising mist) has numerous precedents.

Another poem by the same poet drives the point home. This one, from his *Unaimatsu* (Grave-marking pine, no. 297), is about the death of a daughter, the sort of event for which we might anticipate a less-conventional response. As it turns out, however, Chōshōshi again turns to courtly habits:

I fell asleep	omoitsutsu
thinking about her, and yet—	nuru yo mo au to
she did not appear.	mienu kana
In this world of ours, the dead	yume made hito ya
go even from our dreams.	naki yo naruran

Here the poet draws on an old trope more common in love poems, where thinking of someone while falling asleep might lead to meeting in dreams. But there is nothing iconoclastic in his conception, which is not a gut-wrenching cry of grief but a model of understatement that invokes courtly habits of mind.

In the late-medieval period and on into the Edo period, courtly ideals faded in significance in many ways. Yet the *dai* (topics) of new genres like *haikai* and various forms of comic poetry can often be traced back to courtly precedents, and poets frequently employed parody—always a gesture toward established convention, as a poem from the early haikai collection *Enokoshū* (Mongrel-puppy collection, 1633; no. 1129) by the *haikai* master Matsunaga Teitoku (1571-1653) from the early *haikai* collection demonstrates.

It is the cause	*minahito no*
of all these people napping–	*hirune no tane ya*
the autumn moon.	*aki no tsuki*

Moon viewing was not just a courtly practice, of course, but the centrality of the image of the autumn moon in court poetry cannot be denied, and the humor of the poem obviously plays on a contrast between elegant cause and vulgar effect.

Japanese poems are relatively short, the most famous genres being just seventeen or thirty-one syllables in length. Even the so-called long poems are not truly long. (The longest of the long poems presented in this book, Hitomaro's poem on passing the ruins at Ōmi, is just forty-seven lines.) Scholars point to linguistic reasons for this. Whatever the cause(s), the fact of brevity remains and is connected to a number of phenomena, the most prominent being a trend toward ellipsis and economy of expression, and minimalist rhetoric. For instance, the many suffixes relating to tense, mood, gender, and status that are so important in classical Japanese prose are mostly absent in poetry. Even grammatical subject and point of view must often be inferred from context. But that is not all. In addition to syntactic and grammatical ellipsis, Japanese poetry often displays semantic ellipsis, as is apparent in even a quite ordinary *hokku* from *Taigi kusen* (A selection of *hokku* by Taigi, 1707; no. 707) by Tan Taigi (1709-1771).

For a thief	*nusubito ni*
they ring the temple bell.	*kane tsuku tera ya*
Winter grove.	*fuyu kodachi*

Here the particle *ni* (a versatile particle that can be a locative or directional case particle, a conjunctive indicating cause or contrast, a copular particle or an intensifier, and other things) is rather vague. It is historical knowledge that tells us it probably means that someone at the temple is ringing the bell as an alarm, "because of" a thief. And the last line is literally a noun fragment with no predicate. To arrive at an interpretation of the poem one must thus deal with an elliptical statement: because of a thief, someone strikes the alarm bell, at a temple in a grove of barren trees. But so what? Is the poem just description, perhaps of an actual event? The best guess is that the poet wanted to create a human portrait of a thief finding little cover as he attempts to escape, perhaps as a way to symbolize the basic human predicament, and to show hot desperation in the cold of winter—articulating the essence of a topic being one of the chief purposes of poetry. Beyond that, one might claim that the poem is lightly humorous (something we expect of Edo *haikai*), evoking the image of people in the town around the temple being called out into the bleak winter landscape to protect community interests.

But much remains unresolved. Should we make something of the syntactic break between the first two lines and the last? Do the first two lines indicate that the *neighbors* know why the bell is being rung, or just the *monks*? And might it really imply that the neighbors are not yet outside, that perhaps they are only waking, listening, having trouble leaving their warm beds? One must conclude that one product of elliptical expression is a correspondingly high tolerance for uncertainty, as well as for values such as understatement, subtlety, suggestion, and ambiguity. The poem gives us a sound, an image, and a gesture toward the human world but leaves it at that.

As noted, reading Japanese poetry is often helped by a knowledge of context—i.e., authorship, time, social setting and place, and in many cases conventional topic (*dai*). This does not mean that poems cannot be made to signify without such information, but it does mean that without it some poems may seem opaque and superficial. Knowing context usually adds depth and triggers recognition of metaphor and symbolism. For instance, just the fact that the following Chinese poem from *Kūgeshū* (Ephemeral flowers, before 1388, p. 10) is by the Zen monk Gidō Shūshin (1325-1388) is enough to prepare us for an allegorical reading:

Sparrow in the Bamboos

He doesn't go for the grain in the storehouse,
nor does he peck holes in the landlord's place.
In the mountain groves he can make his living,
perching for the night on a tall bamboo.

Zen poems so often focus on everyday things that the sparrow is no surprise. However, knowing that Zen monks often use allegory makes it easy to see the sparrow as standing for the monk himself or Zen monks in a more general way: not men involved in the worldly affairs of "storehouses" and "landlords" but monks content to make a meager living in "mountain groves," the latter being a conventional metaphor for Zen temples. (Poetry by Zen monks is in fact called Gozan poetry, or "poetry of the Five Mountains," in reference to the governing temples of the Rinzai Zen sect.) And if we know that Gidō was in fact not some obscure mountain dweller but a high-ranking cleric, we can go even further and surmise that his poem is not meant literally at all but as a highly literary portrait of the poet as above the administrative affairs that were in fact the substance of his everyday life.

In addition to authorship, time, and place, many Japanese poems also rely on intertextual references (often in the form of explicit allusion, or *honkadori*) that may be seen as another kind of context. Perhaps this is a universal feature of poetry in the sense that Wordsworth's sonnets gesture toward Shakespeare and Shakespeare's toward Petrarch. In the case of Japanese poetry, however, the gestures are frequently so obvious that we are meant to apprehend them as part of our first experience of the poem. Also, in a general way such gestures toward past tradition are a constant of Japanese poetic culture, in the way that certain famous gardens incorporate the "borrowed landscape" around them as part of their expression. Thus a two-verse *renga* link from *Chikurinshō* (Poems from the bamboo grove, 1476; no. 1264) by the *renga* master Shinkei (1406-1475) "borrows" as a backdrop the following passage from *The Ten-Foot Square Hut* (*Hōjōki*, p. 22) by Kamo no Chōmei (1153-1216) in which he describes his life in the mountains outside Kyoto. "When the weather is good, I climb up to a mountain ridge where I can see the skies far off over my former home [in the city]":

| Now it is my heart | *kokoro no kayou* |
| that journeys at evening. | *yūbe ni zo naru* |

Going out, I gaze—	*tachiidete*
and cannot forget Kyoto	*miyako wasurenu*
in my mountain hut.	*mine no io*

The unknown author of the first verse here was probably not thinking of Chōmei specifically but only of someone or somewhere as evening comes on, alluding most likely to a lover. But in a comment in *Shibakusa* (Grasses on the wayside, 1470, p. 42) about his "linking poem" Shinkei tells us he was thinking of Chōmei, who wrote so thoughtfully, he says, of how difficult it is to leave memories behind. Hundreds of years had passed since Chōmei's time, and countless people had retired to the mountains around the city. The shadows of all of them crowd around Shinkei's lines, all finding it hard to put thoughts of their former lives from their minds.

In Japanese poetry, especially before the Edo period, the basic assumptions about life, its meaning, its challenges and purposes, may in the main be described as Buddhist stoicism, even when a poem is not explicitly religious in content. One reason for the prominence of natural imagery across all genres of Japanese poetry is the belief that the cycles of the natural world teach us fundamental Buddhist concepts such as constant change and transience. This is not to say that Japanese poetry is universally dark and pessimistic. (As Earl Miner pointed out nearly half a century ago, the sense of desolation is often tempered by a spirit of celebration deriving from Shinto animism.)[4] But it is to say that the appreciation of beauty or emotion is often tinged with sadness that comes from knowledge that time is fleeting and all human experience illusory (the relevant term is *mujō*). It is in this sense that one may say that irony is a constituting feature of Japanese poetry. To appreciate the splendor of the full moon is also to recognize that it must wax and wane. A *hokku* from an early *hokku* compendium (*Hokkuchō*, 1614, p. 313) by the linked-verse poet Shūkei (d. 1544) makes the point explicitly.

Falling onto moss	*chirite nao*
they glow again below:	*koke no shitateru*
autumn leaves.	*momiji kana*

Days of glory may end and still come again, but the cycles of the seasons are inevitable: the leaves will fade, as will the moss, in time. Even if nature occasionally tricks us, we know the exception from the rule. The glow of life remains a temporary thing, if more precious for that reason. Rather than despair we confront stoicism.

Anyone reading Japanese poetry quickly notices the prominence of certain recurring natural images, particularly cherry blossoms, the moon, autumn leaves, and snow, that might be termed iconic in the way they point beyond themselves toward large currents of tradition and socio-aesthetic value. And in the same way, one cannot help but notice that the range of subject matter in Japanese poetry, especially before the Edo period, seems rather narrow, involving primarily the four seasons, love, and a few miscellaneous categories such as travel and laments—usually with some human situation or predicament present, whether in the foreground or the background. Rather than dismissing these features of the canon as signifying a lack of creativity, it is worthwhile to see them as revealing the Buddhist idea of change within constancy and to appreciate the challenge of poets to take an established image or idea and somehow "make it new," even if only slightly, as the following *waka* illustrates.

"On 'lingering heat,' for a ten-poem sequence at the house of the Mikohidari major counselor"

Autumn has come,	*aki kite mo*
yet still I must use a fan	*ōgi no kaze o*
to stir the air.	*narasu kana*

> This year the season will begin
> with dewfall first of all.
>
> *kotoshi wa tsuyu ya*
> *saki ni okuran*

In the canons, cool breezes are often the first harbinger of autumn, but the author, Tonna (1289–1372), and his friends at a poetic gathering—who were the first audience for his poem (*Sōanshū* [Grass hut collection], 1359?; no. 424)—knew that sometimes the natural and poetic worlds are out of sync. Another icon would have to do. The topic "lingering heat" is suggested only by the fan, but that is enough. Such subtle manipulations of convention are an essential value in Japanese poetic discourse, where, as in this case, they become a theme in themselves.

Not surprisingly, given the prominence of Buddhist culture and concepts in the Japanese tradition, there are certain Buddhist-inspired thematic constants that arc through both form and content. The most obvious of these is wordplay, specifically punning, which expresses a strong sense of the artificiality of language. And rhetorically this same emphasis of the ultimate indeterminacy of meaning is evident in the techniques of allusion, punning, recasting, and recontextualizing, this last term referring to taking a poem from an "original" source and placing it another textual setting. Usually the sort of relativism suggested by this scenario was not truly subversive in either intent or effect. Rather, it seems to have encouraged a sense of stoicism that comes across in poems in mild rather than stark ways. It is also noteworthy that in a corpus that involves so much rhetorical play, one of the highest terms of praise encountered in poetic commentary and criticism is *ushin*, "sincere feeling." The two terms are not always antithetical, but the tension between them is again a constituting feature of much Japanese poetry. Sometimes the tension is literally the subject of a poem, as in a *hokku* from *Sarumino* (The monkey's straw raincoat, 1691; no. 1861) by the *haikai* poet Nozawa Bonchō (d. 1714):

> Something makes a sound.
> Fallen over, by himself—
> a scarecrow.
>
> *mono no oto*
> *hitori taoruru*
> *kakashi kana*

There is something innately humorous (and spooky) about a scarecrow: a trickster and impostor that looks like us but is not. And Bonchō's poem involves humor as well, arising from the personification involved in saying the scarecrow falls "by himself" (*hitori*). But can one claim personification when an object was created to stand for a person to begin with? Whatever our response, the brief smile of the speaker ends in lonely silence. If he had hoped the sound might signal a visitor, he is in fact left as solitary as the scarecrow, a creature of wood and cloth who cannot share his feelings. The metaphor is unmasked as metaphor, a likeness and nothing more, creating a poem that is playful on the surface but full of feeling at its core.

Of course the preceding list of key words and concepts is not exhaustive. But looking at a final poem through the lens they provide shows how keeping them in mind can be useful. It is a thirty-one-syllable poem from *Kakanshū* (The hazy gate collection, 1793?; no. 469) by an eighteenth-century woman we know as the Wife of Yoshimasa, a woman of samurai background married to a bureaucrat.

"Written on the fifteenth day of the Eighth Month"

From a past unseen	*minu mukashi*
and on into a future	*mizaran nochi mo*
I shall never see—	*kawaraji na*
ever unchanging is the light	*nadataru aki no*
of the renowned autumn moon.	*tsuki no hikari wa*

A simple poem? Yes, in a way, for it may be read as praise for the beauty of the full moon that contains no metaphors, indeed no figurative language at all. But attention to the key words and concepts listed in the preceding helps tease more signification out of the poem. The references to an undifferentiated past and future, for instance, are obviously elliptical, even with the contextual information provided by a headnote that gives us crucial temporal orientation. Furthermore, there is a natural icon from the courtly tradition of elegant expression at the center of the poem, the moon—in this case the full moon, which gestures intertextually toward a long tradition of poems about that image. Nor can it be denied that the poem expresses a tension between permanence and impermanence that is at the heart of the Buddhist worldview. And finally, the poem is also rhetorically playful in the way it draws attention to how the moon may be unchanging, but we—who are in a moment in time between the past and the present, both beyond our sight—are not. Beautiful but also cold and aloof, the moon shines down from above, renowned because it is not subject to the cycles of life that human beings must endure below.

A NOTE ABOUT TRANSLATION

Japanese poems have customarily been recorded in a variety of formats. Here I have followed practices of lineation that have been dominant among translators for many years. In other words, I break poems into lines using an alternating scheme of long and short lines based on the genre in question—five lines in the case of *waka*, three in the case of haiku, and so on. (Historically, Japanese poems were recorded on paper in a variety of formats that practical considerations make too difficult for me to reproduce.) Whenever possible, I also try to adhere to the image order of the originals. In order to show continuity across time and genres, I anchor each of the lines of my translations on the left, with no indentation. For the benefit of students who want to see the poems in Japanese, I have included both Romanized and original *kanji-kana* texts of the poems I analyze in the individual entries that make up the body of the book. Rather than embark on the quixotic task of guessing at the pronunciation of the *kanji* and *kana* in each historical period, I have Romanized texts as one would modern Japanese.

A NOTE ON NAMES

In most scholarly and reference works, Japanese poets are referred to not by their full names (clan or family name plus given name) but by their given names or pen names: thus the medieval poet Fujiwara no Teika is usually referred to as Teika, his given name (which confusingly can also be read Sadaie); and the *haikai* master Matsuo Bashō is usually referred to as Bashō, one of his sobriquets (he had others: Tōsei being the most prominent one). But it should be noted that even a cursory survey of standard works reveals a diversity of practices that makes it impossible to establish a useful rule. (An example: the *renga* master Chiun, who was of the Ninagawa lineage, is nonetheless usually referred to not as Ninagawa Chiun but as simply Chiun, while the modern poet Masaoka Shiki is often referred to by his full name.) To compensate for the confusion, I have used cross-references in the index.

I should also note that there is not uniformity concerning the pronunciation of many names. Until recently, for example, the name of the *renga* poet that I have here rendered as Kenzai tended to be read as Kensai; and in the case of another *renga* poet, Kyūzei, there are two other variants—Kyūsei and Gusai. Insofar as possible, I have followed examples in the most recent reference works.

In the body of this book (chapters 1–7), I give full names in the first instance and thereafter allude to them by their given names or pen names, and I do the same for other people mentioned in the text. In the appendixes, I follow that same practice in each separate entry.

HEADNOTES, TOPICS, AND TITLES

In most original sources, Japanese poems are introduced with headnotes (*kotobagaki*) that offer various kinds of contextual information, including such things as time and place of composition, along with the poem's topic (*dai*) or title, whenever relevant. The distinction between topics and titles is important. *Dai* were conventional, prescribed topics, usually assigned to the poet to treat before actual composition, whereas titles were often assigned after composition. In this book, I translate full headnotes as often as possible, placing them in quotation marks ("Written on the fifteenth day of the Eighth Month"). I also place *dai* in quotation marks: "Snow in front of a shrine." In the case of a *dai* appearing as just part of a headnote, the *dai* is given in single quotation marks, as in "From his many poems on 'blossoms.'" For more details on *dai*, see the appendixes.

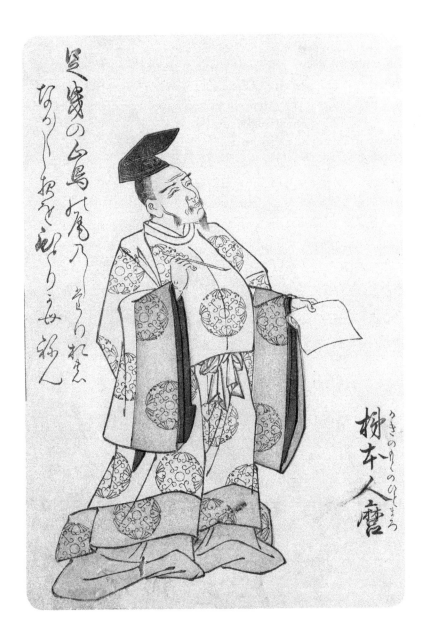

Portrait of Man'yō-era poet Kakinomoto no Hitomaro, from *Nishiki hyakunin isshu azuma ori*, an illustrated text of *Hyakunin isshu* by the eighteenth-century artist Katsukawa Shunshō.

Courtesy L. Tom Perry Special Collection, HBLL, Brigham Young University.

Chapter 1

ANCIENT SONG AND POETRY

ANONYMOUS, *Kojiki* 10: "A song that was a signal for the men of Kume to strike down the men of the Earth Spider clan"

Ah, the great pit	osaka no
at Osaka:	ōmuroya ni
so many the men	hito sawa ni
who have come here,	kiiriori
so many the men	hito sawa ni
who here band together!	iriori to mo
Yet the Kume men	mitsumitsushi
so famed for valor—	kume no ko ga
clubs they will take up	kubutsutsu i
and swords with pommels of stone,	ishitsutsu i mochi
to strike all a fatal blow.	uchite shi yamamu

Envoy

You Kume men	mitsumitsushi
so famed for valor:	kume no kora ga
clubs you must take up	kubutsutsu i
and swords with pommels of stone—	ishitsutsu i mochi
for now is the time to strike!	ima utaba yorashi

忍坂の大室屋に人多に来入り居り人多に入り居りともみつみつし久米の子等が頭椎石椎もち撃ちてし止まむみつみつし久米の子が頭椎石椎もち今撃たば宜し

CONTEXT: This song comes from one of the earliest Japanese writings, *Kojiki* (*Record of Ancient Matters*, 712). In *Nihon shoki* (*Chronicles of Japan*, 720) it is introduced with the following preface (pp. 203-4) concerning the mythical first emperor, Jinmu (whose reign began, according to tradition, in 660 BCE): "When he arrived at the great pit at Osaka, eighty men of the Earth Spider clan, men with tails, waited there in an unruly manner, so the child of the heavenly deity ordered a banquet to be served to them, with eighty stalwarts assigned as servers, each wearing his sword. The stalwarts were told, 'When you hear the song, cut them all down.' This was the song that signaled for them to attack."

The Kume "stalwarts" took their name from a place (near Kashiwara) on the southern edge of the Nara plain, close to Osaka.

COMMENT: Whether the first stanza is addressed to the attackers or describes their action objectively is not clear, but taken in dramatic context the final phrase *utaba yorashi* (If [you] strike now, it will be best!) suggests a second-person voice. The irregular prosody of the first stanza (5-6-5-5-5-6-5-5-5-7-7) reflects an era before standardization. A symbiotic relationship between *chōka* and song is suggested by the presence of a *makurakotoba*, *mitsumitsushi*—"robust" or "valorous"—a "pillow word" that was formulaically applied to the clan name Kume. And we also see other common syntactic structures, parallelism (lines 3–6) and repetition (9–10 repeated in 3–4 of the envoy). Martial subjects appear often in early records but thereafter virtually disappear from poetry, unless one takes into account the song sections of military tales such as *Tales of the Heike* and Noh plays.

ANONYMOUS, *Kojiki* 35–37

Yamato Takeru became a broad-winged plover, rose into the heavens, and flew toward the beach. His wives and children followed in tears, paying no heed to the bamboo grass cutting their feet. This was their song.

Up to our waists	asashinohara
we trudge through bamboo grass.	koshi nazumu
Not through the sky do *we* go,	sora wa yukazu
but on our feet.	ashi yo yuku na

This is another song, from when they waded through the sea.

Up to our waists	umiga yukeba
we trudge through the sea.	koshi nazumu

浅小竹原腰なづむ空は行かず足よ行くな

海処行けば腰なづむ大河原の植え草海処はいさよふ

浜つ千鳥浜よは行かず磯伝ふ

In the broad riverbed	ōkawara no
grasses grow,	uegusa
and in the sea	umiga wa
we drift.	isayou

A song from when the plover flew off and perched on a rock offshore:

The beach plover:	hama tsu chidori
he goes not along the beach	hama yo wa yukazu
but along rocks offshore.	isozutau

CONTEXT: In *Kojiki*, which records the deeds of early emperors and legendary and historical figures, we read the tale of Yamato Takeru, a prince and great warrior who subdued the East Country for the emerging Yamato state. Legend says that as he died he was transformed into a great white bird. In the inscription on his grave in Ise Province, he is called the White Plover.

COMMENT: Many early Japanese poems memorialize important events, public and private, and poems associated with death or death rites are common. According to legend, these songs—neither *chōka* nor *waka* in prosodic terms—were composed upon the death of a great hero of early times. Rather than a bard speaking for the state, however, we hear the dead man's family. The poems are personal and private, but each expresses the same symbolic contrast, between the freedom of the bird and the tearful toil of those left behind. In the first poem, the grievers are impeded by sharp-edged bamboo grass, in the second by the water and grasses, and in the last by the sea again and the rocks. Also in each case, the mourners are subject to danger and pain that affects their bodies. Together the poems amount to an allegory in which the mourners are mired in mortal toil and anguish while the bird soars above, oblivious to their sorrow. Cruelly, the living can still see the dead, just as we retain memories of those who have left us yet are unable to reunite with them.

PRINCE SHŌTOKU 聖徳皇子, *Man'yōshū* 415: "On his way to Takahara Well, Prince Shōtoku saw a dead man at Tatsuta Mountain and wrote this poem to express his sadness"

Were he at home,	ie naraba
he would sleep on his wife's arm,	imo ga te makamu
not a grass pillow.	kusamakura

Yet here he lies, midjourney—	tabi ni koyaseru
alas, poor traveler!	kono tabito aware

家ならば妹が手まかむ草枕旅に伏やせるこの旅人あはれ

CONTEXT: Prince Shōtoku (or Shōtoko; 572–622), regent to Empress Suiko (d. 628), was instrumental in forging strong ties to China and in the adoption of Buddhism as a state religion. This song can be traced back to a story in *Nihon shoki* (p. 198), which is probably the source for a number of other versions in medieval folktale collections, poetry anthologies, and poetic histories. There the prince comes upon a man who is starving and, giving him his own cloak, composes a song:

On Kataoka	shinateru
of the sunlit slopes,	kataokayama ni
he starves for food,	ii ni ete
lying here, overcome—	koyaseru
alas, poor traveler!	sono tabito aware
Have you not parents	oya nashi ni
who brought you into the world?	nare narikeme ya
Have you not a lord	sasu take no
who is staunch as young bamboo?	kimi wa ya naki
He starves for food,	ii ni ete
lying here, overcome—	koyaseru
alas, poor traveler!	sono tabito aware

COMMENT: Why does the poem from *Man'yōshū* (*Collection of Ten Thousand Leaves*, ca. 759) change the man encountered in *Nihon shoki* from starving to dead? One answer is that a dead man is better suited to the category of laments (*banka*), an important subgenre at the time that was linked to beliefs concerning communicating with and supplicating spirits. But another likely reason is that the *Nihon shoki* version comes from a longer story entailing the eventual death of the traveler, who is then buried by the prince but whose body mysteriously disappears, leaving only the gifted cloak behind—a plot that was too long for a thirty-one-syllable poem. Obviously more of that story could have been put into *chōka* form, but it was not. The compilers may have sought to make the poem less a story of starvation and more a Buddhist lament on the fragility of human existence. In this sense, the poem is an example of recycling.

As we read the poem, we find it easy to imagine ourselves in a similar situation. Putting aside Shōtoku's identity as a political leader, we then see the poem less as a paean to the virtue of a particular leader and more a dramatic statement of the more universal problem of death.

THE GRAND CONSORT 大后, *Man'yōshū* 153: "A poem by the grand consort"

You boats on Ōmi Sea,	isanatori
place where men take the great whale:	ōmi no umi o
as you row your way	oki sakete
from far out in the offing,	kogikuru fune
as you row your way	hetsukite
from closer in to shore—	kogikuru fune
do not strain your oars	oki tsukai
in the offing!	itaku na hane so
do not strain your oars	hetsukai
by the shore!	itaku na hane so
You will scare the birds	wakakusa no
he loved so—	tsuma no
My Lord, vibrant as new grasses.	omou tori tatsu

CONTEXT: When Emperor Tenchi (626-672; r. 668-672) died in 672, he and his grand consort had produced no heir. Bloody events involving rivals for the throne followed Tenchi's death, despite his attempts to forestall them, but the poem says nothing about them. Four of the consort's poems appear in *Man'yoshu* and all, including this one, belong to the genre of laments (*banka*).

COMMENT: About half the lines of the grand consort's poem are irregular in length, and the poem has no envoy, indicating that conventions had not developed fully in her time. Again we encounter the rhetorical technique of apostrophe—the speaker talking directly *to* the boats offshore rather than just *about them*—which intensifies the drama of a person soliciting sympathy from objects that cannot offer it. The author also employs parallelism (lines 3-6 and 7-10) in order to portray a world seemingly ranged against her feelings. Her *makurakotoba* connect back to old tradition, lending authority to her sentiments, and ironically suggest a permanence that contrasts with the reality of mortal experience. *Isanatori*—"where men take the great whale"—should not be understood as evidence that whales were found in the waters of a lake, but rather as evidence that some nouns (here *umi*, or "sea," in the proper noun Ōmi no Umi, the Ōmi Sea; modern Lake Biwa) seem to "trigger" use of the epithets almost automatically. The second *makurakotoba*, "of the new grasses" (*wakakusa no*), imagistically prefaces the word *tsuma*, "mate."

Tenchi was forty-five at the time of his death, and hardly young. In this sense, there is nostalgia and poetic convention at work in the poet's conception. The image she creates of herself holding off noisy men threatening the serenity of a place that stands for her husband's memory and may still be a place dedicated to his repose is simple yet profound. One remembers what Fujiwara no Shunzei (1114-1204) said (*Korai fūteishō* [Notes on poetic style, past and present], 1197, pp. 286-87) of Man'yō-era poets: "They let the words come out naturally, yet their words sound deep in feeling and elevated in form." Of course knowing recent political history would have made the poem even more moving for people of her day, and the careful structure of the poem belies the idea that its words have just "come out naturally."

KAKINOMOTO NO HITOMARO 柿本人麻呂, *Man'yōshū* 29-31:
"A poem written by Kakinomoto no Hitomaro when he passed the remains of the capital at Ōmi"

Since that Sage of Old	tamadasuki
bore sway at Kashihara,	unebi no yama no
on the jeweled slopes	kashihara no
that gird Mount Unebi's Peak—	hijiri no miyo yu
since those ancient days	aremashishi
all those born to reign as gods	kami no kotogoto
beneath the heavens	tsuga no ki no
had ruled from fair Yamato:	iya tsugitugi ni
spruce trees in a row,	ama no shita
stretching back generations	shirashimeshishi o
far into the past.	sora ni mitsu
Yet Our Lord left Yamato	yamato o okite
of the vaulted skies,	aoniyoshi
and crossed over the mountains	narayama o koe
of rich-earthed Nara,	ikasama ni
and for reasons of his own	omōshimese ka
—what could they have been?—	amazakaru
established his place of rule	hina ni wa aredo
beneath the heavens	iwabashiru

at Ōmi, that remote land	ōmi no kuni no
of stone-coursing waters,	sasanami no
where he built a grand palace	ōtsu no miya ni
on the shore at Ōtsu,	ame no shita
place of the rippling waves.	shirashimeshikemu
Yes, here, I am told,	sumeroki no
he erected his palace,	kami no mikoto no
our Lord Sovereign	ōmiya wa
who reigned as a very god;	koko to kikedomo
here it was, they say,	ōtono wa
that his grand palace once stood.	koko to iedomo
Yet now spring grasses	harukusa no
have overtaken the grounds;	shigeku oitaru
now haze rises	kasumi tachi
and hides the rays of spring sun	haruhi no kireru
on the many stones	momoshiki no
where the palace once stood—	ōmiyadokoro
a thing sad to look upon!	mireba kanashi mo

Envoys

At Kara Point	sasanami no
in Shiga of the rippling waves,	shiga no karasaki
all is as it was.	sakiku aredo
But we who wait courtiers' boats—	ōmiyabito no
surely we do so in vain.	fune machikanetsu

The broad waters	sasanami no
off Shiga of the rippling waves	shiga no ōwada
may wait, still and deep.	yodomu to mo
But will they ever again	mukashi no hito ni
look upon those people of old?	mata mo awame
	ya mo

CONTEXT: The palace on the Ōmi shore was erected by the aforementioned Emperor Tenchi, who moved there from Mount Unebi in the southern reaches of the Yamato Plain. Tenchi's death precipitated a conflict between his son and his younger brother, the so-called Jinshin Rebellion of 672, which in turn led to the abandonment of the Ōmi capital and the return of government offices to Nara. Hitomaro (fl. 680–700), as a minor court official who wrote poems memorializing imperial processions and hunts, enshrinement ceremonies, and funeral services, would doubtless have known the Ōmi capital. The headnote does not tell us the occasion of this poem, but his voice is semipublic, speaking *to* an audience but also asking questions *for* that audience as well.

COMMENT: To elevate the tone of his poem and the lofty themes it articulates, Hitomaro employs the prosodic devices of parallelism and repetitive syntax. He also refers to famous places, including Mount Unebi in Yamato and places around the abandoned capital at Ōtsu on the shores of the Ōmi Sea (modern Lake Biwa). A number of the places are introduced complete with *makurakotoba*: *tamada-suki Unebi* (Unebi girded with a jeweled halter), *sora ni mitsu Yamato* (Yamato of the vaulted skies), *aoniyoshi Nara* (Nara of the rich earth), *iwabashiru Ōmi* (Ōmi where water courses over stones), and *sasanami no Shiga* (Shiga of the rippling waves). These perform the dual functions of invoking oral traditions of song while also marking the places in question as of historical renown associated with the site of Tenchi's reign. They also expand the poem's scope beyond immediate events to a whole train of history and may have resonated with talismanic significance at the time. However, the speaker also draws our attention toward the natural world. First we see the basic elements of the landscape—sky, earth, stones, and water; then we get a "close-up" view of more transient forms—spring grasses and haze. Only then do we see human beings (except for the emperor, "who reigns as a god"), and then only as an absence: "courtiers" and "people of old" are viewed only in the mind's eye. The grasses and hazes prevail, a scene that related to both politics and to broader human concerns.

At the heart of Hitomaro's conception is the sad end of the Ōmi capital, stronghold of Tenchi's son, where after defeat all the high officers of the court were removed by execution or banishment. The son himself committed suicide, allowing his uncle to rise to the throne as Emperor Tenmu (631–686; r. 672–686). But while gesturing toward these events, Hitomaro also describes the vanity of human ambition, juxtaposed with the more perdurable mountains, seas, and sky. Taken together, Hitomaro's parallelisms, repetitions, and *makurakotoba* create a mood that is philosophical, perhaps even existential, while of course focusing on a particular event for readers of his own time.

YAMANOUE NO OKURA 山上憶良, *Man'yōshū* 63: "A poem written by Yamanoue no Okura when he was in China, longing for home"

Come along, men—	iza kodomo
let us be off, for Yamato!	hayaku yamato e
At Ōtomo Bay	ōtomo no
the pines will be waiting,	mitsu no hamamatsu
pining for our return.	machikoinuramu

いざ子どもはやく日本へ大伴の三津の浜松待ち恋ひぬらむ

CONTEXT: Tradition says that Yamanoue no Okura (d. 733?) may have been ethnically either Chinese or Korean, which might explain his participation in a Yamato state legation that left for China in 702. In the seventh and eighth centuries, travel between Japan and China was varied in purpose but constant, and Chinese influence on Japanese government, religion, language, art, and culture was of overwhelming significance. The poem above was evidently written just before Okura left to return home, probably in 704 but perhaps a few years later, via the official port at Ōtomo (in modern Osaka). Back in the capital at Nara, Okura went on to serve as tutor to the crown prince, and later he was appointed as governor of a province in Kyushu.

COMMENT: Many *Man'yōshū* poems were composed on public occasions, such as imperial progresses, coronations, and memorial services; and often the speakers of such poems were officials speaking in behalf of a group. Although that is not precisely the case in Okura's poem, it is clear that, rhetorically, he is speaking not just for himself but *for*, and *to*, a delegation about to embark on a voyage. The poem is in two parts: the first two lines a call to courage and action, the last three a vision of home intended as motivation. (It is perhaps no accident that Okura skips over the perils of the ocean voyage, training all eyes on the calm waters of the Japanese port. The journey was notoriously dangerous.) Thus the rhetoric of the poem involves what might be called a hortatory voice that emphasizes common identity, desire, and purpose. The emphatic interjection *iza* is a colloquial form that typically begins an admonition, meaning "all right now, let's . . . ," and it is followed by *kodomo*, which in later Japanese often means "child" but here refers to young men, perhaps in this case Okura's staff or compatriots.

After calling his men to attention, Okura goes on in the next three lines to present the destination of the voyage—beloved Yamato, where the pine trees along the shore wait for their return. *Mitsu* is the word for harbor, a name that survived in later times as a place-name in the area at Ōtomo (the latter also functioning as a double entendre meaning also "companions"). Pines and other evergreens were commonly employed to represent patient, enduring steadfastness, an example of how the actual qualities of an object may recommend it as a natural, rather than arbitrary, symbol. Okura concludes by calling to mind loved ones whom he figures as waiting (*matsu*) like the pines (also *matsu*). Thus we encounter another example of a conventional double entendre, or *kakekotoba*, used as a final prod toward action, for Okura and his companions. Employing such devices was part of what constituted a poetic community, then, as now.

ANONYMOUS, *Man'yōshū* 2671

今夜の有明の月夜ありつつも君をおきては待つ人もなし

Though I am up	*koyoi no*
to see the moon lingering	*ariake no tsukuyo*
in the sky at dawn—	*aritsutsu mo*
still tonight I wait, my love,	*kimi o okite wa*
and for no one if not you.	*matsu hito mo nashi*

CONTEXT: *Man'yōshū* is a collection of collections, including those of individual poets such as Kakinomoto no Hitomaro and Ōtomo no Yakamochi (718?–785). But it also contains many anonymous poems from unidentified sources. This poem is from the eleventh chapter of that anthology, which is made up entirely of anonymous love poems and is one of a group of poems that "express feelings in relation to things." In later history, a poem by a known author might be entered as anonymous because of political or class reasons, but in this case authorship is truly unknown.

COMMENT: This poem offers an example of the *jokotoba*, or "preface," constituting the first two lines leading up to the verb *ari*—"to be"—and the statement that is the declarative heart of the poem, "Here I am, waiting for you and only you." Sometimes the content of *jokotoba* has little or nothing to do with the final statement, but in this case the idea of waiting up until the appearance of the dawn moon fits nicely with the speaker's complaint. Since the poem was written in response to a prompt, however, we should probably not take the first three lines literally but instead as a metaphor for frustrated longing.

There is every possibility that this poem was composed for some sort of gathering, but we cannot be sure. What we do know is that the motif of the moon remaining in the sky at dawn (*ariake no tsuki*, appearing in the latter half of the lunar month) would become a common one in love poems, where the convention was to present a man going home at dawn after a tryst or a woman waiting all night for a lover who does not come. The temporal situation of the speaker is ambiguous: either she imagines herself seeing the dawn moon, or she is now witnessing it. The last two lines of the poem, however, are more precise. "Other than you [*kimi*]," she says, "there is no one for whom I wait."

But is it necessary to take the speaker as a woman? In later times, that idea would become more fixed; it was women who waited for men to visit. But even in court society, it was not unheard of for a woman to visit a man under some circumstances, and the language of the poem contains no gender marks. Perhaps, then, we can put aside the question of gender roles and simply focus on the poem as an emphatic statement of resolve and constancy, a theme that comes through frequently in early *Man'yōshū* love poems, as in another anonymous poem (no. 3004) employing the image of the moon:

Only on that day	*hisakata no*
when the moon resplendent,	*amatsumisora ni*
high in the heavens,	*teru tsuki no*
vanishes to beam no more—	*usenamu hi koso*
only then will my love cease.	*waga koi yamame*

KASA NO KANAMURA 笠金村, *Man'yōshū* 1785: "Composed in autumn of the fifth year of Jinki [728], in the Eighth Month"

Rare fortune it is	*hito to naru*
to be born human;	*koto wa kataki o*
yet here I am,	*wakuraba ni*
among those so placed by fate.	*nareru waga mi wa*
And my only thought	*shini mo iki mo*
has been to serve thee, My Lord,	*kimi ga ma ni ma to*
in life, or in death.	*omoitsutsu*
But empty as a cicada husk:	*arishi aida ni*
so were all my plans!	*utsusemi no*
For the sovereign's decree	*yo no hito nareba*
you must meekly obey	*ōkimi no*
and beneath distant heavens	*mikoto kashikomi*
now sojourn afar,	*amazakaru*
to subjugate rustic lands—	*hina osame ni to*
setting off at morn	*asatori no*
as the morning birds give voice,	*asadachishitsutsu*

taking your leave
as your men flock all around—
while I—I stay on,
longing for one who for so long
I shall have no chance to see.

muratori no
muradachi inaba
tomari ite
are wa koimu na
mizu hisa naraba

Envoy

On that day to come,
when you cross Koshi Mountain
amidst falling snow—
pray think back on me, then,
on the one who stayed behind!

mikoshiji no
yuki furu yama o
koemu hi wa
tomareru ware o
kakete shinobase

CONTEXT: Kasa no Kanamura (fl. 715–738) was a courtier from a prominent aristocratic lineage who left behind nearly fifty poems, many of them commemorating imperial events. He wrote the poem here as a proxy for someone who wanted a proper poetic statement to submit to his lord, who was leaving him behind in the capital in order to take up a provincial assignment.

COMMENT: For all but the highest government officials, service in the provinces was an inevitable stage in an aristocratic career. Here Isonokami Otomaro (d. 750?), himself a poet of some renown, although mostly in Chinese, had been called to serve as provincial governor in Echizen Province. That region, located northeast of Kyoto on the "backside" of the island of Honshu along the Japan Sea, was known as a place of heavy snows.

Scholars surmise that Kanamura did not write this poem about himself but instead as a proxy for someone in Otomaro's entourage who was staying in Nara. (Proxy writing was an important feature of the poetic profession.) We do not know whether or not the poem was recited aloud at a farewell banquet, but the voice makes it easy for us to imagine him doing so. The poem is a statement of loyalty while at the same time a plea not to be forgotten, a statement both political and personal. Although there were compensations in the capital city for those left behind, losing access to one's patron could also be dangerous. No doubt the poet was asked by the man being left behind to emphasize loyalty above all else, but his statement is complicated by complex feelings of loss. Kanamura deploys only one set of parallel structures, referring to those who depart with their lord in proper fashion, "setting off at morn / as the morning birds give voice, / taking your leave / as your men flock all around." Not only do they depart, they do so in an orderly way that mocks his contrary feelings.

The man left behind, on the other hand, is presented in a nonparallel sentence that symbolizes estrangement: "while I—I stay on, / longing for one who for so long / I shall have no chance to see." The people following their lord into the provinces show the proper way of things, while the speaker is left in a more confused state. For him, the political world now seems empty. And lurking behind the brief image of order is the fact that the speaker's lord is going off "to subjugate rustic lands," suggesting to readers the danger that awaits those who represent the imperial will in the provinces. The fact was that some of those going off to take up such appointments sometimes lost their lives through illness or in pursuance of duty.

The poem is a study in ironies and competing value systems. The first irony is that someone born in human form, a "fortunate" situation that in Buddhist terms ought to allow for freedoms not granted lower forms of being, should be obliged to relinquish that freedom out of Confucian duty to the sovereign. At the time Buddhism was effectively a state religion whose doctrines were widely accepted among the elite especially. But for officials in the lay world, loyalty to the emperor and to the needs of one's own lineage took precedent: one's "freedom" was constrained by political realities, as signaled by the phrase "for the sovereign's decree / you must meekly obey." It is the sovereign who enlists Otomaro, and Otomaro *must* go just as the speaker for his part *must* stay. And this leads to the second irony—namely, that someone committed to duty should find his dedication compromised by the vagaries of worldly affairs. Fate for a courtier, we learn, is ultimately a political enterprise in which the empty shell of the cicada (*utsusemi*) becomes a symbol of futility. Buddhist doctrine, which teaches the inevitability of trouble, loss, and heartbreak in the world, truly has the final word. The "order" of things is a facade; it cannot be trusted.

In the envoy, as is so often the case in *Man'yōshū*, the poet turns to the natural world for a metaphor to suggest the feelings of the speaker, following a rhetorical pattern that would persist for more than a thousand years. This "restatement" goes a step further in imagining the snowy landscape awaiting the travelers on the harsh shores of the Japan Sea, where those who accompany their lord in his trials will forge bonds denied the man left behind.

ANONYMOUS, *Man'yōshū* 1937-38: "Summer, on 'cuckoo'"

A man of the court,	masurao no
I journey to Asuka,	idetachimukau
former capital	furusato no
and place where a god resides,	kamunabiyama ni
and there hear you sing—	akekureba
in the limbs of the mulberries	tsumi no saeda ni
as the day begins,	yū sareba
in the branches of the pines	komatsu ga ure ni
as evening descends;	satobito no
hear you sing, O cuckoo,	kikikouru made
till the people yearn,	yamabiko no
till the mountainsides resound	aitoyomu made
with their response;	hototogisu
hear you even in the night,	tsumagoi surashi
pining in song for your mate.	sayonaka ni naku

Envoy

Away from your home,	tabi ni shite
you must be missing your mate,	tsumagoi surashi
you, cuckoo, singing	hototogisu
in the Mountain of the God,	kamunabiyama ni
so late into the night.	sayo fukete naku

CONTEXT: "Place where a god resides" probably refers to Thunder Hill (Ikazuchi no Oka), located near the ancient capital at Asuka on the Nara plain. It is one of many famous places (*utamakura*; later, *nadokoro* or *meisho*) that appear in *Man'yōshū*—places that were believed to be honored by representation in song and would later become sites where travelers wrote poems as a way to connect with tradition. The anonymous poet writes about the place but also treats a conventional topic—the cuckoo—as a way to describe his own feelings.

COMMENT: The *makurakotoba kamunabi* (place "where a god resides") harks back to early traditions, but our speaker focuses not on ancient history but on his own feelings in visiting a storied place. While folk beliefs saw the cuckoo as a messenger between the land of the living and the realm of the dead, the speaker imagines the bird missing its mate, concentrating on "present" experience, albeit in an ancient landscape. He ends with a profound evocation of the loneliness that often accompanies reconnection with elements of a past that for all of us can only ever exist in fragments. The rhetorical elements we see at work here would, as we have noted, all become conventional in later tradition, particularly apostrophe ("you, cuckoo...") and parallelism ("in the limbs..., in the branches..."). Together, they heighten the dramatic tension of the poem. Obviously, the bird is not alone in missing someone; so does the speaker. An absence is thus at the heart of the poem, and we are part of it, wondering what (or whom) the speaker wonders about as he listens to a bird singing in the night.

TAKAHASHI NO MUSHIMARO 高橋虫麻呂, *Man'yōshū* 1807-8: "A poem about the maiden of Mama in Katsushika"

In the East Country,	tori ga naku
place where the cocks crow,	azuma no kuni ni
there is a story	inishie ni
that is still passed down today:	arikeru koto to
a tale from the past	ima made ni
of events at Mama	taezu iikeru
in Katsushika,	katsushika no
abode of the girl Tegona.	mama no tegona ga
Hempen robes she wore,	asaginu ni
with blue collars she had made;	aokubi tsukete
and her rough skirts, too,	hitasao o
she wove with her own hands.	mo ni wa orikite
No comb did she have	kami dani mo
to run through her long tresses	kaki wa kezurazu
and no shoes to wear	kutsu o dani
when she walked about.	hakazu yukedomo
Yet none could compare—	nishiki aya no
not even coddled ladies	naka ni tsutsumeru
all decked out	iwaiko mo
in their damasks and brocades.	imo ni shikame ya
Her countenance	mochizuki no
shone like the moon at the full;	tareru omowa ni
when she smiled	hana no goto
it was like flowers in bloom.	emite tatereba

And so came suitors
like summer insects to a flame,
like boats come ashore
in search of a safe harbor
at fall of night.
But what was she thinking
when they pressed her,
that she should despair of life—
life that is so short?
What can she have meant
to abandon herself
and lay her body in a grave
amidst the clamor
of the waves that break onshore?
It is a story
from a distant time, I know,
but to me, now,
it seems it happened yesterday
and right here before my eyes.

Envoy

I see the Well
of Mama at Katsushika
and think of her:
Tegona drawing water,
wearing the pathway down.

natsumushi no
hi ni iru ga goto
minatoiri ni
fune kogu gotoku
yukigakure
hito no iu toki
ikubaku mo
ikeraji mono o
nani to su ka
mi o tanashirite
nami no oto no
sawaku minato no
okutsuki ni
imo ga koyaseru
tōki yo ni
arikeru koto o
kinō shi mo
mikemu ga goto mo
omōyuru ka mo

katsushika no
mama no i mireba
tachinarashi
mizu kumashikemu
tegona shi omōyu

CONTEXT: Takahashi no Mushimaro (precise dates unknown) was probably a petty official, perhaps holding a provincial office in the East Country. He is remembered as one of the few *chōka* poets who wrote something akin to narrative. The story of Tegona, a young woman of beauty so renowned that she attracted suitors even from neighboring provinces, is of ancient origin. Why she chose to kill herself is not clear in the stories, but one version says that she was the victim of a political alliance gone wrong who died to spare her family further suffering. The Well of Mama refers to a well where legend says she drew water. It was located in Ichikawa, Chiba Prefecture. A small shrine to her memory is located there still today.

COMMENT: Mushimaro's story is presented elliptically: a young woman, pursued by suitors, throws herself into the sea. But he chooses not to dwell on that event so much as on a fine description of her "natural" beauty. Then he goes on to the central question: why did she despair of living? The answer has sobering overtones that reveal the tensions of marriage politics. It is not by accident that the poet stresses that Tegona's beauty rivaled that of elite ladies, who were often pawns in power struggles as well. Much is going on beneath the surface.

The poem begins with a pillow word for Azuma, the East Country, where the sun rises (place where the cocks crow), a remote setting that lends itself to legend. The middle lines of the poem—lines 9-12 and 13-16, 21-24—offer parallel sentences that describe her rustic beauty and domestic talents in an orderly fashion. The stock metaphors that compare the girl's countenance to the moon and her smile to blossoms employ images that were already on their way to becoming the chief icons of the Japanese poetic tradition. But there is irony in all of this, and the result is another set of parallel sentences (25-28) that present a predictable (indeed "natural") consequence: suitors who crowd around her, demanding that she make a choice. At this point, the parallelism gives way to less orderly syntactic structures as the poet asks questions of himself and of us as readers. Finally he conjures up the image of Tegona taking her drastic step, but he is left wondering why she went so far. His reaction from a distance is predictable: "life is precious," he implies, "surely she should not have thrown it away." Yet still he is perplexed.

The envoy offers a somewhat different scene, a well where she drew water. Now we have another vision of Tegona, as a young girl of filial virtue who every day went to get her heavy load and take it to her home and family. The image of her wearing down the earth of the pathway with her unshod feet gives us a happier memory that at the same time reminds us of the textures of a life lost.

MIKATA NO SAMI 三方沙弥, *Man'yōshū* 4227: "A poem intoned by Mikata no Sami as commanded by Fusasaki, lord of the Northern Fujiwara, minister of the left (posthumous). It was Kaga no Kogimi who heard the poem recited and passed it on, and later Kume no Hirotsuna, scribe in Etchū Province, did the same."

Hold off, I say:	ōtono no
do not tread upon the snow	kono motōri no
'round the palace of my lord.	yuki na fumi so ne
Not often	shiba shiba mo
do we see snow so deep—	furanu yuki so
snow of a depth	yama nomi ni

that falls only in the mountains.	furishi yuki so
So hold off,	yume yoru na
you men,	hito ya
do not tread upon it—	na fumi so ne
not on *this* snow.	yuki wa

Envoy

Just as now it lies—	aritsutsu mo
so will he wish to see it.	meshitamawamu so
So hold off, I say:	ōtono no
do not tread upon the snow	kono motōri no
'round the palace of my lord.	yuki na fumi so ne

CONTEXT: Mikata no Sami (precise dates unknown) was a Buddhist priest who served as tutor to the crown prince. Fujiwara no Fusasaki (681–737) was a high-ranking court official whose lineage, the Northern Fujiwara, was growing in power at court. The headnote makes it clear that the poem was not written spontaneously but upon request and is to that extent a "staged" piece.

COMMENT: This poem was submitted to Ōtomo no Yakamochi, compiler of *Man'yōshū*, in 750, when he was governor of Etchū Province—a fact that reveals one facet of Yakamochi's method in compiling the anthology. The prosody of the upper stanza is eccentric, containing some lines with too many syllables and others with too few (the full progression is 5-7-7-5-6-5-6-5-3-5-3), showing that even at that time standardization was not complete. The envoy, which *does* follow the standard 5-7-5-7-7 pattern and offers a clear summary of the long poem, may well have been concocted later.

Mikata no Sami was probably asked for a poem describing the snowfall around his master's residence. His response posits a genteel dramatic tension between the world of work and a moment of beauty. A noble palace was a busy place, and in the cold menials had little time for aesthetic contemplation, a province more in the ambit of their master and the poet whose work expressed that beauty in words. As noted, doing proxy work of this sort was a basic duty of the poetic profession. For us, though perhaps not for its author, the poem enunciates an aesthetic "bond" between the two men that assumes a class affiliation.

SHITORIBE NO KARAMARO 倭文部可良麻呂, *Man'yōshū* 4372: "A poem by Shitoribe no Karamaro, presented at court on the fourteenth day of the Second Month by Okinaga no Mahito Kunishima of the senior seventh rank, lower, an assistant in the Bureau of Frontier Guards in Hitachi Province"

At Ashigara	ashigara no
the god will grant me passage,	misaka tamawari
and I will go on	kaerimizu
with never a backward glance,	are wa kueyuku
making my way	arashi o mo
past the Gate Indestructible	tashi ya habakaru
at Fuwa,	fuwa no seki
feared even by rugged men.	kuete wa wa yuku
On Tsukushi's Capes—	muma no tsume
far as horses can endure—	tsukishi no saki ni
meekly I will serve,	chimari ite
and pray only for one thing:	are wa iwawamu
that all may be well	moromoro wa
with you that I left behind,	sakeku to mōsu
till the day when I return.	kaeriku made ni

CONTEXT: We know nothing about the man from Hitachi Province (the northern part of modern Ibaraki Prefecture), Shitoribe no Karamaro, to whom this poem is attributed. Even about the "assistant" (*daikan*) of the headnote we know only that in 762 he was advanced to junior fifth rank, lower grade. At the time, we do know that men between the ages of twenty-one and sixty were sent to Tsukushi (ancient Kyushu) to serve three-year obligatory terms as coast guards. The journey between Hitachi and Tsukushi was more than six hundred miles, and the exigencies of travel and weather made the going difficult and dangerous.

COMMENT: Poems of this sort were collected by—perhaps even solicited by—Ōtomo no Yakamochi when he served in the Ministry of Military Affairs at Naniwa (modern Osaka), the port through which conscripts passed on their way to their postings. Scholars believe that composing such poems may have been a "duty" of sorts, signifying their submission to imperial authority, as is apparent in the phrases "go on / with never a backward glance" and "meekly I will serve." At the same time, however, we notice that the poem expresses the perils of travel, as well as the sheer distance to Tsukushi, alluded to by the pillow word attached to Tsukushi—*muma no tsume*, a place "far as horses can endure." And we cannot help but notice that the poem ends with a prayer for those left behind that hints at resentment. Few men embarked on such expeditions willingly.

Karamaro was unusual in producing a long poem. Most works by guards were in the shorter *waka* form, perhaps indicating that the longer format was beyond the abilities of most men of low birth and little education. Yet sentiments similar to Karamaro's are clearly expressed in the following poems, all taken from a chapter of *Man'yōshū* dedicated to *sakimori no uta* (poems by guards of the capes). In each case we are given the name of the composer and his home district, the first two in Tōtomi and the last in Suruga Province, areas in modern Shizuoka Prefecture; but nothing more.

Man'yōshū 4322, Wakayamatobe no Mimaro, a clerk in the Arama district of Tōtomi

Ah, my woman,	*waga tsuma wa*
surely she must long for me!	*itaku koirashi*
Seeing her image	*nomu mizu ni*
in the water before I drink—	*kago sae miete*
how could I forget her?	*yo ni wasurarezu*

Man'yōshū 4325, Hasebe no Kuromasa of Saya district of Tōtomi

Father and Mother—	*chichi haha mo*
if only they could be flowers!	*hana ni mogamo ya*
Even sojourning	*kusamakura*
with grasses for my pillow,	*tabi wa yuku to mo*
I would hold them as I go.	*sasagote yukamu*

Man'yōshū 4343, Tamatsukuribe no Hirome of Suruga

My own journey	*waro tabi wa*
will be hard going, I know.	*tabi to omehodo*
But for her, at home,	*ii ni shite*
worn haggard by the children—	*komechi yasuramu*
how I feel for my poor wife!	*waga mi kanashi mo*

Scholars point out that the surnames of these poets end in "be," referring to occupational groups subservient to clans. The poems also may imply folk beliefs, one involving the idea that intense longing might make a person "appear" in dreams or, as in this case, as a reflection in water, and the other the custom of using flowers as talismans providing protection to their bearers. To readers, however, the poems present not objective description but direct, domestic and dramatic statements of longing *by* specific individuals *for* individuals—"my woman," "Father and Mother," "children," and again "my poor wife." Particularly effective is the scene of a wife "worn haggard" (*yasuramu*) by her children in the last poem, which does not rely on the mediation of any natural image. Left on her own for three years, a woman would have had to answer the needs of her children alone and probably take care of a house and land as well. Thus we have a poem that concentrates not just on the hardships of travel for the one going away but also on the gender role of a wife who may waste away before he can return. In Karamaro's poem, the barrier at Fuwa (in modern Gifu, near Sekigahara) may be called indestructible, but one could not be so sure of human beings. The focus on the emotional bonds connecting sojourner and home would become a standard feature of travel poems in centuries to come.

ŌTOMO NO YAKAMOCHI 大伴家持, *Man'yōshū* 1626: "A poem by Yakamochi composed in reply to Sakanoue Ōiratsume when she took off a robe she was wearing and sent it to him"

Against cold autumn winds,	*akikaze no*
I shall now put on your robes	*samuki kono koro*
beneath my own:	*shita ni kimu*
a memento of your love	*imo ga katami to*
that may make me yearn the more.	*katsu mo shinowamu*

CONTEXT: Ōtomo no Yakamochi, the son of a poet and prominent court official, compiled *Man'yōshū* as we now know it, no doubt building on the labor of earlier anthologists. In the autumn of 737, when he married Ōiratsume (his own first cousin), the daughter of his chief patron, she sent him robes in order to formalize their relationship, following a nuptial custom of the time. Yakamochi replied with the poem here.

COMMENT: Even as early as the time of *Man'yōshū*, many *waka* were composed in group settings, but then as in later times poetry was also a feature of private correspondence, between lovers but also between friends, colleagues, and so on. Yakamochi's poem is obviously a private one but transparent in conception. When the weather turned chilly each autumn, people put on more layers of robes. Here the speaker does so, but using a robe just sent by his lover rather than his own. Wearing the robe underneath his own of course meant it would be next to his skin, allowing him to come as close to touching her as was possible across distance. Donning each other's robes as "undergarments," the lovers could be quite literally entwined in a mutual embrace that symbolized their union. It is also worth noting that one duty of wives in aristocratic society was to provide their men with new robes each year.

The last two lines of the poem make one think of the witty poems of the era of *Kokinshū* (*Collection of Ancient and Modern Times*, ca. 905) in the way they inject irony into the scenario. First comes the adverbial *katsu mo*—literally, "on the one hand"—which immediately makes one think of "the other hand." (In the translation, the idea is suggested by "yearn *the more*," i.e., more than I would without wearing the robe.) And the verb *shinobu*, the final word of the poem, inflected with a suffix of speculation or conjecture (*mu*), clinches the point: "Wearing this robe next to my body will remind me of you, yes, but on the other hand it also makes me want you—and not just your robes—all the more." Any *katami* ("token" or "memento") must always draw attention to an absent original. It need hardly be said that poems, too, were substitutes, for intimate talk, for intercourse itself, as suggested by the motif of the robes.

In later tradition, love poems often focused in the same way on the confused state of minds in the throes of passion. Here the slight confusion reads more like a pose intended to suggest to us not just passion but also the whimsical intelligence of its author. Such claims of refined sensibility are a constant of the classical *uta* tradition.

LADY KASA 笠女郎, *Man'yōshū* 603: "From among twenty-four poems sent by Lady Kasa to Ōtomo no Yakamochi"

If just loving—	omoi ni shi
if that alone were enough	shini suru mono ni
to make one die—	aramaseba
why, then, I would be dead	chitabi so ware wa
by now a thousand times.	shinikaeramashi

CONTEXT: Lady Kasa (precise dates unknown) was a sometime lover of Ōtomo no Yakamochi, and that is all we know about her. *Man'yōshū* includes twenty-four of her poems, all love poems and all addressed to Yakamochi. Puzzlingly, we have only two replies from Yakamochi to Kasa, a fact that over the years has assisted in casting her as a precursor of the motif of the "waiting lady" that would appear in countless other poems in the future.

COMMENT: Some of the images in Lady Kasa's other poems—in one, the statue of a hungry demon, for instance—are rare in court poetry. But others, from fading dew to pines to cranes, would become standard in the centuries to come, making her one of the first in a long line of women poets known for fine rhetorical skills employed with subtlety and intense feeling. The number and tenor of her poems sent to Yakamochi make it likely that they were truly lovers; and since only the last two poems at the end of the *Man'yōshū* series were written "after they had parted," we can assume that the one here was written before their relationship ended. The rhetorical structure of the poem—which presents a hypothetical premise offered in the first half of the poem, followed by an equally hypothetical (and hyperbolic) conclusion in the second (if A, then B)—would become a common one in court poetry. Such witty propositions, often signaled by the particle *ba* (if, for the sake of conjecture) at the end of line 3 and the conjectural suffix *mashi* (then most likely) at the end of line 5, were particularly common in love poems, which, as mentioned, tend to concentrate on the psychological states of those under the influence of the passions.

The absence of poetic figures or even of images assists in making the poem uncomplicated and direct, a rhetorical statement of emotional "fact." In poems like the following (*Man'yōshū*, no. 594), however, Kasa shows her skill in the employment of imagery (in this case, an early example of the *jokotoba*, designed to introduce a topic in a concrete fashion) in ways that anticipate the future tenor of love poetry in particular.

Around my house	*waga yado no*
the light of sunset shimmers	*yūkagekusa no*
in dew on grasses—	*shiratsuyu no*
dew that fades as vainly	*kenu gani motona*
as do I, for love of you.	*omōyuru ka mo*

おもひにし死にするものにあらませば千度そ我は死にかへらまし

Portrait of Lady Ise, from *Nishiki hyakunin isshu azuma ori*, an illustrated text of *Hyakunin isshu* by the eighteenth-century artist Katsukawa Shunshō.

Courtesy L. Tom Perry Special Collection, HBLL, Brigham Young University.

Chapter 2

LONG POEMS AND SHORT POEMS

LADY ISE 伊勢, *Iseshū* 56: "Written as a poem by Emperor Xuanzong, when the Teijiin emperor had people write poems for a standing screen on various elements of *The Song of Everlasting Sorrow*"

Not yet swept clean,	kurenai ni
the ground of my garden court	harawanu niwa wa
has gone to crimson—	narinikeri
covered over with the leaves	kanashiki koto no
of my lamenting words.	ha nomi tsumorite

CONTEXT: The daughter of a provincial governor of Fujiwara lineage, Lady Ise (fl. 904-938) served in the court of a consort of Emperor Uda's (867-931). More than twenty of her poems appeared in *Kokinshū*, the first imperially commissioned anthology of Japanese poetry, and she would be well represented in many other such collections in the centuries to come. This poem is from a group of five poems on the same Chinese theme in her personal anthology. Standing screens (*byōbu*) were standard furnishings in noble dwellings, used for decoration, to subdivide spaces, for privacy, and as windbreaks. At first, single-panel screens were the rule, but in time multiple-panel folding screens also developed. Unfortunately, no screens from the Heian period survive, but based on later examples we can surmise that Lady Ise's poems for Emperor Uda accompanied illustrations in the *yamatoe* style of the story of Emperor Xuanzong (685-762) of the Tang dynasty, whose infatuation with a low-ranking lady named Yang Guifei led to political unrest and her death. Lady Ise's poem would have been written on a square of paper that was then pasted on the screen as a cartouche.

COMMENT: The story of Emperor Xuanzong and Yang Guifei as told in "The Song of Everlasting Sorrow" ("Chang hen ge," p. 93) by Bai Juyi (772-846) also figures in the background of the first chapter of *The Tale of Genji*, in which Emperor Kiritsubo is similarly infatuated with a woman, although with consequences less dire. We cannot be sure of the content of the painting, but Ise's poem alludes to lines by Bai Juyi describing the state of the palace when the emperor returns home after putting down the rebellion.

> With such sights before him, how could he not shed tears?
> Peach trees blooming in the winds of spring,
> Parasol trees shedding leaves in autumn rain.
> Autumn grasses grow in West Palace and in South Court;
> Fallen leaves cover the stairway, crimson not swept away.

Ise's poem obviously reworks the material of Bai Juyi's original. He employs a third-person narrator, but the headnote to Lady Ise's poem tells us that she put her words in the mouth of the emperor himself. Thus her speaker addresses us from inside the story and "inside" the painting, adapting the perspective rather than simply mimicking the original. Since tears of sadness are often figured as bloodred in hue, the suggestion is that the garden court is covered not only with fallen leaves but also with the emperor's tears.

ŌSHIKŌCHI NO MITSUNE 凡河内躬恒, *Kokinshū* 1005: "A long poem on winter"

The Tenth Month begins,	chihayaburu
when the mighty gods are gone.	kannazuki to ya
And that must be why—	kesa yori wa
why *this morning* first showers fall	kumori mo aezu
with the autumn leaves,	hatsushigure
from skies that though not clear	momiji to tomo ni
are not thick with clouds.	furusato no
From now on, as the days go by,	yoshino no yama no
winds will blow colder	yamaarashi mo
from the mountains of Yoshino,	samuku higoto ni
where once a palace stood.	nariyukeba
Hailstones will scatter all 'round,	tama no o tokete
so many jewels	kokichirashi
sprung from a broken necklace,	arare midarete
while frost freezes	shimo kōri

to make harder and harder	iya katamareru
the garden grounds—	niwa no omo ni
those grounds where winter grasses	muramura miyuru
growing in clumps	fuyukusa no
that show through here and there	ue ni furishiku
will lie beneath white snow,	shirayuki no
falling deeper and deeper still.	tsumori tsumorite
And thus a New Year	aratama no
I will add on to my store—	toshi o amata mo
one of many I have lived through.	sugushitsuru ka na

CONTEXT: Ōshikōchi no Mitsune (d. ca. 925) was a court official. By his time, those wanting to write longer poems had cast the *chōka* aside in favor of Chinese poetry. This poem is one of only six *chōka* included in *Kokinshū*, for which Mitsune served as a compiler.

COMMENT: Mitsune's poem on the *dai* (topic) winter is in fact about advancing age. The narrator, writing in the first month of winter (the Tenth, when the gods leave their own shrines to assemble at Izumo Shrine), imagines images to come: first rain showers and falling autumn leaves, then storm winds, hail, frost, and snow. Although beginning and ending his poem with *makurakotoba* (*chihayaburu kami*, the "mighty" gods, and *aratama no toshi*, "new" or "rough-hewn" year), his diction is unadorned, a conventional rehearsal of seasonal progress that reads like a metaphorical preface (*jo*) for his last three lines of lament. He refrains from affecting a public voice, and gone are the various rhetorical amplifications of poets like Hitomaro. Storied Yoshino, for instance, does appear, but only as a source of storm winds and with no overt hint of its grand history.

KI NO TSURAYUKI 紀貫之 and ŌSHIKŌCHI NO MITSUNE, *Teijiin uta-awase* 13, 14 (Spring: "The Second Month")

Left [winner]

Not truly cold	sakura chiru
is the wind that now scatters	ko no shita kaze wa
the cherry blossoms;	samukarade
and never has the sky known	sora ni shirarenu

snowflakes to fall like these. yuki zo furikeru
   Tsurayuki

Right

Quite overcome waga kokoro
by spring on the mountain slopes, haru no yamabe ni
my heart tarries on: akugarete
staying today, a long, long day, naganagashi hi o
till dusk again makes its end. kyō mo kurashitsu
   Mitsune

CONTEXT: Ki no Tsurayuki (872?–945) and Ōshikōchi no Mitsune were both minor court officials who served as compilers for *Kokinshū* and were known primarily as poets. *Teijiin uta-awase* (Retired Emperor Uda's poem contest, 913) was sponsored by two princesses, each leading a team (called left and right, following the standard pattern), and the event involved music, fine costume, and the display of "landscape trays" as well as poems. The contest was a social and ritual event held at rooms in the imperial palace, where the poems—eighty of them, in forty rounds—were recited aloud in formal fashion by appointed ladies and final "judgments" (*han no kotoba* or *hanshi*) were rendered by Emperor Uda himself. The broad topics for the event were spring, summer, and love.

COMMENT: Tsurayuki's poem plays against the technique of "confusion of the senses" by challenging conventional metaphors in the light of real experience, using a transparent conceit to do so. For we must notice, he proclaims, that the wind blowing through the blossoms in spring is not a cold winter wind; and do we not see that blossoms scattering against a spring backdrop are quite unlike snow flurries in the pallid skies of winter? The poem is a superb example of the rhetorical polish and playfulness associated with the *Kokinshū* style, which was heavily influenced by the witty poetry of the Six Dynasties era in China (220–589). It is also an example of a poem that went through recycling, appearing in the spring book of the third imperial anthology, *Shūishū* (Collection of gleanings [1005–1007]; no. 64).

   Poetry contests—one of the first modes of "publication" in the early days of the tradition—were often spectacles first of all, where the win was awarded on the basis of technical mastery rather than artistic excellence. In this case, a note tells us that the judgment went against Mitsune because of his use of the somewhat archaic phrase *naganagashi hi* (literally, "a long, long day"), which we are told made the "reader" shrug her shoulders and mumble when reciting it. Such things were called *yamai*, poetic "ills" or "faults."

MIBU NO TADAMINE 壬生忠岑, *Kokinshū* 625 (Love):
"Topic unknown"

Since that parting	*ariake no*
when I saw your cold rebuff	*tsurenaku mieshi*
in the late moon's glare,	*wakare yori*
nothing is more cruel to me	*akatsuki bakari*
than the moment of dawn.	*uki mono wa nashi*

CONTEXT: Mibu no Tadamine (fl. 905-950) was a courtier who wrote an influential poetic treatise and served as one of the compilers of *Kokinshū*. His poem is a classic variation on the "morning-after" (*kinuginu*) subgenre, the speaker being a man who is now complaining either about being rebuffed altogether or about a tryst that ended too soon. The poem was later included (as poem no. 30) in *Ogura hyakunin isshu* (*One Hundred Poems by One Hundred Poets*, ca. 1235) and many other collections.

COMMENT: Love as a poetic *dai* is generally portrayed as fraught with yearning (in the beginning) and resentment (later); little attention goes to joyful consummation. Tadamine's conception employs personification, relying on the metaphor of the cold visage of the remaining moon—the so-called *ariake no tsuki*, which rises late in the latter half of the lunar month and remains in the sky at dawn—as a symbol of rejection. To express his idea, Tadamine employs a central pivot structure that an English translation can only suggest: the phrase *tsurenaku mieshi* (appearing distant, cold, unresponsive) modifying both "the moon" as a predicate and "parting" as an attributive clause. Thus we imagine a man on his way home at dawn (a dominant trope in love poetry) looking up at the moon, only to see reinforcement of his unhappiness in its cold light.

It was probably the metaphor of the dawn moon gesturing toward the complex but unarticulated feelings of rejection *over time* that made the author of *Teika jittei* (Teika's ten styles)—an influential text of uncertain date attributed to Fujiwara no Teika (1162-1241), probably falsely, we know now—single Tadamine's poem out as one of only several poems from *Kokinshū* that qualified as examples of the ideal of *yūgen*, or "mystery and depth" (p. 362). Interestingly, one of the others (*Kokinshū*, no. 691) on that same list for that same category (p. 364), by the monk Sosei (d. 910?), is similar to Tadamine's.

Because you pledged	ima komu
that you would come at once,	to iishi bakari ni
I waited all night—	nagatsuki no
in the end greeting only	ariake no tsuki o
the moon of a Ninth Month dawn.	machiidetsuru kana

Here rather than the man going home on the morning after a tryst, we have a woman waiting for a man who never shows. It is common in Japanese poetry for a man to speak as a woman, or vice versa. Classical Japanese poems present no linguistic gender marking, nor do they use honorific or humilific language that would reveal class relationships. Ironically, this made it easier for a man to speak as a woman, or vice versa.

ANONYMOUS, *Kokinshū* 1027 ("Haikai" chapter): "Topic unknown"

葦引の山田のそほづおのれさへ我をほしてふうれはしきこと

You, scarecrow,	ashihiki no
standing in a rice paddy	yamada no sōzu
in foot-wearying hills:	onore sae
what a bother to be wanted	ware o hoshi chō
by even such as you.	urewashiki koto

CONTEXT: *Kokinshū* is made up primarily of thirty-one-syllable, formal *waka*, but its last two books contain a few *chōka*, folk songs, and *haikai no uta*, or "eccentric poems." We know nothing of the specific circumstances of the rather rustic poem here. One imagines a young woman as the speaker—someone so popular that she mistakes a scarecrow for a man in pursuit. Personification and apostrophe were prominent *Kokinshū*-era techniques.

COMMENT: Half the *haikai* poems in *Kokinshū* are anonymous, but we also have *haikai* by prominent poets such as Tsurayuki, and we can assume that most poets occasionally produced humorous works. The humor in early *haikai no uta* tends to be light and usually involves mainstream images, as is the case with the following poems on cherry blossoms from *Goshūishū* (Later collection of gleanings, 1203–1209; nos. 1201 and 1207) by the courtier Fujiwara no Sanekata (d. 998) and a monk named Zōki (also known as Ionushi).

"Topic unknown"

Perhaps a few blossoms	mada chiranu
have not fallen yet, I think,	hana mo ya aru to
and set off to see.	tazunemin
But we best be quiet a bit—	anakama shibashi
we mustn't let the wind know!	kaze ni shirasu na

"Composed when the winds began to blow after blossoms had fallen in his courtyard"

I had thought	ochitsumoru
to go see blossoms piled up	niwa o dani tote
in my courtyard.	miru mono o
How heartless of the storm winds	utate arashi no
to be sweeping them away!	haki ni haku kana

Seven of the twenty-one imperial anthologies include small sections of eccentric poems. Later, in the medieval period, poets would produce comic poems involving bawdy subject matter—what we refer to as *kyōka*—although the term *haikai no uta* persisted. In common parlance, the term *haikai* now usually refers to the Edo-period precursor of haiku.

MURASAKI SHIKIBU 紫式部, "Matsukaze" (The wind in the pines) chapter of *The Tale of Genji* (*Genji monogatari* 2: 393–94)

At dawn, as departure loomed ahead, there was a chill in the autumn wind and insects were busily crying.... Wondering how he would fare alone, the monk was unable to control his feelings.

As we part ways,	yukusaki o
I stop and look down the road	haruka ni inoru
with a hopeful prayer.	wakareji ni
Yet still I am an old man	taenu wa oi no
who cannot stay his tears.	namida narikeri
The Akashi Monk	

Will we both live on	ikite mata
to someday meet again?	aimimu koto o

行く先をはるかに祈る別れ路に堪えぬは老の涙なりけり

生きてまた相見むことをいつとてか限りも知らぬ世をば頼まむ

And if we do—when?
For now, I can only trust
in a future yet unknown.
    The Akashi Lady

itsu tote ka
kagiri mo shiranu
yo o ba tanomamu

CONTEXT: Murasaki Shikibu (precise dates unknown), lady-in-waiting to an empress, wrote all the poems in *The Tale of Genji* herself, always from the dramatic perspective of the characters in her stories. In this case we have poems exchanged by the Akashi monk and his daughter. The occasion is her departure for the capital to enter Genji's household, which means leaving her father behind. The most common form of exchange poem (*zōtōka*) was a "morning-after" poem (*kinuginu*), referring to a message sent by lovers after a night together, but many other occasions also elicited poems.

COMMENT: Corresponding through poetry was a requirement of life for both men and women at court. Here we have an exchange from *The Tale of Genji* involving not lovers but a father and child. Although the old man had always dreamed of his daughter's joining high society, there is inevitably sadness as they part—she to begin life as one of Genji's consorts in the city, he to dedicate himself to Buddhist devotions that he has postponed too long.

The imagery of the poem is what we might expect: without the mediation of a natural image, we see two people looking down the uncertain road ahead. Conceptually, the "parting of the ways" of the first poem is balanced by "meet again" in the second. Fittingly, we note the prayer of a father followed by a daughter's avowal of faith in the future. The old man's prayers for her future had been realized in Genji's advent in Akashi, after all; why should the gods not continue to smile on her in Kyoto? The speakers could not know what readers would learn: that one day the child that was the product of Genji's time in Akashi would become empress, or that, as both feared when writing their parting poems, the monk and his daughter would indeed not meet again.

FUJIWARA NO KINTŌ 藤原公任, *Senzaishū* 1203 (Buddhism): "Like floating clouds"

We liken ourselves—
our bodies, frail and vagrant—

sadame naki
mi wa ukigumo ni

to floating clouds.	*yosoetsutsu*
And all along, in the end,	*hate wa sore ni zo*
that is what we shall become.	*narihatenu beki*

CONTEXT: Fujiwara no Kintō (966–1041) was a poet and court officer who was also one of the most honored scholars of his day. His poem appears in the seventh imperial anthology, *Senzaishū* (Collection of a thousand years, 1188), in the chapter dedicated to Buddhist poems (*shakkyōka*), a subgenre that remained important for centuries. Earlier we encountered Buddhist concepts and paradigms at work in a number of poems, those by Murasaki Shikibu, most obviously. The category had first been separately designated in poetry collections at the end of the eleventh century. At first such poems were included under the heading "Miscellaneous" but later appeared in a separate chapter of their own.

COMMENT: *Shakkyōka* were written in many different contexts: on visits to temples, at gatherings associated with religious services, or for votive sequences, to name a few. Although we lack background information about Kintō's poem, scholars point out a relevant passage of scripture in the *Vimalakirti Sutra* (ca. 100 CE) that lists metaphors for the body, including clouds but also other insubstantial things—dreams, reflections, bubbles on water, echoes, and so on. So common is that kind of metaphor that one might hesitate to cite a particular source were it not for the headnote, which indeed reads like a quotation. Writing poems on passages from scripture was common practice.

As a general context for the poem one must remember that at the time bodies were usually cremated. There were several sites on the outskirts of Kyoto, most notably Toribe Fields, where bodies were burned, thus quite literally becoming "clouds" of smoke. Cleverly, Kintō makes this the overt theme of his poem, which is how a metaphor we often use to describe the frail nature of our bodies and the uncertain qualities of human existence will "in the end" emerge as a literal truth, consonant with the concept of ephemerality, the most basic of all Buddhist teachings. From the beginning, our bodies are fated for decline and death, prey to illness, accident, old age, and ultimate mortality, thus being *sadame nashi*, "impermanent"; and after our mortal frames have been reduced to smoke, leaving only a few bones behind as relics, nature seems to be giving us a lesson by converting our remaining energy into a cloud to be tossed on the wind, briefly, before being absorbed into the "nothingness" of the sky. (The same Chinese character is in fact used for both "nothing" and "sky"—the first variously read as *kara*, *aki*, *munashi*, and *kū*, and the second as *sora*—producing an ironic lexical situation in which the idea of "empty" is "full" of connotations.) Here the word

さだめなき身はうき雲によそへつつはてはそれにぞなりはてぬべき

"sky" does not appear, but it is inevitably in the background whenever the "cloud" is used, being the final destination for all the insubstantial elements of worldly existence.

ANONYMOUS, *Wakan rōeishū* 571: "House in the paddies"

Wasn't it yesterday	kinō koso
we transplanted our seedlings?	sanae torishi ka
And yet already	itsu no ma ni
the leaves of the rice plants rustle	inaba mo soyo ni
in passing autumn wind.	akikaze no fuku

きのふこそ早苗とりしかいつのまに稲葉もそよに秋風のふく

CONTEXT: As already noted, Chinese poetry was composed in Japan from the earliest times. The first three imperial anthologies produced at the Japanese court, dating to early in the ninth century, in fact consisted of Chinese poems exclusively. A later anthology, *Wakan rōeishū* (Songs in Japanese and Chinese, ca. 1018) offers a contrast by including Chinese poems (*kanshi*) written by both Chinese and Japanese poets, along with *waka* by the latter as well. Rather than full Chinese poems, however, Kintō, who put the work together, excerpted just a few lines (usually two), while in contrast quoting *waka* in full. All the poems in the book, whether in Chinese or Japanese, were evidently sung, whether privately or in groups, according to melodies then known in literate society that we can only guess at now. Most of Kintō's poets are canonical figures, from the works of the late Tang dynasty in China and the ninth and tenth centuries in Japan. The poem here actually appeared first in *Kokinshū* (no. 172), as did many of the poems in the anthology.

COMMENT: Kintō often recontextualized poems—i.e., put them under subject categories that do not correspond to their original contexts. The poem included here, for instance, appears in *Kokinshū* among poems on the conventional *dai* of "autumn wind," rather than under the *dai* "house in the paddies." A slight difference, one might say; and perhaps assuming anything about an anonymous poem with no headnote is risky. Yet the fact remains that the new heading directs our mental gaze to farmers living in shacks in the fields rather than the more "elegant" themes of the breezes blowing over the leaves on the rice plants and the imperceptible passage of time. Two Chinese lines (*Wakan rōeishū*, no. 566) by Miyako no Yoshika (834-879) included under the same heading make the contrast even more clear.

Guarding the house, a dog barks at a visitor;
grazing in the fields, cows lead their calves to rest.

As a doctor of letters at the imperial court, Yoshika wrote poems in proper Chinese, with proper Chinese themes and images. Among them were dogs and cows, thought to be too rustic for courtly treatment in *waka*. Many of the poems in *Wakan rōeishū* appear under subject headings not unlike those found in Japanese anthologies—plum blossoms, travel, pines, year's end, and so on. Others, however, resonate more with Chinese traditions—pleasure girls, friends—or neighbors, as we see in a few lines (no. 573) by Bai Juyi, who is credited with more poems than any other poet in the anthology.

Not alone but together, we shall stay till life ends—
and leave a fence for our progeny to share.

FUJIWARA NO KIYOSUKE 藤原清輔, *Shin kokinshū* 1843
(Miscellaneous): "Topic unknown"

If I should live on,	nagaraeba
may I yet recall these days	mata kono goro ya
with tender feelings?	shinobaren
Those times I thought hard long ago	ushi to mishi yo zo
are fond memories to me now.	ima wa koishiki

CONTEXT: Fujiwara no Kiyosuke (1104-1177) was a prominent poet who is now remembered more for his scholarship and activities as a critic and contest judge. The headnote to this poem in his personal anthology says only that Kiyosuke sent the poem to someone "when he [Kiyosuke] was thinking about the past." It is interesting to note, however, that the poem later went through recycling three times: first, for inclusion in his own personal poetry collection (*shikashū*) of more than four hundred poems, put together late in his lifetime, by the poet himself or someone working from his records; then for the eighth imperial anthology, *Shin kokinshū* (*New Collection of Ancient and Modern Times*, ca. 1205); and finally for the most famous of all small Japanese poetic anthologies, the *Ogura hyakunin isshu* (no. 84). Compiled by Fujiwara no Teika in 1216 at the request of a patron, the latter collection would become a primer for practitioners of the *waka* form for centuries to come. It has the distinction of being perhaps the most popular of all poetic texts in premodern times.

ながらへば又この比や忍ばれんうしとみし世ぞ今は恋しき

COMMENT: Natural imagery is a component of most *waka*, but not all. Here Fujiwara no Kiyosuke presents a logical proposition that is in no way dependent upon the "outside" world for its power. He deploys a common two-part structure, with the caesura at the end of the third line, in a riddle-like rhetorical posture, asking, "Why might I later recall the present with positive feelings?" and answering, "Because in time our troubles are covered over by nostalgia, making even the hardest times seem dear." As readers we look first into the future, then move from the present—a time of trouble, we later learn—into another time of trial in the past, and then back to the present, but with a new understanding. Ultimately, though, what we learn is less logical than psychological, which explains why *Teika jittei* (p. 368) would later honor it as an example of *ushin* (deep feeling), a quality of affective richness that Teika felt all proper poems should display. The process described is therefore a reasoning process, while the conclusion goes beyond that to express sentiment.

In *Ogura hyakunin isshu* Kiyosuke's poem is surrounded by laments, a fact that has perhaps tinted interpretations too much over the years. For, in addition to being a lament, the poem is also a pronouncement on the nature of memory. The reader must assume some kind of crisis behind the poem, either for Kiyosuke or the person to whom he sent it (a male relative, the commentaries say), which makes the poem personal on the surface. Significantly, however, we are not told the source of the sadness. A failing love affair, perhaps? Illness? Political conflicts? Disruptions in the natural order? No answer is given, perhaps purposely so. To restrict the poem's scope by being more specific would reduce its power for readers as an insight of universal significance.

TOMOTSUNE 智経, *Hirota no yashiro uta-awase* 53 (round 27): "Snow in front of a shrine"

I shall not trespass	*tamagaki no*
the jeweled fence of the shrine.	*uchi e wa iraji*
Surely the god, too,	*furu yuki o*
would resent any footsteps	*fumimaku oshi to*
on this newly fallen snow.	*kami mo koso mire*

CONTEXT: Tomotsune is identified as a priest in an early document. He probably was associated with Hirota Shrine, which still stands today in Hyōgo Prefecture, near the city of Nishinomiya (literally, "western shrine"). According to legend, the shrine was established by the decree of Empress Jingū in the 300s, upon command of the Sun Goddess, Amaterasu. It was one of the Twenty-Two Shrines of the Home Provinces to which offerings were sent by the imperial court at a festival held during the Second and Seventh Months to pray for a good harvest. Shinto shrines were as important as Buddhist temples in the world of medieval Japan and were often located in old-growth groves that were themselves considered sacred, serving as the earthly abodes of deities. To emphasize their antiquity, shrine buildings were kept simple, even rustic, but every effort was made to keep both buildings and grounds clean, reflecting the fact that one of the chief occupations of priests presiding there was purification rituals.

COMMENT: A curious story lies behind the decision to hold a poetry contest at Hirota Shrine—referred to as just that *Poetry Contest at Hirota Shrine*—in 1172. Two years before, a large event of eighty-seven rounds involving all the major poets of the day, including courtiers, court ladies, and clerics, had been held on Osaka Bay at Sumiyoshi Shrine, which made the god of Hirota so envious, so the story goes, that he expressed his displeasure in a dream that was reported to a monk—who then decided to hold a similar event at Hirota to assuage the spirit of the god. The format of the contest was identical to the one held at Sumiyoshi, involving most of the same poets, *dai*, and the same judge, Fujiwara no Shunzei.

The circumstances of the contest are perhaps suggested by Tomotsune's poem, in which he explicitly expresses a desire not to offend the god. The central idea of the poem, however, perhaps owes more to literary precedent, especially a poem by Izumi Shikibu (precise dates unknown) from *Shikashū* (Collection of verbal flowers, ca. 1151–1154; no. 158) in which she tries to convince herself that it is just as well she is not visited by a tardy lover, "not wanting footsteps to disturb / the snow of my garden court." This explains Shunzei's comment in awarding the poem a win in its round: "Nothing new in conception, but still elegant and refined [*yū*], I should think." The poet's reluctance to sully the beauty of the shrine precincts reveals a proper courtly sensibility, as well as religious devotion, of course; but as we imagine the speaker standing outside the fence, looking in on the grounds in reverie, we also naturally think of the precincts as a sacred space made more so by a layer of pure white snow, a place in which the aesthetic and the spiritual merge together. That it was associated with the most important of all native gods, the Sun Goddess, imbued the poem with an additional layer of cultural significance.

たまがきのうちへはいらじふるゆきをふままくをしと神もこそみれ

SAIGYŌ 西行, *Sankashū* 77 (Spring): "From his many poems on 'blossoms'"

If I had my wish,	negawaku wa
I would die beneath the blossoms	hana no shita nite
in the springtime—	haru shinan
midway through the Second Month,	sono kisaragi no
when the moon is at the full.	mochizuki no koro

ねがはくは花のしたにて春しなんそのきさらぎのもちづきのころ

CONTEXT: Saigyō (1118–1190) was a samurai in the Guards Office of the retired emperor before becoming an itinerant monk in his twenties. He died as he wished, on the sixteenth day of the Second Month.

COMMENT: This poem from the poet's personal collection, *Sankashū* (Mountain home collection, precise date unknown), also appeared in a mock-poem contest, the *Mimosusogawa uta-awase* (The Mimosusogawa poem contest, 1189), which Saigyō submitted to Shunzei, whose comment on the poem is famous: "This poem is anything but beautiful in outward effect, but for its style it works well. Yet a person who has not gone far along the way will not be up to composing in this manner. This is something that can be achieved only after a poet has arrived at the highest level" (*Mimosusogawa uta-awase* 13).

The poem is terse and direct, without adornment, colloquial, and didactic—indeed, as Shunzei says, not beautiful (*uruwashi*) in total effect (*sugata*). The aesthetic term often used to describe such works is *heikaitei*, "ordinary" or "plain," and it is used in a negative sense by Shunzei himself, as well as by Retired Emperor Juntoku (1197–1242) and other medieval critics. In Saigyō's case, however, the direct style succeeds in expressing the ultimate religious desire—to die at the same time of year as the historical Buddha—in terms of two premier icons of the courtly tradition, cherry blossoms and the moon. He believed in the spiritual efficacy of *waka*, in "purifying the heart, eliminating evil from one's thoughts" (*Saigyō shōnin danshō* [Conversations with Saigyō], ca. 1225–1228, p. 271).

Another poem shows that Saigyō could produce poems of conventional beauty and skill. This one (*Shin kokinshū*, no. 1615) was written when he saw Mount Fuji while on the road:

Following the winds,	kaze ni nabiku
smoke rises from Fuji's peak	fuji no keburi no
into empty sky,	sora ni kiete
its destination unknown—	yukue mo shiranu
as too my vagrant passions.	waga kokoro kana

Here Saigyō employs a *jokotoba* in which the first three or four lines of the poem provide a figurative correlative for the idea expressed at the end: "Smoke rising from a peak and then fading off into the sky, at the mercy of the winds," he says, "that is what love is for me." Fuji had been on the list of poetic *meisho* (or *nadokoro*, "famous places") for hundreds of years and remains an icon of Japanese culture today. This poem is listed in *Teika jittei* (p. 366) as an example of the *taketakakiyō* (the lofty style), in direct contrast to the *heikaitei*.

PRINCESS SHIKISHI 式子内親王, *Shin kokinshū* 1124 (Love):
"From among the poems of a hundred-poem sequence"

Oh, I am aware	yume nite mo
that I may appear in his dreams—	miyuramu mono o
but what of my sleeves?	nagekitsutsu
Will he see these wet sleeves, tonight,	uchinuru yoi no
as in sadness I lie down?	sode no keshiki wa

夢にても見ゆらむものをなげきつつうちぬるよひの袖のけしきは

CONTEXT: Princess Shikishi—formally Shikishi Naishinnō (d. 1201)—served as Kamo Virgin in her youth, but after a decade resigned because of illness, thereafter living a somewhat reclusive life. In 1197 she became a nun. She was among those requested by Retired Emperor Go-Toba (1180–1239) to present a hundred-poem sequence in the autumn of 1200. She died very soon after and never saw her poem honored in *Shin kokinshū*.

COMMENT: Princess Shikishi's poem is an example of how the subject of love is often figured through a contrast between the dream world and the world of reality. We can assume that the speaker is not so much Shikishi herself, who was a nun at the time, as a rhetorical extension of herself based on literary precedents and her own experience in the highly codified culture of the imperial court. Writing on *dai* (in this case, love) demanded that one express an idea, usually through a particular and private experience.

Still, though, she was a woman. The setting of the poem is nighttime, when a woman is yearning for a lover whose identity is undisclosed. Perhaps he had promised to visit; perhaps she waits only for a message. In either case she is left alone, musing that while tonight they may not meet in the real world, perhaps she will appear to him in his dreams. Even if she does, however, she stresses that he will not see the reality of her situation. "And suppose I do appear in his dreams," she says, "will he see me the way I am *now*—my sleeves drenched with tears?" The rhetorical question suggests that what the man sees will likely be only an extension of his own romantic fantasies. The reality would be more unpleasant: a woman grieving as she gives in and goes to bed, her sleeves showing her distress. The sleeves are a synecdoche for an entire body wracked with heartache.

In coming years Princess Shikishi would figure in the tradition as the court lady par excellence, evoking effusions like the following from *Kirihioki* (The paulownia brazier, p. 287), a text spuriously attributed to Teika but written well after his death: "How should one describe her poems? A courtier, his countenance rosy and glowing, dances 'The Waves of the Blue Ocean' below the palace steps as autumn leaves fall, his hair adorned with a chrysanthemum beginning to fade." Such a highly romanticized vision, harking back to the image of the ideal Heian-era courtier, Genji, who danced the same dance in the "Beneath the Autumn Leaves" chapter of *The Tale of Genji*, is perhaps the sort of thing Shikishi is actively resisting in her poem. She includes no mention of color, or scent, or sound, and even the image of tears drenching her sleeves must be inferred from context. It is also significant that the metaphor reverses her gender, while aestheticizing it at the same time.

LADY KUNAIKYŌ 宮内卿, *Shin kokinshū* 1199 (Love): "Love, using 'wind' to express longing"

Do you not hear it?	kiku ya ika ni
Even the fickle wind that blows	uwa no sora naru
in the sky above	kaze dani mo
is sure to sound its coming	matsu ni oto suru
to the waiting pines.	narai ari to wa

きくやいかにうはのそらなる風だにもまつにおとするならひありとは

CONTEXT: One of Go-Toba's consorts, Kunaikyō died only a few years after she wrote this poem, still in her twenties. Fifteen of her poems ended up in *Shin kokinshū*. She was among ten poets invited by the retired emperor to participate in a contest in the autumn of 1202, *dai* for which were sent out on the twenty-ninth of the Eighth Month, with a formal "airing" and judgment taking place at Go-Toba's Minase Palace two weeks later—the so-called *Minasedono koi jūgoshu uta-awase* (The fifteen-poem contest at Minase Palace). At that time, *Shin kokinshū* was being compiled and poets did their utmost to produce poems worthy of inclusion in the imperial anthology.

COMMENT: In judgments attached to the contest, Lady Kunaikyō's poem received high praise from both Go-Toba and Fujiwara no Shunzei, the latter calling it "excellent in both idea [*kokoro*] and diction [*kotoba*], from beginning to end" (*Minasedono koi jūgoshū uta-awase*, no. 141). She begins with an enigmatic question to a negligent lover: "How can you not hear what I hear?" Then the speaker answers the question by referring to something the lover *must* hear too: the wind, which despite its reputation for caprice, can still be relied upon (the Japanese is *narai ari*, "to be in the habit or custom of") to let the pines know, through its sound, that it is coming for a visit. As a message, then, the poem says simply, "You are less reliable even than the wind. How long must I wait?" Readers (of the Japanese original, at least) would recognize the presence of two *kakekotoba*: *matsu*, meaning both "pine tree" and "waiting," and *otosuru*, meaning both "announce" and "visit." Also working as a double entendre is the phrase *uwa no sora* (the sky above), which when modifying the "wind" means "fickle."

Despite its rhetorical complexity, the poem is graceful both aurally (the full vowel sounds of *uwa no sora naru* at the center of the poem contrasting well with the more staccato sounds before and after, leading up to a final emphatic and rising *wa*) and syntactically, thus displaying the qualities held to be essential for poetic excellence. Altogether, it is a fine example of the ideal of the "clever style" (*omoshirokiyō*). But Kunaikyō's poem is more than just clever. As Go-Toba remarks, "It is the skillful use of the 'wind' to articulate the *dai* that makes the poem" (*Wakamiya senka-awase* [Wakamiya contest of selected poems] 1202; no. 27). Along with the speaker, we sit inside at night, listening (not seeing: the poem is all sound) to the wind in the pines, anxious for a visitor or at least a messenger. But as the hours go by the wind signifies only disappointment. Anticipation turns to bitterness, and we *pine* with the *pines*, listening in the darkness to sounds that inspire more annoyance than hope. The psychological state of the speaker is thus as intricate as Kunaikyō's rhetoric.

FUJIWARA NO TEIKA 藤原定家, *Shin kokinshū* 1206 (Love)

After his tryst,	kaerusa no
he may think it lights the way	mono to ya hito no
as he returns home.	nagamuran
But I gaze at it, still waiting—	matsu yo nagara no
there in the dawn sky, the moon...	ariake no tsuki

CONTEXT: Teika, son of Shunzei, is known for his interest in aesthetics generally and, in his own poetry, for complex rhetoric and use of symbolism. Here we have a poem of the sort that might appear in a court romance. In another

かへるさのものとや人のながむらんまつ夜ながらの有明の月

poem that involves gender reversal, a woman gazes up at the moon after waiting all night for a man who never came, a man whom she imagines going home, oblivious to her loneliness, after visiting a rival. The moon in the sky at dawn is that same moon that served as a symbol of rejection for Mibu no Tadamine. Indeed, it seems likely that Teika wants us to remember Tadamine's poem, which Teika later recontextualized for his anthology *Ogura hyakunin isshu* (no. 30).

COMMENT: In Japanese, Teika's poem reverses normal syntax by ending not with a verb but with a noun (a rhetorical technique called *taigendome*), creating an unresolved effect popular among poets of the generation of *Shin kokinshū* and on into the late medieval era. The romantic, evocative quality of the poem makes some scholars see Teika's poem as an example of the ideal of *yōen*, or "ethereal beauty," a term that Teika used only a few times and never really defined. What's more, when the poem appears in Teika's list of poems in various styles, it is offered as an example of the ideal of Teika's later years—*ushin*, or "deep feeling." (Frustratingly, the *yōen* style is not included in that list at all.) Since Teika elsewhere says that the quality of "deep feeling" is one that should be present in all styles, the problem is not insurmountable. But the confusion does serve as a caution against reducing our understanding of Japanese poetry to an exercise in mechanically applying aesthetic ideals to poems. A poem by Juntoku (*Juntokuin onhyakushu* [The one-hundred-poem sequence of Retired Emperor Juntoku] 1237; no. 5) that Teika in a short interlinear note *does* praise as an example of *yōen* presents something closer to Shunzei's ideal of *en*, or "loveliness":

I wake from a dream,	yume samete
and through the gaps in blinds	mada makiagenu
not yet rolled up,	tamasudare no
it seeks its way into my chambers—	hima motomete mo
the scent of flowering plum.	niou mume ga ka

There is no direct allusion of human drama here but only the delicate evocation of an elegant situation and an ingenious conception: we expect moonlight in the last line, but instead we get the scent of plum. One suspects, however, that Juntoku—and Teika reading Juntoku's poem—may have been thinking of old traditions that associated plum scent with nostalgic feelings for departed loved ones.

LONG POEMS AND SHORT POEMS

CHIEF ABBOT JIEN 慈円, *Shin kokinshū* 1782 (Miscellaneous):
"From a fifty-poem sequence"

As I muse alone,	omou koto o
why does no one come to ask	nado tou hito no
what is troubling me?	nakaruramu
I look up, and in the sky	augeba sora ni
the moon is shining bright.	tsuki zo sayakeki

おもふことをなどとふ人のなかるらむあふげば空に月ぞさやけき

CONTEXT: Jien (or Jichin, 1155–1225) was the son of a regent and himself became the chief abbot of the Tendai sect, most powerful of the aristocratic sects of Buddhism at the time. The poem here was composed for a poem contest titled *Rōnyaku gojisshu uta-awase* (Contest of fifty poems, between the old and the young) convened by Retired Emperor Go-Toba early in 1201. The first step in the process was the composition of fifty-poem sequences by the ten participants, which were then paired for the contest of two hundred fifty rounds. Jien, at age forty-seven, was on the "old" side. His poem was on the open *dai* of "miscellaneous," which gave poets considerable latitude in choosing imagery. Strictly speaking, the image of the moon would denote an autumn setting, but seasonal description is obviously not the main focus of the poem.

COMMENT: The upper half of Jien's poem is a simple statement of loneliness. We are not told what the speaker is brooding about, only that he wishes someone would come and allow him to unburden himself. The last two lines then give him—and his readers—a reply. In his loneliness, he looks up at the sky and sees the moon shining bright. In this case the brightness (*sayakesa*) is crucial to our understanding. One need only remember the cold glare of the moon in Tadamine's famous poem to conclude that in Japanese poetry the moon does not always offer comfort. But here the brilliance of the moon seems to be answering Jien's query. As scholars point out, the moon shining bright is described in Buddhist discourse as the *shinnyō no tsuki*, "the moon of truth." Since the compilers placed Jien's poem in the "Miscellaneous" book of *Shin kokinshū* rather than in Buddhism, they must have judged it to be less an attempt at doctrinal statement than a poem of praise about the beauty of the moon shining in worldly gloom. It is not surprising, however, that Jien turned to a Buddhist conception for his theme. Several years before, he had been replaced as chief abbot because of political conflicts, but he would be reappointed at Go-Toba's bidding just a few days after the first of the gatherings for the contest took place.

In several medieval lists this poem is offered as an example of the "lofty style" (*taketakakiyō*). One wonders if this is partly because early readers immediately identified the speaker with Jien himself, a man of the highest rank and aristocratic attainments. More than anything else, however, it is the elevated diction of the poem and its sense of grandeur that put it in that exalted category. Rhetorically the lines of the poem take us from the gloom of the speaker's mind up into the sky, and then into the light. The way the upper and lower halves of the poem related to each other not through word association but through suggestion and feeling qualified the poem in the mind of the *renga* master Shinkei (1406-1475) as an example of *soku*, or "distant linking," as explained in his *Sasamegoto* (Whisperings, 1463-1464, p. 122).

FUJIWARA NO IETAKA 藤原家隆, *Minishū* 1776 (Winter):
"'Snow in the pines,' from a fifty-poem sequence at the house of the Reverend Prince Dōjō"

At Takasago	takasago no
the days go by without cries	onoe no shika no
from deer on the slopes—	nakanu hi mo
days that pile up with white snow	tsumorihatenuru
enveloping the pines.	matsu no shirayuki

CONTEXT: Fujiwara no Ietaka (1158-1237) was a regular in the court of Retired Emperor Go-Toba. Like Teika, he served as a compiler of *Shin kokinshū*.

COMMENT: Poetry in the *waka* form is highly intertextual in the sense that it uses fixed lines and phrases that inevitably gesture back toward scores of other poems. But from early in the tradition poets also used a device called, literally, "taking a line from a foundation poem" (*honkadori*). The practice began very early but was particularly conspicuous among poets of the *Shin kokin* age. It was applied in diverse ways, with poets sometimes appropriating only one prominent phrase, sometimes as much as three full lines. Ietaka's poem is an example of the latter, taking three lines (the first three in the foundation poem, which become the last three in the later poem) from an anonymous poem from *Shūishū* (no. 191), written two hundred years before.

Again and again	akikaze no
the winds of autumn blow	uchifuku goto ni

高砂のをのへの鹿のなかぬ日もつもりはてぬる松の白雪

at Takasago—	takasago no
where no day goes by without cries	onoe no shika no
from deer on the slopes.	nakanu hi zo naki

A first reading of Ietaka's poem will focus on the clever way in which he "reverses" the earlier poem by changing just one syllable: *takasago no onoe no shika no nakanu hi ZO* [*naki*] becoming *takasago no onoe no shika no nakanu hi MO* [*tsumori*], which in the translation becomes "no day goes by" and "the days go by." Beyond that, however, Ietaka has also changed the seasonal context, moving from autumn to winter. As a reader one cannot help but imagine the deer of the earlier poem hunkered down somewhere on slopes now covered with snow. Thus Ietaka invites us to hear those distant cries, along with the autumn wind, hovering behind his winter scene. In so doing, he suggests imagery and meaning that are the essence of what Shunzei called *yūgen*, "mystery and depth," while also imbuing his scene with "deep feeling" (*ushin*). The Zen monk and poet Shōtetsu (1381-1459), speaking of layers of meaning, would say that Ietaka's poem was itself the "deepest of all poems" (*Kenzai zodan* [Chats with Master Kenzai], before 1510?, p. 144). The call of the deer—figured as yearning for its mate—was considered especially moving. Ietaka makes it even more evocative by alluding to it only as an absence, in that way fully expressing the feeling of accumulating snow that obscures all.

EMPEROR TENCHI 天地天皇, *Ogura hyakunin isshu* 1

In autumn fields	aki no ta no
stands a makeshift hut of grass	kariho no io no
with its roof of thatch—	toma o arami
so roughly made that my long sleeves	waga koromode wa
are ever wet with dew.	tsuyu ni nuretsutsu

CONTEXT: Emperor Tenchi was the son of Emperor Jomei (593-641). As noted, succession disputes after his death eventually brought his brother, Emperor Tenmu, to the throne. His poem begins Fujiwara no Teika's famous *Ogura hyakunin isshu*, the most famous of all hundred-poem sequences (*hyakushu-uta*), which dates from around 1216 and is thus a prime example of recycling. The *Man'yōshū* original (no. 2174), noted as anonymous, is on the *dai* of dew.

In autumn fields	akita karu
I've made a hut to live in,	kariho o tsukuri

秋の田のかりほのいほのとまをあらみわが衣手は露にぬれつつ

while I harvest grain;
and so my long sleeves are cold,
drenched as they are with dew.

waga oreba
koromode samuku
tsuyu zo okinikeru

COMMENT: This poem has a messy history. The *Man'yōshū* version appears with a slightly altered first line as an anonymous poem in *Shin kokinshū* (no. 454). But the version Teika uses in his anthology comes from *Gosenshū* (Later collection, ca. 951; no. 302), the second imperial anthology, where it is listed as "topic unknown" and attributed to Emperor Tenchi, although he almost certainly did not write it. Prevailing opinion is that the final version dates from the Heian period, along with the attribution to Tenchi, reflecting his importance as the ancestor of all Heian-era emperors. The usual interpretation sees it not as a personal lament but as a didactic display of sympathy for farmers, but that idea probably also comes from Heian times.

The contrasts between the two versions tell us much about aesthetic ideals in Heian and later times. In the *Man'yōshū* version, the speaker constructs his own hut and alludes to actual work in the fields as his purpose, while the later version alludes directly to no such labor; nor does the later version say openly that the speaker "lives in" the hut, leaving that to suggestion, subtlety being a chief feature of late courtly ideals. Also, the *Man'yōshū* version says "sleeves are cold" directly, rather than hinting at that as in the newer version. Finally, there are syntactic breaks or pauses at the end of lines 2, 3, and 4 of the earlier version, while the *Hyakunin isshu* poem has only one break, at the end of line 3, which gives the poem the more elegant flow and rhythm of a formal poem (*hare no uta*). Thus the poem has been revised in a way that would have pleased representatives of later court ideals such as Teika's father, Shunzei, who said that a good poem should have flowing aural qualities when read aloud and that it should be both elegant and moving (*Korai fūteishō*, p. 275). The revised version presents rustic subject matter, but in a more elegant and poignant way; and it eliminates choppy syntax in favor of a more smoothly flowing structure. A prominent medieval list of poems in aesthetic categories (*Teika jittei*, p. 363) lists the later version of the poem under *yūgen*, "mystery and depth."

FUJIWARA NO TAMEUJI 藤原為氏, *Shoku gosenshū* 41 (Spring):
"On 'spring view of a cove,' written in 1250 for a poem contest"

If someone asks me
I shall say I haven't seen it—

hito towaba
mizu to ya iwamu

Tamazu Island,	tamatsushima
where haze spreads over the cove,	kasumu irie no
in spring, in the dim light of dawn.	haru no akebono

CONTEXT: Fujiwara no Tameuji (1222-1286) was son and heir of Fujiwara no Tameie (1198-1275), the latter being the sole compiler of *Shoku gosenshū* (Later collection continued, 1251), the imperial anthology in which the poem here appears. Tamazu Island was located off the coast at Waka Bay (now Wakayama Prefecture) and was the site of a shrine to one of the three gods of poetry, the other being Sumiyoshi Myōjin and Hitomaro.

COMMENT: The poet Tonna (1289-1372) records that the second line of this *waka* originally read, "I shall say I *have* seen it" and was changed to "I *haven't* seen it" by Tameie himself, a small change (from *mitsu* to *mizu* in Japanese). Another anecdote, from *Waka teikin* (Teachings on poetry, 1326?, p. 139) explains, "Rather than describing in detail the features of Tamazushima, the poem seems replete with artistic atmosphere [*fuzei*] as the scene floats up before our eyes. It is the virtue of *uta* to reveal a surplus of meaning in just thirty-one syllables.... In poems with overtones [*yojō*], we see little technique on the surface, but as we recite them, we find more profound pathos and more loneliness."

Leaving something to the imagination of readers is what constitutes the quality of *yojō* (also pronounced *yosei*) in this case, gesturing as it does toward an ineffable experience. And the effect is enhanced by an allusion to an anonymous *Man'yōshū* poem (no. 1215).

Tamazushima:	tamatsushima
be sure to observe it well.	yoku mite imase
What will you say	aoniyoshi
in Nara, place of rich earth,	nara naru hito no
when people ask what you saw?	machitowaba ika ni

Tameie's death left his family in a fractured state. Tameuji was clearly his heir in the court hierarchy and inherited his titles, but his younger brothers challenged his authority. This conflict resulted in the splitting of the lineage into three branches: the Nijō descending from Tameuji; the Kyōgoku descending from Tamenori; and the Reizei descending from Tameie's sons by his last wife, known as the Nun Abutsu (d. ca. 1283). This rivalry continued for more than a century, and the poetic issues it engendered for much longer than that. *Yojō* continued to function as ideal for poets in all those lineages, although more so for the Nijō than for the other lineages, and it would continue as an ideal in *waka*, *renga*, and *haikai*.

THE NUN ABUTSU 阿佛尼, *Izayoi nikki* (p. 195)

Mist was rising over waves breaking on the shore, concealing the many fishing boats on the water from view.

As if to declare,	amaobune
"You may not watch as fishing boats	kogiyuku kata o
ply the waters here!"	miseji to ya
waves rise and crest into mists	nami ni tachisou
at morning, out on the bay.	ura no asagiri

蜑小舟漕ぎ行く方を見せじとや浪に立添ふ浦の朝霧

CONTEXT: Abutsu was a lady-in-waiting to an ex-empress in her youth who later became Fujiwara no Tameie's wife and bore him several children. *Izayoi nikki* (Diary of the sixteenth night moon) relates how she traveled to Kamakura in 1279 in order to bring suit against Tameie's formal heir, Tameuji, for withholding behests made to her sons. The poem above was written as she was arriving in Kamakura on the twenty-ninth day of the Tenth Lunar Month, just two weeks from her departure.

COMMENT: Travel poems are a staple of the court tradition, beginning even before *Man'yōshū*. Many among the nobility, high and low, traveled for official or private reasons, and pilgrimage too was an ordinary part of life. No wonder, then, that travel is a subcategory in even the earliest imperial anthologies (often subsumed under "Miscellaneous") and a frequent *dai* in poetry contests and small anthologies. Our earliest major travel diary is *Tosa nikki* (*Tosa Diary*, 935) by Ki no Tsurayuki, and from his time until the end of the nineteenth century hundreds of other writers left such works. Some record mostly poems, composed at well-recognized *meisho*, while others include substantial bodies of prose. The travel diary of the Nun Abutsu presents a well-balanced mix. She documents thoroughly her journey along the most well-traveled road of the time, writing poems at all the places required by tradition, and concludes with a fairly lengthy description of her life in Kamakura, where she apparently stayed until her death a few years later.

We therefore know that the bay in this poem is at Kamakura and that the boats we see are mostly fishing boats. As the government seat of the shogun and his administrators, established nearly a century before, Kamakura was a bustling place, full of temples, shrines, government offices, residences grand and small, and shopping districts. Abutsu's description shows us not such less-than-elegant and "worldly" sights, focusing rather on a vague view of mists on the sea, which she accuses of actively thwarting any desire she might have to see more of the boats at work. In this way we are denied any view of the labor of the boatmen, instead confronting a pastoral that shows the forces of the natural world colluding to restrict our vision: we continue to gaze out, but further details are left to the imagination. Abutsu's reasons for traveling to Kamakura were worldly, indeed political for the most part, but her poems seldom allude to such matters in any direct way, except in how they establish her bona fides as a poet attempting to secure a place in court society for her sons.

LADY SAKUHEIMON'IN 朔平門院, *Gyokuyōshū* 719 (Autumn): "From among her poems on 'the moon'"

In the growing light	*shiramiyuku*
of an ever whitening sky,	*sora no hikari ni*
its rays fade away	*kage kiete*
and leave only its silhouette—	*sugata bakari zo*
the moon lingering at dawn.	*ariake no tsuki*

CONTEXT: Sakuheimon'in (1287–1310) was a daughter of Emperor Fushimi's (1265–1317) who died in her early twenties and left only a handful of poems. As a member of Fushimi's family, however, she was involved in an important literary faction, the so-called Kyōgoku school, sponsored by Fushimi and the people around him. *Gyokuyōshū* (Collection of jeweled leaves, 1313), fourteenth of the imperial anthologies, enshrines their efforts.

COMMENT: The rhetorical tendencies of the Kyōgoku school are apparent here in the way the author avoids direct reference to a viewer in her poem, not even an adjective (*shiramu*, "whitening," for instance, being presented in verbal form) to represent an emotional response. She also uses no metaphor, no allusion, not even a semantic proposition. Instead, she offers us a scene "as it is" (*ari no mama*), without explicit mediations: the moment of change when the moon is reduced to a pale sphere as the sun rises.

Sakuheimon'in's poem recalls another from her father's personal collection, *Fushimiin gyoshū* (The collection of Retired Emperor Fushimi, mid-fourteenth century; no. 1557), although we do not know which came first.

しらみゆく空の光にかげきえてすがたばかりぞありあけの月

The color of frost	niwa no omo wa
begins whitening the ground	shimo no iro yori
of my garden court;	shiramisomete
and fading, paler all the while—	usuku kieyuku
the moon lingering at dawn.	ariake no kage

Fushimi's poem is like his daughter's in offering no subjective reference to a speaker, no adjectives, only a scene presented "objectively." Kyōgoku Tamekane (1254-1332), a grandson of Tamie's who was the chief theorist of the school, tells us that such an approach is not intended as a version of pastoral but rather an attempt to "become one" with the scene in Buddhist terms, thus capturing the truth of it, in its moment (*orifushi no makoto*). From this we can assume that neither author was intent on rendering a scene from experience—however much experience may have conditioned the process—so much as on presenting an allegory of harmonious union. Sakuheimon'in's poem, in particular, might be described as a meditation on the transformative effects of light. Lacking even the garden of Fushimi's poem, her scene has no immediately human or even earthly reference points, only the expanse of the broad sky high above us as it passes through a process of illumination in which the moon, a brilliant orb in the darkness, is absorbed into gathering sunlight.

KYŌGOKU TAMEKO 京極為子, *Gyokuyōshū* 1535 (Love):
"Written as a love poem"

In sad reverie	mono omoeba
I abandon my writing brush	hakanaki fude no
to its own vain whims—	susabi ni mo
and find that what I write down	kokoro ni nitaru
is like what is in my heart.	koto zo kakaruru

CONTEXT: Kyōgoku Tameko (d. 1316?) was a lady in service to Empress Eifuku (1271-1343), consort of Emperor Fushimi. Along with her brother, Tamekane, she was an artistic leader of the Kyōgoku school. The headnote to this poem tells us nothing of the circumstances behind its composition but gives us a crucial prompt: the *dai* of love. Without that context, we might wonder about the cause of the "sad reverie" of the first line. Thinking about the past? Worldly affairs? Illness? Tameko, or perhaps a later editor, decided to resolve the issue, by implicitly acknowledging the ambiguity: "Written *as* a love poem."

COMMENT: While mainstream love poems tend to employ striking imagery and complex rhetoric, the Kyōgoku school poets with whom Tameko was associated sought to represent the various emotions of love—yearning, anticipation, rejection, resentment, and so on—with fewer verbal mediations, emotions "just as they are" (*ari no mama*). Thus Tameko does not use a natural image to express her mood but something in her immediate surroundings: a writing brush. We see before us a lady sitting by her desk, musing about her relationship with some unidentified man, taking out an inkstone and brush and jotting down something—probably old poems—just to pass the time. Calligraphy practice was a constant in aristocratic life, where the need to write notes and letters was a daily thing. Here, however, the speaker picks up her brush in a moment of boredom, with no particular reason, and finds that her hands and heart are connected. Ironically, we encounter a distracted mind refusing to be distracted.

Although Tameko's poem stands on its own and needs little in the way of explication, knowing that she alludes to a scene from *The Tale of Genji* enriches our understanding—which was the primary and immediate purpose of allusion in traditional court poetics. The scene is from the "Wakana" (Spring shoots) chapter and describes how Murasaki, Genji's companion of many years, turns to brush and ink for distraction when she is feeling vulnerable after Genji has just married the Third Princess. "Setting herself to writing practice, she would find that, quite spontaneously, the old poems flowing from her brush would reveal her worries of the moment, impressing upon her how heavily those things weighed on her mind" (4:81).

The general custom in *waka* poetry was to allude to prose passages rather than poems in *The Tale of Genji*, and in that sense Tameko is following the canons of her day. Yet the passage she chose was not a particularly famous one, which leaves one impressed with how thoroughly she knew the tale.

物おもへばはかなき筆のすさびにも心ににたることぞかかる

TONNA 頓阿, *Tonna hōshi ei* 42 (Spring): "At day's end, after viewing blossoms"

Till evening comes …	kurenaba to
so I thought as I spent the day	omoishi hana no
beneath the blossoms.	ko no moto ni
But how hard it is to abandon	kikisutegataki
the sound of the vespers bells!	kane no oto kana

CONTEXT: Tonna was a man of samurai birth who took the tonsure early to dedicate himself to poetry as a religious Way, living in various cottages in Kyoto,

暮れなばと思ひし花の木のもとに聞きすてがたき鐘の音かな

where he carried on a thriving literary practice involving textual work, teaching, and of course poetry gatherings. "Composing on topics" (*daiei*) was central to medieval poetic culture. Poem contests were still held, and *hyakushu-uta* (sequences of one hundred poems) were still commissioned for poetry gatherings. But even in casual gatherings after such events people often composed extemporaneously (*tōza*) on *dai* chosen by lots, a practice that allowed professional poets like the monk Tonna to show their mettle, as he does in this poem from *Tonna hōshi ei* (Poems by the lay monk Tonna, no. 1357).

COMMENT: Fujiwara no Tameie wrote in *Eiga no ittei* (The foremost style of poetic composition, early 1170s, p. 202) that the challenge of *daiei* was to abide by precedent while adding "something a little different" when occasion allowed. Since "at day's end, after viewing blossoms" demanded treatment of cherry blossoms—the most timeworn *dai* of the entire classical canon—Tonna would have taken it as a special challenge. His speaker begins by presenting himself as waiting but then gives us a sound from day's end, the vespers bells that rang throughout Kyoto at the end of each day. In so doing he focuses on the poetic "essence" of his *dai*, based on precedent and informed imagination, what critics called *hon'i*. Almost certainly he had in mind a poem (*Shin kokinshū*, no. 116) by Nōin (988-1050?):

"Written when he was in a mountain village"

To a mountain village	yamazato no
at evening on a spring day	haru no yūgure
I came, and saw this:	kite mireba
blossoms scattering on echoes	iriai no kane ni
from the vespers bells.	hana zo chirikeru

For Nōin and Tonna, both monks, the temple bell symbolized Buddha's voice calling people away from worldly cares. In Nōin's case the sound transforms the falling blossoms into an allegory of transient beauty in a world of universal decline and death. Tonna, on the other hand, focuses our attention on the irony of how the *sight* of the blossoms is replaced by the *sound* of the bell, how one sensory delight follows another, both teaching the same message. At first, the speaker plans to stay only till dusk, thinking there would be no reason to tarry. But the sound of bells reminds him of Nōin's poem and awakens him to another subtle beauty that only gains in attraction as daylight fades and the blossoms literally recede from view.

PRINCE MUNENAGA 宗良親王, *Rikashū* 366 (Autumn):
"Written when he was looking at autumn leaves, at a time when he was living in a mountain village"

These showers falling	*kokorozashi*
on a path back in the mountains	*fukaki yamaji no*
must have a kind heart—	*shigure kana*
dyeing leaves in autumn hues	*somuru momiji mo*
that only I shall see.	*ware nomi zo miru*

CONTEXT: Munenaga Shinnō (1311-1385?) wrote this poem when he was living away from Kyoto, embroiled in the political conflicts during a period of divided rule between the Northern Court in Kyoto and the Southern Court in the provinces. From 1337 on, he lived mostly in remote places like Yoshino, Shinano, and Echigo, finally passing away, sometime before 1389, in the provinces, far from Kyoto.

COMMENT: The majority of poems written from the *Shin kokin* age onward into the Edo period are on *dai*, and records show that this was true of Munenaga's poems as well. And even when he writes about what is before his eyes, he employs mostly traditional images and ideas and creates a model of *ushin*, or "refined feeling." Yet headnotes do reveal deeply personal dimensions to some of Munenaga's poems. The rain showers in the poem here seem to offer consolation as they do the work of dyeing leaves. Normally, however, a poet would look forward to sharing such beauties with friends in the capital. If there is comfort in the constancy of natural processes, then, there is also a sense of alienation. And somehow the poem gains power because we know that Munenaga is not just creating a poetic conception—which it would be easy to do, adopting the voice of a recluse, for instance—but is actually looking out on a scene that must indeed have felt lonely. While he does not allow the realities of politics to invade his poem, he must have known that readers would know his situation. The final "that only I shall see" is, we know, more than rhetorical posturing for an audience, as is also the case with poems like the following lament, also from his personal anthology, *Rikashū* (Collection of the lord of the Bureau of Ceremonies, ca. 1374; no. 790): "Perhaps because I went to sleep with things on my mind, in my dreams I seemed to see only things of the past. After rising the next morning I wrote this":

Sleep leads to dreams;	*nureba yume*
and waking, to reality.	*samureba utsutsu*

One way, or another,	to ni kaku ni
I never forget the past—	mukashi wasururu
not for an instant of time.	toki no ma mo nashi

A poem in the category of "Reminiscence," perhaps? For Munenaga, living in his hut in the mountains, a happier youth and intervening trials must have been impossible to forget.

SHŌTETSU 正徹, *Sōkonshū* 7061: "Lightning on a dark night"

Even in its glow	terashite mo
my heart remains as ever,	kokoro wa yami no
still in the gloom;	mama nareba
it's for someone besides me—	waga mi no yoso no
this lightning in the night.	sayo no inazuma

CONTEXT: Shōtetsu was born into a samurai family but entered a Buddhist temple as a young man and dedicated himself to poetry as a Buddhist Way. He attracted numerous disciples, including men later known primarily as *renga* poets, including Shinkei. He also had many elite patrons, such as the samurai of the Hatakeyama clan at whose monthly gathering (*tsukinamikai*) he composed the poem here.

COMMENT: Buddhism was a category in the court tradition, but Buddhist ideas and ideals appear in poems written on more secular themes as well. The first thing we notice about this poem by a Zen monk is how skillfully it is structured, with the two elements of the *dai* ("gloom" and "lightning") separated as convention required and with the initial "glow" (the verb *terasu*, the first word in the Japanese) reaching forward to "lightning" (*inazuma*, last word in the Japanese) at the end. Between those poles, we confront a man in the dark. Assuming that Shōtetsu speaks for himself may go too far; the poem was on a *dai* that, if we take its essence to be the brevity of lightning as a natural phenomenon, the poet articulates skillfully.

In Buddhist thought the world is dark by definition, and strict Zen practitioners did not believe in saviors such as Amida. For Zen monks the goal was a moment of enlightenment that—usually after devotion and labor—might come in a flash. Yet the burden of the poem is that *if* enlightenment has come for somebody, it must be for someone else (*yoso*). Ironically, this makes more intense the gloom (*yami*) that remains. A similar idea comes through in another poem on "lightning," also from Shōtetsu's personal anthology, *Sokonshū* (Grassroots collection, precise date unknown; no. 10959):

In the dark of night,	*kuraki yo no*
to whom shall I pour out	*tare ni kokoro o*
what is in my heart?	*amasuran*
Suddenly the clouds blink—	*kumo zo matataku*
a flash of autumn lightning.	*aki no inazuma*

The Buddhist "prompts" of the first poem—glow (*terasu*) and gloom (*yami*)—are absent in this case, but the existential loneliness (*sabi*) remains; and the phrase "to whom shall I pour out / what is in my heart" expresses even more effectively a longing for something warmer than enlightenment—human companionship. The use of the word "blink" (*matataku*), an unusual metaphor, with its human connotations, stresses the point even more starkly. Whatever "eye" the lightning throws on the speaker's very human situation seems a cold one indeed.

INAWASHIRO KENZAI 猪苗代兼載, *Sōgi shūenki* (pp. 459-60)

Dew on the branch tips,	*sue no tsuyu*
raindrops beneath the trees—	*moto no shizuku no*
these are but tokens	*kotowari wa*
of the order of our world,	*ōkata no yo no*
shared by one and all.	*tameshi nite*
Yet when it is a close friend	*chikaki wakare no*
one is parting from,	*kanashibi wa*
somehow the sorrow you feel	*mi ni kagiru ka to*
seems for you alone.	*omōyuru*
Ah, since we met long ago,	*nareshi hajime no*
how much time has passed,	*toshitsuki wa*
months adding up to make years	*misoji amari ni*
more than thirty times.	*nariniken*
In those days far in the past,	*sono inishie no*
so kind was he	*kokorozashi*
that now nothing would I grudge	*ōharayama ni*
to express my thanks—	*yaku sumi no*
not even my life itself,	*keburi ni soite*

which I would gladly give
to rise with smoke from charcoal,
sent from Ōhara.
We were in the East Country,
each on his journey,
but separated so far
that the wind took far too long
to bring me tidings.
Rising from sleep
on my pillow of boxwood,
I was in a dream
and unable to waken.
Still, though, I set off,
toiling over field and hill,
hoping as I went
to witness his form, at least,
after his passing—
while the mountains on the way
showed no hint of care,
replying to my queries
with only the wind in the pines.

noboru to mo
oshimarenu beki
inochi ka wa
onaji azuma no
tabinagara
sakai haruka ni
hedatsureba
tayori no kaze mo
ari ari to
tsuge no makura no
yoru no yume
odorokiaezu
omoitachi
noyama o shinogi
tsuyu kieshi
ato o dani tote
tazunetsutsu
koto tou yama wa
matsukaze no
kotae bakari zo
kai nakarikeru

Envoy

What foolishness
to berate being left behind!
How long will *I* last,
my body a mere dewdrop
left in the wake of a storm?

okururu to
nageku mo hakana
iku yo shi mo
arashi no ato no
tsuyu no ukimi o

CONTEXT: Inawashiro Kenzai (1452-1510) was a *renga* master from Aizu who studied and practiced in Kyoto for some years before retiring to the East Country. His *chōka* memorializes one of his teachers, Sōgi (1421-1502), who died at Yumoto on the eastern side of the Hakone Mountain range without Kenzai's being able to pay his last respects. Sōchō (1448-1532) appended Kenzai's poem to his own account of the master's death, *Sōgi shūenki* (A record of Sōgi's passing, 1502).

COMMENT: In the medieval period *chōka* were often used for laments. Kenzai's poem includes one *kakekotoba* (*tsuge*, meaning both "inform" and "boxwood"), but it is one of *Kokinshū* vintage, and he does not employ other *Man'yōshū* conventions, using neither parallelism nor *makurakotoba*, instead using the medieval technique of *honkadori*. His first reference, given almost verbatim, is to *Shin kokinshū* no. 757, a didactic poem by Archbishop Henjō (816-890), to which Kenzai provides an emotional response.

Dew on the branch tips,	*sue no tsuyu*
raindrops beneath the trees:	*moto no shizuku ya*
these are but tokens	*yo no naka no*
of how in this world we mourn	*okure sakidatsu*
as others go—or go ourselves.	*tameshi naruran*

A second allusion is to an anonymous poem (no. 1208) from *Goshūishū* sent to someone who asked the author "if he would like a gift of charcoal":

Were you so kind	*kokorozashi*
as to pledge me charcoal	*ōharayama no*
from Mount Ōhara	*sumi naraba*
then I would put that warmth to use	*omoi o soete*
in lighting the coals on fire.	*okosu bakari zo*

So playful a poem may seem inappropriate in the context of a lament, but Kenzai sidesteps the humor, alluding only to the "kindness" shown by Sōgi as a teacher ("as great as Mount Ōhara") in order to express his own gratitude. Mount Ōhara was another name for Oshioyama, located west of Kyoto and known for its charcoal kilns.

Kenzai's poem contains no vestige of a public voice, describing a personal grief so intense that even the natural landscape offers no relief. While it does contain a narrative element, then, its "story" focuses less on outside events than on the very medieval themes of transience and Buddhist resignation.

SASSA NARIMASA 佐々成政, *Taikōki* (p. 28)

In the world of men,	*nanigoto mo*
everything has changed—	*kawarihatetaru*

何ごともかはりはてたる世の中を知らでや雪の白く降るらむ

and changed utterly.
And yet, all unknowing,
white snow keeps falling down.

yo no naka o
shirade ya yuki no
shiroku fururamu

We associate *waka* with the culture of the imperial court, but even in the early years many warrior men composed poetry, some, like Saigyō, becoming canonical figures. And by the 1300s most elite warriors participated in poetic culture. This poem, quoted in a work that chronicles the life of Toyotomi Hideyoshi (1536-1598), was written by a retainer to Hideyoshi's predecessor, Oda Nobunaga (1534-1582). His name was Sassa Narimasa (1536-1588), and the occasion was when he was stripped of all but one of his fiefs by Nobunaga's successors. Later, he was commanded to commit suicide.

There is nothing in the vocabulary or rhetoric of Sassa's poem to mark the poem as the effort of a warrior. Our knowledge of the circumstances, however, makes the poem more poignant. It could have been written by anyone that had suffered a loss, of course, but warriors lived peculiarly perilous lives. Particularly in the period of the Warring States (1467-1600), fortunes could be unmade in an instant. A man was more often cast aside because of his entanglements than for his own offenses. Narimasa had been lord of the province of Etchū, on the Japan Sea, in the heart of what is now known as Japan's snow country. But a short note in the chronicle tells us that the poem was not written from imagination alone: "As he watched the snow fall," it says, "he was thinking about times gone by" (*furu koto nagara omoiiderarenikeri*). Although a prose comment, it uses the poetic device of double entendre to good effect, the word *furu koto* meaning both "falling" and "of old." The fact is reassuring in a way: the human world changes, but the patterns of the natural world are oblivious, and life must go on. But Narimasa also means for us to see the falling snow as a symbol of the vagaries of human affairs. As he watches, the snow obliterates the landscape, along with his own accomplishments, which in the new order worked against rather than for him.

According to convention, Narimasa's poem would be categorized as a statement of feeling, *jukkai*. Though no *dai* is mentioned, the sentiment expressed is nothing new. Instead the poem connects with similar statements of the past, offering again a kind of consolation. The characterization of the snow as "unknowing" communicates just the right note of stoicism. Our last scene is the snow falling "whitely," obscuring borders and covering over Narimasa's past, leaving Narimasa's speaker and his readers to look out on a world that is indeed utterly changed.

SEN NO RIKYŪ 千利休, *Rikyū hyakushu* 100

What is *chanoyu*?	cha no yu to wa
It is to heat up water,	tada yu o wakashi
prepare the tea,	cha o tatete
and then to drink it:	nomu bakari naru
know that that is all it is.	koto to shiru beshi

CONTEXT: In late medieval times, the composition of *waka* and *renga* was considered a polite accomplishment for anyone in literate society, and it was virtually a requirement for the practice of many other arts, from Noh drama to *chanoyu* (the tea ceremony). It comes as no surprise that one of the earliest tea masters, Takeno Jōō (1502–1555), was a *renga* master who counted the *renga* poet Sōchō and the court poet Sanjōnishi Sanetaka (1455–1537) among his friends, or that among Jōō's own students was the most famous of all tea masters, Sen no Rikyū (1522–1591).

COMMENT: Doubtless Rikyū did not compose all the poems in the collection (which in its current form was compiled by Gengensai in the 1800s) that bears his name, but there is no reason to think he would have blanched at using poetry for a purpose less aesthetic than educational. For while many artists composed poetry out of a belief that it elevated their spirits, they also employed poetry in more didactic ways, one of which involved using the 5-7-5-7-7-syllable form as a pedagogical device. Arts had rules that students had to learn, and rules were easier to memorize in poetic form. Nor were only "philosophical" teachings the rule; matters of dogma and etiquette (no. 78) were put forward as well.

If serving someone	hanami yori
who has just been blossom viewing,	kaeri no hito ni
then don't display these:	cha no yu seba
paintings of flowers and birds	kachō no e o mo
or arrangements of flowers.	hana mo okumaji

The tea ceremony was typically held in a small room or cottage, and those participating were instructed to banish the outside world from their thoughts and enjoy a moment of simple pleasure that was social, aesthetic, and sensual—just heating water, preparing tea, and drinking, as the poem makes clear. Hence, reminding a guest of the flowers he has just seen or the birds he has just heard in the "real" world would amount to a distraction and perhaps even invite disappointment. (What artistic representation could actually compete with the direct experience of nature?)

The poems in *Rikyū hyakushu* are mostly free of poetic devices: no *kakekotoba*, *jokotoba*, etc. Rather, the poems are subordinated to their educational task. When images appear, they come from the tea room, tea wares, and implements, or flowers and plants that might be displayed in the alcove. Above all, the voice of the poems, from the first to the last, is the voice of a master of a discipline, speaking not privately but as a teacher who is comfortable issuing commands: *know* this, *do* this, *be aware* of this.

KINOSHITA CHŌSHŌSHI 木下長嘯子, *Unaimatsu* 291: "There was no change, none at all, in where she had lived; only she was gone"

Morning and night	*akekure ni*
I do nothing but lament	*sono kiwa bakari*
how she passed away—	*nagekarete*
and still I cannot dispel	*kagiri no sama no*
the look in her dying eyes.	*me o zo hanarenu*

CONTEXT: Kinoshita Chōshōshi (1569-1649), now known as a Kyoto recluse associated with Kōdaiji Temple in the Higashiyama district, was a warlord who retired only after political reversals made it necessary.

COMMENT: According to an anonymous disciple Chōshōshi "wrote whenever he was overcome by feelings, disregarding rules and unconcerned with established convention" (*Kyohakushinhyō* [Reading to the heart of Kyohaku], mid-seventeenth century, p. 109). This comes out most strongly in his personal poems, like the one here, written after the death of his third child by his second marriage, a daughter who fell ill in the spring of 1626 and died a year later, aged just seventeen—a process the poet wrote about in detail and movingly in a memoir he titled *Unaimatsu* (Grave-marking pine). Chōshōshi's poem is explicit in a way that is rare in formal composition. His grief continued into autumn, again documented in poems (nos. 319, 323, 328) distinctive in their direct expression:

Barely seen at all,	*miru to naki*
lightning strikes in the gloom	*yami no utsusu no*
of our reality—	*inazuma ya*

its destination the same	*hakanaki hito no*
as the one who is no more.	*yukue naruramu*

Ailing though she was,	*kozo no aki no*
at this same time last year	*kono koro made wa*
she was still with me—	*ukinagara*
here with me as through the mists	*kirima no tsuki o*
we gazed upon the moon.	*tomo ni mishi kana*

My body weakened	*naki hito o*
by longing for one now gone,	*koiyowaru mi wa*
I gaze at my garden	*iku yo shi mo*
and think my days will soon end—	*araji to zo miru*
vanishing like the white snow.	*niwa no shirayuki*

Lightning, mist, the moon, and snow—all of these will of course come around again in the natural course of things, having a provisional temporality established in the cycles of nature; not so, though, Chōshōshi's daughter, as those images, to his sad frustration, endlessly instruct. The symbols, in that sense, are simply not enough—nor, the many poems suggest, is poetry.

KAMO NO MABUCHI 賀茂真淵, *Kamo okina kashū* 80 (Spring): "Broad plains"

As a lark rises	*hibari agaru*
into spring skies at break of day,	*haru no asake ni*
I gaze, and behold	*miwataseba*
the Broad Plain stretching afar	*ochi no kunihara*
beneath bands of spreading haze.	*kasumi tanabiku*

CONTEXT: In the Edo period there were many competing genres, *waka*, *haikai*, and *kanshi* (Chinese poetry), and many competing movements. In the *waka* form, one of these was *kokugaku*, "national studies," whose members often looked to *Man'yōshū* for inspiration in their own poetry. Kamo no Mabuchi (1697-1769) was one of that movement's founders.

COMMENT: Mabuchi's poem, from his personal collection, exhibits the traits of the *kokugaku* style: elevated diction, lofty imagery, declarative rhetoric, and what was called honest feeling (*naoki kokoro*). His attention piqued by a lark rising into mild spring skies, the speaker gazes out on a broad landscape that is a picture of calm. The *dai* of the poem is archaic, as is the word *asake* (break of day). Furthermore, Mabuchi's calls to mind the ancient imperial harvest rite of *kunimi*, or "surveying the realm," as memorialized in the second poem in Man'yōshū (no. 2), a *chōka* attributed to Emperor Jomei:

Climbing Mount Kagu and Surveying the Realm

Mountains abound	yamato ni wa
in our Land of Yamato,	murayama aredo
yet finest of all	toriyorou
is Kagu of the Heavens.	ame no kaguyama
To its peak I climb	noboritachi
and there survey my realm:	kunimi o sureba
smoke rising	kunihara wa
over broad plains of land,	keburi tachitatsu
seagulls rising	unahara wa
over broad plains of sea.	kamame tachitatsu
How splendid our land—	umashi kuni zo
our dragonfly islands,	akizushima
our Realm of Yamato!	yamato no kuni wa

Like Jomei's, Mabuchi's poem is all sensory, invoking no reasoning process but only celebratory images. He presents a "spring" view, replaces the cooking fires with a lark, but otherwise creates a similar auspicious scene. One remembers what Ueda Akinari (1734-1809), himself a *kokugaku* scholar, said in *Harusame monogatari* (*Tales of Spring Rain*, p. 571) about Man'yō-era poets: "Whatever moved them, they wrote about it without affectation." An exaggeration, perhaps, but one that capsulizes the designs of Mabuchi and other poets of his school, whose project was inevitably involved with the nationalist ideology of the new Tokugawa regime.

OKUN おくん, *Okunshū* (p. 38): "Bedclothes"

In my old age	oiraku wa
I pile on the bedclothes at night,	yoru no fusuma o
layer on layer;	kasanete mo
yet still through my chamber walls	neya no hima moru
seeps the chill of the wind.	kaze zo samukeki

CONTEXT: Okun (1715–1781) was consort to Tokugawa Muneharu (1696–1764), lord of Owari domain. Few Edo-era women left large anthologies of their work, but she left more than four thousand poems—an exception perhaps explained by her high status. The *dai* of bedclothes—which refers to quilts, a variation on what we now call *futon*—was somewhat unusual, but her anthology makes it clear that Okun did not choose the *dai* herself, instead receiving it from her teacher, a Kyoto courtier of the noble Reizei house.

COMMENT: Next to this poem Okun's teacher jotted down, "Based on real feelings, perhaps?" (*jitsujō ka*). A more established *dai* demanded strict attention to precedent, but "bedclothes" allowed more latitude. Okun begins with a blunt comment: *oiraku wa*, "in my old age," which colors everything that follows. First she sets the scene—night; then we see her in her bedchamber, piling on quilts; and then we feel with her the "chill of the wind." In this way we go from outside to inside and then to the wall between inside and outside, where gaps allow in the cold wind. Okun's scene is one that anyone can understand but is particularly designed to capture the reality of the experience of the elderly. It is not a far step to imagine Okun under her quilts, shivering with cold, awake and listening to the wind rattling the walls, as her teacher evidently does.

老くは夜の衾をかさねても寝屋のひまもる風ぞさむけき

The word *jitsujō* was also used in reference to poems of the past, as is clear in an anecdote about Jiun (1673–1753) and his teacher, Mushanokōji Sanekage (1661–1738). It begins with Jiun saying he had in the past not been impressed by the following poem by Tonna (*Tonna hōshi ei*, no. 10) until he experienced a similar scene firsthand.

Morning after morning	asana asana
I go outside, and I listen:	tachiidete kikeba
to where in haze	haru no no no
spreading over spring fields	kasumeru kata ni
a bush warbler sings.	uguisu zo naku

In his *Shirin shūyō* (Leaves from the groves of poetry, mid-eighteenth century, p. 166), Sanekage ratifies his judgment. "Ah, you have achieved a fine insight. At first, the poem may seem bland, but it is actually quite ingenious. After all, a poem must first of all present a new conception. There are many poems about the bush warbler, but you will not find one using the phrase 'morning after morning I go outside, and I listen.' This is the part of the poem on which one should focus attention. It is something new, a poem that expresses the feeling of actual experience [*jitsujō*]."

OZAWA ROAN 小澤蘆菴, *Hokusō sadan* (p. 298)

In 1792, Ozawa Roan took to bed with a serious ailment and was down a long time. During that period a certain rich man who had been his poetry disciple did not come to visit even once, and so when he had recovered... Roan sent the man a letter expressing his anger...

In this world of men	hito no yo no
riches are but dewdrops	tomi wa kusaba ni
on the grasses—	oku tsuyu no
light shining for a moment	kaze o matsu ma no
while we wait for the wind.	hikari narikeri

CONTEXT: Ozawa Roan (1723-1801) was a midranking samurai, born in Kyoto, who in middle age opted for life as a poetry scholar and teacher, living in the Okazaki and later the Uzumasa areas of that city. The scholar Tachibana Nankei (1753-1805) records this anecdote, dating it 1792 in his miscellany *Hokusō sadan* (Idle chats beneath a northern window, 1801); the poem is no. 1608 in Roan's personal anthology, *Rokujō eisō* (ca. 1811). He also notes that after recovering Roan cut off all contact with the man.

COMMENT: In the passage that prefaces this poem, Roan taxed his wealthy friend with a "lack of human feeling," using a phrase (*kokoro ari* or *ushin*) that in poetic discourse is often presented as the summum bonum of poetic identity. One does not usually associate Japanese poetry with such a strident statement of grievance. The anecdote ends with a postscript that reveals some discomfort with Roan's reaction: "Perhaps this sounds a little ill-tempered and harsh, but his anger was not without cause." Whatever the man's reasons, Roan's gibe offers us the very old trope of dew on the grasses, shining for only a moment before being dashed by the wind. Behind the trope is the assumption that the practice of poetry should elevate the sensibility and contribute to the building of character.

Roan was no hidebound pedant; indeed, in his time he was known for his quirky, unconventional style, as is evident from another poem, this one from his personal anthology *Rokujō eisō* (Poems in the style of the Six Notebooks, 1804; no. 1483).

"Hearing the cry of a crow in the distance, in the morning"

| The sounds of things | mono no ne wa |
| are better in the distance. | tōki masareri |

Why, even that crow	*karasu sura*
heard from far, far away,	*haruka ni kikeba*
is a source of true delight.	*okashikarikeri*

Some might fault such a poem for vulgar imagery and colloquial rhetoric (what Roan called *tadakotoba*), but as we see the speaker stopping whatever he is doing to enjoy a moment of sensory experience we recognize a familiar pose that claims for the poet the sort of sensibility that his wealthy student supposedly lacked.

MURATA HARUMI 村田春海, *Kotojirishū* 595: "On the first morning of spring, he washed his inkstone and wrote his 'first poem of the New Year'"

So old am I now	*oigami wa*
that the world seems far away;	*yo ni shi mo utoshi*
no one comes calling	*wabizumi wa*
at my shabby little house.	*hito mo toikozu*
Yet all the same,	*shikaredomo*
I am like everyone else:	*yo no hito nami ni*
I too add on	*atarashiki*
a new year to those gone by.	*toshi o kasanu to*
So I sweep the dust	*fuseio no*
from my squat hut of grass,	*chiri kakiharai*
and cast aside	*kinaraseru*
clothing grown old and worn—	*kinu nugikaete*
waiting for the light	*asahiko no*
of the dear sun to shine down,	*kage machitorite*
facing the direction	*haru no kuru*
from which new spring will come.	*kata ni mukaeba*
Unnoticed by me,	*hitoki tatsu*
buds have begun to appear	*hairi no ume mo*
on my one plum tree	*itsushika to*
where it stands at my front door;	*himo tokihajime*
and on the stakes	*muratake no*
of my bamboo wattle fence	*orikakegaki ni*
a bush warbler, too,	*uguisu mo*
is singing his first song—	*hatsune morashite*
all filling my heart	*onozukara*
with a natural sense of calm.	*kokoro nodokeshi*
And so I say:	*yoshi ya sa wa*

I'm fine with no visitors!
So I've grown old—
what reason is that
    to complain!
It's my good fortune
to live life at my leisure
in a world at peace,
and to once again be here
to greet a new spring—
a spring that begins above,
unspoiled by the weeds below.

Envoy

In happy spirits
I now behold a new spring.
From today on,
my friends will be the flowers
and warblers 'round my home.

towarenu mo yoshi
oinu tote

nani nagekamashi
ureshiku mo
yukurayukura ni
shizuka naru
yo ni nagaraete
mugura ni mo
sawaranu haru o
mata mo mukaetsu

ureshiku mo
haru wa mukaetsu
kyō yori zo
hana uguisu o
waga yado no tomo

CONTEXT: Murata Harumi (1746-1811) was born into the merchant class, but his literary talent emerged early, and he was for a time adopted as the heir of a *renga* master in service to the shogunate. He studied philology under Kamo no Mabuchi, a chief figure in the National Studies movement, and produced work of some distinction. His first love, however, was Japanese poetry in the *waka* form. Along with Katō Chikage (1735-1808), he became a central figure in Edo poetic circles. His personal anthology, *Kotojirishū* (Behind the koto, 1810), put together with the help and at the insistence of students, records more than sixteen hundred *waka* and nearly thirty *chōka*.

COMMENT: Old genres persisted into the Edo period, and most poets could compose *chōka* when occasion demanded. One of those occasions, as seen in the *chōka* of Mitsune, was the advent of a new year, which marked the beginning of spring in the lunar calendar. In premodern Japan, many rituals and celebrations marked the beginning of a new year, one of which was composing a "first poem," in either Chinese or Japanese, or both. In the case of short poems, propitious imagery and sentiments were the rule, but Harumi uses his *chōka* form to produce a personal portrait; no public voice here.

Like Kenzai, Harumi employs no *makurakotoba*: he lauds not a "rough-hewn year" (*aratama no toshi*) but a straightforward "new" year (*atarashiki toshi*); and although he does use some parallel structures, they are not as clearly articulated as they would be in a *chōka* of the Man'yō era. In this sense, his *chōka* is modern, however antique its generic origins. His description of his life in a shabby little house, a *fuseio* with eaves that nearly touch the ground, is as modest as the life it purports to represent. In a few laconic lines, we learn that he is a recluse, old and out of touch with the world of human affairs—a pose, certainly, but true enough of a man who had left behind worldly ambitions. Yet the speaker nearly immediately insists that even in such surroundings, he remains part of the community. Hence he does his chores, as expected of all homeowners, sweeping out his abode, throwing out worn garments in favor of something new, and turning toward the "dear sun" (*asahiko*) as a symbol of renewal. Around him, he chronicles a natural world in harmony with the transition from winter to spring, symbolized by buds coming out on his one flowering plum and a warbler breaking out in song. His hut may boast only a crude fence fashioned from bamboo, but he anticipates coming warmth and color all the same, enjoying the natural sense of security that accompanies those changes.

The last eleven lines of the poem and its envoy, full of optimism and approbation, forgo expressing the melancholy usually associated with old age. "I may be on the fringe of things," the speaker says, "but even as an old man, I should not complain. Thanks to the peace of the world around me, I can bask in the spring sun, safe and sound, enjoying the friends I do have, the flowers and the birds." A shadow of loneliness is thus balanced against a bright spirit of gratitude.

RYŌKAN 良寛, *Ryōkan kashū* 1208: "Holing up for winter"

Below Kugami,	ashihiki no
that foot-wearying mountain,	kugami no yamamoto
I hole up for winter.	fuyugomori
On this ridgeline, that peak,	mine ni mo mine ni mo
the white snow descends,	shirayuki no
piling up, piling up again.	tsumoritsumorite
No more do I hear	tobu tori no
songs from birds flying by,	koe mo kikoezu
and the path people take	satobito no

going back and forth from town—
it has disappeared.
So I shut out the cruel world
and pull fast my gate,
my life barely sustained
by pure waters
flowing down from mountain crags:
a stream sure as plumb lines
struck by Hida carpenters.
Thus I have survived
to greet a new year afresh,
as I do again today.

Envoy

As the night wears on,
the snow must be piling up
on the peak above.
Water gurgling amidst boulders—
even that sound has stopped.

yukikau michi no
ato mo nashi
ukiyo o koko ni
kado sashite
hida no takumi ga
utsu nawa no
tada hitosuji no
iwashimizu
so o inochi nite
aratama no
kotoshi no kyō mo
kurashitsuru kamo

sayo fukete
takane no miyuki
tsumorurashi
iwama ni tagitsu
oto dani mo senu

CONTEXT: Ryōkan (1758–1831), eldest son of a well-to-do farmer, studied in a Zen monastery in his teens but later moved back to Mount Kugami in Echigo, near his hometown. He wrote *chōka*, along with *waka*, *haikai*, *kanshi*, and some free verse. Although he studied in Bitchū (modern Okayama) for ten years and received a certificate of enlightenment, Ryōkan never held clerical office, instead living as a beggar-monk.

COMMENT: Ryōkan's poem, from *Ryōkan kashū* (Ryōkan's collection of Japanese poems, 1835), describes life in a harsh climate but also shows his knowledge of poetic traditions, beginning with a *makurakotoba* ("foot-wearying," applied to mountains), employing parallelism, and including an old metaphor for skill and steadfastness—the carpenters of Hida (in modern Gifu Prefecture), who since early times had been commissioned to do civil projects in Kyoto. The poem's dark tone and elevated rhetoric remind us of Mitsune's famous *Kokinshū*-era *chōka* about the New Year's. Yet the last two lines are characteristically playful, suggesting that Ryōkan may have to get along without the "pure waters" he is used to relying upon.

KAGAWA KAGEKI 香川景樹, *Keien isshi* 974: "On a woman selling firewood"

Come and buy, now!	mese ya mese
buy firewood for dinnertime,	yūge no tsumaki
hurry, get it now!	hayaku mese
The road home stretches far,	kaerusa tōshi
to the village of ōhara.	ōhara no sato

めせやめせゆふげの妻木はやくめせかへるさ遠し大原の里

CONTEXT: Kagawa Kageki (1768–1843; also known as Keien) was born in Tottori but moved to Kyoto in his twenties to make a career as a poet. He studied *waka* under a commoner poet affiliated with the noble Nijō school but was also influenced by Ozawa Roan and ended up breaking with his teacher and establishing a school of his own. Kageki's critical writings show his profound knowledge of the classical poetic canon but also the influence of the neo-Confucian discourse that so dominated the intellectual world of his time, which is evident in his impatience with narrow concepts of rationalism and corresponding encouragement of ideas like *shirabe* (fine tuning or tonal integrity) and *makoto* (sincerity).

COMMENT: Kageki's emphasis on the affective qualities of *shirabe* seems at odds with his championing of the *Kokinshū*, an anthology criticized for its excessive artifice by members of the National Studies movement. And there are many other seeming contradictions in Kageki's writings. Although he praises the rhetorical polish of Heian times, for example, he writes many poems that seem more reminiscent of the "plain words" of Ozawa Roan. The one here would seem to fit into that category.

The character Kageki offers in this poem is one with which any resident of Kyoto—or any city at the time—would have been very familiar. Every day in late afternoon peasants, men and women, from the mountains would walk through the city streets, hawking their products, usually carried on their backs, calling out with words like the ones Kageki puts in the mouth of his subject. Colloquial language of this sort would of course not have appeared in a standard *Kokinshū* poem, but it was not imitation of classical poets that Kageki encouraged so much as their freshness and depth of feeling. Furthermore, he put the poem in the *haikai* section of his anthology, *Keien isshi* (One branch from Master Keien, 1830), thus classifying it as "unorthodox" in the technical sense.

Kageki's poem was written as an inscription for a painting depicting a woman selling firewood. The first three lines of the poem tell us what the people of a neighborhood would hear as she walks by: *mese ya mese*—literally, "Buy, buy!"

To people on any given street the voice would be familiar, probably, in fact, the voice of someone they would see frequently. Then the woman urges her patrons on by warning them that she must soon leave, in a way meant to evoke pity. The "hurry, get it now!" is not just a come-on: Ōhara village, located to the northeast, along the banks of the Takano River, was most likely a two-hour journey, even for an experienced walker. And the walk would come after a long day of labor that began with a hike into the hills to gather wood, probably at dawn. In our minds, we see the long valley stretching out as the sun declines toward the mountains.

TACHIBANA AKEMI 橘曙覧, *Dokuraku gin*

What a joy it is:	*tanoshimi wa*
when I catch a glimpse of something	*futo mite hoshiku*
I simply *must* have—	*omou mono*
and then through pain and effort	*tsuraku hakarite*
come to hold it in my hand.	*te ni ireshi toki*

たのしみはふと見てほしくおもふ物辛くはかりて手にいれしとき

CONTEXT: Tachibana Akemi (1812–1868) was a scholar in the National Studies movement dedicated to study of ancient texts and also a prominent poet. In the Edo period there was a whole subgenre of humorous *waka* called *kyōka*, the origins of which go far back into medieval times, but what we confront in Akemi's poem is not generally called *kyōka*, that term being reserved for poems of elaborate wordplay and often ribald or vulgar subject matter. Akemi's work is instead in the tradition of the drinking poems of Ōtomo no Tabito in *Man'yōshū*.

COMMENT: This poem is the last of a set of fifty-two poems titled *Dokuraku gin* (Solitary pleasures, 1864) that all begin with "What a joy it is" (*tanoshimi wa*) and end (in the Japanese) with "when" (*toki*)—each presenting a declarative statement. The subjects deal mostly with the small delights of everyday life: family, friendship, reading, writing, and joys of the moment, from napping to eating and drinking and enjoying a pipe, and the emphasis is often on sensory experience, stated unabashedly. In the poem here, for example, the final satisfaction is expressed in tactile terms, "to hold it in my hand." Nor does Akemi try to defend his enjoyments as always noble or grand. We have all found ourselves just wanting something, perhaps even something vain or silly, and it is describing such universal human feelings that is the point of the poems. The joys he describes as "solitary" are in no sense known to him alone, though some of them concern feelings we might rather not admit.

Another refreshing feature of the poems is that, like the one here and that following (nos. 14 and 43), they sometimes foreground a topic never treated in orthodox *waka*—namely, finances, or rather feelings related to financial struggle:

What a joy it is:	*tanoshimi wa*
when our empty rice barrel	*akikomebitsu ni*
has new rice in it,	*kome ideki*
and I'm told we have enough	*ima hitotsuki wa*
to last us for a month.	*yoshi to iu toki*

What a joy it is:	*tanoshimi wa*
when there is something I want,	*hoshikarishi mono*
so I take out my purse	*zenibukuro*
and pour out all of my coins—	*uchikatabukete*
and have enough to buy it!	*kai etaru toki*

ŌTAGAKI RENGETSU 大田垣蓮月, *Zōho Rengetsu zenshū* 1 (p. 58): "Composed when she heard that south of Fushimi many men had fallen in battle"

I hear the reports	*kiku mama ni*
and drench my sleeves with tears.	*sode koso nurure*
There by the roadside,	*michinobe ni*
those corpses left on the ground—	*sarasu kabane wa*
they will be somebody's sons.	*ta ga ko naruran*

CONTEXT: Ōtagaki Rengetsu (1791–1875) sold poems inscribed on *tanzaku* and also provided inscriptions on paintings and tea wares. She was born into a samurai family and actually served in a castle in her youth, where she learned polite arts such as poetry and calligraphy. Her first marriage ended in divorce, but not before she bore and lost two children, and when she married again, the result was the loss of two (maybe three) more children and her new husband, within five years. At age thirty-three she became a nun, along with her adoptive father, an administrator at Chion'in, a Kyoto temple of the Pure Land sect. Thereafter she supported herself as a commercial artist, living in the Higashiyama and Kamo areas of Kyoto.

COMMENT: In January of 1868 the forces of the Tokugawa shogun and royalists fought at Toba-Fushimi in a crucial battle leading up to the collapse of the old

聞くままに袖こそぬるれ道のべにさらすかばねは誰が子なるらん

government and the establishment of a new monarchy, the so-called Meiji Restoration. It was at that time that this lament was written. Rengetsu was in her late seventies then, living in the area west of the Kamo River near Jinkōin, well to the north of the battlefield. She is remembered now as a nun of the Pure Land sect, but she knew a great deal about the loss of children and in this and other poems writes at least partially as a mother, which amounts to a kind of gender marking. Laments had been written about war in the past, particularly by clergy, but few so direct in terms of their imagery and sentiment. "Corpse" (*kabane*) was not a word generally used in courtly poetry after *Man'yōshū*.

Many legends have attached themselves to Rengetsu. One involves the following poem (also appearing in her complete works, *Zōho Rengetsu zenshū* 1, p. 58), also written during the years of conflict.

Whether foes or friends,	ada mikata
whether winners or losers,	katsu mo makuru mo
I feel only grief—	aware nari
when I think that all of them	onaji mikuni no
are men of our own realm.	hito to omoeba

The legend is that she wrote this "antiwar" poem and sent it to the great general Saigō Takamori (1827–1877), one of the chief opponents of the shogunate, before he invaded Edo, which moved him so much that he changed his tactics in order to do less damage to the city. One would like to believe the story, both for what it implies about the purposes of poetry and for what it implies about Saigō.

HIGUCHI ICHIYŌ 樋口一葉, *Ichiyō kashū* (p. 319): "False love"

I know, of course,	itsuwari no
that in our world people lie.	yo to wa shiredomo
Yet surely not *you*—	kimi nomi wa
I had thought that of you at least	yo mo to bakari mo
that could never be true.	omoitsuru kana

CONTEXT: Higuchi Ichiyō (1872–1896) is known for a group of stories she wrote in a few short years before her untimely death by tuberculosis. Like many young women of her day, she studied poetry as part of her "finishing," leaving behind a personal anthology (*Ichiyō's Waka Anthology*) of more than three thousand poems. Her poem was actually written on an old *dai*, "false love," which may have been assigned by her teacher. The presence of such poems in the oeuvre of one of the most admired writers of the Meiji era reminds us that old *waka* discourse was still alive at that time, especially for women.

COMMENT: There is a refreshing innocence in the surprise felt by the speaker of this poem, a young person, probably a woman, who lacks experience in the ways of love. Knowing something abstractly and understanding it in real experience are two different things. Ichiyō's conclusion is nothing new; what she wanted to say was not new, but fundamental, as the following poem, composed on the topic "love at first sight," makes clear (*Ichiyō kashū*, p. 320):

Ah, how swiftly	kasugano ni
the spring grasses have come out	moeizuru haru no
on Kasuga Moor,	wakakusa no
as swiftly as I have come	hayaku mo hito o
to take notice of you.	misometsuru kana

Here the place-name (in Nara) is entirely conventional, as is the imagery of grasses coming out in spring fields—a common metaphor for the first stirrings of love. And in the first three lines of the poem Ichiyō even deploys a rhetorical device that takes us all the way back to *Man'yōshū* days: the extended metaphorical preface, or *jokotoba*.

The temptation to read such poems in terms of Ichiyō's own life experience is strong. She was, after all, a young person and must have had such feelings herself. It is equally important, however, to remember that she attended monthly poetry gatherings run by her teacher, where she not only presented her own poems but also heard lectures on the Japanese classics. It would be hard to argue that this "literary" experience was less influential than whatever she experienced in her private life. Well into the modern era, the old mores still held sway in many circles, especially those touching in some way on the education of youth, whose mentors were still likely to conceive of the mastering of an art in didactic terms.

いつはりの世とはしれども君のみはよもと斗もおもひつるかな

MORI ŌGAI 森鴎外, *Uta nikki* (pp. 261-62): "In the trenches"

Low clouds were darkening the sky,	tempering the chill
that had prevailed at midday,	when in growing dusk
drops of rain began to tap	on my south window,

along with another sound—
"Who might it be?" I wondered,
finding there a foot soldier,
who had somehow lost the road
till at last he ended up
After bandaging his wound
on the bed right next to mine
"Up there on the front line,
won't you tell me about it,
Do the frosts of morning
Do the rains of evening
Without any proper roads
do you gnaw day after day
Tell me, is that what it's like?"
made a weary attempt
"You may think me rude, sir,
but just the thought of all that now
The way things are in that place—
I will never speak of them:
not to mother or father.
I shall hide those things inside,
someone's voice, it was.
and had someone look,
wounded in the arm,
and gone in circles
outside our gate.
I laid him down
and asked him this:
in the trenches—
what it's truly like?
fall on your cap?
drench your sleeves?
to bring you food,
on balls of dried rice?
At this the soldier
to shake his head.
for not replying,
brings pain to my breast.
why, if I return home,
not to wife or child,
From now, forever,
in my heart alone."

sora kakikumori
samusa nagomeru
minami no mado o
tomo ni otonau
tare ka kitaru to
kaina irareshi
michi ni mayoite
kadobe ni koso wa
kizu o tsutsumite
narabi fusashime
daiissen no
makoto no sama o
bō ni ashita no
yūbe no ame ni
kate o hakoban
hoshii kamite
ika ni to ieba
kōbe tayuge ni

hiru no ma no
yūyami ni
utsu ame to
koe su nari
misasureba
heisotsu no
tamotōri
kinuru nare
waga toko ni
toikeraku
horinuchi no
katarazu ya
shimo furite
sode hizuchi
michi o nami
hi o ya heshi
heisotsu wa
uchifurite

inamaba nameshi to	obosamedo
omoeba mune zo	itamu naru
kashiko no sama wa	kaeran hi
tsuma ni kodomo ni	omochichi ni
ware wa kataraji	ima yu nochi
kokoro hitotsu ni	himeokite

Envoys

In the trenches,	horinuchi yu
so close is the enemy	keburi tateji to
that the soldiers	ada chikami
keep the stove from smoking	kudo no takigi o
and break their kindling quietly.	sasayaka ni waru

In the trenches,	horinuchi ni
how many nights have they slept so—	iku yo ka netsuru
never neglecting	isasame ni
to leave still tied the laces	yuishi ayui no
that secure their soldier boots?	himo tokazu shite

CONTEXT: Mori Ōgai (1862–1922, legal name Rintarō) was born in a provincial capital just before the Meiji Restoration, to a clan physician. After a traditional education in Chinese classics, he was sent to Tokyo Imperial University to study medicine, along with German and Western science. He graduated in 1881 and went on to study in Germany (1884–1888) on government stipend. As he advanced in the ranks of the medical corps, contributing to the study of Western science and literature in Japan, he wrote stories, novels, and biographies that eventually made him one of the chief literary figures of his time.

COMMENT: Ōgai saw medical service in the Sino-Japanese War of 1894–1895 and the Russo-Japanese War of 1904–1905 and in 1907 became surgeon general of the army. At this time he was known as a translator of German and Scandinavian literature rather than a novelist. But he had read Chinese and Japanese poetry all his life and continued to write even while on campaigns. His *Uta nikki* (Uta diary, 1904) consists of poems written from the field in a variety of forms, ranging from traditional genres to modern "Western-style" verse. The narrative poem here, written at Shilihe, Manchuria, on the seventeenth day of the Tenth Month, in 1904, is an adaptation of the *chōka* form that presents alternating seven- and five-syllable lines but employs lineation perhaps meant to break with old models. Showing his knowledge of the Japanese canon, Ōgai employs archaic grammar, parallelism, and even a *makurakotoba* (*tamotōri*, "going in circles"). Yet we have to question his confidence when his narrator, after using traditional aesthetic rhetoric to describe the trenches of his imagination, is rebuffed by the soldier, who says that he will never speak of his experiences. Is this an example of irony—the speaker admitting the distance between the two men, in terms of rank and class? If anything, the envoys increase the distance between the two men, admitting a chasm that cannot be traversed.

WATANABE JUNZŌ 渡辺順三, *Seikatsu o utau* (p. 383)

> She's dirt-poor, and on top of that, has a worthless husband.
> Worn thin from keeping house,
> my wife nods off for a nap.
>
> *binbō na ue ni kayowai otto mochi / setai ni yaseta / tsuma no utatane*

CONTEXT: Watanabe Junzō (1894–1972) was born the son of a disenfranchised samurai who found work as a grade-school principal but died when Junzō was just twelve. The family moved to Tokyo, where Junzō began working in a furniture store. In 1923 he opened a printing shop of his own but was never anything but a failure at business. Since his early twenties he had been active in literary circles and published his first collection of *tanka*—the term used for 5-7-5-7-7 syllables in modern Japan—in 1927. At a time when artistic lineage still meant a great deal, socially and philosophically, he was associated with the disciples of Ishikawa Takuboku (1886–1912), a proponent of socialist engagement. Watanabe himself would go on to be associated with proletarianism in the 1920s and 1930s and the progressive movements of the postwar era.

COMMENT: The history of *tanka* discourse in the mid-twentieth century resists summary. It was a time when anyone writing in traditional forms had to face questions about their relevance in the modern world, and

貧乏な上にかよわい夫もち
世帯にやせた
妻のうたたね

inevitably there were experiments of all sorts, from the formal to the thematic. Broadly speaking, over time the world of *tanka* was divided—though seldom neatly or completely—between those who pursued *tanka* as a hobby, often participating in some sort of club or association under the direction of a master, and those who thought of it as a truly "serious" art form, on a par with free verse. Watanabe is treated as a "serious" poet. In using unconventional lineation (obscuring a traditional 5-7-5-7-7 syllabic structure) he was following the example of Takuboku. The poem here, from his 1927 book *Seikatsu o utau* (I sing of everyday life), is typical in the way it describes a moment of quotidian languor. Watanabe did not have to exercise his imagination to experience poverty, knowing it firsthand for most of his life. Rather than just himself, however, he often puts his wife in the picture. And another poem, from 1954, "Nihon no chizu" (Map of Japan, p. 390), manages to go beyond personal complaint to social critique.

My poverty—
it began in my parents' times, and continued on;
it's like grime that clings to my body, that's how it seems.
binbō wa / oya no dai yori hikitsugite / mi ni tsuku aka no gotoshi to omou

In a capitalist society, the poet hints, poverty is at bottom a matter of lacking capital and is in many cases an inherited state. The reference to the unbathed masses, whose poverty sticks to them like grime—a layer of caked-on dirt that does not yield easily to removal—is a particularly tactile way of expressing what is after all a physical as much as a social state.

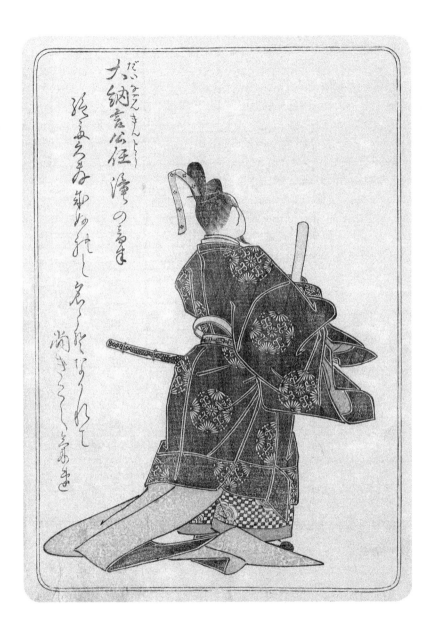

Portrait of Fujiwara no Kintō, an early eleventh-century court poet and musician who compiled one of the first collections of Japanese and Chinese poems for singing; from *Nishiki hyakunin isshu azuma ori*, an illustrated text of *Hyakunin isshu* by the eighteenth-century artist Katsukawa Shunshō.

Courtesy L. Tom Perry Special Collection, HBLL, Brigham Young University.

Chapter 3
POPULAR SONGS

EMPEROR YŪRYAKU 雄略天皇, *Kinkafu* 13

You maiden,	*minasosogu*
fine as flowing waters:	*omi no otome*
hold the vessel tightly, now,	*hodari tori*
hold it firmly.	*kataku tore*
Grip it tightly from below,	*shitagataku*
just as tightly as you can,	*yagataku tore*
you girl holding the vessel.	*hodari torasu ko*

CONTEXT: Some of the earliest songs of the Japanese tradition appear in a small collection titled *Kinkafu* (Songs to accompany the koto), which scholars date to sometime in the late tenth century, although the songs come from much earlier times. Sometimes the songs of the collection suggest allegorical readings, but on the surface the subjects are straightforward: banquets, the hunt, planting, the new year, the beauties of the natural word, and, of course, love and courting.

The introduction to the song here offers two conflicting origin stories. The first says it was composed by Emperor Yūryaku (418-479) in a banquet setting, when a lady of high station (*omi no otome*) served him wine. The second is more convoluted, telling how the emperor's consort composed the song as a lament over members of her clan (the Ōomi) who had been killed in an intrigue against her husband. Scholars tend to favor the former account, first because a similar song is recorded with a similar story in the mytho-historical record *Kojiki* and also because of that story's appealing simplicity.

COMMENT: A notation tells us that the song was known as an *ukiuta*—i.e., a song sung "when pouring sake." We should imagine, then, a woman of high birth

水濯ぐ臣の少女秀瓶執り堅く執れ下堅く弥堅く執れ秀瓶執らす子

given the honor, and the weighty responsibility, of offering wine to a person of some consequence. Doubtless ritual or etiquette was involved in bringing in a wine jar—a large, heavy vessel, the poem implies—and serving libations to an honored guest; hence the concern of the speaker that the maiden hold the vessel firmly as she pours.

Like many early *chōka*, the song displays irregular prosody (four five-syllable lines, two six-syllables lines, and one seven-syllable line), and it also shows its connection to prevailing poetic convention by beginning with a *makurakotoba*. Here that figure—"fine as flowing waters"—introduces the idea of purity, applied both to the sake and to the woman presenting it. Needless to say, the way the emperor encourages her (in a voyeuristic way?) to grip the vessel tightly is suggestive and meant to be so. The reference to her physical embrace of the jar seems especially symbolic when we remember how daughters in elite society of the time were often objects of barter in political maneuvering—what we call marriage politics. Perhaps with this in mind it is not so difficult to imagine the poem as indeed having been written by a woman in grief over the loss of family and perhaps unsure of her own new position. The repetition of various forms of "hold the vessel tightly" on that reading would be a way of reminding herself that she must be careful to hold her place, to play her role well.

ANONYMOUS, *Kokinshū* 1075: "A *torimono* song"

And what damage	shimo yatabi
have the unceasing frosts done	okedo kare sen
to the *sakaki*?	sakakiba no
None—no, the leaves are thriving,	tachisakayu beki
as shall those who serve the gods.	kami no kine ka mo

CONTEXT: In ancient times the imperial government founded a Bureau of Folk Songs tasked with collecting folk songs, regional songs, and sacred songs. Quite naturally, a chapter of such songs was included in *Kokinshū*. The one here is a sacred song (*kami asobi uta* or *kagurauta*). Authorship of the song is unknown, as is the case with all but two of the two dozen in that chapter. The song is identified as in the subcategory *torimonouta*, "presentation songs" that accompanied the offering of auspicious objects before the gods. In ancient times, the *sakaki*, now usually identified with *Cleyera japonica*, seems to have been a more vague reference to various evergreens employed in shrine rituals.

Commentary: *Kagura* were performed at shrines and at the imperial court as part of enthronement ceremonies and twice yearly at the Naishidokoro (Handmaid's Office) and involved the courtly arts of poetry, music, and dance, intended to impress the god and elicit favor. The symbolic origin of the rituals is the mythological story of how the Sun Goddess, sequestered in a cave after an argument with her brother, was coaxed out by dancing, singing, and a decorated *sakaki* tree. Folk versions of *kagura*, which flourished at banquets and at shrines all over the country and are performed to this day, were likely lively affairs. However, things were more staid at court, as is evidenced by the standard prosody of the songs included in *Kokinshū*—almost certainly the result of editing. In this sense, they are prosodically no different from *waka*. The performance we should imagine as the setting of the above poem would have been done at night, probably by torchlight, in a courtyard. A director would dance, with other dancers, a cadre of musicians playing clappers, zithers, Japanese flutes, and *hichiriki* (a kind of oboe), as well as choruses. Performances and the banquets that accompanied them could last all night and involve scores of songs, sung slowly. The poem here is obviously symbolic, functioning as a prayer for favor. The phrase *kami no kine* may be a *kakekotoba* referring both to the trees of the gods (*sakaki*) and, as a homonym, to the *miko* (shrine maidens), who performed among the dancers.

The "presentation song" (*Kokinshū*, no. 1074) that precedes the one here is even more obviously celebratory and simple in conception, a paean of praise that presents again the *sakaki* flourishing in the shrine precincts on an unspecified "holy mountain" (*mimuro*).

しもやたびおけどかれせぬさかきばのたちさかゆべき神のきねかも

Inside the sacred fence	kamikaki no
around the shrine to the god	mimuro no yama no
on its holy mountain,	sakakiba wa
see how the *sakaki* leaves grow,	kami no mimae ni
flourishing before the god!	shigeriainikeri

ANONYMOUS, *Ryōjin hishō* 399

The woodcutter, he's a scary sight!	kikori wa osoroshi ya
He has a rugged look—	arakeki sugata ni
dangling a sickle,	kama o mochi
with an ax in one hand,	yoki o sage
walking along with firewood	ushiro ni shibaki

loaded on his back.	*mainoboru to ka ya na*
And to keep mountain guards	*mae ni wa yamamori*
from approaching head-on—	*yoseji tote*
he has a walking stick as well.	*tsue o sage*

CONTEXT: Our earliest collection of so-called modern songs (*imayō*) comes from Emperor Go-Shirakawa (1127-1192), a fan of songs sung by female street entertainers called *asobi* and *kugutsu*. He titled his collection *Ryōjin hishō* (A secret sheaf of dust from the rafters, ca. 1169). Unfortunately, only a tenth of the original work survives—part of a first chapter of mostly spring songs and the complete second chapter, which concentrates on religious themes. This poem comes from the "Miscellaneous" section in the second chapter.

COMMENT: Songs show a broader swath of life than we see in courtly *waka* and employ a less-polished, colloquial vocabulary. The woodcutter is also evoked in *waka* and *renga* but never in such detail. The song relies on a straightforward sequence of rustic images and contains no poetic devices. Scholars point out that the text mirrors a description of the guardian deity Fudō (Acala in Sanskrit) from the same anthology (*Ryōjin hishō*, no. 284), knowledge of which injects mild humor into the description of the woodcutter.

Fudō Myōō, he's a scary sight!	*Fudō myōō osoroshi ya*
He has an angry look—	*ikareru sugata ni*
dangling a sword,	*kemu o mochi*
with a rope in one hand,	*saku o sage*
walking along with a fire	*ushiro ni kaen*
burning behind him.	*moenoboru to ka ya na*
And to keep evil demons	*mae ni wa akuma*
from approaching head-on—	*yoseji tote*
ah, that fearsome mien!	*gama no sō*

Fudō was a guardian deity whose physical attributes and appurtenances symbolized his readiness to withstand evil—a harsh, wrathful posture, a straight sword, a rope, fire, and a frightful countenance. A woodcutter is a more mundane figure who had need of such a posture. Every day he went into the woods to collect wood, which he carried into towns to sell. Animals and terrain were a constant danger, as were thieves, who might steal either his cargo or his money, and mountain guards, who might restrict his gathering. Imitating the guardian deity was a wise strategy—so the poem suggests.

ANONYMOUS, *Ryōjin hishō* 363

Only the two children,	ōna ga kodomo wa
that's all I've got.	tada futari
My girl, she was summoned	hitori no onago wa
to the kitchens	nii chūjōdono no
of a middle captain,	kuriyazōshi ni
a man of second rank—	meshishikaba
and there she serves.	tatemateki
Her young brother, he was summoned	ototo no onokogo wa
to the swift boats	usa no daiguji ga
of the Shrine Lord	hayafune funako ni
at Usa Hachiman—	koishikaba
and there he works.	madaiteki
Look down on me,	kami mo hotoke mo
gods and buddhas of Wakamiya—	goranze yo
what is it I have done	nani o tataritamau
for you to curse me so?	wakamiya no omae zo

CONTEXT: Emperor Go-Shirakawa, a particular enthusiast of popular song, gives us the names of a few among his courtiers who were *imayō* enthusiasts—for example, Taira no Narifusa (d. 1179) and Minamoto no Sukekata (1113-1188). It appears, however, that they were musicians and not the authors of the songs, which had anonymous origins. The perspective of this song is a person of fairly low social status.

COMMENT: Many songs, including the one here, offer us narratives that employ parallelism—sometimes syntactic, sometimes thematic, sometimes both—reminiscent of patterns observed in the *chōka*. The prosody of the song, however, is highly irregular (six five-syllable lines, but also four eight-syllable lines, three of nine syllables, and one of ten) when viewed in that way. Likewise, the diction is highly colloquial.

Our speaker is a mother presenting a lament on her plight *as* a mother. Significantly, the poem presents not a single natural image and no lyrical flourishes. Instead, it describes a real-world predicament in dramatic and heartfelt terms. Placing children in livings was a duty for parents, of course, and a challenge, and this mother could claim that she has achieved success. Her girl has gone into service of a middle captain of second rank, someone high in the court hierarchy in Kyoto, who uses her in his kitchens. Her son is in less-enviable circumstances, perhaps, working as a sailor, perhaps an oarsman, in the employ of a supervisor at Usa Hachiman Shrine, a large and prosperous Shinto shrine in Kyushu. Yet worldly success does not translate into personal happiness. What the mother in her lonely house feels is not gratitude but resentment, not a blessing but a curse. The particular curse she refers to is one visited upon someone by a dead spirit that demands expiation, but it can fall on someone wholly blameless. Wakamiya is a subshrine where people appealed for expiation of their sins.

ANONYMOUS, *Ryōjin hishō* 302

In spring, I go into burnt fields	*haru no yakeno ni*
to pick herbs	*na o tsumeba*
and there he is, a holy man,	*iwaya ni hijiri koso*
living beneath a cliff—	*owasu nare*
and all by himself.	*tada hitori*
Hey there, holy man,	*nobe nite tabitabi*
we'll meet once in a while	*au yori wa*
in the fields,	*na iza tamae*
but that's not enough—	*hijiri koso*
so come with me!	*iyashi no yō nari to mo*
It's a crude thing, my hut of sticks,	*warawara ga*
but please do come along.	*shiba no iori e*

CONTEXT: It was common practice for monks to withdraw from the world and pursue their devotions in isolation. Here we see a devout man who has taken that step but still finds himself faced with temptations.

COMMENT: This poem begins with the rustic scene of a woman going into the fields to engage in the customary spring activity of gathering young herbs. In that sense the song begins as a praise of new life in the form of plants emerging in fields burned over at the end of the previous harvest season. Spring has come; the snows have melted and people can again enjoy the bounties of the natural world.

But in her trek through the fields the woman finds more than herbs. As she walks along, thinking of her table and the tasty meal to come, the prospect of another sort of pleasure confronts her when she happens on a monk living beneath a cliff. Thus the stage is set for a meeting. The woman and the monk are unidentified; they are types meant to be of universal application. Both live lives of privation, but for different reasons—simple poverty in the case of the woman, one guesses, and religious vocation in the case of the monk.

The woman reveals her attitude with her playful form of address: "Hey there, *holy man*"—or *hijiri*, an honorific title, given to the truly devout but here coming across as a mildly seductive taunt. In every way her approach is cagey: since I live close by, she says, in mock innocence, we are bound to meet from time to time; why not keep each other company? Thus she seeks to erase the distinctions between them, arguing that because they occupy the same environment they may as well occupy it together in the warmth and shelter of her small house, which offers more comfort than the elemental and "natural" environment of a cave. However, we know that for the holy man temptation is waiting in the house of sticks—a place that is "constructed" rather than natural. For a recluse monk, withdrawal from comfort was the whole point, and abstaining from all contact with the opposite sex was a fundamental purpose for fleeing into the wilds in the first place. That we are not told the outcome of the dramatic narrative tells us that the basic conflict the poem poses is constant and endless.

ANONYMOUS, *Ryōjin hishō* 332, 333

332

What is it that clears the heart?	kokoro no sumu mono wa
In autumn, at every hut	aki wa yamada no
in mountain paddies,	iogoto ni
one hears the sound of clappers	shika odorokasu chō
keeping deer away,	hita no koe
that, and the sound	koromo shideutsu
of mallets striking robes.	tsuchi no oto

333

What is it that clears the heart?	kokoro no sumu mono wa
Spring haze, groves of flowers,	kasumi hanazono
the moon in the night,	yowa no tsuki
fields in autumn.	aki no nobe
In the way of love	kamishimo mo wakanu wa
there is neither high nor low:	koi no michi

down through gaps in the rocks
water spills—a cascade.

iwama o morikuru
taki no mizu

CONTEXT: We associate lists with Sei Shōnagon (b. 965?), whose famous *Pillow Book* contains lists of everything from "Clouds" to "Things That Make the Heart Race." One can easily imagine people creating such lists in conversation. "What are things that make you angry?" . . . "What are your favorite flowers?"

COMMENT: These two songs are from the "Miscellaneous" section of the second chapter of *Ryōjin hishō*, and the idea of "clearing the heart" easily fits into a Buddhist scenario. But poets too were advised to clear their hearts before composing, usually by reading classical texts or observing the natural world in order to elevate the sensibility above mundane concerns. Both songs in fact focus on traditional poetic images: huts in mountain paddies, deer clappers (wooden sticks fastened to ropes pulled to make a clapping sound and scare birds and animals away), women beating the wrinkles out of robes with a mallet, in the first poem, and spring haze, flowers, the moon, autumn fields, and water coursing between rocks in the mountains in the second. Yet, however canonical, the things on the lists are well within the experience of normal people. It may seem curious that both poems end with images that evoke love: a woman beating a robe, which was a common trope for longing for a mate away from home, and rushing water, often used as a metaphor for overwhelming passion. But the experience of love was considered a fundamental component of what it meant to be human, and monks often composed on that *dai*. As the songs suggest, love is a universal, and Buddhist thought was highly invested in the contemplation of universals.

ANONYMOUS LITTLE SONGS, from *Kanginshū*

59

How does love feel to me?
Fireflies flickering
above the water,
forlorn fireflies
unable to say a word.

waga koi wa
mizu ni moetatsu
hotaru hotaru
mono iwade
shōshi no hotaru

心の済むものは、秋の山田の庵毎に、鹿驚かすてふ引板の声、衣しで打つ槌の音

心の済むものは、霞花園夜半の月、秋の野辺、上下も分かぬは恋の路、岩間を漏り来る瀧の水

CONTEXT AND COMMENT: In 1518 a recluse who says about himself only that he had lived for more than ten years near Mount Fuji made a collection of 311 *kouta* (little songs) and other songs. (Tradition identifies him as the *renga* poet Sōchō, but no sure evidence for the attribution has been discovered.) He titled his collection *Kanginshū* (Songs from quiet days). The little songs express universal human feelings, often using standard images from the courtly tradition, such as the fireflies in the song here—a straightforward metaphor for smoldering passion that has no voice. The following songs do the same, using images from boats and hail to clouds, the moon, and blossoms.

131

In a slave boat I am rowed along	hitokaibune wa
out on the sea.	oki o kogu
I am to be *sold*, boatman.	totemo uraruru mi o
Could you not row more gently,	tada shizuka ni koge yo
please?	sendōdono

COMMENT: What does gently (*shizuka ni*) mean in such a context? "Take your time, let me have a little calm and peace" before my wretched new life begins.

225

Even the crow	karasu dani
is weary of the world.	ukiyo itoite
Look, see his black robes!	sumizome ni sometaru ya
Yes, he has put on	mi wo sumizome ni
robes of black.	sometari

COMMENT: A recently tonsured person, perhaps looking for comfort, finds it in the natural world: a lowly crow, a vagabond and scavenger, wearing dark robes like a wandering monk.

231

This world of ours:	yo no naka wa
it's hail, that's what it is,	arare yo nō
pattering down	sasa no ha no ue no

on leaves of bamboo. *sarasara satto*
Hail falling, that's what it is. *furu yo nō*

COMMENT: As we walk along, suddenly hailstones fall, pelting us, making us seek for shelter—a metaphor for the nature of life in a harsh world.

235

I want so to tell you, *amari kotoba no*
but all I can say is, *kaketasa ni*
"Look, look, now, *are misainō*
see how fast the clouds go *sora yuku kumo no*
through the sky." *hayasa yo*

COMMENT: A man is with a woman to whom he would like to unburden himself, but all he can manage is a few words about the weather, which happens to resemble his racing feelings.

305

I look at blossoms *hana mireba*
and my sleeves are wet, *sode nurenu*
I look at the moon *tsuki mireba*
and my sleeves are wet. *sode nurenu*
What goes on in my heart? *nani no kokoro zo*

COMMENT: Do we know ourselves where are feelings come from? Somehow all the beauty the speaker sees merely reminds him of feelings of (frustrated?) love.

Edo-period woodblock illustration of Sōgi and other poets composing linked verse at a memorial to Fujiwara no Teika.

From *Ehon yamato hiji*.

Chapter 4
LINKED VERSE

FUJIWARA NO TAMEIE 藤原為家, *Tsukubashū* 335 (Autumn): "Composed for a *renga* at the palace of Retired Emperor Go-Saga on the fifteenth night of the Eighth Month of 1247"

In my mountain home I wait for word from someone— but it never comes.	yamazato wa hito no tayori zo nakarikeru
I hear rustling, and wonder … but no, just wind in the reeds. 　Shōshō no Naishi	so yo to mo sureba ogi no uwakaze
Already, of course, one is prone to lie awake on an autumn night. 　Tameie	saranu dani nezamegachi naru aki no yo ni

山里は人のたよりぞなかりける
そよともすれば荻のうは風
さらぬだに寝覚がちなる秋の夜に

CONTEXT: Fujiwara no Tameie, heir of Teika, was the leader of the court *waka* salons in his day; Shōshō no Naishi was a lady in service to the retired emperor. By this time, people were composing *hyakuin* (full hundred-verse sequences), but the record gives us only fragments. The sequence here was written on a night of the full moon, when literati would often gather together to write poetry and drink sake. Verses 1 and 2, taken together, form a full *waka*, if one views them that way, as do verses 2 and 3.

COMMENT: This sequence of three verses from *Tsukubashū* (Tsukuba collection, no. 1356), the first imperially commissioned anthology of linked verse, displays the kind of pivoting that is central to the act of linking. First we hear the complaint of someone in a mountain village waiting for a person (a lover, perhaps) who fails to appear; to this Shōshō no Naishi's *tsukeku* (linking verse)—expressing a woman's point of view, according to old conventions—adds a hopeful sound that turns out to be only the wind (a conventional link to *tayori*, "word" or "message") in the reeds. But her "reeds" introduces autumn as a category, and it is this to which Tameie responds in his own *tsukeku*, introducing a new speaker and a new context: someone up in the night, plagued by autumn wakefulness. In this way we move from a mountain village in an unspecified season, with no indication of time of day, to a house where someone lies awake on an autumn night, with the sound of the wind acting as a pivot—the same wind, of course, but functioning in different miniplots. One of the reasons the wind occurs so often in linked verse is because it is such a vagabond; it can and does go anywhere, in any season, in any landscape. All of this is naturalistic, reflecting the reality of the wind.

This kind of interpretive pivoting is a constant in linked verse. In this way the first verse in any three-verse sequence is pushed into the distance by a subsequent third verse, which requires us as readers to focus always on just two verses—i.e., the present link. Sometimes the seasonal context may be continued, but even in such cases we are obliged to distance our minds from the imagery and rhetoric of the first verse as we approach the third. Any middle verse thus turns two ways, back to the previous verse and forward to the next, while always stating some independent meaning of its own. One of course wonders what will follow Tameie's verse—as would those in the group more than seven hundred years ago.

JUNKAKU 順覚, *Tsukubashū* 2103 (Autumn *Hokku*): "Composed on the first day of the Seventh Month"

木隠れに秋風みする一葉かな

Beneath a tree,	kogakure ni
autumn wind shows itself	akikaze misuru
in a single leaf.	hitoha kana

CONTEXT: Junkaku (fl. mid-thirteenth century) was a priest and semiprofessional *renga* master who seems to have lived near Kamakura. He probably wrote his verse for a *hyakuin* sponsored by some patron of the military elite or a priest at a temple, or perhaps a noble friend. In the lunar calendar, autumn began on the first day of the Seventh Month, mid-August in the Gregorian calendar, although the tokens of the season did not always manifest themselves so early.

COMMENT: In this *hokku* the autumn wind "offers" us (*misuru* means "to show") a solitary leaf, descending on the wind, as a sign of the new season. In this sense, according to the conventions of *renga*, we are witness to the advent of autumn, with the wind quite literally acting as its agent. But did Junkaku actually see a leaf fall? The conventions of the genre and our knowledge of literary history do not take us that far. But we do know that the author of the *hokku* was obliged to reveal the moment of composition in time (season, that is) and space. Somewhere near the *za*, or place of composition, perhaps in an adjacent garden, the leaves were doubtless beginning to fall, and portraying one descending at an opportune time was well within the spirit of the rules—which make for "informed" rather than unfettered exercise of the imagination.

For readers of Junkaku's time his *hokku* would have called to mind a famous Chinese saying of Zen derivation: "See a single leaf fall, and you know the year is heading toward its end." Thus Junkaku's poem denotes the Buddhist idea that all things are in concert with one another, a single leaf propelling time forward on its inevitable course. As is the custom in linked verse, however, Junkaku's scene stands on its own; recognizing the allusion enriches a reading but is not crucial to our understanding. The possibility of allegorical *hokku* would remain in the tradition, however, as is evident from a *hokku* (*Shōmyōin tsuizen senku* sequence 7, no. 1) by Satomura Jōha (1524-1602) written centuries later, in 1563, commemorating the death of his friend, Sanjōnishi Kin'eda (1487-1563), otherwise known as Shōmyōin.

The clouds clear away	kumo harete
and we are sure of its place:	sadamarikeri na
the moon in the night.	yowa no tsuki

On the surface, this poem presents the scene of clouds clearing the way for the moon. But we are not surprised when in his own commentary Jōha says, "The underlying meaning is, 'In meditation is the sure foundation as one awakens to faith.'" Thus the clouds come to represent impediments to understanding and the moon the ultimate truth revealed when the clouds are cleared away. Again, this interpretation is not the result of free association but of the availability in cultural terms, on a specific occasion, of the moon as a symbol of Buddhist enlightenment, as we have seen in *waka* by Jien and Shōtetsu.

SHINSHŌ 信照, *Tsukubashū* 1128 (Miscellaneous)

| Climbing up the branches | kozue ni noboru |
| go the white dews of autumn. | aki no shiratsuyu |

Low in the pines	yama no ha no
that line the mountain ridge,	matsu no moto yori
the moon comes out.	tsuki idete

梢にのぼる秋のしら露
山の端の松のもとより月出でて

CONTEXT: Shinshō, a monk of unspecified affiliation, was a fourteenth-century *hana no moto* master; i.e., a specialist who officiated at *renga* meetings held beneath cherry blossoms in spring. In *Tsukubashū* this *tsukeku* is listed as anonymous.

COMMENT: In *Sasamegoto* (p. 115) Shinkei lists the *tsukeku* here as an example of the *omoroshirotei* (the clever style), recognizing the wit involved in responding to the riddle "How can dew climb a tree?" Shinshō's answer shows the moon rising behind the trees on a mountain ridge, making the sparkling dew seem as if it were "climbing" up into the branches. The riddle element in the verse provoked the anthologist to place it in the "Miscellaneous" section rather than in "Autumn."

Shinkei's lists do not credit Shinshō with poems in the more sophisticated styles defined by Teika, such as *yūgen*, or "mystery and depth." But he does use that term (see *Sasamegoto*, p. 111) to praise links by Kyūzei (1284-1378).

| We pledged to live together | tomo ni sumamu to |
| here deep in the mountains. | iishi okuyama |

Near a grave site	naki ato ni
I put up a hut of brush	hitori zo musubu
for myself alone.	shiba no io

| Even the sound of the wind | kaze no oto made |
| takes on the chill of dusk. | samuki yūgure |

Autumn begins	aki wa tada
and just waiting for you	hito o matsu ni mo
is pain enough.	uki mono o

The first link depicts a man in a hut near a grave, a sad situation made more poignant when we learn that he will endure the memory of his loss on into the future, thus adding temporal scope and affective depth. The second example literally creates a vantage point from which to regard its *maeku* (previous verse), explaining that the "chill" in the dusk wind comes from the act of waiting itself when winter looms ahead. In neither case is the dramatic context spelled out, creating a sense of the "mystery" in mystery and depth (*yūgen*).

NIJŌ YOSHIMOTO 二条良基, *Tokorodokoro hentō* (p. 285):
"Composed on a visit to Kyūzei's cottage at Ōharano"

Which way to turn?	*izure mimu*
Winds in the autumn leaves,	*arashi no momiji*
snow in the pines.	*matsu no yuki*

いづれ見む嵐のもみぢ松の雪

CONTEXT: Nijō Yoshimoto (1320–1388) was a prominent court official who served three times as imperial regent, but he is best known now as the person most responsible for elevating linked verse to the status of a courtly art. The *hokku* here was congratulatory in nature, praising the iconic beauties around Kyūzei's home in Ōharano. A visit from the regent would have been a signal honor for Kyūzei, a monk of no worldly prominence. But the two men were actually well acquainted. Though worlds apart in status, they collaborated over a period of decades, producing a number of *renga* handbooks and treatises and *Tsukubashū*.

COMMENT: Yoshimoto's *hokku*, which began a sequence that has not come down to us, is a clear example of what is meant by "design" (*mon*), standing out as it does in imagery, conception, and rhetorical polish. A contemporary says that the verse was among the four or five *hokku* Yoshimoto liked most among his own works. By contrast, however, Shinkei, a later *renga* master, records in *Tokorodokoro hentō* (Letters in reply, p. 285) that some people at the time thought the verse so complete a description of the surroundings that it left too little to the imagination. The latter criticism is a formalistic, "literary" one, however: there can be little doubt that as the beginning of a social event the *hokku* was a masterful compliment to Kyūzei as host. In most cases, *hokku* had an immediate, social function first of all. We can be certain that Kyūzei took the verse as the high compliment Yoshimoto intended it to be.

As readers we learn the context of the question in line 1 as we proceed through a series of strong images that we can assume Yoshimoto actually saw before him, although not necessarily in the orderly arrangement suggested by the verse's syntactic parallelism. *Winds* blowing among *colored leaves* and *pines* flecked with *snow*—all this we see in a panoramic view designed to represent the speaker literally turning his head to take it all in, beginning nearby and then moving away into the treetops. The word *momiji*—literally, "red leaves"—evokes all the colored leaves on the oaks and maples (red, orange, brown, yellow) that must have been in Kyūzei's gardens, probably planted against a backdrop of evergreens that would obscure the line between garden and rising mountain slope. Since the description presents images of both autumn and winter, we can assume that the occasion was late in the former or early in the latter. But the poem does not appear in an anthology, so we cannot be sure what seasonal category it would have been placed in. Most likely, though, it would be considered a winter verse because of the snow: pines occur in all seasons, but both snow and leaves falling from the trees (here blown by *arashi*, "strong winds") would indicate that autumn is waning if not gone.

NINAGAWA CHIUN 蜷川智蘊, *Chikurinshō* 1198 (Miscellaneous)

| Ruining his narrow sleeves— | *sebaki tamoto o* |
| the child of a fisherman. | *kutasu ama no ko* |

Going far off	*ōumi no*
into tidelands of the broad sea,	*tōki shiohi ni*
he forages.	*asari shite*

CONTEXT: Chiun (d. 1455?) was a man of warrior lineage (the Ninagawa clan) who served on the administrative board of the shogunal government. He studied *renga* under Bontō, studied *waka* and Zen, and was a prominent fixture in the literary circles of Kyoto.

COMMENT: Both Bontō (b. 1349) and Shinkei write about "close" and "distant" linking (*shinku* and *soku*)—i.e., links (the general term for which is *tsukeai* or *tsukeyō* in Japanese) based on word associations, logic, and dramatic continuity from one verse to another, versus links of mood, and suggestion. And both valorize *soku*. However, it was close linking that provided continuity in a sequence. Chiun's *tsukeku* is a textbook example of how an expert realized the effects of close linking with great subtlety. Most obviously, the verse turns on the contrast between "narrow" and "broad." But *Yuki no keburi* (Smoke above snow, 1482, p. 118), a commentary on *Chikurinshō* (Poems from the bamboo grove, no. 1476) attributed to Sōgi, goes further: "Chiun links the 'broad sea' to 'narrow,' but there is more to it than that. His *tsukeku* focuses on the pitiful plight of the child of a fisherman who makes a meager living by foraging on such broad tidelands. This is a *tsukeku* one should savor." Rather than simply focusing on wordplay, Chiun thus draws us back cinematically, and also explains the reason the boy's sleeves are being ruined, as he drenches them ferreting out anything he can on the sea's verge. The word *asaru*, "to forage," is usually used of birds or animals, and viewed as a single verse the grammatical subject of that verb would probably refer to the animal world rather than the boy. The recasting of grammatical

狭き袂をくたす海士の子

大海の遠き塩干にあさりして

subject is a common device in linked verse and a way to take advantage of ellipsis.

Chiun was doubtless thinking of a famous anonymous poem from *Shin kokinshū* (no. 1703) when he created his link:

Making his life	*shiranami no*
amidst white waves that break	*yosuru nagisa ni*
against the shore	*yo o tsukusu*
is the child of a fisherman—	*ama no ko nareba*
one with no fixed abode.	*yado mo sadamezu*

With this poem in mind, one sees a fuller scene that includes not only the tidelands but also white surf. Moreover, we are left wondering if this child too is without a permanent home. Rather than duplicating the foundation poem, Chiun thus uses it as a supplement, creating images that hover in the background and inspiring further suggestions of deep feeling that go beyond the aesthetic to Buddhist compassion and straightforward human sympathy.

TAKAYAMA SŌZEI 高山宗砌, *Chikurinshō* 1238 (Miscellaneous)

When I look, snow is falling	*mireba yuki furi*
and only the moon remains.	*tsuki zo nokoreru*
A new day dawns.	*akenikeri*
My dreams of yesterday—	*kinō no yume wa*
gone without a trace.	*ato mo nashi*

見れば雪降り月ぞ残れる
明にけり昨日の夢は跡もなし

CONTEXT: Takayama Sōzei (d. 1455) was a shogunal official who served as *renga* laureate and was a teacher to Senjun (1411-1476) and Sōgi. Scholars identify an allusion to a famous scene in the "Asagao" (Bluebell) chapter of *The Tale of Genji* (2:480-85) where the beauty of moonlight shining on snow inspires Genji to declare that sight superior to the glories of spring and autumn.

COMMENT: In *Keikandō* (Stages on the way, p. 140), the *renga* master Kenzai, a student of Sōgi's and Shinkei's, offers a comment on this ingenious *tsukeku* by Sōzei: "[The speaker] awakes to realize that all the colors of a full year—the cherry blossoms, the autumn leaves—all have become a dream, with only the moon and snow remaining. 'Awaken your eyes to the truth!'—that is the idea. The doctrine of 'consciousness only' explains that the myriad things around us are but a dream."

As is often the case in *renga*, here the *tsukeku* seems narratively prior to the *maeku*. It is after realizing his dream has faded utterly that the speaker sees the moon in the snowy landscape, devoid of color. Although the word *odoroku* (awaken) does not appear in the *renga* link, Kenzai's Buddhist interpretation seems reasonable given the high rhetoric of Sōzei's verse. Yet the allusion allows us more than that one meaning. For after Genji taxes his long-suffering wife, Murasaki, with his memories of the women he has been unable to obtain (Fujitsubo, Oborozukiyo, and Asagao—the Lady of the Bluebells that gives the chapter its name), he goes to bed and then awakens from a dream of an angry Fujitsubo that so disturbs him that he commissions Buddhist services for her soul. The poem he composes then—although the *tsukeku* takes nothing directly from it—expresses how he has been troubled by a depressingly brief and unsatisfying dream.

Too tense for sleep,	*tokete nenu*
I lie wakeful and forlorn	*nezame sabishiki*
through a winter night—	*fuyu no yo ni*
unable to complete a dream	*musubohoretsuru*
that ended far too soon.	*yume no mijikasa*

Genji's attitude is not as resolute as the one suggested in Kenzai's didactic reading. And it is significant that what Sōzei's speaker says, too, sounds more like stoicism than resolution, whether or not we recognize the allusion.

SENJUN 専順, **SHINKEI** 心敬, **SŌZEI**, and **GYŌJO** 行助 (from a sequence composed on the fifteenth day of the Third Month of 1453; *Nanimichi hyakuin*)

30 Plum trees bloom in a meadow *mume saku ono no*
    beneath a dawning sky. *akebono no sora*
        Senjun

31 In a mountain hut *yamagatsu no*
    peasants are making wood fires *shiba taku iori*
    in peace and quiet. *nodoka nite*
        Shinkei

32	How noisy is the city world at dusk as the year ends. 　Sōzei	*yo no naka sawagu* *toshi no kuregata*
33	Snow breaks bamboo and leaves a flock of birds bereft of a home. 　Gyōjo	*yukiori no* *take no muradori* *yadoriwabi*

梅さく小野の明ぼのの空
山賤の柴たく庵のどかにて
世の中さわぐ年の暮がた
雪折の竹のむら鳥やどり侘

CONTEXT: Six poets produced the *hyakuin* from which these verses are taken (p. 286), four of whom (the ones quoted here) were among those the later *renga* master Sōgi dubbed the seven sages. Sōzei, as noted, was a warrior and serving as steward of the Kitano Shrine *renga* office, and Senjun, Shinkei, and Gyōjo (1405-1469) were all clerics that were renowned as *renga* experts.

COMMENT: This short sequence, from the central section of the *hyakuin* (see *johakyū* in appendix 1), shows a variety of linking techniques. Senjun begins with a spring tableau of dawn breaking on plum tress in a meadow. Shinkei then adds people to the mix, picking up the tranquil mood of Senjun's verse but going beyond natural description to introduce peasants making morning fires. Sōzei then moves in a slightly different direction by contrasting city and country and activity and tranquility and clearly setting his verse not in spring but in winter. Finally, Gyōjo responds with a scene of snow in bamboos while also shifting from the human to the animal world. All the *tsukeku* involve either conventional associations (*yoriai*) or logical associations: "mountain hut" linking back to "meadow" and "plum trees," "dusk" linking back to "making fires," "snow" linking back to "year's end," "flock of birds" linking back to "noisy," and "bamboo" linking back to "world." (The last of these depends on wordplay involving the homophones *yo*, "the world," and *yo*, "joint of a bamboo"). Relatively speaking, the links are close links and follow well-established patterns, even down to presenting birds in a city setting as noisily looking for nests, as advised by the prominent late fifteenth-, early sixteenth-century *renga* handbook *Shogaku yōshashō* (Choices for beginners, p. 454). Only Sōzei produces a situational "leap." Abiding by the rules, each poet refrains from clashing (*sarikirai*)—i.e., employing words or ideas that encourage connections back beyond its *maeku*.

SHINKEI, *Hyakuban renga-awase* (round 39)

My aching, troubled heart
floats off into empty sky.

omou kokoro zo
sora ni ukaruru

Link 1: My old home gone,
   I see clouds up on the peak
   as a reminder.
      Kyūzei

furusato no
yama no nagori o
kumo ni mite

Link 2: In mountain winds
   blowing through clouds above,
   I watch blossoms fall.
      Shūa

kumo o fuku
miyamaoroshi ni
hana o mite

A crow cries out—
   as on a frosty, moonlit night,
   I lie down alone.
      Shinkei

karasu naku
shimoyo no tsuki ni
hitori nete

CONTEXT: Shinkei was the abbot of a temple in Kyoto who was forced to flee to the East Country because of the Ōnin War and died there. A student of the *waka* poet Shōtetsu and mentor to Sōgi, Kenzai, and others, he wrote some of the finest poetry and most sophisticated literary theory of the late medieval era. Here he engages with a work from a hundred years before his time in which Kyūzei and Shūa (d. 1377?) had each composed links to a hundred *maeku*. Adding his own links to the mix, he titled his work *Hyakuban renga-awase* (Linked-verse contest in one hundred rounds, 1467?). Thus we have links to the same *maeku* by all three men.

COMMENT: The *maeku* is a love verse—whether spoken by a man or a woman, we cannot tell. Kyūzei and Shūa both offer recastings, the former making the "troubled heart" a response to the vanishing of the speaker's home, and the latter a response to wind destroying blossoms. Shinkei, however, remains in the love category. A paraphrase would read, "Beneath a cold moon on a frosty night, as I go to bed alone, I hear a crow cawing in yearning for its mate, my heart, too, feeling as if taken up and buffeted on the currents of the night sky." In a comment, Shinkei glosses his second line as "the chilly, icy moonlight on a frosty night," alluding to his aesthetic of the "chill and icy" (*hiekōritaru*). His *tsukeku* is starker than the earlier two, which join the word *ukaru* (floating off) to "clouds" in more conventional ways. Identification with a crow flying on a cold night, known only by sound and not by sight, is more dramatic than clouds or blossoms.

Crows appear in *renga* more often than in *waka*, especially in winter scenes of black and white. This example from *Shinsen Tsukubashū* (New Tsukuba collection, 1495; no. 2177) is by Nichisei (dates unknown).

| To be in search of lodging: | *yado karu koro zo* |
| what a pitiable state. | *mono aware naru* |

Crows caw at dusk	*karasu naku*
at houses deep in the mountains,	*miyama no sato ni*
dark in falling snow.	*yukikurete*

SENJUN, *Chikurinshō* 556 (Autumn)

| Leaves from *masaki* vines float down | *masaki chirikuru* |
| from a peak, on autumn wind. | *mine no akikaze* |

Where a stag calls	*ojika naku*
from far off in the foothills—	*toyama no oku ya*
there will be rain.	*shigururan*

正木散りくる峰の秋風
男鹿鳴く外山の奥や時雨らん

CONTEXT: Senjun was a Buddhist priest involved not just in *renga* but also in the nascent art of flower arrangement (*rikka*). He studied under the *waka* poet Shōtetsu and was a teacher to Sōgi. Senjun's *tsukeku* alludes to a *kagurauta*, or "sacred song" (*Kokinshū*, no. 1077), performed at court or at Shinto shrines. As noted earlier, during the dance the priest-director held a *masaki* branch.

Deep in the mountains	*miyama ni wa*
the hailstones will be falling.	*arare fururashi*
Here in the foothills	*toyama naru*
the leaves on the *masaki* vines	*masaki no kazura*
have turned a crimson hue.	*irozukinikeri*

COMMENT: Senjun's link is a fine example of close linking based on the natural connections (*yoriai*) between foothills and peaks, stags and falling leaves, wind and rain, and foothills and the colored leaves of the *masaki* vines. He thus transforms the *kagura* scene of the *Kokinshū* poem, moving the speaker from the foothills into the mountains, making hail into rain, and adding the forlorn call of a stag to represent seasonal decline—all with the old court dances hovering in the background. A text attributed to Sōgi praised Senjun's *tsukeku* as embodying both "mystery and depth" (*yūgen*) and "loftiness" (*taketakashi*), but in a delicate, understated way that he prized above all else (*Yuki no keburi*, pp. 122-23, no. 79). "This is what is meant by a superb verse [*shūitsu*]. A superb verse is not something to go chasing after. Sōzei said that he would call this verse the utmost essence of *renga*, and that he never tired of it no matter how often he read it but was in fact more and more moved by it over time. I note this here because these days there are those who might dismiss it as rather plain [*mezurashikarazu*]."

The latter point is one that Sōgi makes repeatedly in his critical statements, particularly when it concerns the work of Senjun. For instance, in *Oi no susami* (A solace in old age, 1479, p. 131) he says, among Senjun's links "are many that appear straightforward on the surface but deep down are full of profound truth." There are probably two things at work behind Sōgi's statements: the first is his experience as a *renga* master who knew how a spirit of rivalry could mar the progress—and the eventual textual outcome—of a *renga* gathering; the second is his grounding in the aesthetics of *ushin*, or "refined feeling," which he saw as the ultimate aesthetic ideal.

SŌJUN 宗順, **RANPA** 蘭坡, **NŌA** 能阿, and **ZŌSHUN** 蔵春, *Kanshō yonen gogatsu nijūhachinichi hyakuin* (p. 40)

A pathway hard to make out,	michi tadotadoshi
beneath grasses growing tall.	kusa takaki kage
Sōjun	
Blossoms fall, and a single hut appears.	hana ochite kokan awawaru
Ranpa	
Out near the fence these days—	magaki no chō no
only the rare butterfly.	mare ni iru koro
Nōa	
Spring grows old, dream of a dream.	haru wa oyu yume no yume
Zōshun	

CONTEXT: Sōjun (evidently of the Hino noble lineage) and Nōa (1397–1471) were both *renga* masters, while Ranpa (1419–1501) and Zōshun (precise dates unknown) were monks in the Gozan ("Five Mountains," or Zen) system, the former being a fixture in the court of Emperor Go-Tsuchimikado (1442–1500). The sequence here, from 1463, is an example of a hybrid subgenre called *wakan renku*, or linked verse written in a mix of Japanese and Chinese. Zen monasteries at the time were large and diverse institutions that served in some ways as universities where many artists and scholars got their education. Training there demanded reading sutras in Chinese, and while some priests looked askance at reading literary texts, others inevitably developed an interest in Chinese poetry, including Chinese linked verse, which in some ways was a model for Japanese linked verse. Typically, a Sino-Japanese sequence involved alternation of Japanese and Chinese verses, as in the case of the four verses in sequence presented here, but the specific "mix" depended on the particular occasion. Here six poets participated, four Gozan monks and two *renga* masters, alternating eccentrically: sometimes a Japanese verse and then a Chinese verse, but more often a Japanese verse and two or three Chinese verses. Altogether, the *renga* masters composed forty-two verses and the monks fifty-eight.

道たどたどし草たかきかげ

花零孤館露

まがきのてふのまれにいるころ

春老夢之夢

COMMENT: The linking between verses in *wakan renku* is no different from that in ordinary linked verse. Taken by itself, Sōjun's verse is in the travel category, while the verses that follow it relate to late spring, with Ranpa coming up with "falling blossoms" as a link to "tall grasses," Nōa "fence" as a link to "hut," and Zōshun "dream" as a link to "butterfly." The last *tsukeku* depends on the well-known story about the Chinese philosopher Zhuangzi falling asleep, dreaming he is a butterfly, and then awakening to wonder if the dream is truly over–i.e., whether he is a man who dreamed he was a butterfly or a butterfly dreaming he is a man. The implication is that the person grows old with the season, living, as in a "dream of a dream." We begin walking toward a hut mostly concealed by grasses, focus our vision on a fence near a dwelling where we see a butterfly late in the season, and then hear an editorial comment implying that our experience is made up of images that in the natural course of things must fade away. Thus the links present a masterful treatment of the theme of *mujō*, "mutability and constant change."

SUGIHARA SŌI 杉原宗伊 and SŌGI 宗祇, *Arima ryōgin kochū*, verses 1 and 2

A warbler sings,
its voice muffled by the mists
that veil the mountain.
   Sōi

uguisu wa
kiri ni musebite
yama mo nashi

The scent of plum blossoms,
in the season of cold frost.
   Sōgi

ume kaoru no no
shimo samuki koro

CONTEXT: The *renga* master Sōi (lay name Sugihara Katamori, 1418–1485) was a samurai and shogunal official who served as laureate of the shogunal *renga* office. He was both teacher and patron to Sōgi. The two men met to compose a sequence (called a *ryōgin*, or *renga* by just two people) at Arima Hot Spring in Settsu Province (present-day Kobe), in the spring of 1482.

COMMENT: Often we don't know the circumstances in which a *tsukeku* was written. In this case we know year, season, and location. Arima was a famous mountain hot spring whose waters were believed to have healing effects. The atmosphere was no doubt relaxed. As laureate of the shogunal *renga* office, Sōi was at the top of the ladder in literati culture, and Sōgi was in the process making a reputation that would allow him to assume that same title some years later, in 1488. The images the men employ—warbler, spring mist, plum blossoms, frost—are highly auspicious and connect back in undeniable ways to *waka* traditions. But it is important to note that Sōi's verse, in this case a *hokku*, also follows the canons in the way it presents a description of the surroundings at the time of composition.

In *Hekirenshō* (Skewed views on linked verse, 1345, p. 45), Nijō Yoshimoto advised that the second verse in a sequence (called the *waki*) should defer in a complementary way to the *hokku*, staying in the same season, not presenting a powerful new image (the moon, snow, the cuckoo, etc.)—in other words, offering an expansion of perspective but only the most subtle sort of change. In his *Sasamegoto* (p. 74) Shinkei endorses Yoshimoto's comments, but in typical fashion he adds that abiding by hard-and-fast rules is difficult, and that one must always keep in mind the people in the *za* and the place of composition. We are not surprised to see that Sōgi follows convention to the letter. As he says in a short comment attached to the this link (see *Arima ryōgin kochū*, p. 20), "The *hokku* is set in early spring, a scene in which the warbler's song is muffled by morning mist that makes the mountain invisible. My verse just presents a description of that time of year."

A later comment points out an allusion by Sōi to *Wakan rōeishū* (no. 65, by Yuan Zhen, 779-831): "A mountain warbler's voice is faint, muffled by mist." Did Sōgi just fail to mention it? A more likely explanation is that the reference was so obvious as to need no response. Those in the know would recognize it; others needed more study.

SŌGI, *Wakuraba* 1125-26 (Miscellaneous)

No one is left to look now,	*hitome taetaru*
deep in the mountain shadows.	*oku no yamakage*
Is the wind thinking,	*hana o kaze*
"These blossoms are *mine*!"—	*waga mono tote ya*
to pass them by?	*nokosuran*

人めたえたるおくの山かげ
花を風わが物とてやのこすらん

CONTEXT: Sōgi (sometimes identified as Inō or Iio Sōgi) was of samurai parentage and began life as a Zen priest but from early on seems to have seen poetry as his vocation. He apprenticed under Sōzei, Senjun, Shinkei, and Sōi. In an exegetical comment in his collection *Wakuraba* (Old leaves, 1481?) on this link, Sōgi says, "With no one to regret their falling, the wind seems to claim the blossoms as its own, and spares them. Something a little different, I think" (*Guku wakuraba*, p. 100, nos. 1280-81). Sōgi's student Sōchō, who also left a comment on the link, describes the idea as something new (*atarashi*), a term of praise that appears only occasionally in *renga* discourse.

COMMENT: Here the *maeku* makes it easy to conjure up a person living in the forest: a recluse, a woodcutter, a peasant, or perhaps a monk in a temple cottage. Perhaps he has had visitors; perhaps people have been passing by for some reason. Whatever the case, everyone has gone, and he is left in the forest darkness, to lament, perhaps, or to savor the quiet—the ambiguity being intentional. But Sōgi's *tsukeku* introduces not a person but the wind and cherry blossoms, and reverses the usual plot. The link is a perfect example of a design (*mon*) verse in terms of imagery, theme, and originality of conception and linking technique. We should notice that Sōgi's link is not just clever; it also involves a statement of feeling. What motivates the wind, the speaker says, is the absence of a human agent to lament the flowers' demise. The personification thus has a point, as the wind does what it can to maintain the symbolic order by postponing its usual work, at least until the appearance of a visitor. In this sense, the link is in the tradition of *ushin* (deep feeling), the poetic ideal that is central to Sōgi's poetics. Another of his links (*Wakuraba* 939–40; "Love"), again involving the theme of absence and subtle feeling, illustrates his affiliations more unmistakably:

| After a long night of pain | *nagaki yo tsuraku* |
| I am weary of waiting. | *machi zo wabinuru* |

He never came,	*konu hito mo*
but he too must see it now:	*miruran mono o*
the moon in the sky.	*sora no tsuki*

Sōchō (*Guku wakuraba*, p. 85) refers to this link as "lovely and deeply moving" (*en ni aware mo fukashi*), using the vocabulary of courtly aesthetics. In the back of his mind may be Teika's famous scene of a woman alone imagining her lover looking up at the moon after a night with a different woman.

KENZAI, *Shinsen Tsukubashū* 3666 (Spring): "Composed on the nineteenth day of the Third Month of 1492, at Shichijō Dōjō"

Blossoms scatter	*hana zo chiru*
in a rush of hue and scent	*kakaran tote no*
we knew would come.	*iroka kana*

花ぞちるかからんとての色香かな

CONTEXT: As noted in chapter 2, Kenzai was a *renga* master from Aizu in the East Country who studied under both Sōgi and Shinkei and practiced in Kyoto for some years, later returning to the East Country. Shichijō Dōjō (also called Kinkōji) was a temple of the Ji (Time) sect, located on Shichijō Avenue in Kyoto. The place was famous for its cherry blossoms, and the 1492 event was no doubt meant to honor the old custom of holding "*renga* parties beneath the blossoms" (*hana no moto renga*). Also participating were Sōgi and a few of his disciples and a number of priests. Although junior to Sōgi as a *renga* master, Kenzai was given the honor of composing the first verse in his capacity as shogunal laureate of the Kitano Shrine *renga* office. Sōgi had resigned from that same office in 1489.

COMMENT: At the time *Shinsen Tsukubashū* was being compiled, Kenzai was among those assisting Sōgi and the courtier Sanjōnishi Sanetaka. In this setting,

Kenzai no doubt was privy to some of the comments of various other people involved, including Emperor Go-Tsuchimikado—who, according to a disciple of Kenzai's, in his *Kenzai zōdan* (Chats with Master Kenzai, p. 122) said of this *hokku* that it was the finest in the entire anthology.

Certain images, most notably the moon and blossoms, were considered so central to the traditions of Japanese poetry that the rules required that they must appear in each *renga* sequence: the moon seven times, blossoms four. For obvious reasons, both images figure frequently in *hokku*, which were supposed to be formal in diction and highly polished and elevated in rhetoric. Thus composing a poem on cherry blossoms constituted a great challenge, thousands upon thousands of *hokku* having been composed on that topic over the centuries. Kenzai responds with a design verse that is highly creative on two counts: first, in the way it includes all the elements for which the blossoms are famous—hue, scent, and the sad beauty of the way the petals scatter on the wind; and second, in the way (through the phrase *kakaramu tote*—roughly, "[knowing] it would be like this") it deftly works in the sense of anticipation we feel before the trees blossom and then again when the blossoms are about to fall. Temporally, the verse begins with the scattering but then goes back to explain that the beauty of that phenomenon lies in the way the hue and scent—and our imaginations—have prepared us to feel more poignantly their denouement.

Some of the earliest *renga* masters, including Shūa, were associated with the Time sect, which was also one of the sects most linked to *hana no moto renga*. Kenzai's choice thus fit perfectly with the setting physically—near the famous groves of the temple—but also discursively with the cult of the cherry blossom connected with that institution.

HINO TOMIKO 日野富子, *Shinsen Tsukubashū* 3704 (Summer):
"Composed for an acrostic *renga* sequence during the year when the Jōtokuin chancellor passed away"

Sadly, I live on,	nagarauru
grieving amidst deutzia	yo o unohana no
in full bloom.	sakari kana

ながらふる世をうの花のさかり哉

CONTEXT: Hino Tomiko (1436-1496) was born into a noble lineage that for generations had provided wives to the Ashikaga shogun, thus working its way into the highest councils in the land and amassing great wealth and power. Her machinations aimed at securing the shogunal position for her son by Ashikaga

Yoshimasa (1436–1490) figured in the conflicts that led to the Ōnin War (1467–1477). Her *hokku* was composed in 1489, not long after the passing of that son, the shogun Ashikaga Yoshihisa (1465–1489) (referred to in the preceding by the formal name of Jōtokuin, given him after death), who had died of illness while on the battlefield on the twenty-sixth day of the Third Month, at just twenty-five years old. Encouraged by Tomiko, he had been very active in poetry circles.

COMMENT: From the earliest times, Japanese poetry has been connected with religious beliefs, in terms of both subject matter and ritual practices. In the case of *renga*, family and friends would meet together to compose memorial sequences for the dead, which would often be presented to temples as votive offerings. Yoshihisa's death was a shock, especially to his mother, who had been a driving force in both his political and poetic activities, the latter including a plan to put together another imperial collection of *waka*. A diary of the time records that when his body was brought back into Kyoto, her wailing inside her carriage could be heard all along the street. She survived for another seven years, however, outliving her husband, Ashikaga Yoshimasa, and remaining a force in political and cultural affairs, especially after the latter's death.

There is a universal quality to Tomiko's *hokku*: surviving the death of a child seems to defy the proper order of things. Hence the verb with which Tomiko begins—*nagarau*, "to live on," which is nearly always used in the context of loss or regret, of being left behind, or of feeling that somehow one has lived too long. Then she chooses the image of deutzia flowers (*unohana*) to convey her grief, employing a *kakekotoba* involving the first syllable of that noun, while also suggesting the first syllable of the verb *ureu*, "to lament." Blooming in summer, the *unohana* bush produces white flowers against a backdrop of pale green leaves, the fluttering of which is metaphorically compared to "turning over" or "returning"—explaining why the flowers are often employed as a motif in travel poems. In Tomiko's verse, however, the flowers "return" to no practical effect. For once, the natural world offers no consolation. The sight of the flowers in full bloom serves only to intensify the speaker's sense of loss. Her son will *not* return. Yet, again, her situation is so conventional that it is easily absorbed into the dynamics of a *renga* sequence.

The Japanese text begins with *na*—first syllable of *namu*, in *namu amida butsu* (Savior Amida—All Hail!)—and is a partial acrostic. The first syllable of succeeding verses would have done the same thing, spelling the phrases out: *na-mu-a*, etc. Unfortunately, the other poems do not survive. Together, we know that they constituted a prayer for the salvation of Yoshihisa's soul.

SHŌHAKU 肖柏, *Shunmusōchū* 248 (Autumn): "Composed for a dedicatory sequence at Kayano Shrine in Settsu, when a drought had persisted for some time"

Does the sky know?	sora ni shiru ya
As we are hoping for rain—	ame o nozomi no
autumn clouds.	aki no kumo

CONTEXT: Shōhaku (1443-1527) was the younger son of a court noble who became a professional literatus, recognized as a disciple of Sōgi's but with a thriving practice of his own involving the teaching of both *waka* and *renga*. Shōhaku lived for many years in Settsu Province, and service as a master of ceremonies at local gatherings was a regular feature of his literary practice. In fact, in the section where this poem appears in *Hokkuchō* (a large compendium of *hokku* compiled later), four of the twelve verses by Shōhaku were written for dedicatory sequences of one sort or another, not including one that is written for a memorial sequence on the death date of Sōgi.

COMMENT: In the preface to *Kokinshū*, first of the imperial anthologies of Japanese poetry, Ki no Tsurayuki claimed for poetry the power to move the emotions of deities, moderate feelings between men and women, and pacify the hearts of warriors, and the use of poetry as a way to petition or placate the gods was a commonplace of Japanese culture (see Sōgi's *Yodo no watari* [Yodo crossing], pp. 294-95, for the perspective of a *renga* master on such matters). In the case of *renga*, the number of dedicatory sequences (*hōraku renga*) that have survived is in fact disproportionally large, for the simple reason that such works were more likely to be carefully recorded and put in safekeeping in the vaults of shrines and temples. Among their number is the most famous of all sequences, *Minase sangin hyakuin* (Three poets at Minase, 1488), in which Shōhaku also participated. In that case the work was presented to Minase Shrine in Settsu Province as a votive offering in honor of the founder of the shrine (or rather the palace that later became the shrine), Retired Emperor Go-Toba, a talented poet and the driving force behind the compilation of *Shin kokinshū*.

The *hokku* of dedicatory sequences nearly always express the supplications of their sponsors, if only obliquely. In this case Shōhaku sees the autumn clouds that we can assume actually to have appeared at the time as a hopeful sign. As a commentary on his personal *renga* collection, *Shunmusō* (Ruminations on spring dreams, after 1515), says, "The very next day it began to rain. The way the autumn clouds trailed along—it was as if *tendō* recognized the request for rain" (*Shunmusōchū*, p. 348).

空にしるや雨をのぞみの秋の雲

The word *tendō* has a range of meanings, from "the Way of Heaven" to the "God of Heaven," and is an interpolation: Shōhaku's poem likewise involves personification but says only "the sky." Shōhaku's *hokku* is more hopeful than confident in its attitude; doubtless so immediate a response to prayer was unusual. Autumn clouds may of course pass by without ever producing rain. In this case, however, he can only have been pleased with the outcome of the event, which reinforced the claims of the *Kokinshū* preface and his own bona fides as a *renga* master.

SŌCHŌ 宗長, *Shinsen Tsukubashū* 1857–58 (Love)

Finding comfort in romance:	*koi ni nagusamu*
ah, the folly of old age!	*oi no hakanasa*
Feelings from the past	*mukashi seshi*
return again as I lie here,	*omoi o sayo no*
awake in the night.	*nezame nite*

CONTEXT: Sōchō was a disciple of Sōgi's who spent his later years mostly in service to the Imagawa warrior clan in Suruga Province. The link here originally came not from a full *hyakuin* but from a pedagogical contest titled *Shichinin tsukeku hanshi* (Judgments on links by seven people, ca. 1490, p. 308) in which Sōgi records and critiques links by seven of his students for a set of *maeku* that he provided as practice.

COMMENT: The word *koi* signifies erotic love. As noted elsewhere, in traditional poetry, love is generally seen as an impediment to Buddhist salvation while also being a fundamental ground of human identity. For this reason, perhaps, love is also one of the most basic subjects of Japanese poetry. In the example here, the complex *dai* of love is further complicated by a highly elliptical *maeku* that contains no definite grammatical subject. This opens up at least two distinct possibilities: either the speaker is an outsider passing judgment on the foolishness of some anonymous old person, or he (or she—once again there is no gender marking) is speaking in the first person, in which case the link becomes a kind of self-censure.

This kind of ellipsis is a fundamental feature of the Japanese language that *renga* poets make great use of as a resource for changing perspective. And, indeed, in the case of this particular link we know that it was created as an exercise for students who would face such ambiguity in the *za*. In the original version, the last word of the *maeku* was not "folly" (*hakanasa*) but "sadness" (*awaresa*), which means that Sōgi probably emended the verse when

恋になぐさむ老のはかなさ
昔せしおもひをさ夜のねざめにて

he put it in *Shinsen Tsukubashū*, a project in which Sōchō also participated. In any case, Sōgi was evidently impressed enough with Sōchō's effort that he offered it (the later version, that is, which he must have thought superior or more appropriate in some way) as an example in another pedagogical work, *Asaji* (Cogon grass, 1500), ten years later. There (p. 332) he paraphrases the link—"Now grown old, I no longer have feelings of love, but at night I lie awake remembering the pleasures of the heart"—and confesses it is "something that one thinks could indeed happen" (*sa mo arinu beku ya*). Thus he sees Sōchō as recasting the *maeku* as first-person censure and takes the link as a lament on the persistence of desire, in the mind if not in the body. The *tsukeku* is a masterful handling of the *dai* of love in Buddhist terms that manages to inspire sympathy in the reader while at the same time recognizing the "folly" of erotic attachment.

Needless to say, Sōchō's verse, on its own, does not indicate that the "feelings from the past" are feelings of erotic love: that interpretation is dependent on the link. A poet tasked with in turn providing a *tsukeku* to his verse could easily "spin" it in another direction: affection for parents, loyalty—an informed imagination being the only limit.

EMPEROR GO-TSUCHIMIKADO 後土御門天皇, SANETAKA 実隆, and CROWN PRINCE KATSUHITO 勝仁親王, *Sanetaka-kō ki*

松たかき軒葉は庭の雪もなし
月ももらじと雲こほる空
音さえて夜の嵐やふけぬらん

Third day of the Twelfth Month, 1497: The accumulated snowfall was delightful. We made the round of palace gardens, enjoying the views.... His Majesty decided we should compose just the first eight verses of a sequence.

Along the eaves	*matsu takaki*
tall pines keep the garden	*nokiba wa niwa no*
free from snow.	*yuki mo nashi*
His Imperial Majesty	

As if to deny us the moon,	*tsuki mo moraji to*
a sky of frozen clouds.	*kumo kōru sora*
Sanetaka	

Colder grows the sound	*oto saete*
of winds in deepening night.	*yoru no arashi ya*
A building storm?	*fukenuran*
The Crown Prince	

CONTEXT: Sanetaka was a courtier-scholar who was a confidant of Emperor Go-Tsuchimikado and tutor to the crown prince (later Emperor Go-Kashiwabara, 1464-1526) but also a friend of commoner *renga* masters such as Sōgi and Shōhaku. In his voluminous diary, *Sanetaka kōki* (Sanetaka's journal, 1474-1536, with gaps), the courtier records these first three of eight verses composed on a snowy night.

COMMENT: The standard medium of *renga* composition from the late 1200s on was the *hyakuin*, or "hundred-verse sequence." In practice, though, people often composed shorter sequences, as in this example. The *hokku* obeys the rules of the genre, using images from its immediate surroundings, revealing the mood of the moment and making a complete statement; so, too, the second verse (the *waki*) and the third verse (the *daisan*), which produce only slight changes in perspective and mood. However, in the case of such an informal, "throwaway" sequence (*iisute*), we can perhaps be forgiven for seeing a unified tableau that relates to the actual setting (snowy pines at the eaves, moon in the sky, storm winds). Sanetaka mentions that before composing their verses the men enjoyed a drink of melted snow and warmed themselves with sake served by palace ladies.

The emperor's *hokku* is the most traditional of the three poems, offering the gentle irony of a garden covered in snow everywhere but beneath the pines next to the house. Sanetaka's "a sky of frozen clouds" is a starker image, which is answered by the crown prince's chilly sound of storm winds late at night. In this case the three verses cannot help but evoke Chinese-style ink-wash paintings of the sort produced by Sanetaka's contemporary, Sesshū Tōyō (1420-1506), although the verbal picture is inevitably more dynamic, involving snow falling and an intensifying storm.

TANI SŌBOKU 谷宗牧, *Kochiku* 381-82

Days accumulate	shitashiki mo
and even one's intimates	tabikasanareba
are friends no more.	utomarete
In morning dew, in evening dew,	asayū tsuyu no
the blossoms fade, then fall.	hana zo utsurou

CONTEXT: Tani Sōboku (d. 1545) was a prominent *renga* master in the poetic lineage of Sōgi who gained great prominence in both Kyoto and the provinces.

COMMENT: An unnamed disciple of Sōboku's explains this link in *Kochiku* (Solitary bamboo, 1540; nos. 381–82).

> This is a masterpiece, a superb poem that was on everybody's lips. The meaning is nothing that unusual. In the beginning, dew is a friend to the cherry blossoms; for in the pattern of things, it is by the blessing of rain and dew that flowers receive their life force, producing the color and scent that are unmistakably their own. Yet it is certain that later it will be because of the dew that the blossoms fade and die. If you think carefully about this principle, you will comprehend that as time goes by one cannot be secure even when it comes to friends.... The decree of the group was to deem this an example of the style of overtones, and it was also one of the author's personal favorites among his works.

したしきもたびかさなればうとまれて
あさ夕露の花ぞうつろふ

In premodern times poems circulated mostly by word of mouth. Japanese poems were short, and powers of memory were a crucial requirement in all fields of endeavor. It is also revealing that the comment harks back to the vocabulary of *uta-awase* judgments, using the classical words for on-the-spot commentary by a group (*shū*) and for issuing an agreed-upon decree (*sata*), and employing the word *yojō* (overtones) as a term of praise. In this case *yojō* refers to the way the link expresses the "overflowing" significance of the *maeku*, showing how general patterns or logical principles (*kotowari*) adhere in the phenomenal world, a precept of neo-Confucian thought. The link is an example of a *soku*, or "distant" *tsukeku*, in which word associations play no prominent role.

Statements of propositional truth in *renga* sequences are often Buddhist in meaning and tone. A link by Sōgi (*Wakuraba*, nos. 381–82) is more explicit than Sōboku's:

Look—see how naturally	onozukara naru
the pattern of things comes forth.	kotowari o miyo
Without a thought,	yadosu to mo
water offers night lodging	mizu wa omowanu
to the radiant moon.	tsuki sumite

Here rather than an adage we have a declaration of doctrine, but the method of linking is similar in that it finds evidence of principle (*kotowari*) at work in the natural world.

HOSOKAWA YŪSAI 細川幽斎, *Kyūshū no michi no ki* (p. 353)

On the eighth [of the Seventh Month] . . . we received word that the master of Honkokuji Temple was going to hold a gathering. He was so persistent that we were powerless to say no, so we stayed the night. I composed this [for the gathering] the next day:

Moonlight spills down—	moru tsuki mo
showing all the more clearly	ima hitoshio no
gaps between the trees.	ko no ma kana

CONTEXT: Hosokawa Yūsai (1534-1610) was the son of an Ashikaga shogun who became heir of the mighty Hosokawa warrior clan. He is one of the most famous of all those who were adept at *bun* and *bu*, letters and arms. In the summer of 1587, Toyotomi Hideyoshi, on his way toward pacifying the whole of Japan, led a massive army of men to Kyushu to bring recalcitrants there into submission, and Yūsai followed him. However military the purposes of the journey, the record Yūsai left—*Kyūshū no michi no ki* (My journey through Kyushu)—is steadfastly literary, narrating his visits to famous sites and the homes of local literati, along with his own *waka* (often about *meisho*) and *hokku* (usually composed for *renga* gatherings).

COMMENT: Yūsai was often asked to provide the first verse for *renga* gatherings held in his honor. Sometimes he begged off and just sent a *hokku*, a common practice since early medieval times, but often—as here at the castle town of Suo Yamaguchi—he was obliged to attend. The season being autumn, he composed a moon verse—perhaps on the spot, perhaps before. (It was common practice to compose a few *hokku* in preparation for a gathering.) We can conclude that it was an evening gathering and that the moon was out, although what the scene presents is not the moon itself but its light silhouetting the trees.

At the beginning of the Fifth Month, when he had visited a temple near another castle town, Yūsai recorded seeing a maple tree in the garden and wrote this (p. 344):

Deep in the forest	miyamagi no
I catch sight of summer:	naka ni natsu o ya
a young maple tree.	wakakaede

Such instances make a pattern: cuckoos call (pp. 344, 354), and Yūsai makes that the center of his poem (not once, but two times); a storm interferes with travel (pp. 352, 353), and he writes a *hokku* on autumn wind. Thus he reveals an element of practice that we can take as a prevailing custom. The ability to work local detail into a *hokku* was highly prized.

After leaving Yamaguchi, Yūsai traveled to Kokufu Tenjin Shrine, where he was again asked for a *hokku*. At first the group planned to compose just eight verses—the first side of a *renga kaishi*; but they ended up finishing a full hundred-verse sequence. He records that they began at the time of the vespers bell and finished up in the middle of the night. The primary image of his *hokku* on that occasion was pine trees, which of course were always found around shrines.

SATOMURA JŌHA 紹巴, *Atago hyakuin* (p. 323)

Fickle affection	tabitabi no	度度の化の情はなにかせん
and shown rarely at that:	ada no nasake wa	たのみがたきは猶後の親
what is one to do?	nani ka sen	
Hard to truly rely on	tanomigataki wa	
is a parent after one's own.	nao nochi no oya	
Jōha		

CONTEXT: Satomura Jōha was a professional *renga* master and the most prominent *renga* figure of his time. His lineage would continue to be dominant throughout the Edo period. The *Atago hyakuin* (One hundred verses at Atago, 1582) was a dedicatory sequence composed at Mount Atago in Yamashiro Province.

COMMENT: Not every *renga tsukeku* involves a natural image. Here the author of the *maeku* (a man named Gyōyū who was a priest at Itokuin on Mount Atago) is probably imagining a lover complaining about ill-treatment. "If affection is shown seldom, and even then is not sincere, what is one supposed to do?" Jōha takes advantage of the vagueness of the statement to cast off love as a category and recontextualize the *maeku*, instead focusing on family relations. The phrase *nochi no oya* means literally a "later parent," a father or mother coming new into the household, usually as a step-parent.

Such stories are common in Japanese literature and folklore, and tense relations between parents and children in the warrior classes were particularly conspicuous because of the complicated political alliances that were almost always involved in marriages. It is worth noting that the occasion for this particular sequence, held at a temple not far from Kyoto in the summer of 1582, was a visit by the warlord

Akechi Mitsuhide (1528-1582), who was actively plotting against Oda Nobunaga at the time. Just a few months later, Nobunaga, surrounded by Mitsuhide's forces, would die by his own hand at a temple in Kyoto. Yet Mitsuhide's triumph was short-lived: he died that same year, which meant that the alliances he had made with the marriage of his own children would collapse and put them in peril. His own wife, along with his son and heir, would be killed at the fortress of Mitsuhide's son-in-law, where they had fled for safety.

Knowing all this, one cannot help but wonder about Mitsuhide's reaction to Jōha's *tsukeku*. But of course the events had not happened yet; and the fact is that Jōha's declaration represented common knowledge to anyone in elite society, in which the frailty of even family relationships was painfully obvious. "Fickle affections" is a phrase that could have described most political alliances, which were based on self-interest and could change direction like the wind. A glance at the annals of the time is enough to show that even parents could not always be trusted, let alone "later parents" without the same bonds of blood. Jōha's verse could easily be stated as a *kotowaza*, or "old saying"—trite but true.

NŌJUN 能順, *Enpō rokunen Hakusan hyakuin* (p. 504): "Composed in the Eighth Month of 1678, midway through autumn, at Yamanaka"

Have a heart, winds,	*yūgiri no*
as you blow evening mists	*nobe ni fuku kaze*
across the moors.	*kokoro seyo*
Sadly caught in sudden rain,	*niwakaame wabishi*
and no lodging in sight.	*yadori mo zo naki*
Nōjun	

夕霧の野辺に吹風心せよ
急雨侘し宿りもぞなき

CONTEXT: Nōjun (1628-1706), son of a priest of Kitano Shrine in Kyoto, was the premier *renga* master of his day. The *haikai* poet Matsuo Bashō (1644-1694) visited him in Komatsu in 1689, during one of his famous journeys. It was to Komatsu that Nōjun eventually retired. He served for a time as chief priest of Kitano Tenman Shrine in Kyoto and also as superintendent of Tenjin Shrine in Komatsu, bastion of Maeda Toshitsune (1594-1558), who governed the three provinces of Kaga, Etchū, and Noto. For Toshitsune, *renga* was part of ritual life, as it had been for generations of Maedas before him. Kitano Shrine in Kyoto, dedicated to the Heian-era statesman-scholar Sugawara no Michizane (849-903), had housed a *renga* office for hundreds of years, and there were Tenjin shrines with similar affiliations all around the country.

COMMENT: Although eclipsed by *haikai* in popular terms, *renga* continued to be composed throughout the Edo period, especially among the samurai elite. This link comes from a sequence composed at a local hot spring involving Nōjun and two other Komatsu locals, the samurai Asai Masasuke and one Ganryū. A colophon records (out of modesty) that the sequence was written for practice (*keiko*) and should be shown to no one, but it was preserved in the storehouse of Komatsu Shrine, far beyond any statute of limitations. Such texts were preserved so that they could be reviewed as part of further study and of course had intrinsic value as votive objects.

The *maeku* in the example here presents a statement by someone whose concern may be aesthetic: a complaint at a view being blocked by the winds blowing mists across the fields. Nōjun's *tsukeku* provides readers with both elaboration and explanation, adding rain showers to the wind and positing a traveler who sees no protection from the elements ahead. (Wind is bad enough; wind plus rain clearly too much.) The link between the verses is a "close" one (*shinku*), cemented by conventional associations ("sudden rain" relating back to "wind" and "mist," "lodging" relating back to "evening" and "moors"), a simple plot, and reasoning. What we see is the integrated scene of a traveler caught without shelter in a rising storm as he crosses fields, along with a sort of riddle made explicit by the apostrophe of the *maeku*: "Why is it that the traveler asks the winds for pity? Because the winds are accompanied by rain showers from which there is no shelter." The first verse is probably in the first person, but the second is ambiguous, a frequent characteristic of the form that allowed for the kind of reorientation that was central to the art of linking.

Late eighteenth-century painting by Matsumura Gekkei of a *haikai* master and students, from *Shin hanatsumi* by Yosa Buson.

Courtesy L. Tom Perry Special Collection, HBLL, Brigham Young University.

Chapter 5
UNORTHODOX POEMS

MATSUE SHIGEYORI 松江重頼, *Enokoshū* 1451 (Winter)

Falling snow
puts makeup on the City:
a Kyoto belle.

furu yuki wa
kyōoshiroi to
miyako kana

ふる雪は京おしろいとみやこ哉

CONTEXT: Matsue Shigeyori (1602–1680) was born in Matsue but spent his adult life in Kyoto as a wealthy merchant. He studied *renga* in his younger years but gained his reputation in *haikai*. Shigeyori's poem shows that already in the early 1600s Kyoto geisha were known for their distinctive white makeup. Although pre-Edo sources contain references to dancers and "pleasure women" who in some ways prefigure the geisha, it was later, in Shigeyori's own time, that licensed entertainment districts were established in cities like Edo and Kyoto; and it was then that the term began to take on its conventional meaning.

COMMENT: What qualifies this *hokku* as *haikai*—i.e., humorous or unconventional verse? Certainly not the first line—literally, "the snow falling down." So much was "snow" the quintessential *kigo* (season word) of winter that according to the rules of classical linked verse it could appear no more than four times in a sequence, unless it was used only figuratively, as in phrases like *hana no yuki*, "a snowfall of cherry blossoms." In Shigeyori's verse, the snow is real, but he immediately stamps his work as a *haikai* effort by a metaphor that would not appear in traditional forms: *shiroi*, or "makeup," specifically the thick white facial makeup worn by geisha. Even in Edo times, some courtiers still wore facial powder, but Shigeyori no doubt refers to women he knew from his own experience of Kyoto culture, gesturing toward a whole world of pastimes and pleasures considered too risqué for traditional genres.

After the establishment of the shogun's government there in 1600, Edo gradually overtook Kyoto as the most important of Japanese cities. Yet many warlords continued to maintain large city estates there, and the many temples and shrines in the city and its environs made it an important site of worship and pilgrimage, as well as tourism. The process of change was thus gradual, and when *Enokoshū* (Mongrel-puppy collection), a large collection of *haikai* from the pre-Bashō era, was published in 1633, Kyoto was still a grand metropolis, known as Miyako, "the capital" (translated here as "the City"), and it was still the preeminent Japanese city of the time. Rather than toward the imperial palace, however, Shigeyori's metaphor gestures toward the merchant and pleasure districts of the city, which were full of inns, teahouses, shops, theaters, and precincts of worldly pleasures. The snow of his first line thus suggests a broad view of the city, appearing pure and white, showing an idealistic scene of the sort described by the poet Murata Harumi (1746-1812), who wrote that under snow "shop streets, too, take on a sudden sheen, reminding one of life in a mountain village and making even the hats and cloaks of tradesmen seem somehow things of beauty" (*Kotojirishū*, p. 609). Shigeyori's mention of the makeup of a geisha, on the other hand, cannot but make us think of another sort of beauty pulsing beneath the makeup, both the makeup of the woman and that of the lively city that she represents.

OZAWA BOKUSEKI 小沢卜尺 and **OTHERS**, *Danrin toppyakuin* 882-85: From the eighth of ten hundred-poem sequences composed in the summer of 1675

82 In bed at morning
    the girl acts shy.
        Bokuseki

asai no toko o
hazuru komusume

83 In fine form
    she goes off to pee—
    hair in tangles.
        Shōkyū

shana shana to
shishi shi ni yukeba
midaregami

84 As the cart leaves,
    wind follows behind.
        Itchō

norimono ideshi
ato no oikaze

85 Harakiri!
    Yesterday, today,
    peaks of cloud.
        Zaishiki

harakiri ya
kinō wa kyō no
mine no kumo

CONTEXT: Ozawa Bokuseki (d. 1695), Deki Shōkyū, Toyoshima Itchō, and Noguchi Zaishiki (d. 1719) were all *haikai* devotees living in Edo. The *Ten Hundred-Verse Sequences of the Danrin School* (*Danrin toppyakuin*) were composed in 1675 and published that same year.

朝ゐの床をはづる小娘
しやなしやなとししに行けば乱髪
乗物出しあとの追風
腹切やきのふはけふの峰の雲

COMMENT: The rules of *haikai*-style linked verse allow for more rapid changes than in classical *renga*, as reflected in these verses by Edo poets, some of them disciples of Nishiyama Sōin (1605-1682), who was himself a transitional figure between classical linked verse and *haikai* and leader of a faction referred to as the Danrin school—literally, "a grove for chatting"—dedicated to an informal style. The first verse presents an inexperienced young woman lingering in bed, perhaps after a night of lovemaking. Shōkyū's *tsukeku* expands that scene, showing a girl trying to act with nonchalant elegance that only draws attention to the fact that she is going to relieve her bladder. Itchō's verse, however, employs no vocabulary that would indicate love as a category: it is only when joined to the previous verse that we see the man in the cart leaving after a night with a woman. Then Zaishiki's verse pivots to another topic altogether, *mujō*, or "transience." Now the girl is forgotten as the cart is recast as a conveyance for the body of a high-ranking man going off to a cremation site, the trailing wind being transformed into the idea of samurai who will be obliged to follow him in death by committing ritual suicide. (The latter is suggested by the word *oibara*, a compound formed by the *oi* of *oikaze* in verse 84 and the *hara* of *harakiri* in verse no. 85). Thus we move from a shy girl to harakiri, all in just four verses, although old associations ("hair" relating back to "girl," "follow" back to "goes," "cloud" back to "wind") still figure in the linking.

MATSUO BASHŌ 松尾芭蕉, *Oi no kobumi* (p. 318)

Ah, the jumble of things
they call back to mind—
cherry blossoms.

samazama no
koto omoidasu
sakura kana

さまざまのことおもひ出す桜かな

CONTEXT: Matsuo Bashō was a man of modest background who in his midtwenties became a professional *haikai* poet. He lived in Edo but traveled widely and left travel records, as well as *hokku*, linked-verse sequences, and pieces of *haikai* prose. Bashō wrote this *hokku* in his hometown of Iga Ueno in the Second

Month of 1688, when he was viewing the blossoms at the villa of Tanganshi, while on the journey later recorded in *Oi no kobumi* (Knapsack notes, 1688). Tanganshi was the son of Tōdō Sengin, the samurai patron of Bashō's youth, whose death in 1666 had precipitated a crisis in Bashō's life that we believe led him to pursue *haikai* as a profession. The setting, already nostalgic because of memories of his deceased parents, was doubly so because of memories of the same garden more than two decades before. The cottage where Bashō composed the *hokku* was thereafter known as Samazama-an, incorporating the first line of the poem.

COMMENT: In *Haikai sabi shiori* (*Sabi* and *shiori* in *haikai*, 1812, p. 385), Kaya Shirao (1738-1791) quotes a remark by his teacher, Shirai Chōsui (1701-1769), that sees an allusion to the "Suma" chapter of *Genji monogatari*, when Genji was in exile. "In Suma, the New Year came, and as the days grew longer, time was heavy on his hands. As the young cherry trees he had planted began to bloom, a few of their blossoms floated on the wind in mild skies, and so many things were called to mind that he was frequently in tears" (2:204).

The technique of allusive variation is not employed in *haikai* as often as it is in *waka*, perhaps because so short a form cannot accommodate a long passage of text. Still, allusions do appear. In this case, Bashō does what ancient poets were counseled to do: to put an old idea in a fresh context. In the tale, the eponymous character gazes out on cherry trees transplanted into his garden just the year before, while Bashō looks at cherry trees from long ago. But the phrase *yorozu no koto oboshiiderarete* (similar to *samazama no koto omoidasu* in Bashō's poem) is vague enough that it could refer as much to Genji's whole life as to his life at Suma. The important thing for Bashō is the idea of blossoms—a yearly marker of passing time—evoking memories for him, as for Genji. Writing about cherry blossoms was a challenge. Bashō's accomplishment is in the way he makes the prominence of cherry blossoms in poetic culture the explicit theme of the poem. What he gives us is not natural description but one man's reaction to a natural scene, one of the hallmarks of Bashō's style. What is he remembering? No doubt his own youth and his patron, Sengin, first of all; but hovering in the background are cherry blossoms in thousands of other poems brought "again to mind."

YAMAMOTO KAKEI 山本荷兮, *Haru no hi* 292-94

34 Gobbling up rice cakes,　　　　*mochi o kuraitsutsu*
　　he celebrates the Reign　　　　*iwau kimi ga yo*
　　　　Tankō

35   Mountains in bloom: *yama wa hana*
     everyone, everywhere   *tokoro nokorazu*
     on holiday.   *asobu hi ni*
         Tōbun

36   Not cloudy, not sunny—   *kumorazu terazu*
     and a lark in song.   *hibari naku nari*
         Kakei

CONTEXT: Yamamoto Kakei (d. 1716) was a samurai and Sugita Tankō, a confectioner; Tōbun's occupation is unknown. All were Nagoya disciples of Bashō. Kakei was the most prominent, a member of the Teitoku school who later became a disciple of Bashō's and, from the mid-1690s onward, forsook *haikai* for *renga*. The links here ended a thirty-six-verse sequence in *Haru no hi* (Spring day, 1686) composed by six men of the Nagoya area, who began their effort at the country cottage of Sugita Tankō, one of the participants, but completed it in the rooms of Yamamoto Kakei, the next day, on the nineteenth day of the Third Month of 1686. Custom dictated that the final verse (no. 36, called the *ageku*) of a *haikai* sequence be in the spring category and that it be propitious in tone. Kakei's *ageku* fulfills both requirements.

COMMENT: One of the dynamics at work in *renku* sequences is between nature and human affairs. (Sometimes the two are referred to as *tenchi ninjō*.) The three verses show that dynamic at work. Tankō creates the amusing scene of someone unceremoniously chomping on rice cakes in honor of the New Year. Rather than adding to that scene visually, Tōbun evokes a similar situation a few months later, as people take the day off to enjoy mountain cherry blossoms—an example of linking by *hibiki*, or "reverberation," with "holiday" serving as an echo of "celebrate." The final verse, by Kakei, however, shows no human involvement at all, instead focusing on the serene, gentle call of a lark in hazy spring skies. In this sense, the last link is a *keikizuke*, or "scenery link," a term that means the same thing it does in *renga* discourse—that is, a natural scene with affective overtones. As a final verse, the singing draws our attention upward in search of the larks, who are traditionally figured as flying so high that they cannot be detected by the human eye. Thus we end the sequence with a kind of benediction, the religious connotations of that word not being inappropriate since the successful completion of a sequence was considered a votive act supplicating for peace and order in the world.

OKADA YASUI 岡田野水, *Arano* 1110 (Miscellaneous)

In autumn, more tears
for a sneak thief's wife.
    Etsujin

aki o nao naku
nusubito no tsuma

Must be daybreak.
From west, from east,
bells sounding.
    Yasui

akuru yara
nishi mo higashi mo
kane no koe

CONTEXT: Okada Yasui (1658-1743) and Ochi Etsujin (b. 1656) were Nagoya merchants. Prominent disciples of Bashō, they in turn practiced as *haikai* masters in their local area. The impetus behind the sequence (from *Arano*, Withered fields, 1689) involved here was a message in the Fourth Month from one Yamaguchi Sodō (1642-1716), who was then living near Mount Hiei, near Kyoto. Letter writing was an art form for literati but also a practical necessity, as all correspondence was undertaken by hand. Runners carrying mail were what kept shopkeepers and innkeepers along thoroughfares in business. As was typical, Sodō wrote a highly literary note, appending a *hokku* that was used to begin a sequence.

COMMENT: Etsujin presents us with the domestic scene of a wife whose tears increase with the coming of autumn—but with a twist, for her husband is a thief. Thieves appear sometimes in *waka*, but only sublimated through the image of *shiranami*, "white waves" or "breakers," and they figure in serious *renga* only rarely. But in *haikai* they are fairly common, probably because they were such a part of the cast of characters in everyday life. But rather than focusing on the thief himself, Etsujin cagily focuses on the man's wife, reminding us that even thieves have families with their own routines. The punishments for thievery were severe and could involve a culprit's dependents.

Yasui's response to Etsujin's brief sketch offers a scene of bells ringing at daybreak that will make moving in a new direction easier for the next participant—what the commentaries call a *yariku*. But in the context of the link, the verse is a variation on the old trope of being kept awake by worries on an autumn night. The first line is thus interior monologue in a highly colloquial idiom: "Must be daybreak, I s'pose." Then comes the explanation for the riddle of the woman's tears: the bells, their warning echoes impinging from all sides. Thus Yasui fills in one of the elliptical corners of the *maeku*. In classical poems, such sounds evoked images

秋をなをなく盗人の妻
明るやら西も東も鐘の声

of temples and often signaled lovers' farewells or suggested scenes of religious life. In Yasui's link, however, the bells inspire worries of a more worldly sort, and the tears are not shed in a romantic or devotional setting. Summer was the best season for thieves, since people were often out late carousing; autumn, always figured as melancholy in poetry, was a more dangerous time as well. Hence the heightened sense of worry. "Why isn't he back yet?" "Has he been injured?" "Or, worse yet, caught?" Finding sympathy for the thief himself may be difficult, but we readily feel sorry for the wife who waits for his return every time he is "at work."

SUGIYAMA SANPŪ 杉山杉風 and OTHERS, *Hatsukaishi hyōchū* 21-23

21 Since first bloom
    he's been counting carts—
    beneath the blossoms.
      Sanpū

saku hi yori
kuruma kazoyuru
hana no kage

22 On the bridge, light rain,
    shimmering like heat.
      Senka

hashi wa kosame o
moyuru kagerō

23 Leftover snow,
    leftover scarecrow:
    uncommon sights.
      Shugen

nokoru yuki
nokoru kagashi no
mezurashiku

咲く日より車数ゆる花の陰
橋は小雨をもゆる陽炎
残る雪残る案山子の珍しく

CONTEXT: Sugiyama Sanpū (1647-1732) was one of Bashō's disciples, as were Senka and Shugen, about whom little else is known. Bashō left few critical writings, but in 1686 he penned a commentary on some of the verses from a sequence involving himself and some of his disciples titled *Hatsukaishi hyōchū* (Comments on the first sequence of the New Year) from which the verses here are taken.

COMMENT: Scholars see Bashō's comments as early articulations of his aesthetic of *karumi*, or "lightness," a term he uses in his characterization of verse 22: "Notice his way of handling the season, lightly and casually [*karoku yasuraka ni*]. What one should do in linking to a blossom verse is to do so straightforwardly, lightly [*yasuyasu to karoku*]." Thus he praises Senka for favoring delicacy over drama. About Shugen's verse Bashō says more: "Again, a spring scene. Restrained linking technique. The worn-out scarecrow standing there, retaining the scent of the fields and rice paddies and orchards, makes for a most touching scene. I call it highly affecting the way autumn and winter remain on into spring, under a light layer of snow" (p. 471).

Here, the terms "a touching scene" (*aware naru keiki*) and "highly affecting" (*kansei nari*) derive from courtly poetics. Elsewhere in the same comments Bashō uses the terms *yūgen*, *taketakashi*, *ari no mama*, *yojō*, and *omoshiroshi*, signaling conscious engagement with courtly traditions. This should be no surprise: among Bashō's stated ambitions was reconnection with the past in spirit, distancing himself from what he attacked as trivial in the *haikai* poetry of more recent times. In this sense, he reversed the medieval dictum of "old words, new heart" (*Eiga taigai*, p. 188), seeking to articulate the high ideals of the past with contemporary vocabulary and subject matter.

MUKAI KYORAI 向井去来, *Kyoraishō* (p. 445)

Nightclothes of fine twill, reflecting sunlight.	aya no nemaki ni utsuru hi no kage
In tears, she looks for little straw sandals— with no success.	naku naku mo chiisaki waraji motomekane

CONTEXT: Mukai Kyorai (1651-1704) was a student of Bashō's who after the latter's death was the leader of the Bashō school in the Kansai area. Records tell us that this link was composed for a thirty-six-verse sequence held at the cottage of the head priest of Kamigoryō Shrine in Kyoto late in 1690. Nine people participated, all disciples or associates of Bashō's. Among them was Sakanoue Kōshun (d. 1701), a disciple of Kitamura Kigin's (1624-1705), one of Bashō's own teachers in his early days as a *haikai* poet. He is probably the source of the following anecdote also recorded in *Kyoraishō* (Kyorai's notes, 1702-1704, p. 445):

When this *maeku* was produced in a gathering, the assembled people were having trouble coming up with a link. The master said, "This verse—it shows a high-ranking woman traveling, I think," and someone came up with a link right away.

Kōshun said, "No sooner did he say it was a high-class woman than someone came up with a *tsukeku*. The way Bashō's disciples got training was something special."

綾のねまきにうつる日の影

泣く泣くも小さき草鞋もとめかね

COMMENT: People in the *za* had to produce verses on the spot, usually within a few minutes. For them techniques were thus not just aesthetic in purpose but also practical aids to composition. In the case of this *tsukeku*, we have an anecdote that illustrates how the idea of *kuraizuke* (linking by social station) assisted in responding to a difficult verse.

The challenge of the *maeku*, composed by a man named Oguri Shiyū (d. 1705), was that it was vague as to any surrounding context, such as who the owner of the "nightclothes of fine twill" was. When no one managed to come up with anything, Bashō offered a hint to set the other participants off in a useful direction by providing an imagined social station and purpose for the owner of the fine nightclothes—a person of substance, on the road, probably staying at an inn. Kyorai then did the rest, coming up with a credible human scene: a rich woman, probably young and perhaps not used to being on the road, still in her nightclothes (or is she perhaps taking them off to get dressed in her traveling clothes?), searching in frustration for her little straw sandals. Thus a *maeku* that offers no more than the single image of twill sparkling in morning sunlight is brought to life, and all thanks to a simple suggestion by the master about *kurai*. The "little" straw sandals is a master stroke, stopping short of saying "pretty" but suggesting the same, while also hinting at youth and inexperience. By the word "high-ranking woman" (*jōrō*), Bashō probably meant to suggest a young married woman. Kyorai's verse gives no pronoun at all, however, leaving leeway for the next person in the linking process.

NAITŌ JŌSŌ 内藤丈草, *Haikai Shirao yawa* (p. 197)

Ōhara Moor.	Ōhara ya
Butterflies out dancing	chō no detemau
in misty moonlight.	oborozuki

大原や蝶の出てまふ朧月

CONTEXT: *Haikai Shirao yawa* (Shirao's night tales about *haikai*, 1833), a collection of anecdotes, offers a story about the creation of this *hokku*:

> This is a verse by Jōsō. When Bashō first heard it, he asked, "I wonder, these butterflies dancing—what would they look like?"
> Jōsō replied, "Last night I actually walked through Ōhara and saw them at it."
> "Well, in that case, the verse is superb," Bashō said, "truly, this *is* Ōhara," and was extravagant in his praise, so it is said.

Naitō Jōsō (1662–1704), a samurai who took the tonsure at a young age to live as a literatus, was among Bashō's chief disciples. Ōhara Moor, just north of Kyoto, was associated with a number of poignant events, especially Lady Kenreimon'in's entry into a hillside temple there after the fall of the Heike clan in the late 1100s. Bashō praised Jōsō's dreamy scene for capturing the essence of the place.

COMMENT: The provenance established by the anecdote in this case states an important principle that goes back at least as far as Fujiwara no Tameie, who in one of his treatises says that there was a special place in practice for poems composed "in accord with actual scenery" (*Eiga no ittei*, pp. 201-2). The nature of Bashō's doubts is not clear (Is he doubting that butterflies actually *dance*? That they come out at night? Or were they perchance moths rather than butterflies?), but he ends up praising the poem in any case.

Without corroboration, determining whether a verse was based on actual observation is difficult, but an early anthology (*Arano*, 1689) offers poems such as these (nos. 447, 570, 654) by obscure disciples of Bashō's that are easy to imagine as "real."

Snow starts to fall
and into the horse stable
go the sparrows.
    Fusen

yuki furite
umaya ni hairu
suzume kana

In a big garden
he's planted just one—
cherry tree.
    Shōsō

hironiwa ni
hitomoto ueshi
sakura kana

Rainy evening:
mosquitoes buzzing around
my umbrella.
    Nisui

ame no kure
kasa no gururi ni
naku ka kana

UEJIMA ONITSURA 上島鬼貫, *Onitsura haikai hyakusen* (p. 211)
(Autumn): "Strolling in the fields"

Autumn wind
blows in and passes by.
People's faces.

akikaze no
fukiwatarikeri
hito no kao

CONTEXT: Uejima Onitsura (lay name Fujiwara Munechika, 1661-1738) was born to a sake brewer in Itami, Settsu Province. He studied medicine as a youth, and at eight years old he began his lifelong dedication to *haikai*. He studied under Nishiyama Sōin but remained an independent figure.

COMMENT: In time Onitsura became disillusioned with the wordplay of the Danrin style, instead arguing that the hallmark of good poetry was *makoto*, "sincerity," a fundamental concept of Confucian dogma at the time that was also of some importance in court poetics. Like poets of the Kyōgoku faction in medieval times (who used that same term), Onitsura wanted objects to speak for themselves, revealing the rhythms of the phenomenal world. But the poem here shows that he was capable of complex conceptions. The first two lines present the most obvious quality of wind: that it blows by. But the word *akikaze*, "autumn wind," of course communicates more than that. For one thing, the autumn wind is by definition a chilly wind, and one that we know blows leaves from the trees and contributes to the general trend toward decay that ends in winter. As a subtle way to tease out these qualities, the poet ends the poem with the evocative phrase *hito no kao*, "people's faces." Thus Onitsura uses the technique of apposition, leaving the task of overcoming the ellipsis to us as readers. The most likely scenario is that as they hear the wind blow by, people turn their faces up from whatever they are doing and notice the change in the landscape, thus coming together, in a way. And the reactions on those faces are various. Some enjoy the sight of things blown on the wind, others feel a sense of foreboding as winter comes on, still others may think about practical tasks that must be done—the possibilities are endless. Instead of the effect of wind on the leaves, then, we are left to imagine its effect on faces.

Onitsura also wrote highly colloquial poems such as the following (p. 220), on the topic "year's end," that invited criticism of the sort leveled at the *waka* poet Ozawa Roan.

You may resent it,	*oshimedomo*
but you'll go to bed, get up—	*netara okitara*
to spring.	*haru de aro*

Some thought such poems went too far. The Zen priest Kyomyōshi Gitō (d. 1730), in a postface to Onitsura's *Hitorigoto* (Talking to myself, 1718, p. 192), disagreed— "The diction of Onitsura's *haikai* is not vulgar but simple and sincere [*makoto*]"— and compared him to the Chinese poetry of Tao Yuanming (365–427) and the Zen of Bodhidharma (fl. sixth century), founder of that sect.

秋風の吹きわたりけり人の顔

146 UNORTHODOX POEMS

NOZAWA BONCHŌ 野沢凡兆, *Bashōmon kojin Shinseki* (p. 264)

A cast-off skiff—	sutebune no
frozen, inside and out,	uchisoto kōru
on an inlet.	irie kana
Bonchō	

CONTEXT: Nozawa Bonchō (d. 1714), a Kyoto physician, was a sometime student of Bashō's.

COMMENT: This haiku by Bonchō, recorded in a compendium of poems by Bashō's disciples put together by Chōmu (1732-1795), calls to mind a *waka* by Shōtetsu on the topic "boat on an inlet":

Owner unknown:	nushi shiranu
at evening, on an inlet,	irie no yūbe
with no one around—	hito nakute
just a rain cloak and a pole,	mino to sao to no
left behind in a boat.	fune ni nokoreru

As recorded by Tō no Tsuneyori (1401-1484) in *Tōyashū kikigaki* (Notes on conversations with Lord Tō, governor of Shimotsuke, 1456?, pp. 340-41), Shōtetsu's poem (*Sōkonshū*, no. 5999) was attacked by the Nijō-school poet Gyōkō (1391-1455) as "the voice of a violent age," in reference to the Mao preface to the Chinese *Book of Songs*. What offended was doubtless the starkness of the scene and the unsparing diction of the phrases *nushi shiranu* (owner unknown) and *hito nakute* (no one around). Shōtetsu paints an objective scene in the *sabi* mode: no metaphor, no figures of speech, nothing to signal a poem in the courtly tradition. Mainstream poems generally treat the subject of loneliness in more sentimental terms.

    Whether Bonchō was thinking of Shōtetsu's poem is not recorded, but we can be sure that Bonchō did not worry about such criticism. In *haikai* "common" objects and the less-elegant aspects of nature and human experience were not regarded as offensive. One thinks of a famous *hokku* by Bashō himself, written near the end of his life, in 1693, and recorded in *Komo jishi shū* (Straw-lion collection, 1693, p. 236):

"First day of the year"

Year in, year out,	toshidoshi ya
the monkey wears the mask	saru ni kisetaru
of a monkey's face.	saru no men

While not objective in its rhetoric, this poem has none of the optimism one expects at the beginning of a new year. The idea of the monkey trapped forever, by decree of nature, behind a face that is comical to human eyes is boundlessly sad. And of course anyone—especially anyone getting on in years—looking at a monkey's face is bound to notice its human qualities and realize that his predicament is not so far from our own. Bashō's reported comment on the verse was, "I was lamenting how people don't make any progress but make the same mistakes year after year" (*Sanzōshi* [Three books], 1702, p. 566).

BONCHŌ AND BASHŌ, *Kyoraishō* (p. 434)

Lower Kyoto:	*shimogyō ya*
snow piles up, and then—	*yuki tsumu ue no*
night rain.	*yoru no ame*

下京や雪つむ上のよるの雨

CONTEXT: As noted, Nozawa Bonchō was one of Bashō's disciples. An anecdote about the poem here recorded in *Kyoraishō* (pp. 434-35) tells us that Bonchō did not compose it alone.

> At first, this poem had no first line. Beginning with the late master, everyone began suggesting lines, and finally this was the one decided upon. Bonchō, however, said, "Hmm," and still wasn't sure.
> The late master said, "Try your own hand, Bonchō—suggest a line. If you come up with anything better, I won't ever say another word about *haikai*."

COMMENT: In this anecdote, revision is presented as a communal activity. Who contributed the first line is not entirely clear, but the story suggests it was Bashō himself. The anecdote has much to tell us about *haikai* culture. First, we see a poet with an incomplete poem, no doubt a common situation; many of Bashō's own poems exist in many versions, some of them arrived at with input from other people. And as we think about poets trying to come up with a beginning line, we notice that Kyorai portrays a model for the master-disciple relationship in which the master prevails, but only after some give-and-take; authority is established through negotiation. And it is not by chance that Kyorai—author of the book in which it appears—is telling such a story as a disciple. The book was written after Bashō's death and served as a claim to succession from the master.

But what is it about the version of the poem quoted by Kyorai that makes it superior? The answer has to do with the connotations associated with "lower" Kyoto, a place well known to the poets. Bonchō's two lines present a natural scene of night rain falling onto accumulated snow but provide no specific setting—and no sense of human involvement or emotion. Establishing the scene as lower Kyoto, the commercial district of the city, always bustling with people, provides both those things, contributing a suggestion of liveliness to the scene and also making an implied contrast with the more upper-class upper section of the city. Thus as readers we imagine shopping districts, merchant tenements, streets and alleyways, rather than the spacious city estates of upper Kyoto, where at a little higher altitude snow might indeed still be falling. In this setting, we visualize slushy streets that add to the "lightness" (*karumi*) of the conception, while also injecting a sense of human involvement. Creating so concrete and evocative a context in just five syllables is no easy task, the anecdote implies. "A mountain village" would work, as would "a fishing village" or a time of day—"as evening descends." But would any of those provide the same affective power and connotations beyond the words, moving beyond the aesthetic to the socio-aesthetic?

KAGAMI SHIKŌ 各務支考, *Zoku Sarumino* 3462 (Miscellaneous)

Sparrows sing	*jikidō ni*
by the monks' dining hall.	*suzume naku nari*
Evening rain.	*yūshigure*

食堂に雀啼なり夕時雨

CONTEXT: Kagami Shikō (1665-1731) was born in Mino Province (modern Nagoya). He had firsthand experience of monastic life, having spent some years at Daichiji Temple in what is now Gifu, a Zen temple where his elder sister had had him placed as a young boy after the death of his father. Why he decided to leave the priesthood is not precisely known, but it seems likely that it was because of a desire to pursue further the more secular studies he undertook at the temple, which would have involved Chinese, along with some exposure to both Chinese and Japanese poetry. He studied in both Kyoto and Ise, at the same time beginning his activity in the world of *haikai*. He became a disciple of Bashō's around 1690 when the master visited Mino on one of his journeys through the provinces. After Bashō's death, he established a school of his own and was considered disloyal by some of Bashō's other major disciples. The poem here is from the "Buddhism" chapter of *Zoku sarumino* (The monkey's straw raincoat II, 1694), an anthology of poems by poets of Bashō's school put together in the autumn of 1694, in Iga, just before Bashō's death. Shikō assisted his master, but as it did not reach final form while Bashō was still living the anthology was viewed with some suspicion by many poets and scholars.

COMMENT: Although in the Buddhism category, Shikō's poem presents a picture of everyday life rather than any doctrine, at least on the surface. Temples were places not just of study and meditation but also of labor of all sorts, especially for those of modest background in the lower ranks, as Shikō would certainly have been. For him, memories of daily life at Daichiji would have been of daily chores, and mealtimes would have been looked forward to as both respite from work and relief from pangs of hunger. Temple fare was notoriously bland, usually consisting of just vegetables and rice, meat being forbidden; but still one can imagine monks eager to receive their bowls. Rather than express this directly, however, Shikō takes an oblique approach, focusing on sparrows, and not inside the mess hall itself but outside. Buddhist doctrine taught that all beings shared in Buddha nature, though at different levels of grace, animals being down the ladder from men. Yet birds and men would of course both have an innate desire for food. The addition of evening showers is important in further establishing season—late autumn or early winter—and mood: the birds would be seeking shelter under the eaves from the cold rain, just as monks would be doing in the dining hall. In the end, Shikō's conception is another example of *karumi*, or "lightness," in the way it focuses on the common sparrow, whose twittering at the eaves in refuge is really little different from the monks inside the hall chatting over their food, all with evening rain coming down outside, imbuing the scene with *sabi*. The fact that by custom the monks would leave some of their precious fare to be set out for their animal neighbors strengthens the metaphorical bond.

KAWAI KENPŪ 河合見風, *Kagetsu ichiyaron* (One night with Kyōka and Chigetsu, 1765?) (p. 81)

There is nothing all that difficult about *haikai*. You just put your evening chats about the heat or the cold into a verse of seventeen syllables.

Such coolness!	*suzushisa ya*
An inner sanctum unknown	*hotoke mo shiranu*
even to Buddha.	*ushirodō*
Kenpū	

涼しさやほとけもしらぬ後堂

In terms of the outer scriptures, *haikai* consoles, while in terms of the inner scripture it soothes the seven emotions. You take what is before your eyes and evoke the forms of mountains, rivers, bays, and seas and the sights of flowers, birds, wind, and moon, everything down to people planting barley in the fields or rice in the paddies.

CONTEXT: Kawai Kenpū (1711–1783), of the Kaga domain, was a student of the Bashō school who also studied *waka* under a master of the Reizei house. This commentary on his *hokku*, from a treatise of uncertain origins titled *Kagetsu ichiyaron*, begins with two important contentions: first, that *haikai* is accessible to anyone, and second that its proper subject is everyday life. Then comes Kenpū's *hokku*, offered as an embodiment of those assertions in its evocation of the everyday experience of coolness, followed by a claim that goes back as far as the *Kokinshū* preface—namely, that poetry should console and soothe by observing the patterns of nature and human affairs.

COMMENT: In all these ways, the comments here claim adherence to old traditions. The reference to the "outer" Confucian classics and the "inner" Buddhist scriptures also connects to the primary moral discourses of the time—the former offering teachings on how to regulate human affairs and the latter metaphysical insights into the nature of human existence and the hereafter. In various Buddhist texts the "seven emotions" are defined as happiness, anger, pity, pleasure, love, evil, and desire, which together define the range of human emotional phenomena, the transcendence of which is one fundamental aim of Buddhist enlightenment.

Kenpū's *hokku* illustrates these claims by offering us not just a natural scene but also a proposition: that the experience of coolness, an everyday thing that virtually everyone has yearned for in the summer heat, offers enjoyment of the sort one might feel in a sequestered worship hall far back in a temple compound—the sort of place, needless to say, that normal people generally could not go. It is important that what the speaker claims is not intellectual—this is not a lecture by some cleric—but affective and sensory, the *dai* being coolness, not "enlightenment" or anything cerebral. Thus Kenpū elevates a simple bodily experience to the level of religious awakening. And to make his rather audacious claim more complete, he adds that such an awakening is not known even by the Buddha himself, a hyperbolic statement along the lines of the famous Zen advice, "If you meet the Buddha, kill the Buddha." Buddha is not a vengeful god and does not mind being abused in the process of instruction.

YOSA BUSON 与謝蕪村, *Buson kushū* 128 (Spring): "Written for a gathering at the Bashō cottage"

While I broke ground,	hata utsu ya
that unmoving cloud—	ugokanu kumo mo
disappeared.	naku narinu

CONTEXT: After the death of his foremost disciples, Bashō's reputation waned for a time, until a revival led by Yosa Buson (1716-1783), who began his career in Edo but gained prominence as a painter and poet in Kyoto during the 1770s. The cottage mentioned in the headnote was located in the grounds of Konpukuji, a subtemple of Ichijōji, a Zen temple in eastern Kyoto that Bashō had visited in his travels. Buson and his friends erected a cottage there in the master's memory in 1776, where monthly poetry gatherings were held.

COMMENT: Buson was a professional painter, and many of his most famous *hokku* present static scenes that could be rendered in pictorial form. This *hokku*, however, involves a flashback of sorts: a plot, in narrative terms, albeit one that is highly elliptical. (Another of the characteristics of Buson is his evocation of short "stories.") In spring, a farmer is out doing the backbreaking work of preparing soil for planting. After some time putting all his energy into that effort, he looks up from the fields and sees that the seemingly unmoving cloud that was in the sky when he began has now disappeared—a skillful way of representing the passage of time and the intensity of the man's labor. What makes him look up we cannot say. Most likely it is simple fatigue, but one can also imagine that the departure of the cloud has allowed the sun to beat down more powerfully, removing the shadow under which he worked. In any case, the scene thus involves a central "absence" and duration of time that no painting could reproduce.

No doubt the bucolic surroundings of Konpukuji inspired Buson's *hokku*, but it is not the only poem he wrote about farming. The lack of pronouns in *hokku* (a feature of Japanese discourse that is particularly conspicuous in poetry) presents the translator with a conundrum: should the perspective be first person, or third? Even if he did not spend time in the fields himself, Buson obviously could imagine himself in such a situation. And another poem, also from *Buson kushū* (A collection of Buson's *hokku*, p. 61), seems more clearly to be written from the perspective of the laborer himself. (Or herself? The possibility cannot be denied, just as one must often leave open the possibility of a plural subject as well).

As I break ground,	hata utsu ya
I still see my house as day ends—	waga mo ie miete
but not for me.	kurekanuru

Pastoral scenes, often involving agricultural connotations, abound in *waka* anthologies, but it is in *haikai* that we see scenes of actual labor. Here the sky is growing dark, but as long as he can see his house through the gloom the farmer knows that he must make use of the light.

152   UNORTHODOX POEMS

KYŪSO 旧礎 and OTHERS, *Sabi, shiori* (pp. 319, 325, 328, 329)

In every inlet,
boats not moving.
Summer rains.
   Kyūso

uraura ni
ugokanu fune ya
satsukiame

Penniless,
I walk through autumn
in Kyoto.
   Kao

zeni nakute
miyako no aki o
arukikeri

Standing still
on an old riverbank—
willow trees.
   Sen'ya (a youth)

furukawa no
kishi ni shizukeki
yanagi kana

It's not as if
my work is done.
Autumn dusk.
   Ryūsui

nasu waza no
tsukuru ni wa arade
aki no kure

CONTEXT: Kyūso was from Kiryū in Kōzuke, and Kao, Sen'ya, and Ryūsui were all from Tajima. We also know that Kao's lay name was Ashida Rokuzaemon and that he died in 1784 at the age of thirty-six. Sen'ya was probably not yet into his teens. *Sabi, shiori* (The "lonely" and "the bent and withered") was compiled in 1776 by a man named Hanabinokoji Ichion (precise dates unknown), a disciple of Buson's. After sections on pedagogy and some anecdotes, Ichion offers nearly a thousand *hokku* by students of Buson and his school, organized by region and author.

COMMENT: The *hokku* in *Sabi, shiori* are not arranged in seasonal categories but have season words, or *kigo*. The poems are thus not a sequence but a list of independent verses. Two of the ones here allude to autumn explicitly, and the other two have unequivocal *kigo*: *satsukiame* (rains of the Fifth Month) and *yanagi* (willows), an icon of spring.

Ryūsui's poem has eight syllables in its second line, rather than the standard seven, but in *haikai* such slight departures were common, and in terms of rhetoric the poems are well within the boundaries of the Bashō school, each in its own way expressing the ideal of *sabi*. Kyūso depicts for us the essence of the feel of the rainy season via the image of boats moored in harbor, unable to brave the weather; and Sen'ya's poem likewise presents us with a scene of natural beauty and feeling. The poems of Kao and Ryūsui, however, show us harsher vignettes of life: a man walking "penniless" through the streets of Kyoto, suggesting circumstances more moving because undisclosed, and a worker whose labors do not cease with the setting sun. The willows in Sen'ya's verse offer a little color, but only against the backdrop of an "old riverbank."

ARII SHOKYŪNI 有井諸九尼 and OTHERS, *Akikaze no ki* (p. 623)

Fourth Month, thirteenth, fourteenth. Passed over Nasu Moor. The autumn fields were unimaginably broad, and just the grasses and flowers we recognized were beyond counting. Standing there, I wrote,

Were you to speak,	*mono iwaba*
what would your voice be like?	*koe ika naran*
Maiden flowers.	*ominaeshi*
Shokyūni	

物いはば声いかならん女郎花

CONTEXT: Arii Shokyūni (1714-1781) was born in Kyushu to a village headman. In her teens she entered into an arranged marriage, as per prevailing custom, but no children came from the union, and around the age of twenty-six she ran away to Kyoto with a itinerant physician and *haikai* poet. After he died in 1762, she became a Zen nun and determined to live as a *haikai* master herself. In 1771, she set out with a priestly traveling companion to visit sites described in Bashō's *Oku no hosomichi* (The narrow road through the hinterlands, 1694), documenting her journey in *Akikaze no ki* (A record of autumn wind, 1772). It chronicles her journey from her home in the Okazaki area of Kyoto, to Edo, Matsushima, and Miyagino, and other places, with long stops along the way.

COMMENT: Shokyūni's *hokku* brings to mind a poem by Bashō's traveling companion, Kawai Sora (1649-1710), about a little girl they met in the fields named Kasane, which the men imagine refers to an eight-pedaled variety of wild pinks (*nadeshiko*). Shokyūni's maiden flowers (prominent in poetry since ancient times) do not come literally to life in the way Sora's pinks do, but she suggests that we at least entertain such a possibility.

Akikaze no ki ends with a small anthology of *hokku* she collected along the way, among them a dozen by women, including these (pp. 627, 632).

If you stopped singing,	*nakariseba*
people could get to sleep—	*hito mo yoku nen*
cuckoo!	*hototogisu*
Ranshitsu	
A warbler calls	*uguisu o*
and hearing its song	*kiku ya inochi mo*
extends my life.	*nagau naru*
Kinshi	

Most women *haikai* poets of the Edo period were in some way connected to a male poet—as wife, sister, daughter, etc. In Shokyūni's case, it helped that her second husband was a *haikai* master, and becoming a nun also eliminated some of the usual gender strictures. Some poems by women were gender marked, but mostly they aimed at broader human relevance that made them equals of men in the *za*.

BAIZAN 買山, *Yahantei tsukinami hokku-awase* (p. 418): "Water birds"

水鳥の猶むつまじく雨の中

Water birds:	*mizutori no*
even chummier	*nao mutsumashiku*
in the rain.	*ame no naka*

CONTEXT: Baizan was from Fushimi, south of Kyoto proper. This poem was composed for a paper contest (not involving an actual meeting of all participants) held in the intercalary Tenth Month of 1786 by Takai Kitō (1741-1789; also known as Yahantei), a disciple of Buson's. It is one of many such contests published by that master, which fulfilled one of his fundamental obligations; namely, getting his students—more than two hundred of them, mostly in Kyoto and its environs, where he had his practice and directed monthly meetings (*tsukinamikai*)—into print. The winning poems were "aired" in woodblock form, along with short critical appraisals by Kitō himself.

COMMENT: If ever one figure dominated a discourse, it is Matsuo Bashō. To this day most histories of *haikai* are structured around him, and his aesthetic values receive more attention than any others in his genre. But recent bibliographic labors have altered our understanding of Edo-era *haikai* in two ways. First, they make it clear that Bashō's practice was eccentric in one way: most *haikai* professionals, of his *and* later eras, made their living through doing what Bashō abandoned after 1680—namely, direct tutoring and "marking" of student work. Second, they encourage us to look beyond Bashō's *hokku* and travel writing to see him too as more engaged in an essentially social profession, even after 1680.

This leads us to pay more attention to poems like the one here from a later time, describing ducks huddling together in the rain. The *dai* in this case was waterfowl, and Kitō attached to it only one word of commentary, *yūen*, a variation on the ancient ideal of *en*, which means something like "beautiful and elegant." Thus, in the world of *haikai*, we have a form, a venue, and a term of praise that link back to the world of *waka* and *renga*. Kitō's comments on another example (*Yahanteihan tsukinami hokku awase*, pp. 358-59) from a monthly competition (dating from two years before), this one by a poet named Sha'en, make the connections just as obvious.

"Departing spring"

Lying ill,	yameru mi no
I am out of sorts	ushirometaku mo
at spring's end.	kure no haru

COMMENT: The feeling of lying in bed, unable to see the colors of spring and resenting the passing of the season, is deeply moving [*aware fukashi*].

This example is not unusual: elsewhere Kitō employs other terms of praise used by Teika (and Bashō), including *yūgen* (mystery and depth) and *yojō* (overtones). Kitō had of course read Bashō, but he had also read the classics of the earlier tradition—as had Bashō, of course—from which the *dai* he assigned were often taken.

KOBAYASHI ISSA 小林一茶 and SUGINO SUIKEI 杉野翠兄,
Issa Suikei ryōgin hyakuin

28	Fireflies—blown by wind on Uji River. Suikei	*hotaru fukichiru* *uji no kawakaze*
29	In moonlit darkness, thin trails of smoke rise from husks of reed. Issa	*tsuki kuraku* *sukumo no keburi* *taedae ni*

30   The wife of an outcast   *eta ga kanai ga*
     makes offerings to the dead.   *tamamukae suru*
        Suikei

31   Autumn crows   *mono kurau*
     set to eat something,   *aki no karasu no*
     cawing away.   *sakebu koe*
        Suikei

32   In dappled dusk light—   *hi no chirachira ni*
     skiff left on the bank.   *kishi no sutebune*
        Issa

CONTEXT: Kobayashi Issa (1763–1827), who in Japan is second in popularity as a *haikai* poet only to Bashō, is known for his attention to little things. His contemporary, Sugino Suikei (1754–1813), was an oil dealer living in Ryūgasaki (modern Ibaraki Prefecture). The sequence the two men composed together is an example of a duo sequence (*ryōgin*).

COMMENT: These verses from a duo sequence show that techniques established by *renga* masters persisted. In verse 28 we see fireflies along Uji River, to which Issa in verse 29 adds a time of day and human inhabitants. Then Suikei redefines Issa's "moonlit" night as the time of Obon, the festival of the dead, when even tanners and other people in "unclean" occupations visit family grave sites with offerings. Linking to his own verse, Suikei then produces a *nioizuke*, or "link by suggestion," that conjures up crows, defined as "unclean" because they eat carrion, in response to the idea of outcasts. Finally, Issa in verse 32 shifts away from Suikei's bloody tableau by the technique of *keikizuke*, using simple apposition to pivot us away from foraging crows to a boat left on a riverbank in evening light, a more elegant scene, surely, and a classic example of a *yariku*, or "kind" link that would make it easier for the sequence to go in a new direction.

TOKOYODA CHŌSUI 常世田長翠, *Ana ureshi* (p. 324)

Barn swallows.	*tsubakuro ya*
How readily today	*kyō wa kinō ni*
becomes yesterday.	*nariyasuki*

CONTEXT: Tokoyoda Chōsui (1753–1813) was a disciple of Kaya Shirao's, whose cottage in Edo he inherited. A native of Shimōsa Province, he left Edo and settled at Sakata in Dewa during his later years.

COMMENT: Most *hokku* present visual scenes, small narratives, or propositions, rather than anything philosophical. Here, however, Tokoyoda Chōsui uses simple apposition to suggest the continuity of time. The poem relies on no standard word associations, metaphors, or other rhetorical devices, presenting only a concrete noun and an abstract statement. As in a link, the first line connects to the final two lines through suggestion, or "scent" (*nioi*).

What qualities of barn swallows suggest the flow of time? In the canons of *haikai*, the word "swallow" indicates spring as a season, a time when the natural world is going through a transition; and we know that swallows often build nests for their young in liminal spaces such as the eaves of houses and outbuildings. Furthermore, we notice them in the morning or the evening, as the human day is undergoing a temporal change. Finally, the word *yasushi*, "readily" or "nonchalantly," might relate to their instinctive behavior, which stands for the seemingly seamless and untroubled order of the natural world.

The use of apposition is a feature of many of the poems in his personal collection, *Ana ureshi* (Ah, a delight, 1816, pp. 322, 327, 330):

Spring day.	*haru no hi ya*
Two people walk together	*tsu no machi suguru*
through a port town.	*futarizure*

Full moon.	*meigetsu ya*
Yesterday the priest	*sō wa kinō no*
was a temple boy.	*chigo narishi*

A snipe cries.	*shigi naku ya*
Gone in passing wind,	*kaze ni kietaru*
a sandy path.	*suna no michi*

This is a world of experience rather than abstract "meaning." Each poem offers juxtapositions that present a transition in time followed by a noun participating in that transition while also remaining static or stationary. One can imagine dramatic contexts (a wandering, a young monk looking at the moon with companions, someone lazily watching passersby on a spring day). But as they are, the poems offer only parataxis—statements not linked by grammar—and leave further combinations to the mind of the reader. The technique would become prominent in the twentieth century.

NATSUME SEIBI 夏目成美, *Sumika o utsusu kotoba* (Moving into a new house, 1814, p. 276)

The place I was moving to was near the entry gate in Asakusa, where I had once lived long before. Located where the Sumida River empties into the bay, along the Kamida River, the place was entirely surrounded by shopping districts, right next to the famous Sensōji Temple. In old age, a person would usually withdraw to a more tranquil place, although there are perhaps many who would prefer the opposite.... Someone told me that having lived so long in solitude I would not be able to stand city noise, but I answered that I would act like an old silkworm and think of the time I had left as time to enjoy.

So short a night!	mijikayo wa
Doing this, doing that—	tote mo kakute mo
time goes by.	sugusu beshi

みじか夜はとてもかくても過ぐすべし

CONTEXT: Natsume Seibi (1749–1816) was unusual in having no primary teacher and truly walking his own way, although he had contact with a number of the poets of his day, most especially Kobayashi Issa. In his sixty-sixth year, Seibi moved from Katsushika, outside the city, to the bustling Asakusa district of Edo, at the request of his children, who were providing his everyday needs.

COMMENT: The son of a wealthy rice broker, Seibi had lived in Asakusa in his youth, but still the adjustment was not easy. In a *hokku* from the same text (p. 276) he opines that even the most common sounds seem different in a new place.

All I hear	kiku koto o
I must hear anew—	mina aratamete
even the cuckoo.	hototogisu

Lame and elderly, Seibi was mostly housebound, and distance made it difficult for him to visit old friends in Katsushika, where he had lived for a decade. As commentary on his new situation, Seibi uses an old phrase, *mijikayo wa*, "So short a night!" Usually that phrase is used in love poems, lamenting the swift passing of a summer night, in words uttered at parting. And Seibi had in fact moved on the sixth day of the Fourth Month of 1814, at the beginning of summer according to the old calendar. But his poem contains no hint of love as a category; rather, it presents the trope of an aging person awake in the night. And he builds on that idea to suggest another connotation of *mijikayo*: the inevitability of time's passage, for everyone, old and young alike. The *sugusu beshi* of the last line is emphatic: time *will* pass by. His ten years in another house are now no more than a dream, and the time back in the neighborhood of his childhood will pass just as quickly. In the summer of the following year, he would write in a colophon to *Haikai nishi kasen* (A western *kasen*, p. 202), "I waste away, prey to every malady, as with each passing year more of my friends die." On the nineteenth day of the Eleventh Month of 1816 he passed away, at his house in Asakusa.

ŌSHIMA KANRAI 大島完来, *Kūgeshū* (p. 459) (Autumn): "Not praying for a long life"

I see the moon	*tsuki o mite*
and this year feel again	*kotoshi mo osana*
like a little child.	*gokoro kana*

月を見てことしもをさなごころ哉

CONTEXT: Ōshima Kanrai (1748–1817; also known as Kūge), born in Tsu Province, was known also by the sobriquet Setchūan the Fourth, signifying that he was the poetic heir of Ōshima Ryōta (1718–1787), master of one of the largest and most prominent *haikai* schools of the eighteenth century. Although Kanrai had begun life as a samurai in Ise, he left that life to come up to Edo to pursue a literary career. He took over Ryōta's Edo practice upon the latter's death in 1787.

COMMENT: The later poems of Ryōta are known for their plain style, and Kanrai's poem is straightforward in that same way. Moon gazing, usually an autumn activity, had been a custom since ancient times, and coming up with a new variation on such an image was a challenge. Kanrai approaches the idea directly, alluding to the moon openly in his first line and then telling us simply how the experience makes him feel. Just as Bashō said that cherry blossoms "call many things to mind," Kanrai finds that the sight of the moon makes him feel as if he were transcending time, feeling again like he did as a child. To complicate his scheme somewhat he employs the particle *mo*, meaning "again, just like before," and with that one syllable extends our vision back across all the years since we first noticed the moon in our youth. While we pass through our lives below, taking on years along the way, the moon, always distant, clear, and cool in demeanor, remains the same.

For Kanrai to leave his living in Ise and opt for life as a *haikai* poet amounted to a religious renunciation of lay life, following a pattern set by medieval poets such as Tonna and Sōgi and later also by Bashō. In an explicitly Buddhist poem from his personal anthology, *Kūgeshū* (Kūge's collection, 1820, p. 456), Kanrai makes the identification of priest and poet explicit:

Born in the world,	umaruru ya
Buddha, Bashō, both—	shaka mo bashō mo
dew on the grass.	kusa no tsuyu

The headnote to this poem says it was written at a tea gathering, another art that was also considered a religious *michi*, or "Way." One thing that all these arts shared in Buddhist terms was a strong sense of the ephemerality of existence in the world. To borrow the metaphor of the second poem, such events shared the lot of all human activities, which in cosmic time last no longer than dewdrops on the grasses—grasses that are seasonal themselves and that will wither and decay as the season progresses. In this sense, the Buddha, the great master Bashō, the dew, and the grasses all teach nonduality: all distinctions being only temporal, and all things ultimately empty. Perhaps it was with this in mind that his disciples chose the title "Flowers of Emptiness" for Kanrai's collected poems.

TAGAMI KIKUSHA 田上菊舎, *Oi no chiri* (p. 31)

For a while	shibaraku wa
I forget even my sins.	tsumi mo wasurete
So cool, the moon!	tsuki suzushi

しばらくは罪も忘れて月涼し

CONTEXT: Tagami Kikusha (1753–1826) was the daughter of a physician in Nagato. She married at age sixteen, but when her husband died just eight years later, she became a nun and poet. Because of the premature death of her husband when she was still in her midtwenties she ended up living as a poet and devotee of the True Pure Land sect of Buddhism who also practiced the art of the tea ceremony. This poem was written early in the Sixth Month of 1780, near Zenkōji Temple (Nagano Prefecture), out of gratitude to a farm couple who had given her shelter.

COMMENT: At the time she wrote her poem, Kikusha was following in the footsteps of Matsuo Bashō in his *Oku no hosomichi*, taking notes for her own travel record, *Oi no chiri* (Knapsack dust, 1782). Yet the content of her poem suggests that her motives were as much devotional as artistic, and the many anecdotes she records about mercies extended to her on the road portray her journey as a pilgrimage. As a True Pure Land nun she believed in the bodhisattva Amida, whose name she recited in the *nenbutsu* ("Savior Amida—All Hail!") as a plea for grace, and we are not surprised that her poem offers a moment of respite provided by a beautiful moon that she says can make us forget—although only briefly, of course—both the summer heat and a world of sin. The moon shining in the darkness of night was frequently employed as a metaphor for Buddhist enlightenment. Here it also stands for the kind ministrations of strangers.

Her travel diary *Taorigiku* (Hand-picked chrysanthemums, 1812, p. 161) records another poem she wrote around the same time that ends with the same line.

At Crone's Crag	*ubaishi o*
I take strength late at night.	*chikara ni fukete*
So cool, the moon!	*tsuki suzushi*

Crone's Crag (*ubaishi*) was a local landmark, a large hump of rock resembling a bent-over old woman that resonates with stories of old people left to die on the slopes of nearby Obasute Mountain. Kikusha decided the next day to climb the mountain trail, where a rainstorm forced her to take shelter between huge boulders, quite literally bent over like Crone's Crag. Fortunately, she was able to "take strength" the next day from another merciful farm family. Kikusha's travel diary documents a whole network of monks, nuns, artists, and poets in villages she traveled through, but she also introduces "people of feeling" (*nasake shiru mono*) from the lower classes. The cool moon of summer, she suggests, shines down on high and low alike, while her identification with Crone's Crag serves as counterpoint, to accentuate the distance between the cool moon above and the fallen world below.

SHIMIZU IPPYŌ 清水一瓢, *Gyoku sanjin kashū* (p. 444): "This year, at the beginning of the Long Month, I left Asakusa...and traveled to Honmoku and on to Sugita, where I made offerings at the grave of my father"

Beside her,	oya no kao
I stare at Mother's face	mamuki ni mitaru
in night's chill.	yosamu kana

親の貌真向に見たる夜寒かな

CONTEXT: Shimizu Ippyō (1770-1840; also known as Gyoku Sanjin, hence the title of his personal collection, *Gyoku Sanjin kashū*), a priest of the Nichiren sect, began his career at Hongyōji in Edo and ended up retiring there after being employed at other temples in Mishima and Kyoto. He was acquainted with both Issa and Seibi. This poem was composed in the "Long" Ninth Month in 1810, when he was visiting his mother in Sugita (now in Yokohama).

COMMENT: Many *hokku* offer the reader objective description, but more intimate feelings are not necessarily proscribed. This seems particularly true when it comes to the experiences of illness, old age, and death. In the following, Bashō (*Nozarashi kikō* [Bones bleaching in the fields], p. 291) writes movingly of seeing a lock of his late mother's hair, as does Issa (*Chichi no shūen nikki* [A record of my father's death], p. 424) of his father's last moments and Seibi (*Seibi hokkushū* [Seibi's *hokku* collection], p. 5) of taking his children to visit the grave of their mother four years after her death.

Held in my hand	te ni toraba kien
it would melt in hot tears—	namida zo atsuki
autumn frost.	aki no shimo
Bashō	

From his sleeping face	nesugata no
I brush the flies away—	hae ou mo kyō ga
today, one last time.	kagiri kana
Issa	

Pointless,	ko o tsurete
dragging my kids along.	yuku kai mo nashi
Frost-covered grave.	shimo no haka
Seibi	

Thus *haikai* continues the memorial traditions of *waka* and *renga*, albeit with more realistic imagery and more colloquial rhetoric. Ippyō's poem concentrates on his mourning mother's face. And what does he see? The signs of old age, no doubt: wrinkles and weathered skin; gray hair, or white; and signs of loss and weariness in the eyes. But all of this must be our contribution to the reading process. A lock of white hair, flies buzzing around a sleeping countenance, a frost-covered gravestone—all are examples of synecdoche, or parts standing for wholes we must imagine for ourselves. Ippyō's concluding "night's chill" (*yosamu*) likewise stands for more than autumn cold.

INOUE SEIGETSU 井上井月, *Seigetsu kushū* 436 (Summer)

Late into night,	*fukete kite*
knocking at the inn.	*yado o tataku ya*
Summer moon.	*natsu no tsuki*

更けて来て宿を叩くや夏の月

CONTEXT: Seigetsu (1822–1887) was of samurai lineage, but one document says he went into poetry when faced with the prospect of farming for a living, perhaps reflecting the disenfranchisement of the warrior class that took place at the time of the Meiji Restoration. He was born in Nagaoka (modern Niigata Prefecture) in Japan's snow country but later lived in nearby Ina, Shinano Province (modern Nagano Prefecture), near Zenkōji Temple. From his late teens on he dedicated himself entirely to *haikai*, taking the tonsure, as was the custom among *haikai* devotees, and traveling to Edo and the Kansai. A twentieth-century compendium of his work, *Seigetsu kushū* (Seigetsu's *hokku* collection), contains nearly thirteen hundred of his *hokku*, along with a short treatise on poetry.

COMMENT: Scholars offer us little help in interpreting the poems of Seigetsu, a little-known regional poet. The poem here, however, asks us only one question: is it the summer moon knocking on the door, figuratively, or an actual traveler? In either case, someone is called to the door by knocking; and in either case our eyes are drawn up to an aloof moon. Like many *haikai* poets, Seigetsu thought of travel as an avocation and knew what it was like to be on the other side of the door with the hope of lodging.

Seigetsu passed away, still in obscurity, before Masaoka Shiki began a campaign to reclaim *haikai* as a poetic genre for a new age. Shiki had harsh words for Bashō, instead championing the works of Buson as models of what he called *shasei*, or "sketching from life." Not so Seigetsu, who participated in memorial services for Bashō and revered him above all poets. One anecdote says that when asked for a copy of Bashō's famous prose piece *Genjūan no ki* (Record of life in Genjū Cottage, 1690), he was able write it out—producing four tightly packed pages—from memory.

In response to Bashō's famous *hokku* (*Oi no kobumi*, p. 312)

A traveler,	tabibito to
that's what I'll be called.	waga na yobaren
First winter rains.	hatsushigure

Seigetsu wrote an allusive variation (referred to as *honku* in *haikai* discourse) that is unequivocal in stating his desire for affiliation with Bashō as a model for life and practice (*Seigetsu kushū*, no. 269).

Count me, too,	tabibito no
among the travelers.	ware mo kazu nari
Cherries in full glory.	hanazakari

Records of his time sometimes refer to him as Unsui Seigetsu—Seigetsu, the Wandering Cloud—indicating that he got his wish.

MASAOKA SHIKI 正岡子規, *Shiki zenshū* (3:312)

That fortune-teller	uranai no
was wrong, it seems,	tsui ni atarade
as the year ends.	toshi kurenu

CONTEXT: Masaoka Shiki (1867–1902) is the most famous of all modern poets in both *tanka* (the modern word for *waka*) and haiku, the latter being the word he insisted upon for modern *hokku* in order to signal a break with traditions of the past. His poem dates from the winter of 1897, when he was suffering with the spinal tuberculosis that would take his life five years later, in his thirty-fourth year.

COMMENT: Even in modern times, many *haikai dai* relate back to earlier poetic discourse. For instance, the "Winter" book of every anthology of *waka* concludes with poems on "the end of the year," a *dai* that for centuries inspired laments such as the following from *Taikenmon'in Horikawa shū* (A collection of poems by Taikenmon'in Horikawa), no. 69, by a late Heian-era lady-in-waiting:

占ひのつひにあたらで歳暮れぬ

What was I thinking,	*mukashi nado*
when in the past I hurried	*toshi no okuri o*
to see a year off?	*isogiken*
As the years keep adding up,	*tsumoreba oi to*
I get older—that is all.	*narikeru mono o*

Our readiness to see the old year off, of course, comes in anticipation of the celebration of the New Year, still today the most important holiday in Japan. But human beings do not truly begin again each year with the calendar and are thus out of sync with the "rebirth" of the natural world, the poet reminds us. For us a new calendar does not truly bring new life.

Shiki's poem is more elliptical and less earnest than Lady Horikawa's, but the two share a sense of foreboding. Shiki, however, was not facing old age but death. He had nearly died in the spring of 1895, and one wonders how hopeful he could have been at the beginning of 1897. But the reading he got from the fortune-teller must have been something more positive than what he actually experienced as the year went on. And it appears that he was no happier the next year, when he wrote another poem (also from his complete works, *Shiki zenshū*, 3:404) on the same idea.

As if laughing	*ningen o*
at us, we human beings—	*warau ga gotoshi*
the year just ends.	*toshi no kure*

Oblivious to our feeble attempts to control it, time just goes by, Shiki says. Shiki faulted Bashō for sentimentality, and in these poems he perhaps shows us what he meant. Fortune-tellers are not the only deceivers, he suggests; we all deceive ourselves by concocting silly conceptions like seasons that mock us as we mistake time's derision for smiles.

NATSUME SŌSEKI 夏目漱石, *Natsume Sōseki nikki* (p. 198)

My two brothers died young, and with not a white hair on their heads. Yet here I am, the hair at both my temples going white, as the thin thread of my life just stretches on.

Still I live,	*ikinokoru*
ashamed of the frost	*ware hazukashi ya*
at my temples.	*bin no shimo*

生残る吾恥かしや鬢の霜

166 UNORTHODOX POEMS

CONTEXT: After a stint as a professor of English literature at Tokyo Imperial University, Natsume Sōseki (1868-1916) went on to write some of the finest novels of the twentieth century, but he also was a close friend of Masaoka Shiki's and wrote haiku. Information from Sōseki's diary (*nikki*) tells us that from August to October of 1910, he was convalescing at the Kikuya Inn at Shūzenji Temple in Izu, suffering from the effects of a bleeding ulcer. This poem comes from his diary, September 14, when he was spending most of his time in bed.

COMMENT: Photos of his time at Shūzenji show an emaciated figure with flecks of white in his hair, and another poem written around the same time (*Nikki*, p. 198) makes it clear that he felt as if the end might not be far off.

Ill on the road,	*tabi ni yamu*
my heart feels night's chill—	*yosamu kokoro ya*
wanting sympathy.	*yo wa nasake*

A literal translation of the last line of this second haiku would read, "In the world, [we need] sympathy," and it comes from a famous saying, "On the road, one wants a companion—just as in the world one wants sympathy" (*tabi wa michizure, yo wa nasake*). One cannot help but wonder if he was thinking of Shiki, gone now eight years, who would have been a comfort on his journey. And we can be certain Sōseki had in mind Matsuo Bashō, from one of whose last poems (*Oi nikki* [Knapsack diary], p. 269) he took his first line:

Ill on the road,	*tabi ni yande*
I wander in my dreams	*yume wa kareno o*
in barren fields.	*kakemeguru*

In an essay about his experience at Shūzenji, Sōseki wrote that writing haiku and Chinese poems during his illness brought him a welcome sense of release from the obligations of normal life (*Omoidasu koto nado* [Things I remember], 1910, pp. 14-17), but the "night's chill" of the second line would seem to reveal darker forebodings. Six years later, on December 9, his bleeding ulcer finally took his life. His last recorded haiku date from just a month before.

YOSHIYA NOBUKO 吉屋信子, *Yoshiya Nobuko nikki* (pp. 277-78): August 1945

蝉も哭き人も泣きけり今日真昼

August 15. Clear. Notice goes out that His Supreme Highness the Emperor himself will make a broadcast noon today. Feels like a weight bearing down on my chest...

At noon, His Highness, for the first time in his own voice, says that the war is coming to an end. I sit in front of the radio, weeping. Hearing the anthem "His Majesty's Reign" was very sad.

The newspaper came at five and I read it. "Lots of imperial warplanes in the skies—sirens blaring—seven warplanes shot down." Such were the reports.

At 11:40 came the final broadcast over the military news.

Cicadas crying,	*semi mo naki*
people crying, too.	*hito mo nakikeri*
Today, at noon.	*kyō mahiru*

CONTEXT: Yoshiya Nobuko (1896-1973) was a romance novelist who wrote openly as a lesbian and was one of the most popular writers of her time. She was an avid practitioner of haiku and a fixture among poets of the form in Kamakura.

COMMENT: Many writers have recorded their reactions to the broadcast in which the emperor himself announced defeat at the end of World War II, often noting how difficult it was to understand the emperor's arcane vocabulary. From her diary (*nikki*), we know that Yoshiya Nobuko evidently understood right away. Like many others, she was relieved but also worried about the future as she listened to the national anthem. The drone of the cicadas, a conventional *kigo*, or "season word," often symbolizes the universal ephemerality of mortal existence, not an inappropriate reference at the time in question; but the addition of human voices, crying not in the night but at midday, makes the poem into a more poignant lamentation over the events of a specific time and place.

A few days later Yoshiya's diary tells us that she attended a haiku gathering at nearby Tsurugaoka Shrine with a number of other writers of the Kamakura community, including Kume Masao (1891-1952), Satomi Ton (1888-1983), Nagai Tatsuo (1904-1990), and others. The group strolled through the grounds of the shrine and found no other people about. Nobuko says that she thought to herself that maybe now that the war had ended it might be possible to begin writing again. The haiku she composed on that stroll (p. 279) is simple on the surface but gains in significance when considered in its historical context.

Only leaves now
on the lotus pond, yet—
I stop to look.

ha bakari no
hasuike naredo
mite orinu

Lotus flowers, another *kigo*, symbolize Buddhist enlightenment. Stopping to gaze on a summer pond where the flowers have not yet appeared she can only have been reflecting about what might be coming in the future, and not only for the pond.

NAGAI KAFŪ 永井荷風, *Kafū haikushū* 731

牡丹散ってまた雨を聞く庵かな

A peony falls
and again I hear rain
outside my hut.

botan chitte
mata ame o kiku
iori kana

CONTEXT: Nagai Kafū (1879-1959) was groomed for business by his father but refused to cooperate. He began as a writer of the naturalist school but went on to write elegies for the grimy alleyways of Tokyo. He also left behind more than eight hundred haiku, the first in 1889, the last in the mid-1950s. In April 1946, when this poem (from the standard collection of his haiku) was written, he was living in Sugano, Ichikawa City.

COMMENT: During World War II, Nagai Kafū published little, but he did keep a diary, where he occasionally complained about the Japanese government. Nor did the war's end not stop him from grumbling, as evidenced by the words he jotted down before recording this haiku on April 28, 1946. The quality of the tobacco being rationed is so bad that it has put him off smoking, he frets, and to make matters worse, the soy sauce isn't salty enough and the miso carries an unpleasant odor—"Conspicuous signs, one must think, of how the nation marches on toward its downfall."

The haiku included here was written one evening at the request of a doctor who was treating Kafū at the time. The pose Kafū adopts is the hoary one of the recluse in his hut of grass. What the speaker is distracted by we do not know—his books? His memories? For whatever reason, he is preoccupied until a falling peony flower interrupts his reverie, drawing attention to what is going on outside. For readers the poem "unfolds" in a conventional but effective way. We begin with the image of a flower falling—a peony, a season word indicating summer—and the rain coming down outside, and only then learn the location of the speaker, an *iori*, or "hut." Thus, in a common ploy, the speaker offers an image that may at first register as visual but then envelops us in sounds—first the heavy "plop" of a peony flower and then the pitter-patter of rain.

By this time Kafū was already publishing stories again—although he could not have known how prominent he would become in the immediate postwar era, when his reputation benefited greatly from his erstwhile belligerence toward the military regime. It is worth noting that after complaining about the tobacco and food he goes on to ridicule the Japanese people at the time for seeking solutions for the present crisis in superficial mimicry of "other cultures," naming China and the West. As the peony was an import from China, one is tempted to undertake a metaphorical reading of his haiku, but that would doubtless be going too far. It appears in Japan as early as *The Pillow Book of Sei Shōnagon* (early eleventh century).

That Kafū put thought into his haiku is apparent from the fact that we have differing drafts. Next to the one here in his composition notebook (*Sōsaku nōto*) is this one (no. 732) that has the same feel but is less clever.

A peony falls	botan chitte
and alone I hear rain	hitori ame kiku
outside my hut.	iori kana

ISHIDA HAKYŌ 石田波郷, *Shūchūka* (p. 38): December 9, "Snow"

Snow falling.	yuki fureri
Falling like bundles	jikan no taba no
of time.	furu gotoku

雪降れり時間の束の降るごとく

CONTEXT: Ishida Hakyō (1913-1969) began writing haiku as a high school student. After two years at Meiji University in Tokyo, he withdrew to devote himself to writing and editorial work. Pleurisy sent him home from the China front during the Pacific War and he never truly recovered, dying at fifty-six. This poem appeared in a collection titled *Shūchūka* (Flowers from alcohol) just months before his death.

COMMENT: Haiku continues to attract both professional poets and vast numbers of amateurs. Many students study under a master, often operating in groups that publish small magazines, and in the mainstream *kigo* are still de rigueur. Hakyō, too, studied under various masters, but the poem here displays a more modernist sensibility, including a season word but also an abstract metaphor that is far in spirit from the nominalist tendencies of Masaoka Shiki. The meaning of the phrase "bundles of time" is crucial but also highly subjective: a reference to the way falling snow makes one notice the passage of time, perhaps? Hakyō was a "serious" poet, and serious poets are allowed obscurities.

Yet still the mainstream is dominated by disciples of Takama Kyoshi, who took over the editorship of Shiki's magazine, *Hototogisu*, and became the preeminent master of his day. The following haiku by Kyoshi disciples display mainstream style (from a collection of *tanka* and haiku from the Shōwa era, *Shōwa shika haiku shi*, pp. 77, 131):

Two kites	tako futatsu
fluttering, fluttering,	chirachira yuki ni
up into snow.	agarikeri
Murakami Kijō	
A wind comes up	kaze fuite
and the butterflies	chōchō hayaku
fly faster.	tobinikeri
Takano Sujū	

Kijō (1865-1938) and Sujū (1893-1976) could not have been more different as people, the former a poor man with a large family who was stricken with deafness at a young age and struggled to make ends meet, the latter a successful physician who became a college professor and dean of a medical school. But they both embraced the teachings of Shiki and Kyoshi, which can be summed up in the word *shasei*, or "sketching from life." Natural imagery figures prominently in each conception, and both poems arise from careful observation rather than the subjective approach displayed by Hakyō. Likewise, both poems concentrate on a moment of change in that outside world, capturing an experience rather than propounding a proposition. Yet there is human involvement—whoever is flying the kites, first of all, and then whoever is witnessing the butterflies—and of course the basic assumption that sensory experience is meaningful to human beings for and in itself.

A MODERN *HAIKAI* SEQUENCE, Kiyūkyoku

23	An image appears,	omokage ni
	but where has he gone?	tatsu hito izuko
	Winter plum blossoms.	tōjibai
	Shimada Shūji	

24	On a frozen roadway, 　the sound of dropped keys. 　　Okai Takashi	*itetaru michi ni* *kii otsuru oto*
25	An old man 　not sure on his feet, 　led by a child. 　　Takano Kimihiko	*ashimoto no* *motsururu oi o* *ji ga tsurete*

面影にたつ人いづこ冬至梅
凍てたる道に鍵落つる音
足もとのもつるる老を児が連れて

CONTEXT: Linked verse has its champions even in modern times. The *kasen* sequence from which these verses are taken was composed by five poets on January 27, 1992, at Chinzansō Hotel in Tokyo. Tsukamoto Kunio (1920–2005), editor of a prominent poetry journal, was master of ceremonies (*sōshō*), acting the role of senior poet and arbiter—still an important role in traditional poetic venues. Each of the poets represented here—Shimada Shūji (1928–2004), Okai Takashi (b. 1928), and Takano Kimihiko (b. 1941)—was also associated with a journal or newspaper poetry column. The day was Mozart's birthday, hence the title, *Kiyūkyoku* (Divertimento). The sequence was recorded in proper traditional form after the event, a photocopy of which appeared, followed by a printed text with commentary, in the April 1992 issue of *Tanka kenkyū*. The article began with a brief history of linked verse and its conventions, written by Mitsuta Kazunobu (b. 1951), a college professor, who subtitled his remarks, "Bashō Cicerone."

COMMENT: Some of the words and images here are from the old lists ("image" and "plum blossoms"), but others ("roadway" and "car keys") denote a modern setting. The links are generally predictable: "frozen" connecting back to "winter," "feet" connecting back to "roadway." Thus we encounter first a statement of loss—someone (whether man or woman is not indicated) who remains unidentified, now only a memory—set in winter, as plum blossoms begin to appear (23); then we see (and hear) that loss concretized in the form of a clumsy old man dropping his car keys (24); finally we see that old man helped by a child (25). Nature melds with the manmade and mechanical, old age joins with youth. The participants agreed to follow Edo-period rules, producing a sequence that employs pivoting and ellipsis and boasts a number of traditional season words, all the while creating a modern feel. The allusion to Mozart may seem strange, but students of Edo *haikai* will remember that *haikai* culture was nothing if not eclectic.

While composing the sequence, the participants also chatted, recording their conversation in the form of a *zadankai*, or "roundtable discussion," which sometimes shows the egos of the participants but also serves to reemphasize the centrality of social exchange in Japanese poetic culture. The verses here elicited the following conversation (as appended to *Kiyūkyoku*, pp. 62–63):

> *Okai*: Is there such a thing as "winter plum blossoms"?
> *Shimada*: These are a little early, you see. Usually plum blossoms indicate spring, but there *are* plum blossoms that bloom in winter . . .
> *Okai*: I wanted to get the word "keys" in. In my head it was car keys.
> *Shimada*: Ah . . . I drop them myself . . .
> *Tsukamoto*: A scent in the verse before, and now a sound: that's a nice progression. We seem to be doing better now than at the beginning.
> *Shimada*: Everyone's getting sharper.
> *Takano*: And quicker.
> *Shimada*: Must be the booze (laughter) . . .
> *Tsukamoto*: How do you all feel about "led by a 'grandchild'"?
> *Takano*: Is something wrong with it?
> *Tsukamoto*: Well, including colloquialisms is all right, I guess, but I feel a certain resistance to using "grandchild" in a *kasen*.
> *Takano*: Well, is that so?
> *Tsukamoto*: How about not "grandchild" but just "child?"
> *Takano*: Okay, then let's change it to "led by a child."

The final version of the sequence shows that Tsukamoto prevailed: "grandchild" became "child." Not all the commentary is like this; the participants occasionally seem to be competing with one another in their knowledge of erudite allusions and popular culture. But the tone is generally light, in keeping with the spirit of the *haikai* of Edo times. All no doubt had in mind the many Edo-period anecdotes of Bashō chatting with his disciples during linked-verse meetings, guiding the composition process gently toward a conclusion that would be a communal statement.

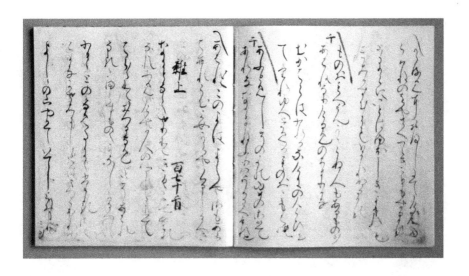

Early medieval handwritten manuscript of Saigyō's personal poetry collection, *Sanka shinjūshū*.

Facsimile edition owned by author.

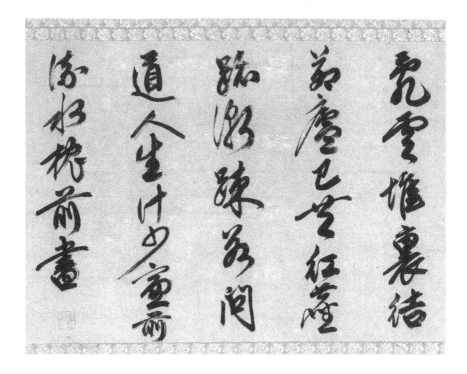

Chinese poem by the early medieval Zen monk Sesson Yūbai, on hanging scroll.

Courtesy Metropolitan Museum of Art and Sylvan Barnet and William Burto, in honor of Miyeko Murase, 2014.

Handwritten poem strip (*tanzaku*) by late medieval court scholar Gojō Tametaka.

Courtesy Metropolitan Museum of Art and Florence and Herbert Irving, 2015.

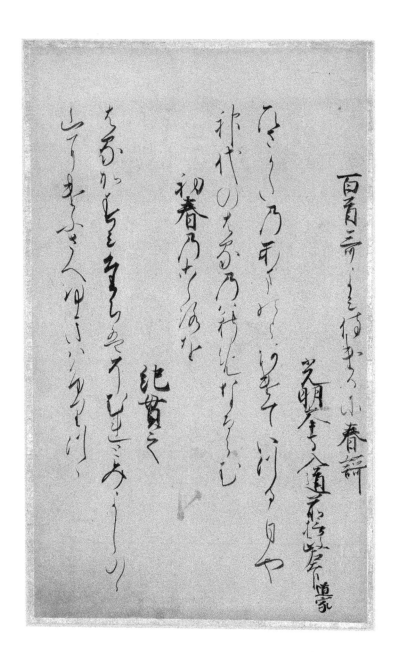

Poems from a copy of *Shoku Kokin wakashū*, eleventh imperial anthology.
Calligraphy attributed to the thirteenth-century poet Abutsu-ni.

Courtesy Metropolitan Museum of Art and Mary Griggs Burke Collection,
Gift of the Mary and Jackson Burke Foundation, 2015.

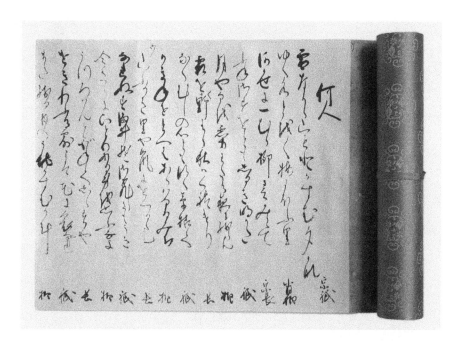

Late medieval handwritten scroll of *Minase sangin hyakuin*, a linked-verse sequence composed by Sōgi, Shōhaku, and Sōchō.

Facsimile edition owned by author.

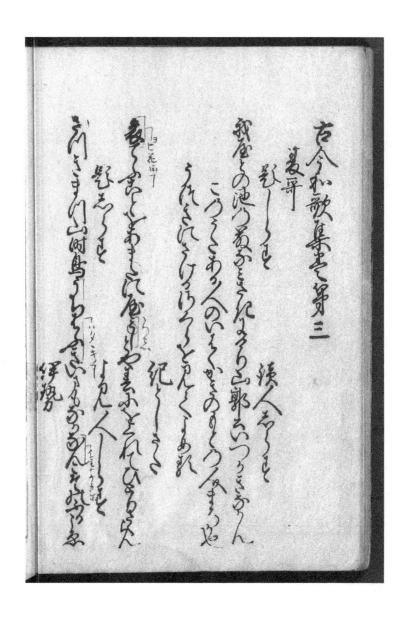

Early eighteenth-century woodblock edition of *Kokin wakashū*.

Courtesy L. Tom Perry Special Collection, Harold B. Lee Library, Brigham Young University.

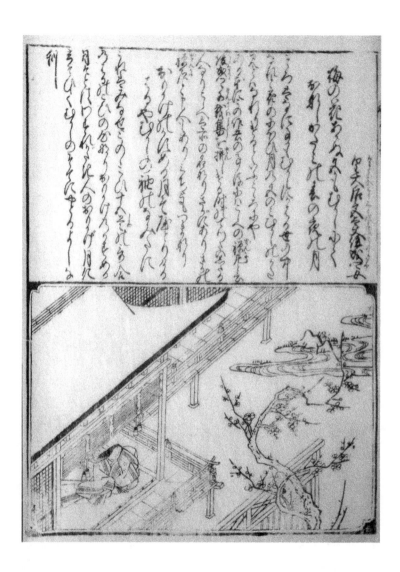

Edo-period woodblock edition of *Jisankachū*, a late-medieval commentary on *waka* by poets of the *Shin kokinshū* era.

Owned by author.

Late Edo-period woodblock edition of *Sansai tsuki hyakushu*, a comic *waka* collection.

Courtesy L. Tom Perry Special Collection, Harold B. Lee Library, Brigham Young University.

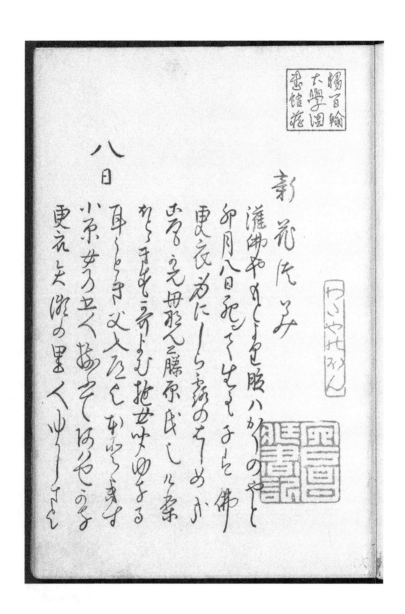

Woodblock edition of *Shin hanatsumi* by Yosa Buson.

Courtesy L. Tom Perry Special Collection, Harold B. Lee Library, Brigham Young University.

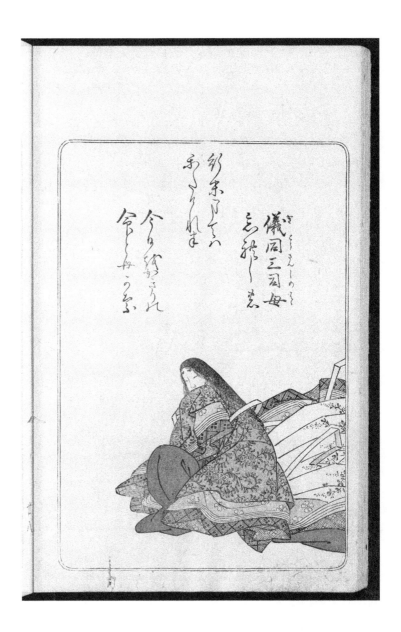

Portrait of the Mother of Minister Gidō, from *Nishiki hyakunin isshu azuma ori*, an illustrated text of *Hyakunin isshu* by the eighteenth-century artist Katsukawa Shunshō.

Courtesy L. Tom Perry Special Collection, Harold B. Lee Library, Brigham Young University.

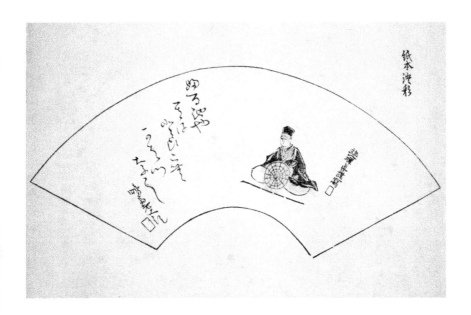

Late Edo-period fan-format portrait of Matsuo Bashō with inscribed poem, from *Ogata-ryū gafu*.

Courtesy L. Tom Perry Special Collection, Harold B. Lee Library, Brigham Young University.

Late Edo-period *tanzaku*-format portrait of Saigyō with inscribed poem, from *Ogata-ryū gafu*.

Courtesy L. Tom Perry Special Collection, Harold B. Lee Library, Brigham Young University.

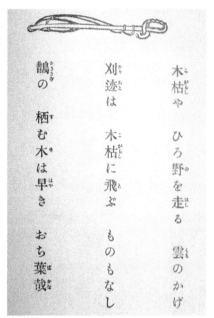

木枯(こがらし)や ひろ野(の)を走(はし)る 雲(くも)のかげ

刈迹(かりあと)は 木枯(こがらし)に飛(と)ぶ ものもなし

鵲(かささぎ)の 栖(す)む木(き)は早(はや)き おち葉(ば)哉(かな)

Poems from *Uta nikki* by Meiji-era literatus Mori Ōgai, with illustration.

Facsimile edition owned by author.

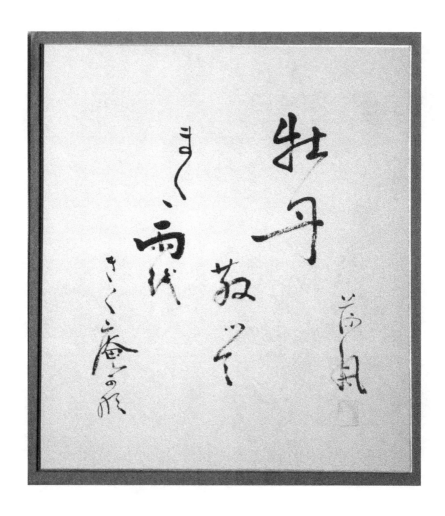

Poem square (*shikishi*) of haiku written by Nagai Kafū in 1946.

Facsimile edition owned by author.

Late Edo-period illustrated *kyōka* anthology *Kyōka roku roku shū*, with illustrations by Utagawa Hiroshige.

Courtesy Metropolitan Museum of Art and Mary and James G. Wallach Foundation Gift, 2013.

Chapter 6
COMIC POEMS

CHIUN 智蘊 and **IKKYŪ SŌJUN** 一休宗純, *Kokon ikyokushū* 1036-1037: "Sent by Chiun to Ikkyū when he wanted to ask about the concept of 'original mind'"

A river may be straight	sugu naru mo
or it may be crooked, still—	yugameru kawa mo
a river's a river.	kawa wa kawa
A Buddha statue, a chapel:	hotoke mo dō mo
they're both the same scraps of wood.	onaji ki no kire

Reply

A river may be straight	sugu naru mo
or it may be crooked, still—	yugameru kawa mo
a river's a river.	kawa wa kawa
A Buddha statue, clogs:	hotoke mo geta mo
they're both the same scraps of wood.	onaji ki no kire
Ikkyū	

直なるもゆがめる川も川仏も堂も同じ木のきれ

直なるもゆがめる川も川仏も下駄も同じ木のきれ

CONTEXT: Chiun's formal name was Ninagawa Chikamasa; he was a shogunal official. Ikkyū Sōjun (1394-1481) was a priest of the Rinzai sect of Zen. Chiun is remembered now mainly as a *renga* poet, Ikkyū as the most audacious of Zen monks.

COMMENT: Why should we call these *kyōka* rather than just Buddhist poems? The men who wrote them might not have seen any generic distinction. But for Edo poets making up anthologies of *kyōka* from earlier times such as

Kokon ikyokushū (Barbaric poems of ancient and modern times, 1666), the poems would qualify as *kyōka* in two ways. First, they present a level of repetition and parallelism that would not generally be found in formal *waka*. Perhaps more importantly, there is enough humor in the poems to justify calling them comic. Still, there is no denying the serious, didactic message: that the original mind encompasses all things, eradicating all distinctions, a point that is endlessly repeated in Zen poems and anecdotes. A Buddhist statue and the building it sits in are both made of wood, as are lowly clogs, Ikkyū says, literally dragging Buddha down into the mud to make his point, and going one step beyond Chiun.

In any form, Ikkyū can be depended upon to be outrageously pedantic.

In this world of ours,	yo no naka wa
we eat and we defecate,	kūte wa koshite
we sleep and get up,	nete okite
and after all of this, well—	sate sono nochi wa
all that's left is to die.	shinuru bakari yo

Whether the historical Ikkyū actually wrote this poem (*Kyōka kanshō jiten*, p. 498) is a moot point. *Kyōka* poets claimed it and were probably not averse to its Zen message.

YAMAZAKI SŌKAN 山崎宗鑑, *Shinsen kyōkashū* 123: "Written when he had a tumor on his back and he was dying"

If someone asks	sōkan wa
where Sōkan has gone to,	dochi e to hito no
just tell them this:	tou naraba
a little something came up	chito yō arite
and he's off to the next world.	ano yo e to ie

CONTEXT: The family name attributed to Sōkan is Yamazaki, perhaps because he lived in a place by that name west of Kyoto for a time. He seems to have died sometime between 1539 and 1541. His name is always listed among the pioneers of humorous poetry, both *kyōka* and *haikai*. Although information about his life is limited, we know that as a young man he was in service to the shogun Ashikaga Yoshihisa, after whose death (in 1489) he took the tonsure and became a *renga* master. For a time Sōkan lived in the Yamashina area, near Kyoto, and later moved to Sanuki Province (modern Kagawa Prefecture) on the island of Shikoku. Records indicate that he had contact with Sōgi and Sōchō, but he is remembered mostly as the compiler of *Inu Tsukubashū* (The mongrel *Tsukuba* collection, early sixteenth century), an anthology of *haikai* links and *hokku* mostly by himself and other poets of his time, all included without attribution.

COMMENT: This poem from *Shinsen kyōkashu* (New *kyōka* collection, 1633) claims to be Sōkan's death poem (*jisei no uta*), and in this case one wonders if the claim may be correct. A tumor usually meant a slow death, leaving one plenty of time to put things in order. The word *yō* is a double entendre, meaning both "errand" or "business to do" and "tumor." The poem appears in a number of early Edo collections with only slight variations.

Kyōka do not always involve the sort of wordplay showcased in Sōkan's death poem. Another poem attributed to him but of more questionable provenance offers a comic complaint about houseguests that could not be more straightforward:

The best don't come,	jō wa kozu
the next best come but don't stay,	chū wa kite inu
the worst stay over.	ge wa tomaru
And the ones who stay two nights—	futayo tomaru wa
they're the worst guests of all!	gege no ge kyaku

In a 1690 essay (*Sharakudō no ki* [A record of Sharakudō], p. 497) Matsuo Bashō alludes to this poem as by Sōkan, but one has to wonder whether the attribution is reliable. A similar poem is persistently associated with the Ichiya-an (One-Night Hut), a small cottage preserved at Kannonji Temple in Kagawa Prefecture, where Sōkan spent his last days. Furthermore, legend says that Sōkan himself never stayed for more than a single night anywhere, although it is impossible to know whether the poem resulted from that story or was partially the source for it. Such doubts aside, the poem represents a common strain of wry commentary that would remain important in *kyōka* on into the Edo period.

SEIHAKUDŌ KŌFŪ 生白堂行風, *Kokon ikyokushū* 421:
"Pent-up feelings of love"

Here I am, then:	ima wa tada
my poor heart in a daze,	kokoro mo horetsu
my body drooping.	mi mo naetsu

| It seems a lot like palsy— | chūbu ni nitari |
| this disease called love! | koi no yamai wa |

CONTEXT: Seihakudō Kōfū (d. before 1688) was born in Osaka. At first he studied *waka* and *haikai*, but by the 1660s he was specializing in *kyōka*. He compiled *Kokon ikyoku shū*, an important early *kyōka* collection.

COMMENT: In Buddhist dogma, eros is illusion, and it is not surprising that already in the *haikai* section of *Kokinshū* we encounter humorous treatments of the subject. One of the most famous (no. 1023) is an anonymous poem that emphasizes its debilitating effects:

From my pillow	makura yori
and from the foot of my bed,	ato yori koi no
love assails me.	semekureba
With nowhere to retreat,	semu kata nami zo
I sit smack in the middle.	tokonaka ni oru

This image is bound to evoke laughter, but, as is also often true in *kyōka*, the situation is sobering. Scholars disagree on whether "love assails me" refers to the speaker's own feelings of love toward someone else or the entreaties of a suitor. Kōfū's *kyōka* also offers us a tragicomic scene. There is nothing funny about *chūbu*, "palsy" or "paralysis"; in most cases it probably refers to the effects of a stroke. The image Kōfū creates, then, is a variation on the state of the speaker in the *Kokinshū* poem, not hemmed in but paralyzed. The word *horu* is a *kakekotoba* meaning both falling in love and to feel vacant or listless, and the verb *nayu* is also used in reference to both physical and emotional enervation.

Some *kyōka* offer even starker descriptions of love's effects. The following (*Kyōka kanshō jiten*, p. 161) was written by a Kyoto *katsurame*, or "maiden of Katsura," referring to women affiliated with shrines in ancient times who in Edo times hawked fish and sake on the streets.

Exhausted by love,	koiwabite
a trout lies low in the stream,	se ni fusu ayu no
wasting away—	uchisabire
reduced to near nothing now,	hone to kawa to ni
nothing but skin and bones.	yasenarinikeri

The metaphor is one that must have come naturally for someone who knew the grind of hauling fish and sake through the streets. Captivity, paralysis, privation: such are the wages of love.

IPPONTEI FUYŌKA 一本亭芙蓉花, *Kyōka godaishū* (p. 251): "Maiden flower"

This flowery maiden—	jorōka ya
every night she is left damp	yogoto ni kawaru
by different dews;	tsuyu ni nure
and what wind will show up next	dotchikaze ni mo
to bend her to its will?	nabiku naruran

女郎花や夜毎にかはる露にぬれどつち風にもなびくなるらん

CONTEXT: Ippontei Fuyōka (1721-1783; also known as Hiranoya Seibei) was born into the Matsunami family in Osaka and began his career there but later moved to Edo. He wrote both *haikai* and *kyōka* and was the compiler of *Kyōka godaishū* (*Kyōka* on five topics, 1781). The setting of his poem is the pleasure quarters. In the 1700s, there were large and prosperous quarters in major cities like Osaka, Kyoto, and Edo, full of teahouses, theaters, shops, and, preeminently, houses of prostitution licensed by the government in an attempt to police the industry. In the quarters, the usual social hierarchies were relaxed to an extent, creating a subculture in which ready cash could mean more than station. However, most women working in brothels were not doing so by choice; often they had been sold into servitude by poor parents. Some managed to find a wealthy patron to buy out their contract, being set up as a mistress but at least escaping the quarters. Many others died of sexually transmitted diseases or childbirth at a young age, leaving only a few to complete their contracts and return to their families or have families of their own.

COMMENT: The *dai* of this poem is *ominaeshi*, "maiden flower." However, the word *jorōka*—which immediately calls to mind the courtesans (*jorō*) of the pleasure quarters—tells us we are reading about more than flowers. And the rest of the poem is similar in the way it offers a series of double entendres: "dampened by dews" implying sexual intercourse; *dotchikaze* meaning both "wind blowing in from who knows where" and men "showing up, out of the blue"; and *nabiku*, meaning both "to bend" in the wind and to submit to someone's will and, literally, "bend over." A more literal translation of the poem that does not interpret the ambiguities might read like this:

> Maiden flowers—
> every night they are dampened
> by different dews,
> and swayed by passing winds
> coming from who knows where.

Obviously, the various situations arising from life in the quarters made for excellent literary material for writers of dramas, fictions, *haikai*, and *kyōka*. The wordplay of Fuyōka's poem is ingenious, but at bottom the poem seems more a graphic comment on the fate of prostitutes than outright humor.

KARAGOROMO KISSHŪ 唐衣橘洲, *Kyōgen ōashū* (p. 264): "Enjoying the cool"

Ah, the coolness—	suzushisa wa
of brand-new tatami mats,	atarashi tatami
of fresh bamboo blinds,	aosudare
of gazing at the new moon—	tsumako no rusu ni
while the wife and kids are out.	hitori mikazuki

涼しさはあたらし畳青簾妻子の留守にひとりみか月

CONTEXT: Karagoromo Kisshū (1744–1802; also known as Kojima Kaneyuki) was a vassal of the Tayasu house (a branch of the Tokugawa) who lived in the Yotsuya area of Edo and sponsored a *kyōka* salon. Many *kyōka* were written on *dai* from the *waka* tradition. "Enjoying the cool" (more literally, "securing a place to cool down"), from a collection titled *Kyōgen ōashū* (Crazy poems on warblers and frogs, 1784), is one such example. Interestingly, most summer *dai* involve images of escape from the heat: a fan, a stream or a spring, a stroll after dark, and so on. Perhaps the most striking summer *dai* are in fact fireflies and lightning, both nocturnal images. Poetry was supposed to elevate and offer comfort, and inspire, after all; there was nothing inspiring about midday in the Japanese summer.

COMMENT: Kisshū's poem involves wordplay only in the last line, where *mikazuki* functions as a *kakekotoba* containing both the verb *mi(ru)* "to see," and *mikazuki*, the moon of the third night in the lunar cycle. And it contains no allusion to a famous poem of the past, although it does perhaps toy with an old saying, "When it comes to wives and tatami, new is best." Otherwise, however, the author uses situational humor. The speaker states his purpose directly, in the first line: *suzushisa wa*, "coolness is..." or "this is coolness." Since we know the poem was a *kyōka*, this obviously reads like a straight line. In serious poetry, something like the cool breeze along a riverbank might follow, but here we expect something else. Two of the things Kisshū offers as sources of relief are images one might encounter in serious poetry: the blinds and the new moon. The other things in his poem are plebian images encountered only in *haikai* and *kyōka*. New tatami mats, their core being made of rice straw, have a fresh smell and are covered in soft rush straw that retains a green tinge for some time—as do *aosudare*, hanging blinds made of bamboo strips. The latter also inevitably call to mind the wind, whether we imagine it blowing through the bamboo—another summer image—or actually swaying the blinds themselves.

Thus the first lines of the poem already articulate the theme of "enjoying coolness." But it is the domestic scene of the last two lines that truly makes the poem, and makes it indubitably a *kyōka*. For the humor—light humor, in this case—in the scene comes from the idea of a family man taking advantage of the absence of his wife and children to relax completely and enjoy the cool in a way that normal circumstances would not always permit. Ultimately, enjoying the cool thus comes to mean not just finding a place that is cool but also having the leisure time to sit and experience it. After seeing the tatami and feeling the wind in the blinds under a crescent moon, we see a husband and father with a little time to himself to enjoy it all.

YOMO NO AKARA 四方赤良, *Shokusan hyakushu* 54

I bag one bird	*hitotsu tori*
and then I bag two birds,	*futatsu torite wa*
cook 'em, and eat 'em!	*yaite kuu*
Then no quail cries from the grass	*uzura naku naru*
at Fukakusa Village.	*fukakusa no sato*

CONTEXT: Ōta Nanpo (1749–1823; also known as Shokusan) was one of the premier literati the late Edo period. Of samurai background, he gave up *kyōka* in middle age in order to become more respectable.

COMMENT: Fukakusa (Deep Grasses) is an area south of Kyoto associated with a famous story about how the poet Ariwara no Narihira (825–880), who, tired of a woman he had been seeing there, asked her in a rather cruel poem whether her garden would become a "wild field" if he were to leave. Her reply (*Kokinshū*, no. 972) coyly (and disarmingly) said,

If it become a field,	no to naraba
I will cry out as a quail	uzura to nakite
as the years go by.	toshi wa hemu
Surely for hunting, at least,	kari ni dani ya wa
you will come this way again.	kimi wa kozaramu

The story ends by saying that Narihira was so impressed that he decided not to leave. Forever after, Fukakusa was associated with that romantic vignette, becoming one of the "famous places" of the classical canon.

Ōta Nanpo knew that most readers would know the story of Narihira and Fukakusa. But the poem he parodies is not the one from the ancient classic but an allusive variation on the story by Fujiwara no Shunzei (*Senzaishū*, no. 259):

"Written as an 'autumn' poem for a hundred-poem sequence"

Daylight fades away,	yū sareba
and the autumn wind on the fields	nobe no akikaze
pierces to the core:	mi ni shimite
a quail cries from the deep grass	uzura naku nari
of Fukakusa Village.	fukakusa no sato

Nanpo's poem, from his *Shokusan hyakushu* (One hundred poems by Shokusan, 1818), is a typical *kyōka* in the way it relies on double entendres (*tori* meaning both "bird" and "take" and *naku naru* meaning both "cry" and "cease to exist"). But it also involves allusion, one of the most fundamental techniques of *kyōka* poets, and less for purposes of creating a mood of mystery and depth (*yūgen*) than for repartee and parody. Akara's poem neatly dispels any romantic expectations readers might have about the romantic past of Fukakusa by catching the quail and serving them up for dinner.

FUSHIMATSU NO KAKA 節松嫁々, *Tokuwaka gomanzaishū* (p. 307):
"Forgetting to return home from beneath the blossoms"

It's all right, I say:	yoshi ya mata
so the house *does* go to ruin	uchi wa no to nare

ひとつとりふたつとりては焼いて食ふ鶉なくなる深草の里

and become a field.	*yamazakura*
Still I won't expect you home	*chirazu wa ne ni mo*
till those mountain blossoms fall.	*kaerazaranan*

CONTEXT: The given name of Kaka (1745–1810) was Matsuko. She was the daughter of a samurai in service to the shogunate and wife of Akera Kankō (1740–1800), a prominent dramatist and *kyōka* poet. Since ancient times, cherry blossom season was a time of celebration, when people would party beneath the blossoms, sometimes for days. The *dai* of this poem is a line by the Chinese poet Bai Juyi, appearing in *Wakan rōeishū* (no. 18), a mid-Heian-era collection containing *waka* and couplets from famous Chinese poems arranged by subject matter.

> Beneath the blossoms, I forget to go home—taken by beauty;
> Before the sake barrel, I get tipsy—urged on by spring wind.

COMMENT: On the surface, Kaka's poem (which comes from a 1785 collection whose title means something like "a second collection of fine *waka* of ten thousand years," alluding to a book that had appeared just two years before) seems to describe its subject as someone who is so entranced by beauty that he forgets about the demands of normal life. A comment penned in next to the poem in one text, however, explains that the situation was more complicated: "This poem," it says, "was written when her husband, Akera Kankō, had spent a number of days in the Yoshiwara quarter without coming home." Once again, as so often in *kyōka*, we encounter allegory: her husband is enjoying a different kind of flower, and not in the mountains but in some brothel in the pleasure quarters. And once again, a hint of this comes in the form of an allusion to a poem already referred to in relation to Yomo no Akara's poem about eating the quail at Fukakusa (where anciently a woman had lamented her abandonment by a man with the image of her house "becoming a field"). Obviously, Matsuko shows a more forgiving attitude, or perhaps resignation and maturity. Rather than berating her man, she archly reassures him, implying that she will be waiting when he does decide to return home. Her poem in fact reflects the attitude toward the pleasure quarters displayed by society as a whole, which stressed the role of such places in keeping the passions in their place and out of the home, where Confucian ideals were supposed to prevail. Indeed, one might say that she is telling him that he really must get his appetites in check before resuming his place as the head of a proper household.

The broad appeal of *kyōka* as a genre is attested by the fact that many were written by women. As in *haikai*, these women were often related to men (as wives, daughters, etc.) active in literary affairs, but the place of poetic expression

よしや又うちは野となれ山桜ちらずはねにもかへらざらなん

in social correspondence meant that being able to display one's wit in poetic form was a valuable asset.

ANONYMOUS, *Kamuri sen* (p. 315)

What a racket!	*yakamashii*
There's lots of treasures on this poor street.	*takara no ōi binbōmachi*

やかましい　宝の多い貧乏町

CONTEXT: In the late 1600s, humor was invading conventional *haikai* as surely as it was *waka*, in the form of *kamurizuke*, a subgenre in which students were given the first line of a *hokku* (five syllables) and asked to finish it (adding seven- and five-syllable lines). Often these exercises read like riddles, and the responses were lightly humorous in tone.

COMMENT: The key to this poem is a saying from medieval times, "Children are a treasure." The examples below need no such elucidation, except perhaps to note that they draw materials and themes from common life. As is often the case with comic poetry, the poems (*Kamuri sen*, pp. 285, 288, 298, 323, 327) are presented anonymously.

Before your eyes	*me no mae ni*
the wonder of a painter birthing a beauty.	*fude ga bijo umu eshi no myō*
Shakily	*burabura to*
he balances the load with one rock.	*taranu katani ni ishi hitotsu*
In fine weather	*yoi hiyori*
old folks on a walk go far from the house.	*zashiki o oi no tōaruki*
From time to time	*tokidoki ni*

her hands stop their sewing,	nuu te no yodomu
thinking of home.	kuni no koto

he shakes off the snow	miburui o suru
from his straw cloak.	yuki no mino

All smiles	nikoniko to

watching bridal preparations—	yomeirigoshirae
an invalid.	miru chūbu

ANONYMOUS, *Yanagidaru* (p. 132)

A single ant:	ari hitotsu
and the young miss is down	teijo shitaobi
to her underclothes.	made hodoki

蟻一つ貞女したおびまでほどき

CONTEXT: Alongside *kyōka* and *kamurizuke*, another humorous version of *haikai* also emerged in the mid-Edo period, called *kyōku* or, more commonly, *zappai* (miscellaneous *haikai*). Originally, these 5-7-5 poems were written in response to *maeku*, but by the time Karai Senryū (1718-1790) published his landmark collection, *Yanagidaru*, in 1765, the *maeku* were no longer being recorded. The more common word for the genre, *senryū*, derives from Karai Senryū's name. *Yanagidaru* (Willow keg) is the name given to series of collections (167 in all) published between 1765 and 1848. The poem here appeared in an edition of the anthology in the early 1800s.

COMMENT: We do not know what elicited this poem, the point of which is to show a young woman who, though physically mature, has not yet truly grown up. We also do not know the author of the poem; in *Yanagidaru* poems are anonymous. Like the majority of *senryū*, the poem shows us a scene from the human comedy; indeed, the collection gives us a cross section of plebian life in the Edo period: husbands, wives, children, widows, brides, priests, merchants, physicians, farmers. But it is a mistake to think that *senryū* poets were somehow entirely cut off from poetic traditions. Icons like cherry blossoms and the moon appear often, although often in parodies of one sort or another. And sometimes a *senryū*, like the following from a collection titled *Mutamagawa* (Mutama River, p. 212) compiled by Kei Kiitsu (1695-1762), alludes directly to a famous poem from the past.

The man next door—	*tonari o ba*
he's no one at all to me,	*hito to omowazu*
as I forget the year.	*toshi wasure*

In terms that are unmistakable, this poem makes sense only as a response to a *hokku* (*Oi nikki*, p. 268) written by Bashō at the end of 1694, when he was ill and dying.

Autumn deepens.	*aki fukaki*
The man just next door—	*tonari wa nani o*
what does he do?	*suru hito zo*

Critics argue about whether Bashō's poem is meant as a bleak commentary on the human condition or something more whimsical. (Probably it is both.) But it cannot help but to lead readers to profound questions. Do we ever know people, or do we just pass them by? Are we trapped in our own realities? On the surface the *senryū* dismisses such issues. Its last line, *toshi wasure* (literally, "to forget the year just past") refers to a year-end party at which people get drunk and put the old year and its troubles behind them. But it clearly engages with Bashō and protests too much. If it is meant as humor, it is humor of a dark sort.

ASŌ JIRŌ 麻生路郎 and UCHIDA HYAKKEN 内田百閒

雨の色黄昏の色かなしき日

The color of rain,	*ame no iro*
the color of the dusk sky.	*tasogare no iro*
Dismal day.	*kanashiki hi*

CONTEXT: Asō Jirō (1888–1965) was involved in the so-called progressive movement (*shinkeikō*) in *senryū*. He was born near Hiroshima but lived mostly in Osaka.

COMMENT: In the late Meiji period, the *senryū* poet Nakajima Shichirō (1882–1968) said, "I want to make *senryū* into poetry. Poetry is what our age demands" (*Senryū nyūmon*, p. 82). Around this time, new currents were creating a discourse less invested in wordplay and more centered on realism and subjectivity, as clearly illustrated in the poem here (*Senryū nyūmon*, p. 132).

Still, humor has remained a major feature of *senryū*, and often it is earthy humor of the sort found in a famous example by literary jack-of-all-trades Uchida

Hyakken (1889-1971). It appears in his essay "Nagai hei" (The long fence, 1938) and centers on a subject that comes up frequently in comic poetry—*tachi shōben*, peeing at the roadside. The passage below (p. 400) begins the essay:

> It's still cold out, so the time for peeing on the roadside hasn't even come around yet; and probably I shouldn't be talking about doing such a thing in the city no matter how balmy the weather. But even if I myself don't indulge, the fact is that on occasion I do catch sight of other men doing so. Which must be why on every fence of any length you see a sign carrying some message enjoining people not to pee there.
>
> I have read a *senryū* that goes,
>
> | | |
> |---|---|
> | A long fence: | *nagai hei* |
> | suddenly I feel the urge | *tsui shōben ga* |
> | to take a pee. | *shitaku nari* |
>
> Very insightful, I find myself thinking—though I must admit that if I happen to remember the poem when I am walking by a long fence, the memory in itself awakens that certain urge.

Needless to say, part of the joke here is pretending that someone else wrote the *senryū*, because it was something the author would know nothing about. The essay goes on to describe various funny signs found here and there instructing men to "Respect public morals—do your peeing in the privy," and so on, and then relates comical incidents involving the practice. Some of these, as one might expect, involve drunks, but Hyakken is quick to add that he is speaking from the experience of being out with drunks and "not because I have ever done such a thing myself" (p. 407).

Detail from Edo-period illustration of *Wakan rōeishū*, an early eleventh-century anthology of poems in Japanese and Chinese.

Courtesy L. Tom Perry Special Collection, HBLL, Brigham Young University.

Chapter 7

POEMS IN CHINESE

PRINCESS UCHISHI 有智子内親王, *Honchō ichinin isshu* 145:
In Response to Emperor Saga's "Mount Wu Looming High"

> Mount Wu is lofty, its slopes sheer;
> I gaze upon it—ah, how high it towers!
> Peaks of green and waters ocean-blue loom ahead;
> from deep purple skies streams gush down.
> Dark clouds engulf all at morning;
> incessant rains pour down at dusk.
> And there is more: monkeys crying at dawn—
> cold voices in the limbs of old trees.

CONTEXT: Uchishi Naishinnō (807-847) was the daughter of Emperor Saga (786-842). She served as Virgin at Kamo Shrine from 810 to 831. Unusually for a woman of her time, she was known for her Chinese poems. The Mount Wu (Wushan) of her poem, located in the Yangtze Gorges, has been known since ancient times as a place of mystery and legend. She most likely knew of it from a rhapsody (*fu*) by Song Yu (ca. 319-298 BCE). That poem tells of how King Xiang, visiting Gaotang Shrine with Song Yu, was out walking when he saw a pillar of mist rising from a shrine on the mountain. Song Yu then told the story of a former king who, while staying in that same area, was visited by a divine maiden in a dream, who lay with him and the next morning told him that she could not tarry, but that he should remember her when he saw the clouds on Wushan in the morning and the rain in the evening. After hearing the story, Song Yu wrote his rhapsody, which paints Mount Wu complete with tigers, dragons, alligators, and wizards.

巫山高且峻
瞻望幾岩岩
積翠臨蒼海
飛泉落紫霄
陰雲朝晻曖
宿雨夕飄颻
別有曉猿斷
寒声古木条

COMMENT: Princess Uchishi's poem (an example of *lüshi*, "regulated verse") begins with the mountain, which for her existed only in the imagination. She then enumerates peaks, rivers, waterfalls, and the obligatory clouds and rain, referring only vaguely to the mystery of the site. Her final couplet adds just one thing to the scene: "monkeys crying at dawn—/ cold voices in the limbs of old trees." Hers is a starker landscape that evokes a hidden world via a technique similar to allusive variation (*honkadori*) in *waka*.

Emperor Saga's court produced a great deal of Chinese poetry. Uchishi's half brother, Crown Prince Masara (808–850; later Emperor Ninmyō), also showed talent. His "Snow Falling in a Quiet Courtyard" (no. 141 in *Honchō ichinin isshu*, a late seventeenth-century collection of Chinese poems by Japanese poets) was written when he was seventeen. It offers description and is similar rhetorically, but without any mythological overtones.

> Dark clouds gather on the myriad peaks;
> white snow floats on winds in the palace grounds—
> falling damp but freezing harder still on the flagstones,
> soundlessly, calmly descending from the sky.
> Cinnabar it cancels out, making all white,
> painting over differences, making all the same.
> Sitting quietly, I observe this by myself,
> as the stones disappear from sight.

PRINCE SUKEHITO 輔仁親王, *Honchō ichinin isshu* 261: Woman Selling Charcoal

> Just now I heard her—an old lady peddling charcoal;
> her village is far away, off in the Ōhara hills.
> In thin robes she climbs steep slopes, harsh winds at her side;
> under cold skies at dusk she heads home, moon in front of her.
> Amidst white snow, she raises her voice at crowded crossways;
> in the autumn wind, prices go up among ramshackle houses.
> For what she sells, most favor buying from a stout young man;
> how one pities her, seeing those white flecks in her hair.

CONTEXT: Sukehito Shinnō (1073–1119) was a prince who did not succeed politically and in his last decade lived in seclusion, writing poetry in both Chinese and Japanese. His *lüshi* offers a variation on "The Charcoal Seller: An Attack on the

Purchasing Tactics of the Palace" by the Tang poet Bai Juyi, who was especially popular among Japanese courtiers.

COMMENT: Bai Juyi's work is social critique, presenting an old man herding an ox loaded with charcoal pursued by palace agents who force him to sell his cargo for a pittance. Sukehito's poem is a variation on that idea that presents us with an old woman and says nothing about an ox or a cart. And rather than being stuck on a muddy road, we see her hawking her charcoal through the streets. Only the last line contains a hint of critique in suggesting that she suffers because of her gender and age. The poem also presents the name of a famous place—Ōhara, northeast of Kyoto proper. All the major images associated with the period when autumn is becoming winter in court poetry are presented: harsh winds, cold skies, snow, and autumn wind, adding the moon to indicate time of day.

Many poets wrote both *kanshi* and *waka* and some *renga* as well, so one wonders if the *renga* master Shinkei had Sukehito's poem in mind when he composed his famous scene (*Chikurinshō*, no. 1258) of a charcoal seller too poor to afford his own products:

A pitiful sight:	*aware ni mo*
smoke rising at evening	*mashiba oritaku*
from a brushwood fire.	*yūkeburi*
His charcoal sold at market,	*sumi uru ichi no*
a man heads back into the hills.	*kaerusa no yama*

The first verse here includes the word *aware*, which Sukehito uses in its verbal form, *awaremu*, and his scene seems closer to the mood of Sukehito's than to that of Bai Juyi. The better conclusion, however, is that Shinkei was aware of both scenes, which hover together around the edges of his ink-wash tableau.

HINO TOSHIMOTO 日野俊基, *Honchō ichinin isshu* 326:
Before Execution at Kuzuhara Hill in Kamakura

The saying is ancient:
there is no death, no life.
For ten thousand *li* clouds dissipate;
the Yangtze's waters flow clear.

古来一句　無死無生　万里雲尽　長江水清

CONTEXT: Hino Toshimoto (d. 1332) was a scholar in service to Emperor Go-Daigo (1288–1339), in whose rebellion against the warrior government he was implicated—not just once, but twice. The first time he escaped death, but when another plot was revealed he was not spared. He was executed in the Sixth Month of 1332 at Kuzuharagaoka in Kamakura.

COMMENT: This poem is an early example of a *jisei no ku*, or "death poem." Often such poems are of dubious origin, but some accounts do show people writing such didactic poems immediately before death, on the battlefield or the execution grounds. Toshimoto evidently wrote two, the Chinese poem here and a *waka* recorded on a plaque at Kuzuharagaoka Shrine:

Before autumn has come	aki o matade
my life fades like a dewdrop	kuzuharaoka ni
at Kuzuhara Hill—	kieru mi no
though I leave some regrets	tsuyu no urami ya
behind me in the world.	yo ni nokoru ran

Toshimoto's Chinese poem, a highly elliptical example of the *shi* form, begins with a statement of stoicism, evoking a grand image of the Yangtze River, meant to contrast with the insignificance of a single human life. As a scholar, he no doubt wanted to be remembered for his skill in Chinese, which the poem demonstrates. His Japanese poem, probably intended for family, is different indeed: here we encounter not stoicism but a hint of regret, expressed not in grand imagery but in a dewdrop.

Toshimoto had a brother, Suketomo, who was also involved in the 1332 plot and was also put to death, after banishment to the island of Sado in the Japan Sea. He, too, left a Chinese quatrain (*Honchō ichinin isshu*, no. 325):

> The five aggregates achieved only fleeting form;
> the four elements now return to nothingness.
> I offer my neck to the white blade—
> to be severed in one blast of wind.

Suketomo refers us to the Buddhist concepts of the five aggregates (*goun*), or *skandhas*—form, sensation, perception, mental formations, and consciousness—and then to the four elements of earth, water, fire, and wind. His final image is obviously meant to slice through all such distinctions. His Chinese poem is as stoical as his brother's.

ZEKKAI CHŪSHIN 絶海中津, *Shōkenkō* 5:
Waiting for a Friend Who Doesn't Show Up

> You promised to come and visit,
> so night after night I fret, waiting for you.
> Clouds and rain come fitfully—
> rambling, staying or going as they please.
> In mountain dusk, autumn's voice comes early;
> my attic room is empty, vapors deep around it.
> In the quiet I sit, no one here to chat with me;
> and my zither, it just hangs there on the wall.

許我一來尋
懷君數夜吟
粉粉雲雨跡
汎汎去留心
山暮秋聲早
樓虛水氣深
知音今寂寞
壁上掛孤琴

CONTEXT: Zekkai Chūshin (1336–1405) was a priest who served at the very apex of the hierarchy of the Rinzai sect of Zen, which arrived in Japan in the late twelfth century and was of central political and cultural importance throughout the medieval period, especially among the military aristocracy. The name Gozan, "Five Mountains," originated in China, where five Zen temples ("mountains") were designated as preeminent. Nanzenji, Shōkokuji, and Tenryūji were among the designated temples in Kyoto, as were Kenchōji, Engakuji, and Jūfukuji in Kamakura. Many Zen priests traveled to China to study, often staying for long periods, and Zen temples quite naturally became centers of Chinese learning that produced many artists (the *renga* master Sōgi and the ink-wash painter Sesshū, for instance) as well as priests who wrote poetry, usually in Chinese.

COMMENT: Zen poems resemble *waka* of the same time in focusing on natural imagery but often employ less than elegant imagery. Sometimes the poems articulate religious ideas, while sometimes they reflect the Zen belief that enlightenment was to be found in the quotidian rather than in "otherworldly" experiences or rituals. Here there is no overtly religious symbolism at work, unless one thinks of the dusky autumn landscape as standing for oncoming decline and death. Alternatively, one might take the last lines as a statement of grudging stoicism.

Zekkai's *lüshi*, from his personal collection (whose highly allusive title means something like "scraps of straw no more substantial than plantain leaves"), has a strong sense of speaker, as is often true in Gozan poems. Many Zen meditation exercises (*kōan*) presented quirky models of behavior, and those qualities shine through to one degree or another in many Gozan poems as well. In this case, however, Zekkai presents us with a very ordinary person in an ordinary situation, and one that reveals nothing about his own status. The trope of a lonely person waiting for a visitor who doesn't show up appears frequently in court poetry as well. There the figure is a melancholy one, however, while Zekkai's speaker is more whimsical. Essentially, the poem presents us with a complaint—"Are you no better than fitful clouds and rain? I wait here alone as autumn deepens, so depressed that I don't even take down my zither to play." Similar complaints are often found in love poems in the *waka* form, of course, but here the headnote tells us that it is a friend that the speaker waits for and not a lover.

The "attic room" probably refers to a small second-story chamber where friends might gather together to chat, write poetry, drink sake, and get a nice view of the moon.

SON'AN REIGEN 村菴霊彦, *Chūka jakuboku shishō* 142:
From Afar, I See a House Where Trees Are in Flower, and Go Right In

遥認桃耶又杏耶 造門不問是誰家 一春身似狂胡蝶 処処相過為有花

> Far off, I see them—peach trees, or maybe plums?
> I go in the gate, not asking whose house it is.
> While spring lasts, I am a crazy butterfly:
> I go in, I pass by—all for the flowers.

CONTEXT: Son'an Reigen (1403-1488; also known as Kisei Reigen) was a Rinzai priest associated with Nanzenji. His poem, from a collection of poems by Chinese and Japanese monks compiled in the mid-1500s, is a *kudai kanshi* that takes a line from a Chinese poem as its topic, a practice as common in *kanshi* as in *waka*, where the device was called *kudai waka*. Reigen builds his quatrain (*jueju*) on a line from Bai Juyi recorded in *Wakan rōeishū* (no. 115):

> From afar, I see a house where trees are in flower, and go right in:
> rich or poor, known to me or not, it doesn't matter.

COMMENT: While noting Bai Juyi's verse, a commentary on Reigen's poem by a Zen priest of the mid-1500s says the meaning (*kokoro*) of Reigen's poem derives more from an allusion to the story of how the Daoist sage Zhuangzi falls asleep, dreams of being a butterfly, and after waking is not sure whether he is a man who dreamed he was a butterfly or a butterfly dreaming he is a man. In this way Reigen presents himself as a carefree spirit captivated by spring flowers. The speaker's avowed indifference toward worldly hierarchies ("not asking whose house it

is") is again typical of Zen, and his dedication to aesthetic experience puts him in
the lineage of the medieval priest Saigyō, who likewise declared his freedom (*Shin
kokinshū*, no. 86) from the usual obligations of social life:

That pathway I marked	yoshinoyama
when last year I made my way	kozo no shiori no
into Yoshino—	michi kaete
I abandon now to visit	mada minu kata no
blossoms I have not yet seen.	hana o tazunen

Another poem by Son'an (*Chūka jakuboku shishō*, no. 188) presents us with a summer flower, the peony, and involves a similar claim that pits the poet against those of more conventional taste:

Behind a small house, a new bloom: shaped like jewels of ice.
I wonder: did rain wash the rouge away?
In the grand houses, they compete in reds and purples;
but this kind of elegance—this they know nothing of.

Appreciation of flowers from which the vivid colors have been washed away, the poet suggests, is something denied to those wealthy enough to get whatever they want.

ISHIKAWA JŌZAN 石川丈山, *Shinpen fushōshū*-a 260:
About the Earthquake of the Summer of 1662

Word is, when the earth of the capital shook,
shopkeepers and nobles all dashed about in fear.
Mountains crumbled, the ground cracked, waters all around rose;
but the birds in the sky—they didn't even know it happened.

CONTEXT: Like Kinoshita Chōshōshi, the samurai Ishikawa Jōzan (1538-1672) offended his patron and was forced into retirement at a young age. Before retiring to Higashiyama he was a scholar to the Asano clan in Aki Province. Rather than immediately withdrawing into seclusion, however, he studied Confucian thought and served in the retinue of a daimyo for a time, then retired to a cottage in the eastern hills of Kyoto and devoting himself to Chinese poetry. The earthquake of 1662—probably greater than seven on the Richter scale—struck the capital on the first day of the Fifth Month, when he was eighty years old.

聞説京城大震時　市朝驚怖急奔馳　山崩地裂水皆立　惟有翔禽不敢知

COMMENT: Writing in Chinese allowed a poet to write about topics never contemplated in *waka*, such as the 1662 earthquake, which destroyed the Great Buddha at Hōkōji Temple and the stone bridge across the Kamo River at Gojō Avenue. Even in the mountains Jōzan must have felt the shaking, but it was in the crowded streets of the city below that the greatest damage took place; and the poem offers little concrete description of the event, instead employing only conventional phrases. The attitude is clinical rather than compassionate, the words of a distant observer. The last line suggests that as an old recluse Jōzan identified more with the birds flying above the fray than with the frantic crowds below. He was old and done with the worlds of status and commerce.

Another, more personal poem from his *Shinpen fushōshū*-b (The Fushō collection, revised edition, 1676, p. 178) was also written when Jōzan was living in his villa, the Shisendō, which he had adorned with the portraits of thirty-six Chinese poets he had commissioned from a member of the Kanō school.

Being Ill on a Summer Night

My body declines, my life nearing its end;
my heart is tranquil, but at night—no sleep.
The frogs croaking, the cuckoos calling—
in chorus with the rain, they blast my ailing pillow.

This poem does include seasonal icons and is closer to the *waka* tradition in feel. Even more so, however, its image of rain "blasting" the pillow where he lies ill reminds one of the Gozan poets. Chinese poetry in the Edo period embodied all such influences and was as important intellectually as court poetry, boasting a large number of practitioners and occupying an important place, especially among Confucian scholars but also among men of samurai birth.

OGYŪ SORAI 荻生徂徠, *Soraishū* (p. 202): Farmhouses on a Cove

The roadway follows the cove bank, winding along;
around the farmhouses here, fences are rare.
The banks are so low farmers can wash their tools;
when the skies are clear, it's here people dry fishing clothes.
The little ox loaded with firewood stops to drink;
a small boat loads up harvested barley, then heads home.

Kids play in the sand on the shore;
the gulls are used to them and don't fly away.

CONTEXT: Ogyū Sorai (1666–1728) was one of the premier Confucian scholars of his time. After retiring from government service in 1709, he established his own academy, where he led a "back to the classics" movement, meaning the Chinese classics and early Chinese kings. It was one of many schools at the time. His approach emphasized the need for law and authority but also personal cultivation rather than more openly political activities.

COMMENT: One of Sorai's ideals, culled from the Chinese *Book of Songs*, was *fūga*, "courtly elegance," a term that was also used by Matsuo Bashō. Sorai's conception of *fūga*, however, focused more on the civilizing effects of poetry, meaning both that the content of poetry should be life affirming and positive and that the composition of poetry had an elevating effect on the poet. And his attitudes are apparent in the lifestyle he catalogues in the example here, from his personal collection, a regulated verse (*lüshi*) that presents us with a kind of investigation of things ("immediate manifestations of being") that when properly perceived reveal the order behind the surface of sensory experience. The topic of "cove" (*irie* in Japanese) is common in *waka*: one remembers Shōtetsu's use of the image in a stark winter setting, for instance. But Sorai's poem concentrates not on the water so much as on people, who are noted as an absence in Shōtetsu's conception but are very much present in Sorai's. In this way Sorai suggests that the water is not only beautiful but also integral to the daily life of people: farmers, fisherfolk, ox herds and their oxen, harvesters, kids, and gulls, all of whom make brief appearances, making up a lively tableau. He mentions weather once ("when the skies are clear"), but only to represent the rhythm of life in such a place and to suggest that his description is not meant as a "sketch" of just one moment but rather a composite, as an idealized state of being presented in parallel sentences that represent order. Above all, what we see in his poem is labor and the utility of water, until we get to the children, who have achieved a kind of symbiosis with the gulls, symbolizing innocence and natural harmony.

In Sorai's thought, achieving such harmony with the constantly changing realities of the natural world was the ultimate human goal. His view of human nature, while stressing the need for the kind of behavior inculcated by social and governmental institutions, allowed for personal engagement with important classical texts of the Confucian tradition and the development of individual

門巷隨江曲
田家籬落稀
岸低洗耕具
雨霽晒漁衣
小犢負薪飲
扁舟刈麥歸
兒童沙上戲
鷗狎不高飛

talents. Predictably, his waterside scenes concentrate on the "lower" orders of civilized society, which he saw as providing the ultimate foundation for an orderly state.

GION NANKAI 祇園南海, *Nankai Sensei shibunshū* (p. 208): Expressing My Feelings

In my inn, the gloom of evening is beyond bearing;
wind blows frost-laden leaves as high as the second floor.
Thick-billed crows fly low in drizzle of dusky hue;
geese fly close as fulling sounds ring out in the autumn sky.
The season's tokens are so right they surprise a traveler from afar;
with no hope of fame, I give myself to the floating life.
As to future plans—what will become of me?
Who will take pity on me, a boat unmoored?

客舍黃昏不耐愁
風吹霜葉入山樓
鴉低暮色瀟滿雨
雁傍砧声處處秋
節物尤能驚遠客
功名空自托浪遊
後來心計竟何事
身世誰憐不繫舟

CONTEXT: Gion Nankai (1677-1751) is considered one the finest painters in the Nanga style, a Japanese rendering of the so-called Southern School of Chinese painting (Nanzonghua). He was born into the family of a samurai-physician in Wakayama but from a young age was interested only in the arts. In his early twenties he committed an offense that put him in seclusion for a decade; thereafter, he worked as a Confucian scholar, dedicating himself to the life of a *bunjin* (literatus, connoisseur) and eschewing political affairs. Poetry, calligraphy, and music: these were his obsessions, which he sought to integrate into a lifestyle. Not surprisingly, he believed that the proper subject of all the arts was a realm of beauty and pleasure above the mundane world. The poets he most admired in the Chinese canon were Tang-dynasty masters such as Li Bai (701-762). He had little use for what he considered to be the overly rational poetry of the Song dynasty (960-1279).

COMMENT: This poem as taken from a modern edition of his works, *Nankai Sensei shibunshū* (Writings of Master Nankai), was written when Nankai was on the road and can easily be compared to famous *waka* on the ennui associated with the topic of travel. The setting is an inn; the season is late autumn or winter; the time of day, evening. In all, it is a monochromatic scene rendered with great artistry. The crow, considered an inelegant image in *waka* was not so in Chinese poetry; together with the wild geese, it draws our attention to the sky, as the sound of women fulling robes—an autumn task associated with lonely wives in traditional poetics—adds to the sense of gloom. All of this could of course be rendered in a painting, but the final lines of the poem shift our attention from the outer world with an "editorial" comment, noting that the landscape he sees is almost too perfect in terms of traditional motifs and ending with abstract statements that could not be expressed in pictorial form.

In the midst of this is the poet himself, a traveler and as such someone with no worldly ambitions, abandoning himself (*taku su*) to a floating life (*rōyū*), which is neatly symbolized by the unmoored boat, tossed on the waves. How much of the landscape was actually before Nankai's eyes is impossible to say, although the phrase "the season's tokens are so right" introduces a hint of reflexive play into his conception. The goal of painting and poetry in literati discourse was ultimately expressive rather than representational, and the scene Nankai presents is meant to convey his feelings rather than a realistic landscape. The title of his poem is a compound that appears frequently in *waka* and *renga* as well, where almost always we encounter not happy but melancholy thoughts.

KAN CHAZAN 菅茶山, *Kōyō sekiyō sonshashi* 117:
First Day of the New Year

> My two siblings are still alive,
> and I have lived six of ten decades.
> I still hope to meet with pleasures,
> but life is a risk—what else can one say?
> Ditches flow with muddy spring rains;
> fields are thick with midday fog.
> Once again I greet soft spring light;
> birds join in with drinking songs.

CONTEXT: Kan Chazan is the sobriquet of the Confucian scholar Suganami Tokinori (1748–1827). He was born in Bingo Province (modern Hiroshima Prefecture) and after studying in Kyoto and Osaka spent much of his life there. Among his friends were Yosa Buson and other literati figures. He was sixty-one years old when he wrote this *lüshi* and was no doubt feeling his age, although he would live on for two more decades. His Confucian academy (which he dubbed the Village School of Yellow Leaves and Evening Light [Kōyō Sekiyō Sonsha]—the source of the title of his personal collection of 1812) in Kannabe,

同胞二人在
百歳六分過
楽事要相及
浮生附奈何
萬渠春水濁
四野午烟多
復値韶光至
禽声入酔歌

Bingo Province, was thriving. Twelve years before, he had turned over the family business, a sake brewery, to his brother so that he could dedicate himself to his scholarship, teaching, and, of course, poetry.

COMMENT: Chazan's poetry is known for its gently subjective tone and focus on everyday life, including words and images sometimes regarded as too common and vulgar for "upright" and properly Confucian poetry. His setting in this case is New Year's Day, which came in what is late January or early February in the modern calendar. It was the holiday of all holidays across all segments of society. Although often the weather did not show any sign of it, New Year's was figured as the beginning of spring and treated as a time of renewal with family gatherings and trips to shrines and temples.

Chazan's poem begins with sober reflection. He has been fortunate, he tells us: he and his sisters (named Chiyo and Matsu, records inform us) are still living; and he still anticipates experiencing joys ("enjoyable things," which implies everyday, including ordinary, things, wine, women, and song, rather than more idealistic forms of happiness). But he is quick to add that life is uncertain. The word he uses is *fusei*, literally a "floating life." In that sense his poem is only cautiously optimistic. The spring rains, which signal the end of winter cold and the advent of a season of rebirth, are not presented in the usual propitious terms: we see ditches of muddy water and fields thick with fog. If we feel a sense of new life in the scene, then, we realize that the perspective is more that of a farmer than of a traditional court poet, a landscape rendered in rustic terms and not as an elegant tableau designed to more explicitly symbolize notions of peace and order. And in his last lines we see the same thing: while acknowledging the soft light of spring, Chazan mixes the songs of drunks with birdsong. Thus in every respect the poem is earthy by comparison with standard *waka*, resisting the traditional associations of old aesthetic ideals.

RAI SAN'YŌ 頼山陽, *San'yō shishō* 96: Arriving Home

On a backstreet, I trudge through mud,
amidst tendrils of dawn rain.
Approaching home, I feel uneasy;
spying my house, I feel even more unsure.
I hear my wife's footsteps, a country girl's steps,
and feel such joy that I become sad.
For two years I have not returned home;

my face is yellowed and dark from the world's dust.
She makes to heat water and wash my feet,
but the firewood is damp, and the fire won't start.
But damp firewood—that's no bother;
I'm just glad to be with her again.

CONTEXT: Rai San'yō (1780–1832) was a Confucian scholar born in Aki Province (Hiroshima). He studied under his own father, also a scholar, and then other scholars, including Kan Chazan. In addition to Chinese poetry, he also wrote an important history of Japan. His stubborn behavior led to house arrest for three years and later disinheritance. By 1811, however, after turning down Kan Chazan's offer to adopt him as his heir, he had a school of his own in Kyoto. In 1815, he moved with his family into a house near the intersection of Nijō Avenue and Takakura Street in Kyoto, but he often traveled. The poem here was written after a long absence.

COMMENT: This poem from San'yō's personal collection of Chinese poems, published in the year of his death, presents a very personal story. After two years, the speaker—San'yō himself, there can be no doubt—is nervous about returning home; and the closer he comes, he tells us, the more unsettled are his emotions. His wife may resent having to raise children and manage a household without his support. Perhaps he wonders if she will have aged, or is concerned about what she will make of him—or both. The "world's dust" (*jin'ai*) comes up frequently in Chinese poetry as a symbol of the filthy nature of the worlds of politics and commerce, in particular. San'yō says, graphically, that that dust has soiled his face.

The speaker characterizes his wife with one word, *sansai*—literally, a "mountain wife"—implying a contrast between the different worlds they live in, his intellectual, hers domestic. But then the tension dissolves as she plays her "proper" wifely role and prepares to wash the dust of the roads from his feet. Whether this is done lovingly or not is something we are not told, but it would be hard to think of it as anything but a moment of intimacy: a simple act of physical contact that would allow the ice to start breaking. And the final lines express relief. When the fire won't start, the two people have a quiet time together, probably in silence—and just as well. He can savor a moment of physical relief, pay a little attention to his wife, and admit to himself that he is happy for domestic joys that he has all but forgotten.

窮巷蹂深泥
曉雨方絲絲
近家情卻怕
旧寓認還疑
山妻記足音
喜極反成悲
両歳始帰到
塵埃面目黒
温湯洗吾脚
薪湿火伝遅
薪湿且不妨
唯喜会有期

Appendix 1
TECHNICAL TERMS

ageku 挙句. Last verse. The last verse of a *renga* sequence.

banka 挽歌. Lament. Usually written to commemorate a death. A subgenre in *Man'yōshū* times. The tradition continued into the Edo period, although later the term used was generally *aishōka* 哀傷歌 (or *aishōku*). Nakao Kaishi (1669–1731) wrote such a poem (*Haikai sabishiori*, p. 358) after the death of Matsuo Bashō (1644–1694).

Anything at all	*nanigoto mo*
and I find myself in tears.	*namida ni narinu*
Hut, in winter.	*fuyu no io*

byōbu uta 屏風歌. Screen poem. Poems written for inscription on standing screens, which were used as privacy barriers, windbreaks, and decoration in elite households.

chōka 長歌. Long poem. Poems of more than five lines in length, consisting of alternating five- and seven-syllable lines, concluding initially with a 7-7 couplet; often followed by one or more *hanka*, or "envoys." A major genre during the seventh and eighth centuries, thereafter appearing sporadically in travel writings and as a form for the expression of lament.

chokusenshū 勅撰集. Imperial anthology. The first imperial anthologies were of *kanshi*, but most literary histories begin their accounts with *Kokinshū*. The last of the imperial anthologies was compiled in the 1430s, although attempts to put together imperial anthologies were made into the early Edo period. Generally speaking, only highly formal poems were included in such anthologies. The nobility are better represented than any other social group, but there are exceptions, a notable one being the itinerant monk Saigyō (1118–1190), ninety-four of whose *waka* were included in *Shin kokinshū* (no. 1205), the most of any poet in the anthology.

The first three anthologies (*sandaishū*) carried more weight in the tradition than any others, although in time *Shin kokinshū* also gained many champions.

dai 題. Prescribed poetic topic. Some basic *dai* (flowers, travel, love, snow, etc.) first appear in *Man'yōshū*, and from the time of *Kokinshū* until the twentieth century, formal *waka* and *waka* composed at gatherings were generally on topics. Kamo no Chōmei (1153–1216) says, "In poetry, one must understand the meaning of topics,"[1] and the subject is of universal concern in critical writing. Over time, certain topics were standardized and canonized, the most important umbrella topics being the seasonal topics, love, and miscellaneous themes like travel and Buddhism. From medieval times onward, topics for elite gatherings had to be chosen by the members of poetic houses, who paid strict attention to precedent. Gradually, simple topics such as cherry blossoms developed into complex topics such as "seeing first blossoms" and "cherry trees in full bloom along a mountain river." Topics would generally be passed out beforehand (see *kendai* in this appendix), but from early on poets also drew topics (*tandai* or *saguridai*) for composition on the spot (see *tōza no uta*). Composition on *dai* was also practiced in various contexts in *renga* and *haikai*. Anthologizers in the world of *haikai* often organized material in chapters of *hokku* by *dai*, according to predominant imagery or logic, even when the *hokku* was not written on a *dai* in the first place. Furthermore, many *dai* from the court tradition served in *haikai* as *kigo*. See also *daiei* in appendix 2.

daisan 第三. Third verse of a *renga* sequence. See also *hokku, waki*.

fu 賦. Rhapsody or rhyme prose. A long, descriptive Chinese poem involving lines of various lengths, using extensive parallelism.

fuzei 風情. Artistic atmosphere or idea. Often related to *yojō* and *fūryū*.

haikai 俳諧. Comic, unorthodox, or eccentric poems. A general term for humorous or unconventional poetry that in the 1500s began to be used to refer to comic or unorthodox *renga* and in the Edo period often referred to what we now call haiku.

haikai no uta 俳諧の歌. Comic, unorthodox, or eccentric *waka*; a subgenre of *waka*. Poems containing nonstandard vocabulary, abundant wordplay, or humorous rhetoric or subject matter. Such poems appear in *Man'yōshū*, but the category emerges fully only in *Kokinshū*.

haikai renga 俳諧連歌. Comic, unorthodox, or eccentric *renga*; a subgenre of *renga*. Poems containing nonstandard vocabulary, abundant wordplay, or humorous rhetoric or subject matter. Much early *renga* was humorous, but the subgenre did not fully emerge until the late medieval period.

hanka, kaeshi uta 反歌. Envoy. A 5-7-5-7-7-syllable poem appended to the end of a *chōka*, often summarizing or restating its contents.

han no kotoba, hanshi 判詞. Judgments or words of judgment. Words of explication and criticism appended to poem contests. Sometimes participants at an event made comments (*shūgihan*) that were later written up; more often major poets and scholars were assigned the task of awarding wins and penning statements of judgment. In the golden age of the poem contest (twelfth and thirteenth centuries), Minamoto no Shunrai (1055-1129), Fujiwara no Mototoshi (d. 1142), and, preeminently, Fujiwara no Shunzei (1114-1204), served as judges, using aesthetic terms and ideas that became central to the courtly poetic tradition, which continued to be of relevance into the Edo period.

hare no uta 晴の歌. Formal or public poem. *Waka* written for formal, public occasions such as poem contests or small commissioned anthologies. The ideal was a poem that expressed its topic fully, was dignified in diction and subject matter, and had no poetic "faults" (*yamai*). Fujiwara no Tameie (1198-1275) lists the following poem by Shunzei (*Shin kokinshū*, no. 677), written for a sequence requested by a prince, as an example of formal composition.[2] The setting Shunzei chose was a hoary mountain on the Yamato Plain near Nara that was associated with events in ancient history, and the images he employs—snow, *sakaki* trees (branches of which were used in imperial ceremonies), and moonlight—are among the most iconic of the tradition.

The sacred *sakaki*	*yuki fureba*
high up on the mountaintop	*mine no masakaki*
are buried under snow;	*uzumorete*
and polished by the moonlight—	*tsuki ni migakeru*
the Heavenly Peak of Kagu.	*ama no kaguyama*

Grand celestial imagery, lofty rhetoric, dignified subject matter—this descriptive poem was clearly intended to impress the man who commissioned it.

The concept carried over into *renga*, although often referring more to considerations of class than formality. In a fifteenth-century beginner's handbook of uncertain authorship, we read, "Formal meetings are sure to involve nobles and adepts," and that in such settings students should be modest and restrained.[3]

hokku 発句. The first or initiating verse of a *renga* sequence. A handbook for beginners dating from the mid-1400s counsels poets to remember that *renga* is a social art: "In writing a *hokku* one should carefully study the look of the meeting place and accommodate the weather; if you do that, your *hokku* will sound like it emerges from the meeting place and be of interest. An overly clever *hokku* will make it seem that you are running through old poems in your head and put a damper on things."[4] Here the influence of *waka* poetics, as expressed by Fujiwara no Tameie, is obvious: "When composing extemporaneously at a gathering, you should describe the scenery and surroundings at the moment."[5] According to convention, each *hokku* had to indicate the season of composition and the mood of the gathering—proper and dignified for formal events, somewhat more relaxed in more intimate settings. *Hokku* were often contained in separate chapters in anthologies, and in time the subgenre developed its own identity, leading in the Edo period to what we now call haiku.

hon'i. See appendix 2.

honkadori. See appendix 2.

hyakuin 百韻. Hundred-verse *renga* sequence. The standard format of linked-verse composition. Early on, shorter sequences were the rule, and even in the late medieval period poets sometimes produced just a few links in casual settings, but references to *hyakuin* appear as early as the early 1200s. Our first full examples of the form date from the time of Nijō Yoshimoto. Longer sequences—*senku* 千句 (thousand-verse sequences) and *manku* 万句 (ten-thousand-verse sequences)—were essentially made up of separate *hyakuin*. The rules of the genre relate almost exclusively to the hundred-verse format.

hyakushu-uta 百首歌. Hundred-poem sequence of *waka*. The first such small anthologies began to appear in the late tenth century. They were generally commissioned works, often solicited by an elite patron. Other "numbered" anthologies—of fifty poems (*gojisshu-uta*), etc.—also appeared. Such works became resources for imperial anthologies.

iisute 言捨て. A short *renga* sequence dashed off for amusement. Sometimes only the first three verses of such a sequence were recorded, but often the verses were not recorded at all. The term is also used sometimes to mean a "cast-off" poem that was not meant to be taken seriously but just composed and cast off.

imayō 今様, *imayōuta* 今様歌. Modern song. Documents evince the popularity of various kinds of song from the earliest times. The term *imayō* refers specifically to songs popular among the aristocracy from the 1100s and on into the medieval period. The songs usually consisted of eight or twelve alternating seven- and five-syllable lines and were considered a form of amusement.

ji. See *jimon* in appendix 2.

jisei no uta 辞世の歌 (also *jisei no kanshi*, *jisei no ku*). Death poem. Poem written just before death in some cases, but often simply the last poem a person wrote.

jo, joshi, jokotoba 序, 序詞, 序詞. A metaphorical preface incorporated into the first few lines of a poem. Often the material of the preface is metaphorically related to the theme, scene, or idea of the final lines, but sometimes not.

johakyū 序破急. A term used in *renga* commentary and criticism, meaning prelude, breakaway, and presto. The idea was that at the beginning of a sequence, the pace of composition should be smooth and subject matter and technique relatively formal, giving way to more experimentation and variety during the middle eighty or so verses, all leading to a fairly rapidly flowing conclusion. Great variations on this pattern no doubt existed, but the general idea of a three-part structuring of a *renga* session is consistent from the mid-fourteenth century onward. The same concept appears in the discourses of music and Noh drama.

jueju 絶句. Quatrain. A four-line Chinese poem, with rhyme usually occurring in the second and fourth lines.

kagurauta 神楽歌. Sacred song. Songs sung at shrines or at the imperial court on ritual occasions.

kakekotoba 掛詞. Pivot word. A technique involving the use of a double entendre—a homonym or partial homonym that functions as the end of one phrase and the beginning of another.

kanshi 漢詩. Han poem. A general term for Chinese poetry written by the Japanese.

kasen 歌仙. A thirty-six-verse *renga* or *haikai* sequence. Our earliest references to this shorter alternative to the hundred-verse *hyakuin* come in the early 1500s. The form became especially popular in the time of Bashō and later.

kayō 歌謡. Popular song. A general term for various kinds of lyrics set to music.

keiki 景気. Scene or scenery. Sometimes used to mean simply natural description, but more often something like "evocative scenery" or scenery of affective resonance or atmosphere. (See also *keikyokutei* in appendix 2.)

kendai 兼題, *kenjitsu no dai* 兼日の題. A conventional topic distributed to participants invited to a planned poetic event (*kenjitsu no kai* 兼日の会) beforehand, in contrast to *tōza no dai*, topics drawn for extemporaneous composition. Usually, four or five topics were sent out, which would be aired together, constituting a sort of informal poem contest.

ke no uta 褻の歌. Informal *waka*, written casually or for personal occasions, in contrast to *hare no uta*. A famous example comes from Fujiwara no Teika (1162–1241):

Composed when he went with other courtiers to see the blossoms in the Imperial Palace compound, after he had served many years in the Guards Bureau:

Spring upon spring,	*haru o hete*
I have watched your blossoms fall	*miyuki ni naruru*
like snow, cherry trees.	*hana no kage*
As I grow old, here in your shade,	*furiyuku mi o mo*
do you too feel pity for me?	*aware to ya omou*

Retired Emperor Go-Toba (1180–1239) had high praise for this poem as a statement of personal feeling (*jukkai*), using the terms *yasashi* and *omoshiroshi*.[6]

He noted that Teika said it was not one of his own favorites and felt it was not appropriate for an imperial anthology, although it did finally appear in *Shin kokinshū* (no. 1455, a lament).

kigo 季語. *Renga, haikai, haiku.* Season words. Required in all *hokku*. Lists of acceptable items were available in various handbooks and are still used by haiku poets today.

kireji 切字. *Renga, haikai, haiku.* "Cutting words." Particles and verb suffixes (*ya, kana, keri, ramu*, etc.) that assist in making every *hokku* or haiku an independent statement.

kodai kayō 古代歌謡. An umbrella term for sacred songs (*kagurauta*), eastern songs (*azumauta*), planting songs (*taueuta*), *saibara*, and other works recorded in gazetteers (*fudōki*), and compilations from *Nihon shoki* to *Man'yōshū* and later anthologies.

kokoro 心. A word of broad connotations, signifying heart, feeling, mind, meaning, idea, conception, and so on. Often used in contrast to *kotoba*. The tension between *kokoro* and *kotoba* was basic to Japanese poetics. Already in the early eleventh century, poets—competent poets, that is—were instructed to concentrate on *kokoro* but were also told that if they had trouble coming up with interesting ideas they should aim for something that is at least formally polished and pleasing.[7] Generally speaking, *waka* and *renga* poets subscribed to the counsel of Shunzei and his son Teika to use "old *kotoba*, new *kokoro*," while some *haikai* poets sometimes reversed the dictum or abandoned it altogether.

kotoba 詞. A term of broad connotations, signifying diction, rhetorical technique, vocabulary, materials, and so on. Often used in contrast to *kokoro*.

kotobagaki 詞書. Headnote. The note preceding a poem in a written text, often including contextual information, conventional topic, textual source, and the name of the author.

kotowari 理. Principle, logic, cleverness. A concept derived primarily from Chinese discourse, particularly the vocabulary of neo-Confucianism. Sometimes used in a positive way in describing a poem as "making sense," but also used in a derogatory sense in reference to poems that were too clever or lacked subtlety, as in an example noted by Asayama Bontō (b. 1349):

One should compose verses in such a way that the diction is graceful and profound, and in which the wording is crisp and flows well. This poem is instructive:

Showing us gaps in the snow—	*yukima o misuru*
clumps of grass in the fields.	*nobe no wakakusa*

This verse is so intent on displaying *kotowari* that it lacks class: it's like tying a rope around something that's already nailed shut. "Showing" is too boorish.[8]

kouta 小唄. "Little songs" of the Muromachi era and later, which were strongly associated with women performers and were one of the influences on Noh drama and were popular among all social classes. Early on, accompaniment was provided by bamboo flute, but in the Edo period they were accompanied by samisen and had a strong affiliation with women's dance.

kudai waka 句題和歌. A *waka* written with a line from a Chinese poem as a *dai* (topic).

kyōka 狂歌. Madcap or zany *waka*. A subgenre of *uta* that began to emerge in the medieval era but came into full form only in the Edo period. *Kyōka* generally involve elaborate wordplay and subject matter considered too colloquial or vulgar for standard *uta* and sometimes parody well-known poems of the past.

kyōku 狂句. Madcap or zany *haikai*. See also *senryū*.

lüshi 律詩. Regulated verse. Eight-line Chinese poem of five or seven characters per line, with a single rhyme generally occurring in the second, fourth, sixth, and eighth lines.

makurakotoba 枕詞. Pillow word. Formulaic phrases of five syllables preceding certain nouns, such as *ashihiki no yama*, "foot-wearying mountains." By the time of *Kokinshū*, the precise meaning of these mostly archaic expressions was generally unknown.

meisho, nadokoro 名所. Famous places in the Japanese canon. It was virtually obligatory for poets to write poems about places they visited on their travels, and most *renga* sequences also included *meisho*.

mon. See *jimon* in appendix 2.

musubidai 結題. Compound topics involving more than one item, such as "moon above a lake." See also *daiei* in appendix 2

renga 連歌. A subgenre of *waka* that maintained the same aesthetic conventions. A communal form of poetry in which participants produce alternating 5-7-5 syllable stanzas to make up a string of linked verses. *Haikai* linked verse was referred to as *renku*.

saibara 催馬楽. Literally, "horse-readying music," referring to songs sung when tribute from the provinces was sent to the imperial court.

sakimori no uta さきもりの歌, 防人の歌. Poems by frontier guards; literally, "guardians of the capes." Written mostly by men posted to guard duty in the southern islands, where fear of invasion from the continent continued into the 700s.

sama, yō 様. Poetic style. At times the word is also used to mean "manner" or "scene."

sarikirai 去嫌. Clashing. Shorthand for rules of *renga* that require spacing of words, images, and ideas within sequences so as to avoid repetition (*rinne* 輪廻). A synonym is *uchikoshi o kirau*, "avoiding links back to the next-to-last verse."

senryū 川柳. Comic or unorthodox *haikai*. A subgenre of *haikai*, sometimes called *zappai*, or "miscellaneous" or "parodic" *haikai*, distinguished not only by broader humor but also by the absence of season words (*kigo*).

shakkyōka 釈教歌. Buddhist poem. Sometimes used in reference to any poem with strong Buddhist content, but also referring more narrowly to poems on lines from sutras or depicting Buddhist practices contained in separate chapters in imperial and other anthologies.

shi 詩. Earliest form of classical Chinese poem. Of indeterminate length, usually made up of four-character lines.

shikimoku 式目. The rules of linked-verse composition. From very early in its history, the culture of linked verse, which was in the beginning a game of sorts and would always display some aspects of play, produced rules for behavior in the *za* (no chatting, no napping, etc.) and for the proper conduct of a sequence. Over time, these rules became quite numerous and, to the minds of moderns especially, arcane and trivial. At bottom, however, the ideal behind the rules is simple: variety in technique and subject matter, within the general boundaries of the courtly poetic tradition, reflecting on one level an attempt to offer an overview of that tradition, on another level an attempt to analyze that tradition in aesthetic terms, and on still another level, at least in the case of some poets, an attempt to carry out an aesthetic meditation grounded in Buddhist philosophy. In practical terms, this led to stipulations concerning the seriation, intermission, and repetition of words and categories.

shirabe 調. Tone or fine tuning. An enigmatic term that originates in considerations of rhythm and rhyme in Chinese poetry. In the early days of the *waka* tradition it referred to the aural quality of poems, usually rendered into English as "tone" or "tuning." In the poetics of Edo-era poets such as Kagawa Kageki (1768–1843), however, it developed connotations related to ideas of purity and sincerity (*makoto*) while retaining some sense of relation to the euphonic quality of poems.

shū 集. Collection, anthology. Along with twenty-one imperially commissioned anthologies of *waka* (*chokusenshū*), the Japanese archives also contain literally thousands of other kinds of collections, small and large, from the personal anthologies of individual poets (*shikashū*) to anthologies representing groups (*shisenshū*), and in all genres. This tradition continues today, as witnessed by numerous modern editions of poetry such as the ten-volume *Shinpen Kokka taikan*, which includes indexes for every single line of the poems in the imperial anthologies, and a similar indexed collection of the linked-verse canon, *Renga taikan*, now in the process of publication.

sugata すがた, 姿. Variously translated as "total effect," "configuration," "overall effect." Generally referring to the effect upon the reader of a poem taken as a whole in both thematic and aesthetic terms. Chōmei begins his essay on the subject by admitting, "It is difficult to comprehend the total effect [*sugata*] of a poem," but he then gives an instructive comment: "For example, what one sees in the sky at dusk in autumn has neither color nor sound, so one may wonder about exactly the source of its *sugata*, and yet one finds oneself shedding tears."⁹ He probably has in mind a poem by Saigyō (*Shin kokinshū*, no. 367):

A puzzlement:	*obotsukana*
just what is it, one must ask,	*aki wa ika naru*
how might one explain	*yue no areba*
how somehow in the autumn	*suzoro ni mono no*
one finds oneself feeling sad?	*kanashikaruramu*

tanka 短歌. Short poem. Another word for *waka* appearing sporadically from the earliest times; the word most widely used for *waka* since the earlier twentieth century.

tei 体, 躰; sometimes pronounced *tai*. Style or mood. Usually used to in correlation with aesthetic terms of praise: the style of mystery and depth (*yūgentei*), the lofty style (*taketakakiyō*), the style of refined feeling (*ushintei*), and so on. Beginning in the eighth century, poets and scholars began distinguishing a number of different styles, and the so-called ten styles associated with the names of Mibu no Tadamine (fl. 905-950) and Teika had considerable impact on both practice and exegesis in the Kamakura period and later. Sometimes the term is also used to mean scene. The word *yō* is a synonym.

tōza no uta 当座の歌. Extemporaneous *waka*. *Waka* composed extemporaneously, usually on a topic shared with others. Masters of the art were expected to perform well on such occasions, and much of training was aimed at developing the ability to respond quickly and with impressive results. The atmosphere of *tōza* composition was often more relaxed than at formal events. Often topics were drawn by lot (*saguridai*).

tsukeai 付合, *tsukeyō* 付様. Link, linking, or connection. The word refers to the most fundamental practice of linked verse—namely, the joining of verses together in sequence. Many *renga* handbooks and treatises are dedicated to the examination of this fundamental technique, often through the offering of examples of different kinds of linking—by wordplay, by idea, by logic, by suggestion, etc. Sometimes synonymous with *tsukeku*; also sometimes used synonymously with *yoriai*.

tsukeku 付句. Link or linked couplet. The name for both the second verse in a two-verse "link" and the two-verse couplet itself.

tsukinamikai 月並会. Monthly meeting. From the mid-medieval period on, many poetry masters, as well as imperial, noble, and warrior houses, held monthly meetings that gathered together their salon. Typically, some topics were handed out beforehand (*kendai*), with others being "drawn" on the spot, for extemporaneous composition (*tōza*). Later, many houses also held monthly *waka* or *renga* meetings, as did *haikai* masters of the Edo period.

uta 歌. Japanese poetry, in this book used in reference not just to the 5-7-5-7-7 form that was the primary genre of Japanese court poetry until modern times but also to Japanese poetry of all genres.

uta-awase 歌合. Poem contest. In the Heian era, poem contests were actual social affairs, in which two groups of people, constituted as factions of the left and right, met together and wrote poems on *dai* (conventional topics), with judgments rendered on-site. This model remained in play for centuries to come. In later eras, however, many variations emerged. The poet Saigyō, for instance, made paper contests of his own poems and requested judgments—including commentary—by Shunzei and Teika; and around that same time, the time of *Shin kokinshū*, some very large contests were held in which the poets never met for a complete "airing" of poems.

The poem contest was a form of publication for poets, and such contests—at which only highly formal poems were acceptable—became resources for those putting together various anthologies, including imperial anthologies, for which similarly proper poems were favored by compilers in most cases. The *hanshi*, or words of judgment, often appended to the written records of contests, are important documents in the history of poetics and courtly aesthetics.

Various contest formats were also employed among *renga* poets, although not as prominently; in the world of *haikai*, however, the *hokku-awase* was of considerable importance throughout the Edo period.

utamakura 歌枕. Literally, "pillows for poems." Until the mid-Heian era, a generic term for formulaic words used in poetry such as *makurakotoba*. Later, however, the term referred to famous places that were seen as appropriate for poetic description. The list of the Buddhist monk and poet Nōin (b. 988), who was known as a traveler, includes places mostly in the area around Kyoto (Arashiyama, Fushimi Village, Katsura River, Asanohara) but also remote places in Michinoku (Shirakawa Barrier) and Dewa (Yasoshima). See also *meisho*.

waka 和歌. Short poem of 5-7-5-7-7 syllables. Also used in reference to all Japanese poetry in traditional forms.

waki 脇. The second verse of a *renga* or *haikai* sequence. *Renga* pedagogy compared the first three verses of a sequence to a social event, the *hokku* being offered by the guest, the *waki* by the host, and the *daisan* by a companion of the guest.[10] (In any given case, this scenario might realistically describe a *renga* gathering, but not always so.) The implication was that the second verse should "defer" to the *hokku*, staying in the same seasonal context and using restrained style and rhetoric.

The third verse should move the sequence forward, but only in subtle ways and not in a way to upstage the first two verses. See also *hokku*.

yamai 病. Poetic faults or "ills." Various forms of mostly syntactic, aural, or semantic features identified as displeasing in aesthetic terms, usually in the context of formal composition for poem contests and elite social gatherings.

yamatouta やまとうた, 和歌. The Japanese reading of *waka*.

yariku. See appendix 2.

yoriai 寄合. Conventional associations. Related to *engo* ("associated" words), a term used in *waka* criticism in reference to words such as "blossoms" and "scatter" that have an obvious real-world relationship but also to words linked by precedent. *Yoriai* appears in *renga* criticism primarily in reference to various semantic, lexical, and logical associations between words, images, and ideas. Some are seemingly natural ("dream" and "see," for instance, or "sky" and "rain"), while others are dependent upon long-established precedent ("snow" and "cherry blossoms") or explicit sources (Suma and zither, based on scenes in *The Tale of Genji* describing Genji's life as an exile.) Linked verse is often described as *yoriai no bungei*, "an art of associations"—referring both to the fundamental importance of linking in *renga* as a genre and to the fact that people came together in "association" in the *za*.

za 座. Literally, "seat" or "seating"; venue. Used in reference to the place where a poetry gathering was held and also to mean the gathering itself. Of particular importance in *renga* discourse, in which aesthetic and social assumptions nearly always involve the idea of communal effort that in some ways was thought of as a performance. As Bontō says in a work made up of teachings he had heard from Nijō Yoshimoto, "Since art [*geinō*] is a time for people to mingle together, there should be no feelings of inferiority at all, nor should one feel proud just because one has produced something."[11]

zōtōka 贈答歌. Exchange of *waka*. Poems written between two people, the second usually responding rhetorically and thematically to the other.

Appendix 2
AESTHETIC IDEALS AND DEVICES

It would take at least a book-length study to give a comprehensive definition of the aesthetic ideals of the Japanese poetic tradition. Here I list only a few prominent terms as a way to map out the contours of Japanese poetic discourse. For examples and definitions I have looked to poem contests, essays, handbooks, and treatises, many of which were written not as literary criticism but as instruction for students, and beginning students at that. Still, they offer us a good window on the meanings of the terms in their proper historical contexts. It should be remembered, however, that many of the aesthetic ideals encountered in such texts were used not analytically but as terms of praise. And inevitably, different poets and critics did not always agree on how terms might be defined.

Another point to remember is that often terms do not claim to identify objective qualities so much as features that resound with the sensibility of the reader (or auditor)—an intersubjectivity. As Earl Miner says, "Both the condition and the appreciative sensibility are implied."[1] The working assumption is that to identify a quality such as loftiness (*taketakashi*) a reader or auditor must have the aesthetic capacity to respond to that quality, the model being one of resonance. Especially in premodern times, poetry was a matter of the refined sensibility and was believed to have a civilizing effect. It is not without significance that one of the paramount poetic ideals of the entire tradition—*ushin*, or *kokoro ari*, to be possessed of heart, sincerity, refined feeling—is commonly used in reference to both poems and people.

In addition to terms of praise, I have also included technical terms such as *honkadori*, or "allusive variation," the uses and ramifications of which are aesthetic.

ari no mama 有のまま. *Waka*, *renga*, and *haikai*. A phrase that usually refers to poems of direct description or expression, presenting things "as they are"; i.e., without rhetorical devices or adornments. Although the phrase is occasionally used as a pejorative, from as early as the *Yakumo mishō* (1221?) of Emperor Juntoku (1197–1242), it is invoked in a positive sense, meaning roughly composing something directly or spontaneously.

Often description of a natural scene is involved, but not always. A commentary on *The Tale of Genji* by scholars of the Sanjōnishi lineage, for instance, uses the term in reference to a poem in the "Kiritsubo" (The Paulownia Pavilion) chapter of that tale (1:99) written by Genji's mother when, ill and failing after persecution by other imperial ladies, she leaves the palace and retires to her home.[2]

The time has come	*kagiri tote*
and so in sadness I depart	*wakaruru michi no*
and leave you behind,	*kanashiki ni*
though what I wish for my life	*ikamahoshiki wa*
would be a different course.	*inochi narikeri*

This is a direct statement of sentiment, with no attempt at elegant repartee, no figurative language, and no natural imagery.

Yet natural imagery is a staple of poems in the *ari no mama* mode. Nijō Yoshimoto (1320–1388) states as a general truth that "if one looks out on the scenes presented by the wind, clouds, trees, and grasses right before one's eyes and composes on things just as they are [*ari no mama*], one will come to understanding."[3] And the *renga* master Sōgi (1421–1502) characterizes the following scene of natural description (*Shin kokinshū*, no. 594) by Minamoto no Michitomo (d. 1227) as "a poem that presents things as they are [*ari no mama*], lonely and cold."[4]

"On 'the moon at dawn,' from Kasuga Shrine poem contest"

Here in the frost	*shimo kōru*
that freezes upon my sleeves,	*sode ni mo kage wa*
moonlight lingers on—	*nokorikeri*
as it used to in the dew	*tsuyu yori nareshi*
shining in the sky at dawn.	*ariake no tsuki*

This poem offers not straightforward description but a subjective comment involving a reasoning process on a natural situation.

More often, however, the term *ari no mama* is invoked when a poem offers more "pure" description of a landscape or a state of mind, as in a poem by Retired Emperor Hanazono (1297–1348), offered as an example by the warrior-poet Imagawa Ryōshun (1326–1420).

"On 'winter wind,' from a poem contest dated 1343"

I arise from bed	okite miru
and see as dawn strikes my eaves	asake no nokiba
the white of frost—	shimo shiroshi
my body feeling the chill	oto senu kaze wa
of a wind that makes no sound.⁵	mi ni samuku shite

Obviously, there is a human subject involved in this (or any other) poem, and it involves reasoning process to understand that the wind makes no sound because the instruments it usually uses to amplify its sound—the branches of trees and bushes—are so frozen that they do not move. Still, what the poem offers is primarily observational and aesthetic rather than semantic, and the "truth" involved is more experiential than empirical (see *makoto*).

The ideal of *ari no mama* is often associated with arguments between the Kyōgoku and Reizei schools of the late medieval period with which Hanazono and Ryōshun were affiliated. A set of teachings of the Reizei house states the idea succinctly: "The most fundamental of styles is based on describing things just as they are [*ari no mama*], with no adornment."⁶ An attack by the Nijō house summed up the Kyōgoku approach in the same way: "They don't avoid poetic ills, don't steer away from improper topics or proscribed words, and don't bother with adornments; they just use everyday language and write about the scene they see right in front of their eyes."⁷ But the general tendency to do justice to the world "out there," especially the world of natural phenomena, is evident across all factions in the late medieval period and plays into the poetics of *renga* as well. A statement revealing the attitude appears in the writings of the *renga* master Asayama Bontō (b. 1349) in reference to the following verse by Shūa (d. 1377):

Thanks to the wind,	kaze areba
a boat expected tomorrow	asu no tomari ni
has arrived now.	fune no kite

Bontō prefaces his comments by saying that people say Shūa's work is "clever" and "adorned." In this case, however, he says that the poet is more than clever, producing an example of *ari no mama* that is ratified by real-world experience. "There is nothing unusual about a boat arriving early," he argues, "because of a following wind."⁸

Although not usually analyzed in terms of Kyōgoku poetics, a haiku by the modern poet Takahama Kyoshi (1874-1959) usually viewed as an example of *shasei* in fact models the ideal of *ari no mama* as realized in that medieval school exactly:

Sunlight plays	*kiri hitoha*
on one paulownia leaf—	*hi atarinagara*
as it falls.⁹	*ochinikeri*

A few synonyms for *ari no mama* that appear in medieval sources are *ganzen*, *me no mae*, and *ma no atari*—"right in front of the eyes." A comment on a poem by Tani Sōboku (d. 1545), recorded by a disciple on the basis of conversations with the poet himself, provides an illustration.

"For a gathering sponsored by Hekidōsai at Odani Castle north of Lake Biwa"

In the garden, waves;	*niwa ya nami*
and above the miscanthus,	*obana ga ue ni*
an island offshore.	*okitsushima*

This is the place as it is, right before the eyes [*ganzen*]. The lake lies there before your eyes [*me no mae*], and this presents that vista—that is all.¹⁰

The more philosophical dimensions of *ari no mama* in the poetics of Kyōgoku Tamekane (1254-1332) seem to be absent here. Instead, the verse functions as a way to praise a host and draw the attention of all participants in a sequence to the beauty of their surroundings.

In the Edo period, the term comes up in *haikai* discourse and also in the writings of the popular samurai-poet Kagawa Kageki (1768-1843), who offers an inflection on the usual interpretation of the term. When describing actual scenery (*jikkei*), for instance, he says, the point is not to merely to describe "what one sees or hears just as is [*ari no mama*]" but rather to describe one's own subjective feelings just as is, without resorting to ornament.¹¹ One of his most famous *waka* (*Keien isshi*, no. 390) illustrates the point, presenting the poet very much "in" the scene:

As if moonlight	*teru tsuki no*
were cascading down on me—	*kage no chirikuru*
that is how I feel.	*kokochi shite*
As I travel through the night,	*yoru yuku sode ni*
how snow piles onto my sleeves!	*tamaru yuki kana*

aware あはれ; also *mono no aware* 物のあはれ. *Waka*, *renga*, and *haikai*. Moving, touching, sadly beautiful, pathetic. In works like *The Tale of Genji* and *The Pillow Book of Sei Shōnagon*, the word *aware* is used by characters (and narrators) to mean "moving" and is often used in reaction to scenes of beauty tinged with feelings of ephemerality. In poetic discourse, the word tends to be used in rhetorical situations that arise from sudden awareness of fleeting beauty, often perceived in slight fluctuations in quotidian experience.

An early medieval usage of *mono no aware tei* appears in a list[12] where the following poem (*Shin kokinshū*, no. 765, "Laments") by Fujiwara no Sanesada (1139-1191) is given as an example.

"Gazing at cherry blossoms at Hōkongōin during the spring after the mother of Kinmori had passed away"

Gazing at blossoms,	*hana mite wa*
I feel in no great hurry	*itodo ieji zo*
to make my way home.	*isogarenu*
No one is there, after all,	*matsuramu to omou*
to await my return.	*hito shi nakereba*

Often poems offered as examples of *aware* involve explicit statement of emotion, but in this case feeling emerges only from the poet's situation. The fact that the poet is responding to the ultimate sadness of death—of his wife, in this case—is appropriate, for at its foundation *aware* is related to a Buddhist understanding of the uncertainty of human existence. Poems characterized as moving in effect often involve a melancholy state of mind ensuing upon loss, separation, privation, etc. Interestingly, another medieval list categorizes Sanesada's poem as an example of *ushin*, "deep feeling" (see *ushintei*).[13] These two terms are contiguous along the broad spectrum of aesthetic terminology.

In *renga* treatises and commentaries, *aware* usually refers to a scene or situation that is explicitly sad, often indicated directly by vocabulary. In a mock poem contest Sanjōnishi Sanetaka (1455-1537) uses it in reference to a link (*Kabekusachū*, nos. 1041-42) by the *renga* master Sōchō (1448-1532) that provides a specific dramatic setting for the tears of the verse to which it is linked.

| Even at the Buddha's name | *hotoke no na ni mo* |
| the tears come falling down. | *namida ochikeri* |

Little remains now	*tomoshibi no*
of the light of my lamp	*nokori sukunaku*
as the year ends.	*toshi kurete*

Sanetaka's comment is, "Refined and graceful in both feeling and diction, and touching [*aware*] in total effect."[14] The effect [*sama*] emerges from the way the emotion of the *maeku* is subtly contextualized in the link.

Aware also comes up frequently in *haikai* discourse. One example comes in praise by Yosa Buson (1716–1783) for a *hokku* by a disciple, Matsuoka Shisen (b. 1742), as *aware fukashi*, "deeply moving,"[15] no doubt in reference to the poignancy implicit in a scene of morning glories in full bloom.

Morning glories.	*asagao ya*
Yesterday, today,	*kinō kyō ni*
in full bloom.[16]	*sakitsukusu*

The great nativist scholar Motoori Norinaga (1730–1801), a rough contemporary of Buson's, is well known for employing the term *mono no aware* as well. For him the phrase meant the "deep feeling" that things in the world evoke in the sensitive human being and, despite his strongly nativist affiliations, clearly relates to Buddhist ideas of transience. Rather than in the poetry of his own day, however, he saw it at work in some poems of *Man'yōshū*, in *Shin kokinshū*, and in *The Tale of Genji*.

daiei 題詠. *Waka*, *renga*, and *haikai*. Writing poems on prescribed topics, or poems written on prescribed topics. Generally speaking, from the earliest times the challenge of *daiei* was understood as precise articulation of the topic, adhering to its essence (see *hon'i*). This attitude is apparent in the "words of judgment" (*hanshi*) on the following round of a poem contest (*Shōji ninen jūgatsu tsuitachi uta-awase*) held in the Tenth Month of 1200 by Retired Emperor Go-Toba (1180–1239). On this occasion, all those participating in the event voted on judgments (*shūgihan*), but it was Fujiwara no Teika (1162–1241) who wrote the words up, and scholars assume that his opinions prevailed. The difference between the two poems, the first by Minamoto no Tomochika (precise dates unknown) and the second by Fujiwara no Takasuke (precise dates unknown), is obvious: the winning poem contains all the words of the topic (morning, withered, and field), whereas the loser concentrates more on a path through the fields and rather than "withered" uses "frost."

"Morning on a withered field"

Left

In frost so deep,	*fumiwakeshi*
he may stray from the pathway	*ato sae shimo ya*

that others have trod—   mayouran
a traveler at morning   asa tatsu nobe o
searching his way through the fields.   tadoru tabibito
   Tomochika

Right [winner]

When morning comes,   wakeshi no no
he gazes afar at grasses   chigusa no hate o
on fields he passed through— kesa mireba
his heart withering within   kokoro ni karenu
as colors fade on the flowers.   hana no iriro
   Takasuke[17]

The difference is not great, but one thinks that perhaps the poem of the left was written on the topic "frost on a path through the fields." In the poem of the right, the phrase "heart withering within" is not that ingenious, but because it expresses the topic more unequivocally, we awarded it the win.[18]

The dominance of *daiei* in poetic practice and discourse cannot be overestimated, but it is also not true that all poems were written on *dai*. Sometimes poets wrote on immediate experience, and poems were also used in correspondence, in travel records, and so on. Furthermore, some poets were explicitly known for their "personal" poems not written on topics, among them the great priest-poet Saigyō (1118-1190), for instance, and Kenkō (d. ca. 1352), author of *Tsurezuregusa* (*Essays in Idleness*), who wrote the following (*Kenkō hōshi shū*, no. 74):

"Written when he saw gulls at play on an evening when the surface of the sea was utterly calm"

Off the beach at dusk   yūnagi wa
not a wave is to be seen.   nami koso miene
Far, far away,   harubaru to
gulls fly over the seashore: oki no kamome no
rising, falling, that is all. tachii nomi shite

It should perhaps be noted that in his own day Kenkō was considered somewhat less of a poet than Tonna (1289-1372), who was a true master of writing on topics, but still he was prominent in literary circles and was so admired that records say people memorized many of his poems.

Kōun (d. 1429) makes it clear that the ideal was to call to mind actual experience in the composing of *daiei*. "When you are in a poetry gathering and faced with composing on a topic, you should compose with the scenery of the place around you—the patterns of the clouds, the sounds of the wind, or the rain you have just heard—in your heart, and come up with a poem that is unusual in style and expresses some new idea."[19] Some *Shinkokin*-era poems employed natural imagery symbolically, but the mainstream of later medieval poetry stressed an approach informed by actual experience to lend a sense of sincerity. And, as noted in chapter 2, *Shirin shūyō* (mid-Edo) records a relevant conversation between Mushanokōji Sanekage (1661-1738) and his disciple Jiun (1673-1753) about the following poem on the topic "bush warbler at morning" by Tonna (*Tonna hōshi ei*, no. 10):

Morning after morning	asana asana
I go outside, and listen:	tachiidete kikeba
to where in haze	haru no no no
spreading over spring fields	kasumeru kata ni
a bush warbler sings.	uguisu zo naku

As Sanekage argues, this poem shows that even in poems on topics "new conceptions" were prized, and also that the feel of "actual experience" (*jitsujō*) was important.[20]

But what is it that is new in Tonna's conception? The answer hinges on his allusion to an anonymous poem in *Kokinshū* (no. 16):

Setting up house	nobe chikaku
in a place not far from the fields,	iei shi sereba
I hear the voices	uguisu no
of bush warblers singing,	naku naru koe wa
morning after morning.	asana asana kiku

With this poem in mind, we realize that Tonna's poem affirms his own identity as a person of feeling seeking proper aesthetic experience, while also ratifying the claim of the older poem to a basis in real experience rather than mere imagination.

Dai continued to be fundamental to Japanese practice among *waka* poets until the modern period and played a role in other genres as well. In *renga*, *dai* were assigned for *hokku* being composed for *senku* and *manku* (thousand-verse and ten-thousand-verse sequences). Furthermore, anthologies of linked-verse *hokku* organize verses according to traditional *dai*, as do *hokku* in *haikai* discourse in Edo times. *Haikai* poets often met to compose *hokku* (as opposed to sequences) on topics, many of them coming directly from the traditional canon. For instance, Takai Kitō (1741-1789) records a number of anecdotes involving composing on topics. "When some people got together and divided up topics involving "plum blossoms," I drew "plum blossoms beneath the moon.'"

As if driven mad	*mume ga ka ni*
by the scent of plum—	*kuruu ga gotoshi*
clouds around the moon.	*tsuki no kumo*

Because my poem dealt with only the surface of the topic, only expressing a sense of lingering cold, people didn't offer much praise.[21]

It is worth noting that Kitō's note of disappointment about the reception of his verse shows that still in the mid-Edo period poets were concerned about how well a poem expressed its topic.

A final note: sometimes *haikai* poets seem to use *dai* and *kigo* (season word) interchangeably. Kaya Shirao (1738-1791), for instance, lists poems including the phrases *hototogisu* (cuckoo), *akikaze* (autumn wind), and *samidare* (summer rains) as examples of *uta dai* and poems including *sumōtori* (sumo wrestler), *kannenbutsu* (praising Amida in the cold), and *watanuki* (unpadded kimono) as *haikai dai*, adding that *waka* poets use only *uta dai*, whereas *haikai* poets can use both.[22] All the words appear in standard lists of season words. Echoing Matsuo Bashō (1644-1694), Shirao also encourages *haikai* poets not to revert to the triviality of early-Edo *haikai*, but, even while writing on *haikai dai*, to compose poems of elegance and *yūgen*. A comment by Kitō on a *hokku* by his disciple Shunpa (d. 1810) illustrates the attitude:

"Third Month of 1786"

On "warm"

Still it's warm—	*atatakaki*
as the sky is gone	*higure no sora to*
to dusk.	*narinikeri*

At first glance, not an impressive poem, but it expresses the real feeling of spring warmth coming from above, unfolding smoothly and without artifice, achieving a quality appropriate to the first verse in an anthology.[23]

Aristocratic poets of the Edo period continued to compose on topics into the Meiji period, and the same was true of many commoner poets. Yet there were poets such as Tachibana Akemi (1812-1868) who saw composing on *dai* as too confining and sometimes jettisoned the practice.

en 艶. *Waka*, *renga*, and *haikai*. Charming, lovely, delicately evocative. The term is especially important in the aesthetics of Fujiwara no Shunzei (1114-1204). Retired Emperor Go-Toba (1180-1239) famously described Shunzei's own poems as possessing "charm [*en*], profound meaning, and also pathos [*aware*]."[24] The following poem by Jien (1155-1225) describing the subtle natural transition from summer to autumn, written for a poem contest held in 1193, provides a glimpse into what it meant to Shunzei, who acted as judge (see *Roppyaku-ban uta-awase*, round 312):

"Autumn, round 6—'lingering heat'"

Summer remains here,	*aki asaki*
in the still shallow rays	*hikage ni natsu wa*
of autumn sunlight;	*nokoredomo*
but where dusk darkens the fence	*kururu magaki wa*
wind blows over the reeds.	*ogi no uwakaze*

Adherents of the scholarly Rokujō house were dubious about the phrases *aki asaki hikage* (shallow rays of autumn sunlight) and *kururu magaki* (dusk darkens the fence), but Shunzei had no objection to either phrase and characterized the *kururu magaki* in positive terms: "On the contrary, it sounds charmingly beautiful."[25] It was probably the syntax, which might be rendered in unnatural English as "darkening fence," that offended one side and impressed the other. The word *magaki* generally refers to a wattle fence of bamboo or tree branches, usually found around a cottage. Thus the poem suggests the presence of a feeling subject.

In *renga*, the term *en* often refers to scenes of great beauty that have courtly resonances. For instance, a link by Sōchō (1448-1532) praised by Shōhaku (1443-1527) as charming presents a woman remembering her lover by his scent (*Sōchō hyakuban renga-awase*, p. 62).

A sad thing it is—my dream,	*honoka naritsuru*
now nearly faded away.	*yume no awaresa*
Only a scent	*tamakura no*
on my arm he used for sleep—	*kaoru bakari o*
all that remains.	*nagori nite*

Yet the renga master Shinkei (1406–1475) suggests that for himself, at least, *en* can emerge even from rustic scenes, scenes that otherwise might be offered as examples of his idea of the cold and spare (*hieyase*). "Nothing is more charming than ice. The fine scenes [*fuzei*] of a thin layer of ice on a rice field after harvest, or icicles hanging from the aging eaves of a roof thatched with cedar bark, or grasses and bushes encased in frozen drops of dew in a withered field—are these things not captivating and charming [*omoshiroku en ni mo haberazu ya*]?"[26]

Matsuo Bashō (1644–1694) uses the word *en* only a few times, implying something like "gentility." In a poem contest, he praises a poem by Kusakabe Kyohaku (d. 1696) as "refined and charming [*yū ni shite, en nari*]."

Where to go	*izukata ni*
for a little holiday?	*yukite asoban*
Year-end cleaning.[27]	*susuharai*

Susuharai—literally, "brushing the soot away"—refers to year-end cleaning, which by convention was done on the thirteenth day of the Twelfth Month. Kyohaku's verse presents the somewhat pathetic plight of someone who has no place to go while the cleaning is done. There is humor in the situation, but *yū* and *en* emerge from the association with old calendrical traditions and the image of the subject ruminating on where to go.

fūga 風雅. *Waka*, *renga*, and *haikai*. Courtly elegance, proper poetry, poetic spirit. From the beginning *fūga* was closely associated with the idea of a proper "courtly" life grounded in ancient Chinese ideals and high standards of taste as well as rules of order and propriety. The definition by Nijō Yoshimoto (1320–1388) is decidedly didactic: "If the content of a verse is upright and the words subdued, then it will blend with the voices of an orderly world. This is what is meant by *renga* of courtly elegance."[28]

Matsuo Bashō (1644–1694) and his disciples sometimes use the term to mean poetry—proper, serious poetry, that is—in a general sense. Thus Bashō and his followers claimed that the spirit of *fūga* animated all genres of poetry: "Chinese poetry, *uta*, *renga*, *haikai*—all are *fūga*."[29] And in a famous statement, Bashō says that *fūga* is found in the work of the artists he admires most across generic boundaries. "The *waka* of Saigyō, the *renga* of Sōgi, the paintings of Sesshū, the tea of Rikyū—the same thing that runs through all of these. Things that cleave to *fūga* follow creation and befriend the four seasons."[30]

A related term is *furyū* 風流, which in early times derived from Chinese concepts and seems to have meant something like an elegant life, grounded in court lifestyle, etiquette, and aesthetics. It is a close synonym of *miyabi*, "courtly taste."

In Bashō's school it is sometimes used to mean poetry: "The one quality that flows through what the world calls *furyū* is this: you are moved by something and let it work on your feelings, in the end breathe it out in words as a poem. This is the foundation of Chinese poetry, *uta*, *renga*, and *haikai*, and if you allow not a thread of the personal into it, that is what is called true art [*fūga*]."[31]

heikaitei 平懐躰. *Waka, renga, haikai*. The ordinary or plain style. The word is used in a negative sense, meaning "ordinary" or "prosaic" by Fujiwara no Shunzei (1114-1204), Retired Emperor Go-Toba (1180-1239), Emperor Juntoku (1197-1242), Tonna (1289-1372), and Kōun (d. 1429). However, sometimes it also appears as a more neutral term, in reference to certain works of Saigyō (1118-1190), in particular,[32] who uses the word in a positive way himself.[33] Among his poems, the following is often mentioned as an example of the "ordinary" style.[34]

As if to say	nageke tote
"Suffer!" moonlight shines down—	tsuki ya wa mono o
but that cannot be.	omowasuru
Yet that is where my crying eyes	kakochigao naru
seem to want to look for blame.	waga namida kana

Since it appears in both in *Senzaishū* (no. 929) and *Ogura hyakunin isshu* (no. 86), compiled respectively by Shunzei and his son Fujiwara no Teika (1162-1241), this poem cannot be easily dismissed. Yet it should also be remembered that Go-Toba, Shunzei, and others stressed that Saigyō was an exceptional talent whose style was not a good model for younger poets.[35]

Among later medieval poets, it was Shinkei (1406-1475) who used the term *heikai* in a positive sense, in reference to his own *waka* (*Kanshō hyakushū*, no. 77) no less.

"Love, using the image of 'bridge'"

Over the ages	furinikeru
Itada Bridge has descended	yoyo no itada no
into ruin,	hashi yori mo
yet more obvious still	koboruru mono wa
is the way my tears fall down.	namida narikeri

This poem is a *shinku* [closely linked poem; see *shinku soku*] and ordinary, but still it holds some interest. This, too, is one style.[36]

Another of Shinkei's poems (*Kanshō hyakushū*, no. 56) that he characterizes as "entirely in the *heitai* style"[37] suggests a connection to his "chill" aesthetic (see *hieyase*).

The desolate scene	*susamajiki*
of a heavy, frigid sky,	*sora no keshiki mo*
and the sound of wind:	*kaze no oto mo*
both bring with them the sadness	*kanashisa souru*
of winter, now surely come.	*fuyu wa kinikeri*

One remembers again that in one of his essays Shinkei says that "nothing is more profoundly moving or refreshing than water" and "nothing is more elegant than ice."[38] The elevation of the mundane and seemingly ordinary into artistic significance was clearly part of his project.

Heikai also comes up occasionally in *haikai* discourse, usually pronounced not as *heikai* but as *konashi* and often refers to unconventional or somewhat forced treatment of serious topics. In a positive sense, however, the idea was also instrumental in the developments of *karumi*, or "lightness," in the poetics of Matsuo Bashō (1644–1694).

hieyase 冷え痩せ. *Waka* and *renga*. Cold and spare. An ideal particularly for the *renga* master Shinkei (1406–1475), who uses a number of similar terms—*hiesabi*, *hiekōritaru*, *samuku yasetaru*, etc. In one of his works (*Tokorodokoro hentō*, p. 290), he praises a *hokku* by Mashita Mitsuhiro (d. 1441) as an example of what he means.

Blow on, storm winds—	*fuke arashi*
in those reeds faintly sparkling	*ogi ni honomeku*
in moonlit dusk.	*yūzukuyo*

Like this one, many of the poems Shinkei identifies with the term and its synonyms present stark, cold imagery, but his student Inawashiro Kenzai (1452–1510) says that is not enough: "When it comes to what in the world of poetry we call *hieyase karabitaru*, there are many who say it is a rotting willow, a withered plum tree, frost falling on a bridge, or a night of snow and ice. If that were true, how easy it would be."[39]

The implication is that the most important element in this mode is rhetorical restraint: not just cold imagery but also spare style and chilly feeling. One of Shinkei's own (*Chikurinshō*, no. 418) links perhaps illustrates the point:

> On the path, no footsteps show— *fumu to mo mienu*
> as dew hardens into frost. *michi no tsuyu shimo*
>
> No one passes by *yuku hito mo*
> and the night goes silent *shizumaru tsuki no*
> in white moonlight. *shiroki yo ni*

Shinkei's link in this case contains no inherently cold image, although one might say it "borrows" the frost of the *maeku*; but at the center of it is a pared-down image of night quiet that makes for the chilly effect. Elsewhere Shinkei himself argues that "in summer, when one sits by pure flowing water or by a spring, one feels a chill; and when one hears the word 'autumn water' one also feels cool and refereshed."⁴⁰

A late Muromachi *renga* handbook attributed to Sōgi (but perhaps a compendium of sorts including teachings of Shinkei and Kenzai as well) includes words of caution about the chilly mode: "For novices, to be too fond of creating the effect of *hiesabitaru* will retard their progress in the art."⁴¹ It was probably considered the province of true masters.

hon'i 本意. *Waka*, *renga*, and *haikai*. Essence or essential nature. Sometimes the term is used to refer to the accumulated "precedents" related to a word or image; sometimes it is used in the more abstract or philosophical sense of "essence." In the late medieval period *hon'i* comes up mostly in reference to the proper treatment of specific topics (*dai*), words or images, but sometimes it is evoked in a more general way, as when Asayama Bontō (b. 1349) says that a verse in which someone asks for clouds to cover the moon is contrary to *hon'i*.⁴² Obviously, this reveals a conservative attitude toward tradition and a strong commitment to the maintenance of a harmonious community of poets, sharing a common past as inscribed in the canon.

A statement by the *renga* master Satomura Jōha (1524–1602) is apposite. "In spring, great winds may blow and rainstorms arise, but to make the winds calm and the rainfall gentle—this is to adhere to *hon'i*. Again, spring days may on occasion be short, but in *renga* the practice is to describe them as long and languorous."⁴³

Haikai poets, who often defined themselves in opposition to old strictures, were more likely to ignore old conventions. Yet the persistence of season words in *haikai* shows that the old prescriptions were still at work in various ways in *haikai* discourse. And, ironically, the "newness" of *haikai* is in fact often dependent upon our knowledge of *hon'i*, as is apparent in the following example (*Iozakura*, p. 117).

My dream, shattered—	*yume karete*
by a dog barking far off	*hatsuaki inu no*
as autumn begins.	*tōne kana*

This poem by Mizuta Saigin (d. 1709) obviously challenges our expectations concerning two things. First is the topic/season word "autumn begins," which in earlier times would have been treated with more elegance; and second is the sound that wakes the speaker from sleep, which in *waka* or *renga* would usually be the wind or a bell sound, and certainly not a dog. In this sense the verse is quite literally constructed by toying with *hon'i*. The same is often true in comic forms.

honkadori 本歌取. *Waka*, *renga*, and *haikai*. A form of explicit intertextual reference involving the appropriation of a line or lines from an earlier "foundation poem" (*honka*) in order to create an allusive variation on the original. Generally speaking, one or two lines would be "borrowed," and borrowing too much was frowned upon. The following is a classic example of the technique in a poem by Fujiwara no Teika (1162-1241) written in 1198 (*Shin kokinshū*, no. 40) for a sequence commissioned by Reverend Prince Shukaku (1150-1202):

All across the sky	*ōzora wa*
the scent of plum blossoms moves	*ume no nioi ni*
like spreading haze;	*kasumitsutsu*
yet it is not clouded over—	*kumori mo hatenu*
the moon on this night in spring.	*haru no yo no tsuki*

This highly evocative description of the moon shining dimly in the haze of a night fragrant with the scent of plum blossoms might even be called surreal. But Teika knew that his readers would recognize that it was grounded in allusion, the lines *kumori mo hatenu / haru no yo no tsuki* coming from a poem by Ōe no Chisato (dates unknown; the poem was written in 894 but appears as *Shin kokinshū*, no. 55) in only slightly varied form.

On the line "Neither shining, nor clouded over—the murky moon":

| Not shining clear | *teri mo sezu* |
| and yet not clouded over | *kumori mo hatenu* |

is the murky moon	haru no yo no
on this night in springtime—	oborozukiyo ni
a thing beyond compare.	shiku mono zo naki

Teika also knew that readers would recognize the line from a Chinese poem by Bai Juyi (772-846) that had served as Chisato's topic (*dai*), making for another layer of allusion. Whereas Chisato does little more than restate the topic, adding a word of praise, however, Teika engages with it by adding the fragrance of plum blossoms spreading through the night, obeying the general requirement that allusive variations should in some way "make it new." And the resonances of the poem do not stop there, for Teika cannot have been unaware of a scene in the "Hana no en" chapter (Under the cherry blossoms) of *Genji monogatari* (1:246) in which the sister of Kokiden, one of the women the eponymous character is pursuing, quotes Chisato and thereafter in the tale is known as Oborozukiyo, "Lady of the Murky Moon." Thus Teika's poem represents not just *honkadori* but also *honzetsu*, allusion to a tale or other prose source. It is because of these layers of reference that Teika's poem is often elicited as an example of a poem with *yojō* (overtones). The kind of allusive variation it displays is especially important in the *Shin kokin* era but continues as a prominent technique in both *waka* and *renga* into the future.

Honkadori in *renga* functions much the same as it does in *waka*, with the same goal of not simply repeating the content of the foundation poem but also either echoing it in subtle ways or engaging with it creatively. An example of the latter comes from *Kochiku* (nos. 541, 542), the personal anthology of Tani Sōboku (d. 1545):

As I gaze out	nagametsutsu
into unending nightfall—	taenu yūbe o
it pierces to the core.	mi ni shimete
Who says a mountain village	tare uki yori to
is better than the cruel world?	iishi yamazato

This link obviously contains an allusion to an anonymous poem from one of the "Miscellaneous" books of *Kokinshū* (no. 944), a poem that any poet in Sōboku's day would have committed to memory.

Things are forlorn	yamazato wa
in a mountain village—	mono no sabishiki
surely that is so;	koto koso are

but life there is easier	*yo no uki yori*
than back in the cruel world.	*sumiyokarikeri*

As a commentary says, Sōboku's link enters into a dialogue (*mondō*) with the poem, disputing the idea that the lonely life in a mountain village is easier than life in the cruel world. "Who says so?"

Haikai poets also use *honkadori* as a technique. Matsuo Bashō (1644–1694), however, especially in his mature work, often seems to have favored a vague kind of intertextuality over actually borrowing lines, hence his praise of an anonymous poem that appeared in a poem contest from the late 1670s.

Loneliness—	*sabishisa ya*
it comes down to this:	*tsumaru tokoro wa*
autumn dusk.[44]	*aki no kure*

Rather than alluding to one particular poem, this *hokku* refers to scores of poems from the classical tradition, beginning with at least *Kokinshū*. The author of the anonymous *hokku* is unknown, and rather than point out the allusions Bashō simply says, "Coming to the understanding of the idea of the ephemerality of all things [*jakumetsu*] through the loneliness of an evening in autumn is deeply moving [*aware fukashi*]."[45] One cannot help but think that all this was on Bashō's own mind when just a few years later (in 1680) he composed a *hokku* (*Arano*, no. 737) that is generally considered to inaugurate the Bashō style:

On a bare branch	*kareeda ni*
a crow comes down to roost.	*karasu no tomarikeri*
Autumn dusk.	*aki no kure*

Bashō's *hokku* is generally seen as polemical: a declaration that *haikai* imagery—a crow, here—could fit into the longer tradition represented by "evening in autumn," which stood for nearly eight hundred years of poetic history. Thus general resonance with literary canons is more important than reference to any particular text.

Allusion across poetic genres was not common, but it did occur, as the following *waka* (*Keien isshi*, no. 796) by Kagawa Kageki (1768–1843) attests:

What did he mean	*furinikeru*
talking about that old pond?	*ike no kokoro wa*
I don't know.	*shiranedomo*

But even now you can hear	ima mo kikoyuru
the sound of water.	mizu no oto kana

No student of Japanese poetry could miss the reference here to one of Bashō's most famous *hokku* (*Haru no hi*, no. 316), which—as Kageki's poem wryly suggests—had already generated much interpretive attention even by the mid-1800s.

At an old pond	*furuike ya*
a frog takes a plunge.	*kawazu tobikomu*
The sound of water.	*mizu no oto*

honzetsu 本説. *Waka*, *renga*, and *haikai*. Allusive variation on a scene from a tale or other prose work. Such allusions are commonplace in *waka* as well as in *renga*, and somewhat less frequently in *haikai*.

One example of the technique elucidated by Nijō Yoshimoto (1320-1388) refers to scenes from the "Yadorigi" (Ivy) chapter of *The Tale of Genji* (5:393-402) that involve Niou and Nakanokimi meeting in the former's Nijō mansion in the autumn, as the crickets make her miss her former "mountain home" in Uji.

Voices weary from lamenting—	*nagekiyowaritaru*
crickets at the end of day.	*higurashi no koe*

In sad autumn,	*uki aki ni*
who is it that would be off	*tare yamazato o*
to a mountain home?	*tazenuran*

As Yoshimoto says, this link carries only the "vestige" (*omokage*) of the Genji scenes, "calling them to mind only vaguely."[46] The link uses phrases from several poems and prose passages, evoking the episode as a whole.

The word *honbun* 本文 is a synonym of *honzetsu*, often referring to allusion to lines from Chinese texts.

hosomi 細み. *Haikai*. Spare, slender, bereft, forlorn. Matsuo Bashō (1644-1694) is reported to have said of the following *hokku* from *Sarumino* (no. 1668) by Yasomura Rotsū (d. 1738), "The verse has [the quality of] *hosomi*."[47]

Are even the birds	*toridomo mo*
in bed for the night?	*neitte iru ka*
Yogo Sea.	*yogo no umi*

Here in the skies above the Yogo Sea, a lake north of the much larger Lake Biwa, we see no birds, which we can imagine dotting the waters below, already retired for the night. Some scholars posit a connection between *hosomi* and the ancient term *kokorobososhi*, "desolate and forlorn" or "in low spirits," but here the focus is more on the spare, monochromatic imagery of the poem and its accompanying mood of chilly loneliness.

jimon 地文; *jimon no uta* 地文の歌, *jimon no renga* 地文の連歌. *Waka*, *renga*, and *haikai*. Background and design. A term derived from weaving that was first used in reference to the composition of *waka* sequences (particularly the *hyakushu*, or one-hundred-*waka* sequence), encouraging poets to create a fairly small number (ten to twenty) of striking poems and then create less-striking efforts as a "background" (*ji*) against which the "design" (*mon*) could stand out. The same technique was recommended for the composition of *renga* sequences, although critics and commentators seldom stopped to clearly define their terms. Still, there can be no doubt that, just as variety of subject matter and technique was important in the *za*, so was the ideal of a mix of aesthetic textures.

Especially in formal venues, some images—blossoms, the moon, and snow, for instance—were more likely to be elevated into design verses than, say, field grasses or swamp water or sparrows. A comment by a disciple on a link by Inawashiro Kenzai (1452-1510) makes it equally clear, however, that it was not so much the predetermined nature of materials that decided the issue as how they were treated in the linking process.

Back in the mountains,	*okuyama ni*
a meager life, hard to bear—	*kurashiwabitaru*
holed up for winter.	*fuyugomori*
Hailstones striking the window,	*mado utsu arare*
withering wind at the eaves.	*noki no kogarashi*

The *maeku* is a background verse. With the words "hailstones" and "withering wind" we move into design. The meaning is that one finds life hard to bear hearing the hail and wind.[48]

The comment makes it clear that design relates not just to imagery but also to style, rhetoric, and dramatic content. It is as much the spare syntax—really nothing more than juxtaposition—and aesthetic minimalism of the link as the harshness of the scene that makes the scene stand out. Ultimately, it is the whole effect of the link against the backdrop of the *maeku* by which we as readers "move into design."

Furthermore, when it came to *renga*, it is clear that the terms were sometimes used in regard to linking technique and not just the aesthetic qualities of individual verses. A treatise on linking techniques by Sōgi (1421-1502) implies this when it says that *mon no tei* involves, "bringing flowers into bloom on withered trees, attaching flowers to clouds... having tree cutters lament cutting trees in spring and grass cutters so sensitive that they search for ways to avoid harvesting the autumn grasses—that is the essence of this style."[49]

From the beginning, those who used the term *ji* probably did not mean that background verses should be considered inferior to design verses, but only less impressive. Fujiwara no Tameie (1198-1275) said that "always a truly excellent poem has nothing arresting [*omoshiroki*] about it,"[50] and Asayama Bontō (b. 1349) expressed the same idea: "Not every link should be fine [*yoshi*]. Composing *ji renga* [background links] is crucial. The *ji renga* of an adept will be simple, correct in diction, and have a pleasing quality about it [*mezurashiki fuzei*]. The *ji renga* of someone unskillful will be disappointing, like the pines at Sumiyoshi."[51] Sumiyoshi was a famous *utamakura* with which pines were nearly always associated—something so predictable as to be considered disappointing.

It is in the writings of Tonna (1289-1372) that we begin to see the emergence of "background" composition as a positive aesthetic aim. "Most people understand a poem that has some outstanding quality as design and a straightforward poem that does not stand out as background. But if we define a good poem as one that is gentle, beautiful, and lofty, then we should call such a poem design and refer to a poem that has some outstanding quality as background."[52]

In the work of Sōgi (1421-1502) and his poetic lineage, considerable stress was put on the composition of background links as an essential part of training and practice. This in turn led to similar attitudes among later *haikai* poets, including Matsuo Bashō (1644-1694), who not only adhered to the ideal in his linked verse but also adapted it to the organization of *hokku* anthologies.[53]

karumi かるみ. Haikai. Lightness. An ideal embraced by Matsuo Bashō (1644-1694) in his last years. For him, it seems to have been not a matter of subject matter but one of simplicity and understatement in rhetorical treatment, without reliance upon erudite references or the distraction of figurative language. He is quoted as saying that the effect was like "looking at shallow water in a gravel-bottomed stream"[54]—implying a contrast with a river where the water courses by over rocks and boulders.

A verse (*Zoku sarumino*, no. 3449) Bashō composed in the summer of 1694, the year of his death, serves as an example of the ideal. "He was in Ōtsu in the summer, when a letter came from his older brother, asking him to come home to celebrate the Festival of the Dead."

The whole house goes,	*ie wa mina*
staffs in hand, white-haired—	*tsue ni shiraga no*
to visit graves.	*hakamairi*

Here humorous detail—old people tapping their way along—might be said to "lighten" the mood of what could easily be portrayed in more somber terms, given the nature of their journey.

Although we have only hints about Bashō's conceptions, it is clear that he used *karumi* in contrast to *omomi*, or "heaviness," referring to poems that were heavily rhetorical and literary, and that *karumi* implied certain qualities of character—modesty, stoicism, and a quiet and casual demeanor.

keikizuke 景気付. *Renga* and *haikai renku*. Linking through scenery. Treatises offer a number of variations of this technique, one of the most prominent being linking scene to scene, as illustrated in a link (*Chikurinshō*, no. 1496) by Sōzei (d. 1455):

At day's end, a bell sounds,	*kane o kagiri ni*
the sun already gone down.	*hi koso irinure*
On a far mountain,	*tōyama no*
amidst the clouds of evening—	*yūbe no kumo ni*
a temple appears.	*tera miete*

This is a close link that might be said to simply expand the dimensions of a suggested landscape. However, the link also continues a theme and mood.[55]

In *haikai renku*, linking through scenery continued to be a prominent technique. Matsuo Bashō (1644-1694) sometimes uses the word *keshiki* as a synonym for *keiki*,[56] but he also uses the older term, as in his praise for a link by his disciple Rika (precise dates unknown) presenting a scene of Tadasu Grove in the southern Kamo area of Kyoto.

A shrike calls once—	*mozu no hitokoe*
and evening sun gives way	*yūhi o tsuki ni*
to the moon.	*aratamete*

| At a Tadasu sweets stall | *tadasu no ameya* |
| autumn grows cold.⁵⁷ | *aki samuki nari* |

Here we encounter no figurative language, no affective words, just a landscape, although the presence of the sweets stall adds a dimension of everyday life.

keikyokutei 景曲体; also *keiki* 景気. *Waka*, *renga*, and *haikai*. Other synonyms are *keshiki* and *nari*. Scenery or atmosphere. In *Guhishō*, an essay attributed to Fujiwara no Teika (1162-1241), the term *keikyoku*, a synonym of *keiki*, is explicitly identified as belonging to the larger category of *miruyōtei*, "the style of visual description."⁵⁸ The word *keiki*, which appears in both *waka* and *renga* discourse, sometimes means simply "scenery," but more often it is a term of praise referring to "beautiful or emotionally charged scenery" and usually implying the creation of an atmosphere of symbolic overtones. The anonymous author of *Gukenshō* says, "What we call the *keikyokutei* is to bring out the particular attractions of each of the seasons—that is the kind of poem that qualifies."⁵⁹

Kamo no Chōmei (1153-1216) says that "in what the world usually calls a good poem... a scene floats up against the sky" the way a stitched patterns stands out against a background in weaving.⁶⁰ He offers a famous poem (*Kokinshū*, no. 409) often attributed to Kakinomoto no Hitomaro (fl. ca. 680-700) as an example:

In the dim, dim light	*honobono to*
in the early morning mists	*akashi no ura no*
on Akashi Bay,	*asagiri ni*
a boat fades behind the isles—	*shimagakureyuku*
my heart going in its wake.	*fune o shi zo omou*

Certainly this poem presents natural description, but, as Chōmei notes, it is also "replete with overtones" that suggest separation and heartache.

The *renga* master Sōzei (d. 1455), drawing on medieval *waka* treatises, used *keikyoku* as a term of praise for links using natural scenery that "appear to be shallow but are deep."⁶¹ And the idea of *keiki* as atmosphere that surrounds a poetic scene is also of great importance to Shinkei (1406-1475) and Inawashiro Kenzai (1452-1510). But *renga* masters sometimes discouraged overreliance on scenery. Nijō Yoshimoto (1320-1388) wrote that "if one uses words skillfully and creates rich conceptions, then one can create masterful *renga* without using scenery."⁶² Yet at the same time, Asayama Bontō (b.1349) taught that "one is unlikely to produce something truly interesting without scenery and overtones."⁶³

A *hokku* by the renga master Shōhaku (1443-1527) is identified as an example of *keiki* by a disciple:

Scented with plum,	*mume ga ka ni*
haze spreads among the skiffs	*irie kasumeru*
out in the cove.	*obune kana*

An ingenious description of the area in front of a gate; a scene of skiffs in a cove where haze faintly scented with plum is spreading over the water. A *hokku* that presents a beautiful scene.⁶⁴

Here it is probably the idea of haze carrying the scent of plum that elicited the praise, which expands the concept beyond the strictly visual to include the olfactory and by implication perhaps all the senses.

In the poetics of Matsuo Bashō (1644-1694), *keiki* was used in both an analytical sense and as a term of praise. In a general way, he thought of scenery verses as "lightening" the tone of a sequence, playing a role much like *ji* verses.⁶⁵ Hattori Tohō (1657-1730) quotes the master as praising the following *hokku* by Mokudō (1666-1723) as a superb model of the ideal.

Spring wind.	*harukaze ya*
The sound of water moving	*mugi no naka yuku*
through a field of wheat.	*mizu no oto*

Lest we take the ideal of *keiki* too lightly, however, Bashō adds a word of warning to students: "People think scenery verses are easy, but this is off base. This is a matter that requires great care. In *renga*, the term used was *keikyoku*, and masters of the past refrained from composing such verses, limiting themselves to one or two in a career. They were being strict with their students, because *keiki* verses are so easy to mimic. In *haikai* we are not as strict as they are in *renga*. They were strict because it is so easy for *keiki* verses to sound antique."⁶⁶

Surely "one or two in a career" is an exaggeration, since in another statement Bashō said, "As for my verses, I use nothing but *keiki*."⁶⁷ But the warning reminds us as readers to look carefully at scenic verses, which often contain subtly affective elements. A "spring wind" is a mild and welcome thing, and the gurgle of water unseen but flowing in a field of wheat stands for life and the harvest.

Masaoka Shiki (1867–1902) was a major proponent of *keiki* in *hokku*, which he associated with Yosa Buson (1716–1783).

kokorozuke 心付. *Renga* and *haikai*. Nijō Yoshimoto (1320–1388) defines this technique as "linking only by *kokoro*, casting off any word links or assocations."[68] The technique demanded subtlety and rhetorical skill and thus was not recommended for beginners; but it was expected of masters. Sōgi (1421–1502) elucidates the method in a commentary on a link from his own *hyakuin* dating from 1495:

| A hovel at Naniwa, | *naniwa no koya wa* |
| thatched rudely with reeds. | *ashi no karibuki* |

Living here now	*sumikaete*
where once was a capital—	*miyako no ato no*
only common folk.	*iyashiki*

Here it appears that nothing links back to a hovel rudely thatched with reeds, but the term "common folk" holds the link together. I think this is what is referred to as *kokorozuke*.[69]

The link in this case may contain no formulaic association with anything in the *maeku*, but the scenes fit together well and are similar in mood.

In the world of *haikai renku*, especially of the Bashō school, the general trend was toward more emphasis on linking by suggestion (*nioi* and its synonyms), which can be conceptually traced back to the ideals of *kokorozuke*, *soku* (distant linking), and *yojō* (overtones). A commentary by Matsuo Bashō (1644–694) on three verses from a sequence by his disciples gives a sense of things.

Lightning flashes	*inazuma no*
in gaps between trees:	*ko no ma wo hana no*
like blossom's glow.	*kokorobase*
Kyohaku	

To link "between trees" to lightning is very clever [*omoshiroshi*]. Indeed, one might call lightning "flowers on an autumn night."

In a field, a cast-off priest	*tsurenaki hijiri*
opens his knapsack.	*no ni oi o toku*
Kifū	

This is a superb verse, either on its own or as a link. Just as lightning strikes in the chilly gloom of night, a priest is making his bed in the fields. What people call the new way of looking at things in *haikai*—this is what it comes down to.

Hordes of people—	*hito amata*
getting things ready	*toshitorimono o*
for New Year's.	*katsugiyuku*
Yōsui	

This is a superb verse: it takes the night a priest is unable to find lodging and makes it into the last night of the year. That is original of itself. And the scene of people bustling around, transporting things in preparation for the New Year, just as the priest beds down in the fields—that is one of the finer links of recent times. One should appreciate the way the link transforms the *maeku*.[70]

In the traditional vocabulary of *renga* poetics, these links would be called *kokorozuke*. In other words, there are no automatic or formulaic links between words in the verses. Instead, as Bashō makes clear, the poets have *created* links by (re)interpreting the *maeku*: the priest and his knapsack do not have any necessary relationship to lightning strikes or flowers, nor are there any sure formulaic connections between the priest and his knapsack and people bustling around at year's end.

kotobazuke 詞付. Renga. Linking by words, usually in contrast to *kokorozuke*, or linking primarily by *kokoro*. A cousin of *yoriaizuke* but generally hinging on very specific word associations ratified by tradition. Inawashiro Kenzai (1452–1510) gives an example (*Chikurinshō*, no. 1129) by his teacher, Shinkei (1406–1475).

| Rain will be coming, no doubt: | *ame ni ya naran* |
| the sound of the wind blowing. | *fuku kaze no oto* |

Out in the paddies	*sue nabiku*
where tall bamboos are swaying—	*tanaka no take ni*
the song of a dove.	*hato nakite*

These verses fit well together as scenery, wind blowing in bamboos near rice paddies before rain. But Kenzai explains that the question of why rain will be coming is answered by a specific word association between "rain" and "dove" that is based on an old popular saying, "The song of the dove summons rain."[71]

In one of his essays Shinkei himself criticizes Asayama Bontō (b. 1349) for links in which the verses are just placed next to each other with no subtle connections and challenges the conventional dichotomy of *kokoro* versus *kotoba*: "There should be no such thing as a link that is not a *kokorozuke*. What we call close links and distant links in *waka*, these are all *kokorozuke*."[72]

makoto まこと, 実, 誠. *Waka*, *renga*, and *haikai*. Truth, sincerity, honesty. This word appears in the *Kokinshū* preface and in many medieval writings. Fujiwara no Tameie (1198-1275), in a treatise by Tonna (1289-1372) is reported to have said to a student, "You should put *makoto* above all else, and be sure you adhere to the principles of the world [*dōri*]."[73] The concept figures greatly in the thinking of Kyōgoku Tamekane (1254-1332), for whom direct apprehension of the "truth" is the whole purpose of poetry: "Whether it be a scene of cherry blossoms, the moon, break of day, or end of day, one should become the thing one is confronting and reveal its *makoto*."[74] In his own work, this often yields poetry of careful observation without the distraction of figurative language, as is demonstrated in the following (*Gyokuyōshū*, no. 2220):

"Mountain hut in the wind"

Wind from the mountain	yamakaze wa
blows over my bamboo fence	kakio no take ni
and goes on its way:	fukisutete
then from pines on the peak	mine no matsu yori
it echoes once again.	mata hibiku nari

Makoto continued to be important into the Edo period, partly under the influence of Zhu Xi Confucianism, in which it was figured as the metaphysical ground for virtuous behavior. The term is used in critical writings by the court poet Karasumaru Mitsuo (d. 1690) and other elite poets writing in the *waka* form, but it was also used by Matsuo Bashō (1644-1694), who is quoted as saying that *makoto* was the foundation of serious poetry (*fūga*) in all forms and that it was the quality that synthesized the dynamic forces of *fueki ryūkō*, "the unchanging and the changing." Nativist scholars and plebian poets as disparate as Ban Kōkei (1733-1806) and Tachibana Akemi (1812-1868) also used the term to mean sincere and straightforward expression of one's own feelings, in opposition to what they considered the excessively rhetorical, mannered works of many of their contemporaries.

It is perhaps in the writings of the *haikai* poet Uejima Onitsura (1661-1738) that *makoto* received its most complete hegemony, as revealed in his famous dictum,

"There is no *haikai* outside of *makoto*"[75] and in injunctions to "Let your spirit traipse through the skies and experience the *makoto* of snow, the moon, and cherry blossoms."[76] In poems like the following (*Onitsura haiku hyakusen*, p. 198) he created "objective" tableaux reminiscent of Tamekane: "Written on the spot in response to Reverend Kūdō, who had asked him, 'Just how is that you perceive your own *haikai*?'"

Out in the garden,	*teizen ni*
blooming whitely—	*shiroku saitaru*
camellias.	*tsubaki kana*

Implicit in Onitsura's *makoto* is the idea that it appeals to the individual poet in even the smallest and most seemingly insignificant of things and events, revealing that the most profound truth of all is the principle of constant change.

mirutei 見躰, *ken'yō* 見様, *miruyōtei* 見様躰. *Waka* and *renga*. The style of visual description. See also *keikizuke*. A seemingly unproblematic term, but it should be remembered that the Nijō school interpreted it to mean not spare and realistic description but rather description rendered with elegant and courtly refinement, as in an early poem (*Shūi gusō*, no. 755) by Fujiwara no Teika (1162-1241) recorded in a medieval commentary of the Nijō school as an example of the ideal.

"From a hundred poems on ten topics"

From between the clouds	*yūdachi no*
of an evening thundershower,	*kumoma no hikage*
sunlight starts to show;	*haresomete*
on the slope in front of me—	*yama no konata o*
a white egret passing by.	*wataru shirasagi*

A scenic poem [*keiki*], in the style of visual description. The idea is that the egret looks all the more white because it is flying in front of green mountains.[77]

The poem alludes to lines from a Chinese poem, "Two yellow warblers sing in green willows; a line of white egrets rises into the blue sky" by Du Fu (712-770),[78] thus adding an extra layer of richness and evocative power to the scene. This is even more obviously true of a poem (*Shin kokinshū*, no. 340) by Fujiwara no Kiyosuke (1104-1177) listed in a medieval text as in the visual style.[79]

"Composed for a hundred-poem sequence presented to Retired Emperor Sutoku"

Through a thin mist—	*usugiri ni*
flowers wet with morning dew	*magaki no hana no*
on my wattle fence.	*asajimeri*
Who was it that once declared,	*aki wa yūbe to*
"In autumn, it is evening"?	*tare ka iikemu*

This is not natural description so much as a subjective comment on natural description, alluding in the last line to a statement in the famous preface to *The Pillow Book of Sei Shōnagon*,[80] but still it focuses on the beauty of the scene itself, rather than on symbolic or emotional referents.

The term *keiki* used in *waka*, *renga*, and *haikai* commentary and criticism can be seen as an extension of *mirutei*. But in 1452 Sōzei (d. 1455) is still using the old term in reference to a *tsukeku* by Asayama Bontō (b. 1349).

Again a change begins	*mata kawariyuku*
in autumn's lonely mood.	*aki no sabishisa*
Off through the leaves	*ko no ha fuku*
storm winds blow toward miscanthus,	*arashi no sue no*
clustered in far fields.[81]	*murasusuki*

nadaraka なだらか. *Waka* and *renga*. Smooth, gentle. A term used by Minamoto no Toshiyori (1055-1129), Fujiwara no Akisue (1055-1123), and others and picked up later by Fujiwara no Tameie (1198-1275), who declared that "a poem of fine total effect [*sugata*] is one that has smoothly flowing diction [*kotoba nadaraka ni iikudasu*] and is highly refined."[82] The ideal was important in Nijō poetics in the late medieval period, which stressed what modern scholars call *heitanbi* (elegant simplicity). Among the poems Tameie lists immediately after his pronouncement is one by Fujiwara no Shunzei (1114-1204; *Senzaishū*, no. 1151) that indeed unfolds smoothly as a simple statement of a profound truth.

"On 'deer,' written for a hundred-poem sequence of laments"

From this world of ours	*yo no naka ya*
there is no path of escape.	*michi koso nakere*
Even in the mountains	*omoiiru*

where I go to flee my cares	yama no oku ni mo
I hear the call of a stag.	shika zo naku naru

A later poem (*Saishōsō*, p. 433) by Sanjōnishi Sanetaka (1455-1537), written in 1524, shows that the ideal was still in effect.

"On 'the beginning of summer'"

So cool it is	asamidori
as it blows across leaves	wakaba o wataru
green with new growth.	suzushisa wa
No longer is it the wind	hana ni itoishi
I hated in the flowers.[83]	kaze to mo nashi

Rather than straightforward natural description, we encounter here a flowing statement of the simple truth of how immediate, subjective context conditions our response to natural phenomena.

nioizuke にほい付. *Haikai*. Linking by scent. An extension of the idea of *yojō*, or "overtones," inherited from court poetry. The notion is that a "scent" can drift from one verse to another, becoming the basis for a link. Hattori Tohō (1657-1730) offers as an example the first two verses of a linked-verse sequence (*Hisago*, nos. 1472-73) involving Matsuo Bashō (1644-1694), Hamada Chinseki (d. 1737), and three other disciples.

Too confusing,	iroiro no
they have so many names.	na mo magirawashi
Spring grasses.	natsu no kusa

Jolted by wind,	utarete chō wa
a butterfly wakes.	me o samashinuru

Tohō says the link is based on the "scent" of the word *magirawashi*, "confusing," which suggested to Bashō the idea of a sleeping butterfly being suddenly thrown into confusion by the wind in the summer grasses.[84] It is easy to imagine the butterfly as actually out in the grasses, but the link does not go that far: it simply catches the scent of "confusion" in the previous scene and creates a corollary.

In another comment on a link by Bashō from the same anthology (*Hisago*, nos. 1450-51) that is commonly noted as an example of *nioizuke*, Tohō explicitly mentions overtones.

In autumn wind	akikaze no
people in the boat cringe	fune o kowagaru
at waves' sound.	nami no oto

| Where the geese head: | kari yuku kata ya |
| White Sands, Young Pines. | shiroko wakamatsu |

Here the poet takes on the surplus feeling [*kokoro no amari*] of the *maeku* and articulates it through scenery [*keshiki*].[85]

The place-names Shiroko and Wakamatsu are located on the coast in what is modern Mie Prefecture. Each evokes a natural image—white sands (*shiroko*) and young pines (*wakamatsu*).

Nioizuke is sometimes used as a comprehensive term for Bashō's variety of *kokorozuke*, or "linking by feeling or suggestion," encompassing other terms such as *hibikizuke* (linking by echo), *omokagezuke* (linking by vague allusion), and *utsurizuke* (linking by transference).

okashi をかし. *Waka*, *renga*, and *haikai*. Witty, novel, amusing, interesting. The term implies creativity in conception and rhetoric and is one of the commonest terms of praise in poem contests and commentaries. Minamoto no Toshiyori (1055–1129) uses it in reference to a poem by Minamoto no Kunizane (1069–1111) from a poem contest held in 1100.

"Round 13, on 'love at night'"

Overwhelmed by love,	omoi amari
I gaze out and see a sky	nagamuru sora mo
of gathering clouds.	kakikumori
Even the moon, it would seem,	tsuki sae ware o
is intent on shunning me.[86]	itoikeru kana

Okashi is a quality of most good poems, and its use does not necessarily imply contrast with, for example, *aware*. In his judgment of a poem in a contest held in 1172, Fujiwara no Shunzei (1114–1204) explicitly refers to the following poem by Inbunmon'in Chūnagon (precise dates unknown) as "deeply moving" (*aware fukaku*), but also amusing in total effect (*sugata okashi*).

"Lament"

To the river depths	minasoko ni
my body has now sunken,	waga mi wa shizumi
arrived at its end.	hatenuredo
Yet endlessly the currents	ukina o nagashi
carry on my sullied name.[87]	seze zo kawaranu

Okashi does not appear quite as often as *omoshiroshi* in either *renga* or *haikai* discourse, but Yosa Buson (1716–1783) is still using the term in a critique of *hokku* by his disciple Teramura Hyakuchi (1748–1836) in the late 1700s.

Stormy winds.	kogarashi ya
Baggage is transported,	funeni wo uma ni
boat to horse.[88]	tsumi kawaru

What makes the verse effective is of course the stormy winds, which blow at the clothing of the teamsters and lend a sense of urgency to their labor—an amusing observation, according to Buson.

omoshirotei 面白躰. *Waka*, *renga*, and *haikai*. The clever, ingenious, or arresting style. A term usually applied to the conception or rhetoric of a poem. The medieval poet and scholar Kōun (d. 1429) praises the following poem (*Shin kokinshū*, no. 359) by Fujiwara no Yoshitsune (1169–1206) as "achieving a profound level of cleverness, of the sort beginners should not hope to approach."[89]

"On 'autumn evening,' composed for poem contest of hundred-poem sequences"

I was not musing,	mono omowade
so where could it have come from—	kakaru tsuyu ya wa
this dew on my sleeves?	sode ni oku
Ah, but I *was* gazing out	nagametekeri na
on an evening, in autumn.	aki no yūgure

The amusing quality here derives from the speaker's tears, shed spontaneously in response to an action (gazing out at the sky on an autumn evening) that the tradition defines as inevitably sad. In that sense it is a play on convention, though nothing that even approaches sarcasm or cynicism. Indeed, one might even read a sense of weariness into the last two lines that serves to keep the attitude wistful and sincere.

One challenge for the beginning reader of Japanese poetry is that the ingenious quality of a poem assumes recognition of conventions and the canon. The following poem attributed to Tonna (1289-1372),[90] for instance, is not incomprehensible on its own but gains greatly in interest if one recognizes the way it cleverly engages a famous earlier poem (*Shūishū*, no. 15) by Taira no Kanemori (d. 990), quoted here immediately after Tonna's:

For you to visit—	towaruru mo
why, surely this is something	itodo omoi no
I did not expect,	hoka nare ya
the flowers on my high plums	tachie no ume wa
having now scattered and gone.	chirihatenikeri

Composed for a screen painting depicting visitors coming to a house where plum blossoms were in bloom:

Ah, it must be	waga yado no
that you saw the high plum trees	ume no tachie ya
blooming 'round my house:	mietsuran
never had I expected	omoi no hoka ni
that you would come and visit.	kimi ga kimaseru

Kanemori's poem gently accuses the visitor in the screen painting of being more interested in enjoying the plum blossoms than their owner. Tonna's poem, on the other hand, is more in the nature of compliment, suggesting that his visitor has more admirable motives.

A certain amount of creativity was of course required to succeed in either *waka* or *renga*. In the latter, cleverness is especially important in the creation of links. An anonymous commentator[91] praised the following link (*Chikurinshō*, no. 767) by the *renga* poet Gyōjo (1405-1469) as *omoshiroshi*.

| A lingering figure, | tatazumu kage zo |
| visible in the moonlight. | tsuki ni miekeru |

Enough, so be it!	yoshi saraba
Before the rumors begin,	kaerusa isoge
I will hasten home.	na ya moren

The *maeku* in this case presents objective description: someone, or something, is lurking in the moonlight. Gyōjo ingeniously decides to create a love verse, putting words in the mouth of a man who is so wary of being discovered that he decides to hurry along home. No doubt we are to imagine him waiting outside a woman's house for a way to visit undetected. For whatever reason—rejection, or simply bad timing—he is forced to give up.

sabi さび, *sabitaru* さびたる. Waka, renga, and haikai. Lonely, forlorn, desolate, bleak. A noun form derived from the verb *sabu*, "to be deserted, old and worn, rusty," and the adjectival verb *sabishi*, "lonely." The verb form appears often in poems and is not as explicitly an aesthetic term as, say, *yūgen*.

A poem by Saigyō (1118-1190) from a mock poem contest judged by Fujiwara no Shunzei (1114-1204) illustrates the ideal. It is, as Shunzei says, a poem of deep resonances that produces "a total effect of loneliness [*sugata sabitaru*]."[92]

In the long Ninth Month	nagatsuki no
the light of the moon shines down	tsuki no hikari no
late into the night.	kage fukete
In the fields skirting the slope	susono no hara ni
a stag is calling.	ojika naku nari

Here the imagery is spare and monochromatic, the phrasing direct and unadorned; and the scene is literally devoid of any direct statement of human presence.

Yet usage of the term is not always so linked to stark natural imagery. In his judgment on the following poem on the topic of lament by Jakunen (b. 1119?), Shunzei praises "the overall effect as lonely and desolate [*sugata sabite kokorobosoku*]."[93]

"Lament"

Awake in the night,	nezame shite
I find all around me sad.	mono zo kanashiki
Ah, how few are they—	mukashi mishi
people I saw in days gone by	hito wa kono yo ni
who still remain in the world.	aru zo sukunaki

In this case the effect of *sabi* emerges more from direct statement and the depiction of a state of mind than from external features in a landscape.

In *renga* criticism and commentary, *sabi* is not used as an aesthetic term so much as a descriptive one. A link by Inawashiro Kenzai (1452-1510) is glossed by his student as *sabishiki tei nari*, which may simply mean "a lonely scene" but may also mean "in the mode of loneliness."[94]

| Who might it be, all alone, | *tare karagoromo* |
| striking mallet upon robe? | *hitori utsuran* |

So cold blows the wind;	*kaze samuku*
and out on my ruined eaves	*aretaru noki no*
I see dewdrops.[95]	*tsuyu o mite*

A synonym of *sabi* that appears in commentaries occasionally is *karabitaru*, meaning "sere, desiccated, or withered," which harks back to *Santai waka* (no. 1202) by Retired Emperor Go-Toba (1180–1239). Kenzai uses the term in reference to a *tsukeku* (*Chikurinshō*, no. 197) by Ninagawa Chiun (d. 1448).[96]

| He fastens his aging gate | *furuki kado sasu* |
| as spring ends in falling dusk. | *haru no kuregata* |

Out in the weeds	*yomogiu ni*
wind blows in from the pines—	*matsukaze fukite*
blossoms all gone.	*hana mo nashi*

Sabi continued to be used as a term of praise into the Edo period, although in *haikai* discourse the ideal went through rather predictable inflections. For Matsuo Bashō (1644–1694), it was the formula of *sabi* plus light humor that was the very essence of *haikai*. Mukai Kyorai (1651–1704) said this about the term, offering an example from among his own *hokku* that he said was praised by Bashō.

> *Sabi* is the hue [*iro*] of the verse; it does not mean only a lonely verse. Imagine an old man in armor on the battlefield, or wearing fine clothing at a banquet—still his age will be apparent. *Sabi* can be there in a lively scene or in a quiet scene. An example is by Kyorai:
>
> | Blossom guards | *hanamori ya* |
> | poke white heads together | *shiroki kashira o* |
> | for a chat. | *tsukiawase* |
>
> Master Bashō said, "The hue of *sabi* emerges well here' and was very pleased with the verse."[97]

The white-headed old men chatting together beneath the blooming cherry trees obviously contrast with the flowers that surround them, symbolizing temporality and drawing attention to the theme of human aging and decline, but only in the most gentle way.

In a work published in 1812, Kaya Shirao (1738-1791) still uses terms like *okashi* and *yūgen*, as well as descriptive phrases deriving from *Shinkokin*-era aesthetics such as *hosoku karabitaru* (spare and withered), which he employs to praise a *hokku* (*Arano*, no. 968) by Bashō.[98]

"Written when visiting someone's house"

As I thought:	*sareba koso*
a house crumbling at will	*aretaki mama no*
beneath frosts.	*shimo no yado*

This poem was written when Bashō was on a visit to Tsuboi Tokoku (d. 1690) in his hut, an out-of-the-way place where Tokoku was living after running afoul of the law. Again, "a house crumbling" is not something one would find in classical poetry, but beyond that the resonances with medieval poetry of more elevated diction are obvious.

shasei 写生. *Haikai*, *tanka*, and haiku. Sketch, sketching from life. A term used by Masaoka Shiki (1867-1902), which he came to after serious engagement with painting, Western and Asian. Among other things, Shiki recommended that poets take walks and write haiku in response to scenes along the way, a practice still common today, especially among amateur haiku poets. Discursively, the idea is closely related to both *ari no mama* (things as they are), *makoto* (truth, sincerity) and to the emphasis in Bashō's approach on being attentive to actual phenomena, sharing with those ideals the sense of subjective engagement with objects and events. The following poem written in 1894 is an example from Shiki's own works, which was the direct product of his walks in the Negishi district of Tokyo.

Farmers harvesting.	*ine karu ya*
Above cremation grounds,	*yakiba no keburi*
no smoke today.	*tatanu hi ni*

How pleasant it seems to go notebook and pencil in hand to stroll on the outskirts of Negishi, relishing the mystery of sketching things [*shasei*] firsthand.[99]

shinku soku 親句疎句. *Waka* and *renga*. Close linking and distant linking. Another concept, like *ji* and *mon*, that derives from medieval *waka* discourse. In several treatises, *waka* whose upper and lower halves adhered through explicit word associations, reasoning, or syntactic relations were referred to as *shinku* (close verses), while halves less obviously linked were called *soku* (distant verses). Different factions and poets often differed in their opinions of which of the modes should be the ideal. The unknown author of the thirteenth-century treatise *Guhishō* dismissed *shinku* as too ordinary: "Poems in the *shinku* mode usually are too conventional in their phrasing, making connections like leaves growing from branches that rise from the foot of the tree, and therefore are no more than ordinary, rarely amounting to anything unusual."[100]

The author of *Kaen rensho kikigaki* (1315), on the other hand, attacked *soku* as too obscure.[101] Speaking broadly, poets of the Nijō faction seem to have favored close verses, while the Kyōgoku and Reizei factions embraced *soku* more readily, as is reflected in a comment from an essay attributed to a member of the latter: "Someone said *shinku* are seldom truly excellent, but among *soku* there are many fine poems. True? I wonder."[102]

Poems like the following (*Shin kokinshū*, no. 38) by Fujiwara no Teika (1162-1241) in which the two halves are linked primarily by contiguity and could each be taken separately—indeed, almost like two verses in a *renga* sequence—were referred to as *soku* (distant verses):

On this spring night,	haru no yo no
the floating bridge of my dreams	yume no ukihashi
has broken away:	todae shite
lifting off a mountain peak—	mine ni wakaruru
a cloud bank in empty sky.	yokogumo no sora

Shinkei (1406-1475) gives us our most original definition of close and distant linking in linked verse: "*Shinku* is having form, *soku* is formless; *shinku* is the Buddhist teachings, *soku* is Zen."[103] He, too, was of the opinion that most truly excellent *waka* were *soku*, perhaps showing the influence of his teacher, Shōtetsu (1381-1459), who had studied under a Reizei master.[104] For whatever reason, he championed the idea of distant linking in *renga* more than any other master, producing a number of superb examples himself, such as the following, which was called a model of the technique by Sanjōnishi Sanetaka (1455-1537) and elicited a comment from Sōgi (1421-1502):

Smoke rises up	keburi tatsu
from a mountainside village,	fumoto no sato no
hidden in the trees.	kogakurete

A skiff lies abandoned	*obune suteoku*
by an inlet at day's end.	*e koso kurenure*

Here the link does not accommodate the *maeku* at all. If one simply puts the two scenes next to each other, they look like a Chinese ink painting, and there seems to be no gap between them. This is a style of its own, and among Shinkei's verses one will find many like it. But this is very much the skill of a virtuoso. If a beginner develops a penchant for this kind of thing, a certain disjointedness will be sure to result.[105]

From the following statement by Inawashiro Kenzai (1452–1510), one of Shinkei's premier students, we know that Sōgi's characterization is genuine: "If you just put two verses of scenery next to each other, they will end up linked in feeling."[106] But Sōgi's passage is less an endorsement than a word of caution, no doubt representing the experience of a working *renga* master who was concerned that young poets, in particular, should master close linking thoroughly before attempting anything more sophisticated—which was something that Shinkei echoed in a general way in his own writings. In one of his essays Shinkei also noted that both *shinku* and *soku* in the end must be linked by feeling, or *kokoro*.[107]

Most links in any *renga* sequence were of course *shinku*. A link by Sōgi (*Guku wakuraba*, no. 923) shows that even "close" links could be complex.

Confusion, enlightenment—	*mayoi satori wa*
it's a matter of the heart.	*kokoro ni zo aru*
The evening bell rings	*yūgure no*
at a temple in the fields—	*nodera no kane ni*
as someone waits.	*hito machite*

The *maeku* in this case articulates an unequivocal Buddhist message, but long precedent dictates that the *tsukeku* be categorized as love. (Hearing a temple bell announce evening while looking forward to meeting a lover is a common trope.) The link depends on the conventional association of evening bell and temple back to the word *satori*, "enlightenment." Together, the verses nonetheless present a complex state of mind that mixes themes: the bell either brings a tryst to mind or a call to something else.

The kind of linking later favored by Bashō (1644–1694) and his disciples, often referred to as *nioizuke* (linking by scent), may be thought of as an extension of the idea of *soku*. (See *nioizuke*.) Yet above all, Bashō taught that "linking" was basic to linked verse: "Never did a single one of his verses not link."[108] He had harsh words for those who simply lined up verses without bothering to link them and quoted a statement by Shinkei as his authority about some poets in ages past: "They would just put the moon, blossoms, and the snow haphazardly, and when verses make no links to their *maeku*, it's like lining up dead people all decked out in fine clothing."[109]

shiori しほり or *sabishiori* さびしほり. An enigmatic term related to and often coupled with *sabi*. Withered and bent, shriveled, or, more expansively, a quality that adheres as a sort of pathos in ordinary, everyday things. Matsuo Bashō (1644-1694) is reported to have said that the following poem (*Zoku Sarumino*, no. 3472) written by his disciple Morikawa Kyoriku (1656-1715) had the quality.[110]

Those ten dumplings—	*tōdago mo*
how small they are now.	*kotsubu ni narinu*
Autumn wind.	*aki no kaze*

The ten dumplings (*dago*, or *dango*)—typically sold on a string or skewer—were sold at a particularly arduous stretch of the Tōkai Road running from Edo to Kyoto, near Utsunoyama Pass, which is where Kyoriku composed the verse, in the autumn of 1692. The "sensitivity" shown in the verse is to two groups suffering as the cold weather sets in: vendors, who are challenged to make a go of it when the number of customers declines, and travelers. The crucial component is that all of this is accomplished through a small and transient object that ironically has a kind of warmth to it, dumplings. The image is also a fine example of *karumi* (lightness).

shūitsu 秀逸, *shūka* 秀歌, *shūku* 秀句. A masterwork or tour de force. Not restricted to any one style, but superb, excellent; synonymous with *mon* in some cases. Sometimes used in reference to poems involving outstanding wordplay. Many poets use *shūitsu* and *shūka* as terms of praise, meaning "superb," while using *shūku* in reference to poems of (overly) conspicuous wordplay.

Kamo no Chōmei (1155-1216) analyzes a poem (*Shūishū*, no. 224) by Ki no Tsurayuki (d. 945) as a *shūitsu* partly because it is not contrived:

Overcome by love,	*omoikane*
I go out in pursuit of her—	*imogari yukeba*
the river wind	*fuyu no yo no*
so cold in the winter night	*kawakaze samumi*
that the plovers are crying.	*chidori naku nari*

No poem has more allusiveness [*omokage*] than this one. One person said that, "Even on the twenty-sixth day of the Sixth Month, in the worst heat of the year, if I chant this poem I feel cold." Generally speaking, however graceful in idea or diction a poem may be, anything that seems contrived is a failing. This poem is like trees on a peak—not something constructed—or grasses in the fields—not something dyed—or the way flowers show their various colors in the fields in spring or autumn. It is a superb poem [*shūka*], in the way it brings things together naturally, expressing itself in a straightforward way.[111]

tadagotouta ただ事歌, 徒事歌. *Waka* and *haikai*. *Waka* in colloquial style. In the *Kokinshū* preface, *tadagotouta* is introduced as a style of composition, signifying a "correct" style. In later texts, however, the word comes to mean "direct and unadorned," and it is often used as a pejorative signifying the synonym "everyday language" (*tadakotoba*) indistinguishable from prose. A Nijō critique of a poem (*Gyokuyōshū*, no. 1005) by Kyōgoku Tameko (d. 1316), sister and ally of Kyōgoku Tamekane (1254-1332), is dismissive:

"From among her winter poems"

Following the wind,	*kaze no nochi*
hail falls in a sudden burst—	*arare hitoshikiri*
passing quickly by;	*furisugite*
then again, from between the clouds,	*mata murakumo ni*
spills light from the moon.	*tsuki zo morikuru*

It's as if the author means to say something in everyday language. One could say this isn't a poem at all.[112]

Poets of the Kyōgoku persuasion would of course have considered the poem's directness admirable. But a comment by Sōzei (d. 1455) on a link by Kyūzei (1282-1376) makes it clear that the somewhat slightly tentative connotations of the term persisted even among progressive poets.

| I cannot make my way | *ukiyo no naka wa* |
| out of the cruel world. | *ide mo yararezu* |

In bamboo growing	*kuretake no*
in the shade of a mountain:	*hayamagakure no*
moon in a window.	*mado no tsuki*

This link uses *tadakotoba* [of the *maeku*] yet creates an effect of polished beauty. The association is one that no kind of beginner would fail to think of.[113]

As a student of Shōtetsu's (1381-1459), Sōzei was no doubt somewhat sympathetic to Kyōgoku poetics, but his admiration was reserved for more refined rhetoric.

It was not until the Edo-period poet Ozawa Roan (1723-1801) that *tadagotouta* gained another true champion. "To speak of what one is thinking of at the moment, in the language one normally uses, in a way that makes sense—that is what I call *uta*."[114] In his case the approach often translates into rustic scenes, like the following poem (*Rokujō eisō*, no. 595) set in the farmland north of Kyoto.

"Composed when he was visiting Ono with a friend and came upon peasant women carrying firewood on the mountain path near Jakkōin"

She's just like me,	waga goto ya
all grown old and tired out—	oite tsukareshi
this peasant woman	shizugame no
going home late down the path	okurete kaeru
in the mountains of Ono.	ono no yamamichi

Roan began his career studying under a master of the noble Reizei house, but poems like this one so offended his teachers that he was later excommunicated.

taketakakiyō 長高様. *Waka*, *renga*, and *haikai*. The lofty, grand, or dignified style. Often the term is used in reference to poems that show grand vistas, usually accompanied by elevated rhetoric, dignified subject matter, and simple, somewhat archaic diction and phrasing. The following two poems are obvious examples. The first (*Gyokuyōshū*, no. 701) is by Princess Shikishi (1149-1201) and the second (*Kinkaishū*, no. 34) by Minamoto no Sanetomo (1192-1219).

"From a hundred-poem sequence"

Where are they going,	izukata e
those wild geese calling out now	kumoi no kari no
in the clouds above?	suginuramu
Far off in the western sky	tsuki wa nishi ni zo
the moon is going down.	katabukinikeru

"Written on 'spring moon at an old capital'"

Who is living here,	tare sumite
who gazes out in reverie?	tare nagamuran
At the moon shining	furusato no
on a spring night in Yoshino,	yoshino no miya no
capital in ancient days.	haru no yo no tsuki

The first of these poems presents only imagery: wild geese whose calls take the reader's eyes up to clouds in the heavens, and the moon declining majestically on the far horizon. Sanetomo's poem is more conceptually complex, but it, too, includes the grand image of the moon shining down, this time on the mountain recesses of Yoshino, a place with a long history whose name conjures up events of ancient times.

In *renga*, the term is often used in praise of individual verses, *hokku*, or *tsukeku*, but sometimes it is applied to linking technique that enhances a lofty atmosphere. In the following link (*Tsukubashū*, no. 156) by Kyūzei (1282-1376), for instance, a *maeku* elevated in diction and dramatic in theme elicits an equally lofty *tsukeku*.

"Composed when a hundred-poem sequence was held at the home of the regent"

Contemplating, I realize:	omoeba ima zo
that the end has now come.	kagiri narikeru

Out in the rain,	ame ni chiru
blossoms fall as dusk descends	hana no yūbe no
with mountain winds.	yamaoroshi

Here Kyūzei answers, "What is it that has come to an end?" with the highly traditional image of cherry blossoms in a stormy sky. The link contains time-honored imagery, rain, blossoms, evening, mountains, wind, and the phrasing of the verse is smooth and elegant. The link was regarded as an example of *taketakashi* by Asayama Bontō (b. 1349)[115] and praised in a somewhat later treatise of unknown authorship as also displaying both mystery and depth (*yūgen*) and overtones (*yojō*),[116] another indication that such terms were not mutually exclusive.

In his evaluation of the following *hokku* by his disciple Takarai Kikaku (1661-1707) Matsuo Bashō (1644-1694) uses the word *taketakashi*:

Haze fades	kasumi kiete
and Fuji stands naked—	fuji o hadaka ni
fleshy with snow.	yuki koetari

Looks like the first verse for an anthology, expansive and lofty. It is a scene of early spring, not hazy, and the way Fuji appears right before one's eyes [*ari no mama*], " fleshy with snow," is novel indeed.[117]

The words "naked" and "fleshy" mark Kikaku's verse as *haikai*, but still the poem presents a grand vista that he feels worthy of the term *taketakashi*. Decades later Takai Kitō (1741-1789) goes a step further in describing a *hokku* by Itō Shintoku (1633-1698) as both *yūgen* and *taketakashi*.

Thin cloud cover—	usukumori
and beneath, fine groves	kedakaki hana no
of cherry trees.[118]	hayashi kana

ushintei 有心躰; *kokoro aru tei* 心有る躰. *Waka*, *renga*, and *haikai*. The style of deep feeling, refined feeling, sincerity. A quality of refined emotional power that according to medieval texts attributed to Fujiwara no Teika (1162-1241) was felt necessary in all properly courtly poems (*Maigetsushō*, p. 128). The term does not appear in the judgments to poem contests or commentaries as often as *aware*, *okashi*, or *yū*, but that may be because it was a quality that was assumed and not often singled out.

Tonna (1289-1372) says that the Nijō school deems the following poem (*Gosenshū*, no. 1240) by Archbishop Henjō (816-890) the very model of *ushin*.[119]

"Written when he had first shaved his head as a priest"

Surely my mother	tarachine wa
did not imagine me thus—	kakare tote shimo
when she drew me near	mubatama no
to stroke my hair as a boy,	waga kurokami o
my tresses of jet-black.	nadezu ya ariken

Taking the tonsure and giving up on worldly ties and ambitions was innately a somber act, but rather than depicting the event directly Henjō approaches the subject by conjuring up the nostalgic image of his mother stroking his hair as a boy, thus adding a sort of narrative depth to the scene and a strong sense of nostalgia. This kind of subtlety or restraint is a constitutive element of the "refined feeling" implied by the term *ushin*.

Tonna emphasizes that same quality of emotion arising from reflection in one of our longest definitions of the term: "One should take care in understanding the style of deep feeling. People in recent times take something of arresting style that is exciting and skillfully done as the style of deep feeling. But that is incorrect. Thinking carefully about things—whether it be the feelings we have about the wind, clouds, grasses, and trees or the rise and fall of fortunes in the world of human affairs—that is what I would call the style of deep feeling."[120]

A poem by Emperor Go-Murakami (1339-1368) provides another example, this one in which the poem itself expresses deep feeling while at the same time claiming the capacity for refined feeling in its speaker (*Shin'yōshū*, no. 1141).

"Topic unknown"

By a cock's crow	*tori no ne ni*
I am roused from my sleep,	*odorokasarete*
and in the quiet	*akatsuki no*
I lie awake as dawn comes—	*nezame shizuka ni*
thinking about the world.	*yo o omou kana*

Once again, in *renga*, the highest praise goes to links that display the ideal, especially in the writings of Sōgi (1421-1502) and his disciples. Sōgi identifies one such example (*Chikurinshō*, no. 206) by Nōa (1397-1471) and adds a few words of analysis:

One so familiar, yet now gone—	*narenishi hito mo*
into the world of dreams.	*yume no yo no naka*

Mountain blossoms.	*yamazakura*
And then only green leaves	*kyō no aoba o*
to gaze on alone.	*hitori mite*

Here the sense of the link is that as one gazes out on nothing but green leaves on branches far back in the hills—that is, after the cherry blossoms have all scattered from the trees in full bloom one had gotten so used to—one sees that those who grew accustomed to the blossoms are in that same world of dreams. The idea is one of overwhelmingly deep feeling, expressed in diction that is also extraordinary. This is the kind of verse one should savor.[121]

Sōgi himself aimed at achieving the effect of *ushin* in all his work. Early in his career, in a letter to a disciple, he went so far as to record one of his own works (*Wasuregusa*, nos. 1621-22) as an example of what he meant by the term.[122]

| The pathway dwindles away | michi kasuka naru |
| by an old temple in Saga. | saga no furudera |

Perhaps he thinks:	kaeru na to
"You living in the cruel world—	ukiyo ya hito o
you'd best not return."	omouran

The "refined feeling" in this link is attributed by the speaker of the *tsukeku* to a hermit living in Saga whose resolution is strong enough to allow the path to his hut to dwindle away in order to discourage visitors—or at least, that is what the speaker guesses. The way the statement is offered as a surmise softens it and results in a note of subtlety.

As late as 1786, the *haikai* master Takai Kitō (1741-1789) uses *ushin* to describe the following link by himself and Miura Chora (1729-1780):

Briefly I stop,	tatazumeba
and more snow comes down	nao furu yuki no
on the night road.	yomichi kana

| Coming up behind— | waga ato e kuru |
| people, their voices cold. | hito no koesabu |

This *hokku* presents a scene that focuses only on the snow piling up on a night road. Truly, if you get tired and stop walking and just stand for a moment, you do feel like the snow starts falling harder and you mustn't stop, and so you instinctively start moving on.... As for the second verse, it presents a deep feeling: you are walking or standing on a night of heavy snow and think that you are the only one out, but then there is someone behind you, and you hear a cold-sounding voice saying, "Damn this snow!"[123]

The comment makes it clear that in this context *ushin* refers to the suggestion of human feeling implied by *koesabu*, "cold-sounding voices." It is a *kokorozuke*, relying not on verbal associations but responding masterfully to the feeling of the previous verse in a way that seems so natural that the verses quickly seem to literally belong together.

yariku やり句. A "kind" verse. A verse designed to move a *renga* sequence in a different direction. Nijō Yoshimoto (1320-1388) says the term applies not only to verses that "open" a sequence when it seems "stuck"[124] but also to verses that shift to a distant or "open" perspective or "cast one's thoughts into the distance," and Sōgi (1421-1502) uses the term in reference to a link that moves from one category into another—"kindly shifting" from "seasonal links" to "love."[125]

The following example comes from a solo sequence by Inawashiro Kenzai (1452-1510) in which the previous three verses (including the *maeku* given here) all offer spring scenes, employing such images as the bush warbler, blossoms, a spring morning, and the New Year. Kenzai creates a simple verse without any natural imagery at all, creating a pivot to move forward in the sequence into new possibilities:

Out in the world, too,	yo no naka mo
all pass from the ending year	mina aratama no
to one sparkling new.	toshi koete
Once again, I grow older—	nao furimasaru
and what else am I to do?[126]	mi o ika ni sen

Here Kenzai does little more than expand the scene, expressing a very ordinary sentiment: no figurative language, no reasoning, no high diction. He alludes to a *Kokinshū* poem (no. 28)—a frequent strategy in the case of *yariku*—but merely repeats it, rather than engaging with it.

Springtime arrives,	momochidori
with its scores of little birds	saezuru haru wa
chirping out their songs	monogoto ni
and renewal all around—	aratamaredomo
except here, where I grow old.	ware zo furiyuku

In some articulations, *yariku* seems to mean "simple" or even "offhand," while it is sometimes used synonymously with *jirenga*, or "background verses" (see *Yashima Shōrin'an naniki hyakuin*, p. 205). This same kind of thinking is apparent in a quote from the *haikai* poet Uejima Onitsura (1661-1738):

In the *za*, at a time when one or two clever links have been created, most people will put some extra effort into the next link, hoping to produce something even better; only the rare person will nonchalantly produce a *yariku*. If everyone is struggling to create a fine verse, it becomes less likely that a fine verse will be produced. In the wake of a straightforward verse—that is when another fine verse will appear. Contributing a *yariku* at the right moment is something beyond the abilities of the inexperienced.[127]

Whether in *renga* or *haikai*, the *za* remains a social space in which all participants are expected to think of the group—and the text it will produce—before themselves.

yasashi やさし. *Waka*, *renga*, and *haikai*. Gentle, graceful; often paired with *en* (charming, lovely) and *aware* (moving). Retired Emperor Go-Toba (1180-1239) alludes to the following poem (*Shin kokinshū*, no. 1303) by Gishūmon'in no Tango (dates unknown), who "wrote many graceful poems."[128]

"Composed on 'love: meeting, then not meeting,' for a poem contest held in the Third Month of 1201"

"I will not forget"—	*wasureji no*
so you said, but what has become	*koto no ha ika ni*
of the words you spoke?	*narinikemu*
The dusk I waited for came—	*tanomeshi kure wa*
bringing only autumn wind.	*akikaze zo fuku*

Here the "gentle" quality comes from the restrained rhetoric and the tonal delicacy of the final line.

Yasashi appears in *renga* commentaries as well. Shinkei (1406-1475) uses it in one of his essays in reference to a link without known authorship.

Blossoms scatter	*sakura chiri*
and colored leaves fall and rot	*momiji kutsuru*
in a mountain village.	*yamazato ni*

| All alone, as daylight ends— | *hitori kureyuku* |
| blasts of withering wind. | *kogarashi no kaze* |

The way this link is done is graceful. Nothing links back to blossoms or colored leaves, but in the end the verses are well linked.[129]

In this case, the *maeku* presents two important images, cherry blossoms and colored leaves. Rather than linking to either or both of them more specifically, however, the poet uses a winter image that smoothly moves on from spring and autumn into dusky winter. Thus we end up with three images, all of ancient origin in the courtly tradition, presented in a simple, delicate conception based on the simple progress of time.

In his judgment of a *hokku* contest, Matsuo Bashō (1644-1694) says of the following poem by Takarai Kikaku (1661-1707), "The blossoms far off in the fields in Meguro—very *yasashi*. The idea of having already seen the blossoms at Ueno and Yanaka is apparent outside the words of the poem."[130]

Searching blossoms.	*sakuragari*
Today let's get a guide—	*kyō wa meguro no*
to Meguro.	*shirube seyo*

Here the meaning of *yasashi* seems closer to "elegance" or even "gentility," perhaps. The point is that whoever is the subject of the poem is someone who truly enjoys the beauty of the cherry blossoms, enough to go away from the groves in the heart of Edo.

yasetaru tei やせたる躰. *Waka*, *renga*, and *haikai*. The spare, sere, or desolate style. In one of the few documents we have that show an attempt to compose poems that explicitly embody prescribed aesthetic qualities, Retired Emperor Go-Toba (1180-1239) used the term *hosoku karabitaru*, "spare and withered," a synonym for what later was referred to as *yase* or *yasetaru tei*. This poem (*Santai waka*, no. 16) by Fujiwara no Yoshitsune (1169-1206) is among those composed for Go-Toba's exercise.

In a field of reeds	*ogihara ya*
the autumn wind, late at night,	*yowa ni akikaze*
blows over dewdrops—	*tsuyu fukeba*
jewels unforeseen, falling	*aranu tama chiru*
onto my bedding of straw.	*toko no samushiro*

In late medieval times, in the writings of Shinkei (1406-1476), in particular, the spare style would become important as an influence in the development of his core concept of the aesthetic of "coldness" (*hie*).

yōen 妖艶, *yōenbi* 妖艶美. *Waka*. Ethereal charm. An extension of the ideal of *en* articulated by Fujiwara no Shunzei (1114-1204) usually involving rich imagery and complicated syntax, with little overt emotion. In his *Kindai shūka* (*Superior Poems of Our Time*, 1209), Fujiwara no Teika (1162–1241) says that both *yōen* and *yojō* are lacking in the work of poets of the Kokin era, implying these are more recent development in courtly poetics. In the judgment of an *uta-awase* held in 1232, Teika uses it in reference to a spring poem by Shunzei's Daughter (d. after 1252), singling out the phrase "morning frost."[131]

"On 'haze above a river,' for a poem contest held at Iwashimizu Shrine"

Even more chilly	*hashihime no*
grows morning frost on the sleeves	*sode no asashimo*
of the Bridge Princess;	*nao saete*
and blowing over the haze—	*kasumi fukikosu*
the wind on Uji River.	*Uji no kawakaze*

What goes beyond Shunzei's *en* in this case is a very rich tableau of images combined with the highly romantic associations of an allusion to the first of the so-called Uji chapters of *The Tale of Genji*, which concentrate on the melancholy lives of sister princesses living in that area south of Kyoto. Beyond that, the scene evokes the image of Princess of Uji Bridge, a mythological figure. Teika's focus on the term "morning frost" is no doubt meant to praise the originality of placing so cold an image in the center of a spring poem. The overall effect of the poem is one of profound beauty tinged with antique charm and an air of romantic potential.

The word *yōen* appears seldom in poetic discourse after Teika, who used it only in his final years. Two centuries later, however, Ichijō Kaneyoshi (1402–1481) used it to describe the overall effect and diction of a poem by Emperor Go-Hanazono (1419–1470).

Gazing from afar,	*magaikoshi*
I once mistook for clouds	*kumo no yosome no*
those cherry blossoms—	*hanazakura*
blossoms brought to mind again	*omoi zo izuru*
by white snow on the peaks.[132]	*mine no shirayuki*

Go-Hanazono's short meditation on memory and sensory confusion involves layers of imagery that are mirrored in highly elliptical syntax. In the original poem the phrase *hanazakura* functions as a pivot of sorts, at the same time ending the first three lines and then beginning the last three—"seen-from-afar cherry blossoms" and "cherry blossoms that are called to mind again [by] white snow on the peaks."

Whereas many other terms from the *waka* tradition—*aware*, *omoshiroshi*, *taketakashi*, and *yūgen*, for instance—appear frequently in *renga* and *haikai* discourse, appearances of *yōen*, again, are rare.

yojō or *yosei* 余情; *kokoro no amari* 心の余. *Waka*, *renga*, and *haikai*. Overtones, overflowing feeling, reverberations. Sometimes identified as a separate style but more often a quality of poems in other styles, especially *yūgen*, *ushin*, and *sabi*. One of the earliest appearances of the term is *Waka kuhon* (post-1009) by Fujiwara no Kiyosuke (1104-1177), where the following anonymous poem (*Kokinshū*, no. 1077) is listed as an example.[133] Kiyosuke does not explain himself, but most scholars argue that the overtones are a product of the way the poem presents the imagined, as opposed to immediately witnessed, scene of hail falling in the mountains:

Deep in the mountains	miyama ni wa
the hail must be coming down.	arare fururashi
Here in the foothills	toyama naru
autumn colors appear now	masaki no kazura
on the leaves of the vines.	irozukinikeri

Another classic example of a poem replete with overtones is this one by Fujiwara no Teika (1162-1241; *Shūi gusō*, no. 1658) composed in 1198 for a fifty-poem sequence commissioned by Reverend Prince Shukaku (1150-1202). Like many poems associated with *yosei*, this one involves an allusion:

Alone, I hear	hitori kiku
raindrops fall on a stairway	munashiki hashi ni
now deserted—	ame ochite
as the path I took coming	waga koshi michi o
is buried by withering winds.	uzumu kogarashi

This poem might also be analyzed as an example of *sabi*, but the "deserted stairway" inevitably suggests depths not revealed, and also constitutes an allusion to the following evocative lines by the late-Tang-dynasty poet Zhang Du from *Wakan rōeishū* (no. 307) on the topic of falling leaves:

In autumn's third month, how long the palace water clock drones on!
Raindrops fall on the deserted stairway.

How will my home garden fare, ten thousand leagues away?
Leaves lie deep outside my window.

That the Chinese poem is incomplete and known only in fragments perhaps adds to the sense of overtones.

Medieval poets used this term from the *waka* tradition in several ways. Nijō Yoshimoto (1320-1388) defines the term as, "Leaving something unsaid, thus creating something of interest because of its overtones."[134] And the sense of the term by Imagawa Ryōshun (1326-1420) in reference to the following highly atmospheric link created by Kyūzei (1282-1376) is clearly synonymous with earlier usages:

The night must be growing late— no one is making a sound.	*yo ya fukenuran hitooto mo sezu*
In hazy moonlight, in the tidelands of a bay— a moored boat.[135]	*tsuki kasumu shiohi no ura tomaribune*

Why is the person up so late in the night? Is he—or she—waiting for someone? And does the boat signify a visitor? The link is thus based on enhancing a mood latent in the *maeku*, creating suggestions of meaning and emotion of the sort encountered in poems of the *Shin kokin* era.

At other times, however, commentators use the word "overtones" to refer to a poem that *itself* seems to function as a reverberation or aesthetic extension of a famous *waka*, a variety, in other words, of allusive variation. A link (*Kochiku*, nos. 441-42) by Tani Sōboku (d. 1545) illustrates the method.

Outside my hut door even the sun pales in thin mist— the mountains lonely.	*kusa no to ni hi mo usukiri no yama sabishi*
Far away, I see someone on a rope bridge, on a peak.	*ochikatabito o mine no kakehashi*

Here the *maeku* does not contain any allusion of itself, but in the last line—"the mountains lonely"—the author saw an opportunity to evoke a famous travel scene by Fujiwara no Teika (1162-1241; *Shin kokinshū*, no. 953).

"Written as a 'travel' poem"

With autumn wind	tabibito no
blowing back the flowing sleeves	sode fukikaesu
of a traveler,	akikaze ni
how lonely in evening light	yūbe sabishiki
is the bridge up on the peak!	yama no kakehashi

In Teika's poem, the vantage point of the speaker is not clear: it could be taken as third-person description from a distance, or something more immediate, a narrative close-up of what is going through the mind of the traveler as he crosses a plank bridge over a perilous gorge. In Sōboku's verse, however, the vantage point is clarified: a man stepping out the door of his lonely mountain hut looks up through pale mist to spy someone far away crossing a bridge, as Teika's traveler did. Thus a sort of potential latent in Teika's scene, one of its overtones, is realized in a *renga* link.

Matsuo Bashō (1644-1694) used the word in reference to poems that used allusion or finely inflected ambiguity to suggest things beyond the surface. Mukai Kyorai (1651-1704) quotes him as saying that a *hokku* "should not say everything,"[136] following the example of Shōtetsu, who wrote virtually the same thing: "The best poems are those that leave something unsaid."[137] Furthermore, Bashō's penchant for linking by "scent" (*nioizuke*) may also be closely correlated to the rhetorical creation of overtones. The *haikai* poet Kagami Shikō (1665-1731) makes the identification explicit: "*Yojō* is a term used in *waka*; in *haikai*, we use the words *hibiki* [echo] and *nioi* [scent]."[138]

Writing at the beginning of the nineteenth century, the Nationalist scholar Ishiwara Masaakira (d. 1821) is still using the term *yojō*, citing as an example a poem from *Shin kokinshū* (no. 1666) by Kojijū (fl. ca. 1160-1180) that describes a nun at her morning devotions, picking anise to place on her altar:

Wet now from dew	shikimi tsumu
on anise I picked at riverside	yamagawa no tsuyu ni
in the mountains:	nurenikeri
such are my ink-black sleeves	akatsukioki no
when I arise at dawn.	sumizome no sode

His explanation is that the phrase "arise at dawn" (*akatsukioki no*) "makes one think of tears shed on the speaker's sleeves when she parted from a man in her younger days."[139]

yoriaizuke 寄合付. *Renga* and *haikai*. Linking by associations—i. e., by established connections between words, images, or ideas, as an example (*Chikurinshō*, no. 105) by Ninagawa Chiun (d. 1448) demonstrates.

| Gradually engulfed by haze: | *kasumikometaru* |
| forest groves, tree after tree. | *kigi no muradachi* |

Headed toward the scent	*minu hana no*
of blossoms not yet in view,	*nioi ni mukau*
I cross the mountain.	*yama koete*

First and most obviously, the season is spring and involves the two paramount indexes of the season: haze in the first verse complemented by blossoms in the second. Furthermore, the verses are linked by the semantic associations between "engulfed by haze" and flowers "not yet in view," as well as "forest groves" and "mountain." As Inawashiro Kenzai (1452–1510) says in *Keikandō* (p. 124), being able to link verse to verse in this way was the most fundamental requirement of participation in *renga* composition. Needless to say, this required education in the canons of Japanese poetry.

yū 優, *yūbi* 優美. *Waka*, *renga*, and *haikai*. Polished, highly refined, and elegant; related to *fūryū*. One of the most frequently encountered terms in both judgments and commentaries; a courtly kind of beauty, usually involving well-established, elegant imagery, polished to a high sheen, and implying the activity of a highly refined and courtly sensibility. Fujiwara no Akisue (1090–1155) applies it to the following poem (no. 24) by Minamoto no Kanemasa (d. 1128?) in the *Naidaijin-ke uta-awase* poem contest in 1119.

"Evening moon"

So meager the light	*yūzukuyo*
from the early evening moon.	*tomoshiki kage o*
Yet how it enchants	*miru hito no*
the heart of one gazing up—	*kokoro wa sora ni*
as if rising into the sky!	*akugarashikeri*

In his judgments on a poem contest, Fujiwara no Shunzei (1114–2004) praises the following poem (*Shin kokinshū*, no. 23) by Fujiwara no Yoshitsune (1169–1206) as "coming across as refined [*yūbi*] in total effect and diction."[140]

"Lingering cold"

In the sky above,	sora wa nao
haze has yet to appear	kasumi mo yarazu
and the wind is cold;	kaze saete
it has the feel of coming snow—	yuki ge ni kumoru
a moonlit night, in spring.	haru no yo no tsuki

Rather than simple description, Yoshitsune offers a sort of aesthetic reveling in a natural scene as mediated by courtly traditions—sky, haze, wind, snow, moonlight, all modulated by the seasonal context of spring.

The word *yūbi*, "refined beauty," is a synonym of *yū*. Sōchō (1448-1532) uses it to praise a link by Sōgi (1421-1502).

My feelings go deep	kokoro fukaki mo
yet are shallow after all.	asaku koso nare
Deep in the mountains	okuyama ni
I find cherry trees in bloom—	ireba hana saki
and people living there.[141]	hito sumite

In this case the speaker of the *maeku* is not clearly defined, but the link makes him into "a person of feeling" who cannot escape his own gentility. Sōchō says, "The effect of the link is to create a scene right before our eyes; furthermore, it is a peerless example of *yūbi*."[142] The speaker's heart was committed to leaving the world behind, but when he confronts the beauty of blossoms and people living near the cherry groves, he realizes that his resolve was shallow after all.

A usage of *yū* by Takahashi Riichi (d. 1783), in reference to a *hokku* by Matsuo Bashō (1644-1694), tells us something about how the ideal was often inflected in *haikai* discourse. The *hokku* was composed on a journey in 1684, well known because it appeared in his travel record *Nozarashi kikō* (Record of bones bleaching in the fields, 1685, p. 285):

At roadside	michi no be no
a rose mallow flower—	mukuge no uma ni
eaten by my horse.	kuwarekeri

Riichi adds that this *hokku* has the touch of humor (*okashimi*) proper to *haikai*, but then says that Bashō "softens" (*yawaragu*) and adds refinement (*yū*) to the poem by means of its articulation (*tsukuri*).¹⁴³ Frustratingly, he doesn't explain himself, but most likely he means that the way Bashō presents it, there is something elegant in the scene, something that draws attention to what is a common autumn flower first of all, only then introducing a nonchalant horse. One can even say that it represents a small epiphany in which the poet gains more appreciation for the fragile beauty of the rose mallow as he sees it disappear.

yūgen 幽玄. *Waka*, *renga*, and *haikai*. Mystery and depth, profound feeling or meaning. This term of praise, which poets borrowed from Buddhist texts, involves a type of beauty that has about it something of the mysterious or ineffable. The term was given one of its most elegant definitions early on, in an essay by Kamo no Chōmei (1155-1216):

> When it comes to the *yūgen* style ... the essence of it is overflowing feeling [*yojō*] that appears outside the words of the poem, scenery that is there but not overtly present in the poem's conception. If one's idea is of deep significance and one's words have attained the heights of elegance, then excellence will have been achieved as a matter of course. The sight of the sky on an autumn evening has no color and no voice; yet without realizing why, the tears well up in one's eyes ... Through the mist one gets only glimpses of autumn mountains, but, ah, how enchanting, how alluring are the colored leaves as they appear in the mind—surely superior to what one would see with one's eyes. What challenge is there in stating one's idea overtly, praising the moonlight as "shining into every corner," or blossoms as "glorious."¹⁴⁴

Fujiwara no Shunzei (1114-1204) also used the term, albeit sparingly; and so did his son, Fujiwara no Teika (1162-1241), the latter in reference to a poem (*Shin kokinshū*, no. 533) by Minamoto no Toshiyori (1055-1129) that he praised as "ineffably beautiful, with images faintly hovering in the background and a most lonely atmosphere."¹⁴⁵

In my home village	*furusato wa*
all is buried by leaves fallen	*chiru momijiba ni*
at autumn's end;	*uzumorete*
in memory fern on my eaves	*noki no shinobu ni*
the autumn wind is blowing.	*akikaze zo fuku*

No doubt it is the idea of someone listening to the wind blowing at autumn's end that elicited the term "lonely" (*sabishiki*) from Teika. His use of *yūgen*, however, is inspired by the word *shinobu*, or memory fern, which grows on eaves not well tended, so suggesting passage of time. And the word *shinobu* can also mean to yearn for, to remember, or to conceal, adding to the sense of deep feeling hinted at but not fully expressed.

Yūgen persisted as an ideal into the late medieval era, in *waka* and in *renga* (and in Noh drama), in virtually all factions. Kōun (d. 1429), for instance, praises the following poem (*Shoku goshūishū*, no. 192) composed for a screen painting by the conservative figure Nijō Tameyo (1250-1338) as having all the qualities of the true style of the highest level of *yūgen*.[146] It is a deceptively simple poem on the surface—until one connects it to an earlier work by Murasaki Shikibu (precise dates unknown; *Shin kokinshū*, no. 191), quoted here immediately after Tameyo's poem.

Once and once only	*hototogisu*
a *hototogisu* called	*hitokoe nakite*
in Kataoka Grove—	*kataoka no*
passing by just this moment	*mori no kozue o*
up in the tops of the trees.	*ima zo sugunaru*

Once at dawn, when she was in seclusion at Kamo, someone said, "I wish a cuckoo would call"; she looked up and saw the beauty of the treetops in Kataoka Grove.

While I wait here	*hototogisu*
for the voice of the cuckoo	*koe matsu hodo wa*
in Kataoka Grove,	*kataoka no*
I may well be drenched	*mori no shizuku ni*
by dews falling from above.	*tachi ya nuremashi*

The "ineffable depth" Kōun sees in Tameyo's poem derives from the way the cuckoo reminds the reader of how people in the same place three hundred years before had made a wish that is realized—in the imagination, of course—only today, and only once. Also involved is the fact that Tameyo's poem was composed for a "putting on the train ceremony" (a rite signifying attainment of adult standing for women) for a princess (Senseimon'in, 1315-1362), which made the allusion to court culture of the distant pass astute and appropriate. The multiple mediations are part of the effect.

The other poet closely associated with *yūgen* is Shōtetsu (1381-1459), who invoked it in describing the following poem—one of his own (*Sōkonshū*, no. 3098). Obviously he meant it less as praise than as analysis, and it cannot be by chance that his brief words of exegesis hark back to Chōmei in a circular fashion.

Flowers bloomed and fell	sakeba chiru
in the space of just one night,	yo no ma no hana no
as if in a dream—	yume no uchi ni
leaving no confusion now	yagate magirenu
about white clouds on the peaks.	mine no shirakumo

This is a poem in the style of *yūgen*. Mystery and depth is something that is in the heart but unexpressed in words. The moon veiled in thin clouds, or the bright foliage on the mountains concealed in autumn mists—such poetic conceptions are regarded as having the effect of mystery and depth. But if one asks in which particular feature the mystery and depth is to be found, it is difficult to specify exactly.[147]

In *renga* discourse, *yūgen* is applied less frequently than, say, *omoshiroshi*, or even *en*, and it is used more often by men who were not just *renga* poets but also *waka* poets, such as Shinkei (1406-1475) and Sanjōnishi Sanetaka (1455-1537). Yet Sōgi (1421-1502) still mentions it as part of his recipe for poetry, along with *taketakashi* and *ushin*; and it remained an important ideal.[148] It usually implies a beautiful natural setting, themes of loss and separation, understated rhetoric, and a hint of courtly culture and values. Shinkei singles out a link (*Zoku Sōanshū*, no. 653) by Tonna (1289-1372) as an excellent example.[149]

All but deserted—	furusato to
yet still in the old village	naru made hito no
people live on.	nao sumite

| Wind blowing in the reeds | ogi fuku kaze ni |
| and someone beating a robe. | koromo utsu nari |

The word *furusato* has a range of meanings, from old capital (there were many such places in the areas around Nara and Kyoto that had been capitals long ago), to hometown, to, literally, an "aging village." The first verse does not commit itself—it could be an abandoned capital, but it could just as well be a village abandoned for some other reason. Already the scene is replete with visions of an imagined past, but all the verse tells us is that—inexplicably—people persist in living there. Rather than providing an explanation, Tonna adds to the sense of mystery by introducing a woman beating a robe on a fulling block somewhere in the distance. Who she might be, why she might be living there, whether she is alone or not—these are questions that he does not answer, producing a sense of mystery and a depth of feeling that are the essence of *yūgen*.

Matsuo Bashō (1644-1694) uses the word *yūgen* frequently in his contest judgments, and in a statement quoted by Morikawa Kyoriku (1656-1715) makes it clear that *yūgen* still functioned as a positive value in the world of *haikai*. "In composing *hokku* one should adhere to the orthodox style. Take what you see and hear, and make a verse from that. You should communicate feeling through *yūgen* expressed in loneliness and delicacy [*yūgen no sabihosomi miekakete*]."[150]

NOTES

INTRODUCTION

1. The statement appears in a 1928 letter to Seymour Adelman of Trinity College. *The Letters of A. E. Housman*, ed. Archie Burnett (Oxford: Clarendon Press, 2007), 68.
2. *Shōtetsu monogatari*, 202. Here and elsewhere throughout this book Japanese sources are cited in abbreviated form. Full bibliographic information is available in "Sources of Japanese Texts" in the back matter.
3. I should note that I have not changed *waka* to *uta* in long-established compounds such as *uta-awase* (poem contest), *sakimori no uta* (songs by guardians of the capes), etc., nor have I altered quotations in which the term *uta* rather than *waka* is used.
4. Earl Miner, *Introduction to Japanese Court Poetry*, p. 11.

APPENDIX 1: TECHNICAL TERMS

1. *Mumyōshō*, p. 179.
2. *Eiga no ittei*, p. 203.
3. *Shogaku yōshashō*, p. 448.
4. *Shoshinshō*, p. 411.
5. *Eiga no ittei*, p. 201.
6. *Go-Toba no in gokuden*, p. 149.
7. *Shinsen zuinō*, p. 26.
8. *Chōtanshō*, p. 166.
9. *Mumyōshō*, p. 242.
10. *Gojūshichigajō*, p. 203.
11. *Chōtanshō*, p. 166.

APPENDIX 2: AESTHETIC IDEALS AND DEVICES

1. *An Introduction to Japanese Court Poetry*, p. 161.
2. *Sairyūshō*, p. 12.
3. *Gumon kenchū*, p. 148.
4. *Sōgi jisankachū* 57.
5. *Rakusho roken*, p. 106.
6. *Reizeike waka hihikuden*, p. 216.

7. *Kaen rensho kikigaki*, p. 73.
8. *Chōtanshō*, p. 199.
9. *Gendai haiku*, p. 44.
10. *Kochiku* 6.
11. *Kagaku teiyō*, p. 153.
12. *Sangoki*, p. 318.
13. *Teika jittei*, p. 368.
14. *Sōchō hyakuban renga-awase*, p. 50 (round 40).
15. *Kuhyō*, p. 305.
16. *Kuhyō*, p. 305.
17. It appears that the poem attributed to Takasuke here was actually written by Asukai Masatsune (1170-1221).
18. *Shōji ninen jūgatsu tsuitachi uta-awase*.
19. *Kōun kuden*, p. 48.
20. *Shirin shūyō*, p. 83.
21. *Shin zōdanshū*, pp. 404-15.
22. *Haikai sabishiori*, p. 351.
23. *Yahantei tsukinami hokku awase*, p. 458.
24. *Go-Toba no in gokuden*, p. 145.
25. *Roppyaku-ban uta-awase*, round 312.
26. *Hitorigoto*, p. 61.
27. *Tsuginohara*, p. 466.
28. *Tsukuba mondō*, pp. 81-82.
29. *Sanzōshi*, p. 524.
30. *Oi no kobumi*, p. 311.
31. *Ari no mama*, p. 154.
32. See *Tōyashū kikigaki*, p. 84. See also *Shogaku yōshashō*, p. 452.
33. *Saigyō shōnin danshō*, p. 408.
34. See, for instance, *Hyakunin isshu ōeishō* (no. 86), the first of the medieval commentaries on *hyakunin isshu*, by Fujiwara Mitsumoto.
35. *Go-Toba no in gokuden*, p. 145; Shunzei, *Mimosusogawa uta-awase*, round 7.
36. *Kanshō hyakushū* 77.
37. *Kanshō hyakushū* 56.
38. *Hitorigoto*, p. 61.
39. *Renga entokushō*, p. 102.
40. *Hitorigoto*, p. 61.
41. *Shogaku yōshashō*, p. 445.
42. *Chōtanshō*, p. 187.
43. *Shihōshō*, p. 233.
44. *Jūhachi-ban hokku-awase* 10.
45. *Jūhachi-ban hokku-awase* 10.
46. *Gekimōshō*, p. 69. The link is attributed to Kyūzei.
47. *Kyoraishō*, p. 514.
48. *Seibyō senku chū*, p. 234.
49. *Renga shotai hidenshō*, pp. 461-62.
50. *Eiga no ittei*, p. 207.
51. *Chōtanshō*, pp. 177-78.
52. *Gumon kenchū*, p. 154.

53. *Uda no hōshi*, pp. 608–9.
54. *Betsuzashikijo*, p. 125.
55. See *Chikubun*, p. 271.
56. *Kyoraishō*, p. 507.
57. *Hatsukaishi hyōchū*, pp. 474–75.
58. *Guhishō*, p. 293.
59. *Gukenshō*, p. 356.
60. *Mumyōshō*, p. 243.
61. *Hana no magaki*, p. 99.
62. *Renri hishō*, p. 40.
63. *Shoshin kyūeishū*, p. 85.
64. *Ōtabon Shunmusōchū* 52.
65. *Aki no yo hyōgo*, p. 477.
66. *Uda no hōshi*, p. 614.
67. *Aki no yo hyōgo*, p. 477.
68. *Hekirenshō*, p. 38.
69. *Yodo no watari*, p. 285.
70. *Hatsukaishi hyōchū*, p. 474.
71. *Keikandō*, p. 134.
72. *Oi no kurigoto*, p. 381.
73. *Seiashō*, p. 310.
74. *Tamekane-kyō wakashō*, pp. 160–61.
75. *Hitorigoto*, p. 96.
76. Preface to *Takasunagoshū* (1692).
77. *Shūi gusō shōshutsu kikigaki*, p. 75.
78. See *Shūi gusō shōshutsu kikigaki*, p. 162.
79. *Teika jittei*, p. 372.
80. *Makura no sōshi*, p. 3.
81. *Hana no magaki*, p. 99.
82. *Eiga no ittei*, p. 204.
83. Itō Kei, modern editor of the text, uses the word *heimei* to describe the poem.
84. *Sanzōshi*, p. 580.
85. *Sanzōshi*, p. 586.
86. *Kunizane-kyō no ie no uta-awase*, round 13.
87. *Hirota no yashiro uta-awase* 173.
88. *Kuhyō*, p. 299.
89. *Kōun kuden*, p. 58.
90. Quoted in *Rakusho roken*, p. 107.
91. *Chikubun* 634, p. 208. Most likely the author is Kenzai.
92. *Mimosusogawa uta-awase* 40.
93. *Hirota no yashiro no uta-awase* 142.
94. *Seibyō senku chū*, p. 296. The comments are generally regarded as close to Kenzai's own.
95. *Seibyō senku chū*, p. 296. Poem no. 43 in ninth *hyakuin*.
96. *Keikandō*, p. 136.
97. *Kyoraishō*, p. 513.
98. *Haikai sabishiori*, p. 360.
99. *Dassai shooku haiku jō shō*, p. 23.
100. *Guhishō*, p. 298.

276 NOTES TO APPENDIX 2

101. *Kaen rensho kikigaki*, p. 112. Authorship is attributed to either Rokujō Arifusa (1251–1319) or some other Nijō partisan.
102. *Sangoki*, p. 351. See also Imagawa Ryoshun's *Rakusho roken*, pp. 95–97.
103. *Sasamegoto*, p. 123.
104. In *Sasamegoto* (p. 121) he quotes a text spuriously attributed to Teika in support of his position.
105. *Chōrokubumi*, pp. 83–84, and *Shinonome*, p. 317.
106. *Renga entokushō*, p. 89.
107. See kokorozuke in this appendix. *Oi no kurigoto*, p. 381.
108. *Kyoraishō*, p. 507.
109. *Uda no hōshi*, p. 617; *Sasamegoto*, p. 68.
110. *Kyoraishō*, p. 514.
111. *Mumyōshō*, p. 245.
112. *Kaen rensho kikigaki*, p. 117.
113. *Hana no magaki*, p. 93.
114. *Furu no nakamichi*, p. 46.
115. *Shoshin kyūeishū*, p. 60.
116. *Renga shotai hidenshō*, p. 486.
117. *Inaka no ku-awase*, p. 456.
118. *Shin zōdanshū*, p. 412.
119. *Seiashō*, p. 215.
120. *Seiashō*, p. 215.
121. *Oi no susami*, p. 115.
122. *Chōrokubumi*, p. 88.
123. *Tsukeai tebikizura*, p. 433.
124. *Chirenshō*, p. 121.
125. *Yodo no watari*, pp. 283–84.
126. *Seibyō senku chū*, p. 265.
127. *Hitorigoto*, p. 23.
128. *Go-Toba no in gokuden*, p. 147.
129. *Shinkei hōin teikin*, p. 393.
130. *Inaka no ku-awase*, p. 457.
131. *Iwashimizu wakamiya no uta-awase* 2.
132. *Hōtoku ninen jūichigatsu sentō uta-awase*, round 32, p. 281.
133. *Waka kuhon*, p. 32.
134. *Hekirenshō*, p. 39.
135. *Rakusho roken*, p. 98.
136. *Kyoraishō*, p. 437.
137. *Shōtetsu monogatari*, p. 172.
138. *Jūronibenshō*, p. 241.
139. *Nennen zuihitsu*, p. 364. Masaakira misquotes the second line, which should be "on anise picked by a mountain path" (*yamaji no tsuyu ni*).
140. *Roppyaku-ban uta-awase* 23.
141. *Shitakusachū* 7 and 8.
142. *Shitakusachū* 7 and 8.
143. *Moto no shimizu*, p. 126.
144. *Mumyōshō*, pp. 242–43.
145. *Kindai shūka*, p. 43.
146. *Kōun kuden*, p. 60.

147. *Shōtetsu monogatari*, p. 224.
148. *Azuma mondō*, p. 226.
149. *Sasamegoto*, p. 111.
150. *Biwaen zuihitsu*, p. 76.

SOURCES OF JAPANESE TEXTS

Place of publication is Tokyo unless otherwise noted.

ABBREVIATIONS

CKS	*Chūsei karonshū*, ed. Hisamatsu Sen'ichi. Iwanami Bunko, 1985.
IRRS	*Rengaronshū*, ed. Ijichi Tetsuo. 2 vols. Iwanami Bunko, 1985.
KHT	*Koten haibungaku taikei*, ed. Hisamatsu Sen'ichi et al. 16 vols. Shūeisha, 1975.
KKSH	*Karon kagaku shūsei*, ed. Sasaki Takahiro et al. 20 vols. Miyai Shoten, 1999.
KRRS	*Rengaronshū*, ed. Kidō Saizō. 4 vols. Miyai Shoten, 1972-1990.
NKBT	*Nihon koten bungaku taikei*, ed. Takagi Ichinosuke et al. 102 vols. Iwanami Shoten, 1957-1968.
NKBZ	*Nihon koten bungaku zenshū*, ed. Akiyama Ken et al. 51 vols. Shōgakkan, 1970-1976.
NKT	*Nihon kagaku taikei*, ed. Sasaki Nobutsuna and Kyūsojin Hitaku. 10 vols., 5 suppl. vols. Kazama Shobō, 1977-1981.
SKKT	*[Shinpen] Kokkai taikan*, ed. Taniyama Shigeru et al. 10 vols. 1983-1992.
SNKBT	*Shin Nihon koten bungaku taikei*, ed. Sasaki Akihiro et al. 106 vols. 1989-2005.
SNKBZ	*Shinpen Nihon koten bungaku zenshū*. 88 vols. Shōgakkan, 1994-2002.
TBT	*Teihon Bashō taisei*, ed. Ogata Tsutomu et al. Sanseidō, 1962.

Akikaze no ki—KHT 14.
Aki no yo hyōgo—TBT.
Ana ureshi—KHT 16.
Arano—SNKBT 70.
Arima ryōgin kochū—Kaneko Kinjirō, ed. *Sōgi meisaku hyakuin chūshaku*. Benseisha, 1985.
Ari no mama—KHT 14.
Asaji—KRRS 2.
Atago hyakuin—Shimazu Tadao, ed. *Shinchō Nihon koten shūsei* 54. Shinchōsha, 1979.
Azuma mondō—NKBT 65.
Bashōmon kojin shinseki—KHT 9.
Betsuzashikijo—excerpted in Komiya Toyotaka et al., eds., *Shin Bashō kōza*, 6. Sanseidō, 1995.
Biwaen zuihitsu—KHT 16.
Buson kushū—NKBT 58.
"Chang hen ge"—Takaki Masaichi, ed. *Chūgoku shijin senshū* 13. Iwanami Shoten, 1972.
Chichi no shūen nikki—NKBT 58.

Chikubun—Yokoyama Shigeru, ed. *Chikurinshō kochū*. Kadokawa Shoten, 1978.
Chikurinshō—SNKBT 49.
Chirenshō—IRRS 1.
Chōrokubumi—SNKBZ 88.
Chōshōshi zenshū—Yoshida Kōichi, ed. *Choshoshi zenshū*. 6 vols. Koten Bunko, 1972–1975.
Chōtanshō—IRRS 1.
Chūka jakuboku shishō—SNKBT 53.
Danrin toppyakuin—SNKBT 69.
Dassai shooku haiku chō shō—Masaoka Shiki. Haishodō, 1902.
Dokuraku gin—SNKBT 93.
Eiga no ittei—CKS.
Eiga taigai—CKS.
Enokoshū—SNKBT 69.
Enpō rokunen Hakusan hyakuin—in Tsurusaki Isō et al., eds., *Hakusan manku, shiryō to kenkyū*. Hirayama Hime Jinja, 1985.
Entokushō—KRRS 4.
Furu no nakamichi—SNKBT 68.
Fushimiin gyoshū—SKKT 7.
Gekimōshō—IRRS 1.
Genji monogatari—NKBZ 12–17.
Gojūshichigajō—KRRS 4.
Gosenshū—SKKT 1.
Goshūishū—SKKT 1.
Go-Toba no in gokuden—NKBT 65.
Guhishō—NKT 4.
Gukenshō—NKT 4.
Guku wakuraba—Kaneko Kinjirō, ed. *Renga kochūshaku shū*. Kadokawa Shoten, 1979.
Gumon kenchū—KKSH 10.
Gyoku sanjin kashū—excerpted in NKBZ 42.
Gyokuyōshū—SKKT 1.
Haikai nishi kasen ato—Ishikawa Shinkō, ed. *Natsume Seibi zenshū*. Izumi Shoin, 1983.
Haikai sabishiori—KHT 14.
Haikai Shirao yawa—excerpted in Shibata Shōkyoku, ed. *Shōmon no hitobito*. Iwanami Bunko, 1986.
Hana no magaki—KRRS 3.
Haru no hi—SNKBT 70.
Hatsukaishi hyōchū—TBT.
Hekirenshō—NKBZ 51.
Hirota no yashiro uta-awase—SKKT 5.
Hisago—SNKBT 70.
Hitorigoto [Onitsura]—Fukumoto Ichirō, ed. *Onitsura no hitorigoto zen'yakuchū*. Kōdansha Gakujutsu Bunko, 1981.
Hitorigoto [Shinkei]—SNKBZ 88.
Hōjōki—SNKBT 39.
Hokkuchō—Morikawa Akira, ed. *Hokkuchō*. Koten Bunko, 1984.
Hokusō sadan—Miuru Osamu, ed. *Nihon zuihitsu zenshū* 4. Kokumin Tosho, 1927.
Honchō ichinin isshu—SNKBT 63.
Hōtoku ninen jūichigatsu sentō uta-awase—SNKBT 47.
Hyakuban renga-awase—Yunoe Sanae, ed. *Hyakuban renga-awase, Kyūzei, Shūa, Shinkei, hyōshaku*. Izumi Shoin, 1990.

Hyakunin isshu ōeishō—see Yoshida Kiwamu. "Honkoku hyakunin isshushohō." *Ōsaka Sangyō Daigaku Sangyō Kenkyujo Shohō* 2 (1978): 16–42.
Ichiyō kashū—NKBT 8.
Inaka no ku-awase—TBT.
Iozakura—excerpted in NKBZ 42.
Iseshū—SKKT 3.
Issa Suikei ryōgin hyakuin—KHT 15.
Iwashimizu wakamiya no uta-awase—SKKT 5.
Izayoi nikki—SNKBT 51.
Jūhachi-ban hokku-awase—TBT.
Juntokuin onhyakushu—SKKT 7.
Jūronibenshō—excerpted in *Basho kōza* 2. Sanseidō, 1956.
Kabekusachū—Kaneko Kinjirō, ed. *Renga kochūshaku shū*. Kadokawa Shoten, 1979.
Kaen rensho kikigaki—KKSH 10.
Kafū haikushū—Katō Ikuya, ed. *Kafū haikushū*. Iwanami Shoten, 2013.
Kagaku teiyō—NKBT 94.
Kagetsu ichiyaron—KHT 14.
Kakanshū—SKKT 6.
Kamo okina kashū—SKKT 9.
Kamuri sen—Tsukamoto Tetsuzō, ed. *Shinsen senryū kyōshi shū*. Yūhōdō, 1923.
Kanginshū—SNKBT 56.
Kanshō hyakushū—SNKBZ 49.
Kanshō yonen gogatsu nijūhachinichi hyakuin—Kyoto Daigaku Kokubungaku Kenkyūshitsu, ed. *Muromachi zenki wakan renku sakuhin shūsei*. Kyoto: Rinsen Shoten, 2008.
Keien isshi—SKKT 9.
Keikandō—KRRS 4.
Kenkō hōshi shū—SNKBT 17.
Kenzai zōdan—KKSH 12.
Kindai shūka—Fukuda Hideichi, Itō Masayoshi, and Shimazu Tadao, eds. *Kanshō Nihon koten bungaku* 24. Kadokawa Shoten, 1976.
Kinkafu—NKBT 3.
Kinkaishū—SKKT 4.
Kirihioke—NKT 4.
Kiyūkyoku—*Tanka kenkyū* 49, no. 4 (April 1992): 28–67.
Kochiku—Kaneko Kinjirō, ed. *Renga kochūshaku shū*. Kadokawa Shoten, 1979.
Kojiki—NKBT 1.
Kokinshū—SKKT 1.
Kokon ikyoku shū—SNKBT 61.
Komo jishi shū—excerpted in NKBZ 41.
Korai fūteishō—NKBZ 50.
Kotojirishū—SKKT 9.
Kōun kuden—KKSH 11.
Kōyō sekiyō sonshashi—SNKBT 66.
Kūgeshū—excerpted in NKBT 89.
Kūgeshū—KHT 16.
Kuhyō—KHT 12.
Kunizane-kyō no ie no uta-awase—SKKT 5.
Kyōgen ōashū—excerpted in Hamada Giichirō and Morikawa Akira, eds., *Kanshō Nihon koten bungaku* 31. Kadokawa Shoten, 1977.

Kyohakushinhyō—Yoshida Kōichi, ed. *Chōshōshi zenshū* 4. Koten Bunko, 1973.
Kyōka godaishū—excerpted in Hamada Giichirō and Morikawa Akira, eds. *Kanshō Nihon koten bungaku* 31. Kadokawa Shoten, 1977.
Kyōka kanshō jiten—Suzuki Tōzō, ed. Kadokawa Shoten, 1984.
Kyoraishō—NKBZ 51.
Kyūshū no michi no ki—SNKBZ 48.
Maigetsushō—NKBT 65.
Makura no sōshi—SNKBT 25.
Man'yōshū—NKBZ 2–5.
Mimosusogawa uta-awase—SKKT 5.
Minasedono koi jūgoshu uta-awase—SKKT 5.
Minishū—SKKT 3.
Moto no shimizu—KHT 14.
Mugi wo wasure—SNKBT 70.
Mumyōshō—KKSH 7.
Mutamagawa—Tsukamoto Tetsuzō, ed. *Shinsen senryū kyōshi shū*. Yūhōdō, 1923.
Nagai hei—Uchida hyakken. Chikuma Shobō, 1991.
Naidaijin-ke uta-awase—SKKT 5.
Nanimichi hyakuin—Yokoyama Shigeru, ed. *Shinkei sakuhin shū*. Kadokawa Shoten, 1978.
Nankai Sensei shibunshū—NKBT 89.
Natsume Sōseki nikki—*Sōseki zenshū* 25. Iwanami Shoten, 1979.
Nennen zuihitsu. Miura Osamu, ed. *Kandenkō hitsu, Nennen zuihitsu, Yūkyō manroku*. Yūhōdō, 1915.
Nihon no chizu—excerpted in Kubota Masabumi, ed. *Gendai meika sen*. Shinchōsha, 1976.
Nihon shoki—NKBT 67.
Nozarashi kikō—NKBZ 41.
Ogura hyakunin isshu—SKKT 5.
Oi nikki—excerpted in NKBZ 41.
Oi no chiri—in Ueno Sachiko, ed. *Ueda Kikusha zenshū*. Izumi Shoin, 2005.
Oi no kobumi—NKBZ 41.
Oi no kurigoto—KRRS 3.
Oi no susami—SNKBZ 88.
Okunshū—Nagasawa Mitsu, ed. *Nyōnin waka taikei* 3. Kazama Shobō, 1978.
Omoidasu koto nado—*Sōseki zenshū* 17. Iwanami Shoten, 1975.
Onitsura haikai hyakusen—Fukumoto Ichirō, ed. *Onitsura no hitorigoto zen'yakuchū*. Kōdansha Gakujutsu Bunko, 1981.
Ōtabon Shunmusōchū. See *Shunmusōchū*.
Rakusho roken—KKSH 11.
Reizei kuden—KKSH 11.
Renga shotai hidenshō—KRRS 2.
Renri hishō—NKBT 66.
Rikashū—SKKT 7.
Rikyū hyakushu—Ayamura Shōko. *Kaite oboeru Rikyū hyakushu*. Tankōsha, 2007.
Rokujō eisō—SKKT 9.
Roppyaku-ban uta-awase—SNKBT 38.
Ryōjin hishō—SNKBT 56.
Ryōkan kashū—Yoshino Hideo, ed. *Ryōkan kashū*. Toyo Bunko, 1992.
Sabi, shiori—KHT 14.
Saigyō shōnin danshō—KKSH 7.
Sairyūshō—*Genji monogatari kochūshaku taisei* 5. Nihon Tosho Sentā, 1978.

Saishōsō—excerpted in *SNKBT* 47.
Sanetaka-kō ki—Takahashi Ryūzō et al., eds. *Sanetaka-kō ki*. 13 vols. Zoku Gunsho Ruijū Kanseikai, 1957-1967.
Sangoki—*NKT* 4.
Sankashū—*SKKT* 3.
Sanseidō Edo senryū benran—Satō Yōjin, ed. Sanseido, 1998.
Santai waka—*SKKT* 5.
San'yō shishō—*SNKBT* 66.
Sanzōshi—*NKBZ* 51.
Sarumino—*SNKBT* 70.
Sasamegoto—*NKBZ* 51.
Seiashō—*KKSH* 10.
Seibi hokku shū—Ishikawa Shinkō, ed. *Natsume Seibi zenshū*. Izumi Shoin, 1983.
Seibyō senku chū—Kaneko Kinjirō. *Renga kochūshaku no kenkyū*. Kadokawa Shoten, 1974.
Seigetsu kushū—Fukumoto Ichirō, ed. *Seigetsu kushū*. Iwanami, 2012.
Seikatsu o utau—excerpted in Kubota Masabumi, ed., *Gendai meika sen*. Shinchōsha, 1976.
Senryū nyūmon—Bitō Sanryū. *Senryū nyūmon: Rekishi to kanshō*. Yūzankaku, 1989.
Senzaishū—*SKKT* 1.
Sharakudō no ki—*NKBZ* 41.
Shibakusa—Yokoyama Shigeru and Noguchi Eiichi, eds. *Shinkeishū ronshū*. Kisshōsha, 1948.
Shichinin tsukeku hanshi—*KRRS* 2.
Shihōshō—*IRRS* 2.
Shikashū—*SKKT* 1.
Shiki zenshū—Kawahigashi Hekigodō, ed. *Masaoka Shiki zenshū*. 22 vols. Kaizōsha, 1929.
Shinkei hōin teikin—*KRRS* 3.
Shin kokinshū—*SKKT* 1.
Shinpen fushōshū-a—*SNKBZ* 86.
Shinpen fushōshū-b—*NKBT* 89.
Shinseki kaishi—*NKBZ* 41.
Shinsen kyōkashū—*SNKBT* 61.
Shinsen Tsukubashū—Kaneko Kinjirō and Yokoyama Shigeru, eds. *Shinsen Tsukubashū: Sanetaka-bon*. Kadokawa Shoten, 1970.
Shinsen zuinō—*NKBT* 65.
Shin'yōshū—*SKKT* 1.
Shin zōdanshū—*KHT* 14.
Shirin shūyō—*KKSH* 15.
Shitakusachū—Kaneko Kinjirō, ed. *Renga kochūshaku shū*. Kadokawa Shoten, 1979.
Shogaku yōshashō—*KRRS* 2.
Shōji ninen jūgatsu tsuitachi uta-awase—*SKKT* 5.
Shōkenkō—*SNKBT* 48.
Shoku gosenshū—*SKKT* 1.
Shokusan hyakushu—Hamada Giichirō, ed. *Ōta Nanpo zenshū* 1. Iwanami Shoten, 1985.
Shōmyōin tsuizen senku—Kaneko Kinjirō. *Renga kochūshaku no kenkyū*. Kadokawa Shoten, 1974.
Shoshin kyūeishū—*KRRS* 3.
Shoshinshō—*KRRS* 2.
Shōtetsu monogatari—*NKBT* 65.
Shōwa shika haiku shi—*Shōwa shika haiku shi, Masaoka Shiki kara Tanikawa Shuntarō made*. Matsui Takaya, ed. Mainichi Shimbunsha, 1978.
Shūchūka—quoted in Masaki Yuko, ed., *Gendai shūku*. Shunjūsha, 2012.

Shūi gusō—SKKT 3.
Shūi gusō shōshutsu kikigaki—Ishikawa Tsunehiko, ed. *Shūi gusō kochū* 2. Miyai Shoten, 1986.
Shūishū—SKKT 1.
Shunmusōchū—Kaneko Kinjirō, ed. *Renga kochūshaku shū*. Kadokawa Shoten, 1979.
Sōanshū—SKKT 4.
Sōchō hyakuban renga-awase—Yamagishi Tokuhei et al., eds. *Katsura no miya bon sōsho* 18. Tenri: Yōtokusha, 1968.
Sōgi jisankachū—in Kurowaka Masataka and Sookyoung Wang, eds., *Jisankachū toshū shūsei*. Ōfūsha, 1987.
Sōgi shūenki—SNKBT 51.
Sōjinbon wakuraba. See *Wakuraba*.
Sōkonshū—*Shikashū taisei* 5. Meiji Shoin, 1974.
Soraishū—NKBT 89.
Sumika o utsusu kotoba—Ishikawa Shinkō, ed. *Natsume Seibi zenshū*. Izumi Shoin, 1983.
Taigi kusen—excerpted in *NKBT* 92.
Taiheiki—NKBT 34-36.
Taikenmon'in Horikawa shū—SKKT 3.
Taikōki—quoted in Watanuki Toyoaki, *Sengoku bushi no uta*. Kasama Shoin, 2011.
Takasunagoshū—Fukumoto Ichirō, ed. *Onitsura no hitorigoto zen'yakuchū*. Kōdansha Gakujutsu Bunko, 1981.
Tamekane-kyō wakashō—NKBT 65.
Taorigiku—KHT 16.
Teijiin uta-awase—SKKT 5.
Teika jittei—NKT 4.
Tokorodokoro hentō—KRRS 3.
Tokuwaka gomanzaishū—excerpted in Hamada Giichirō and Morikawa Akira, eds. *Kanshō Nihon koten bungaku* 31. Kadokawa Shoten, 1977.
Tonna hōshi ei—SNKBT 47.
Tōyashū kikigaki—NKT 5.
Tsuginohara—TBT.
Tsukeai tebikizura—KHT 14.
Tsukuba mondō—NKBT 66.
Tsukubashū—Fukui Kyūzō, ed. *Tsukubashū*. In *Nihon koten zensho*, 81-82. Asahi Shimbunsha, 1948-1951.
Uda no hōshi—KHT 10.
Unaimatsu—Yoshida Kōichi, ed. *Chōshōshi zenshū* 2. Koten Bunko, 1972.
Uta nikki—*Mori Ōgai shū* 1, *Nihon kindai bungaku taikei* 11. Kadokawa Shoten, 1974.
Waka kuhon—NKBT 65.
Wakamiya senka-awase han no kotoba—SKKT 5.
Wakan rōeishū—NKBT 73.
Waka teikin—KKSH 10.
Wakuraba—Kaneko Kinjirō and Ijichi Tetsuo, eds. *Sōgi kushū*. Kadokawa Shoten, 1977.
Wasuregusa—Kaneko Kinjirō and Ijichi Tetsuo, eds. *Sōgi kushū*. Kadokawa Shoten, 1977.
Yahantei tsukinami hokku-awase—Nagai Kazuaki, ed. *Tsukinami hokku-awase no kenkyū*. Kasama Shoin, 2013.
Yakumo mishō—NKT 3.
Yanagidaru—excerpted in Tsukamoto Tetsuzō, ed. *Shinsen senryū kyōshi shū*. Yūhōdō, 1923.
Yashima Shōrin'an naniki hyakuin—Yamagishi Tokuhei et al., eds. *Katsura no miya bon sōsho* 18. Tenri: Yōtokusha, 1968.

Yodo no watari—KRRS 2.
Yoshiya Nobuko nikki—excerpted in Iwaya Daishi, *Kamakura, Zushi*. Kōdansha, 1980.
Yuki no keburi—Yokoyama Shigeru, ed. *Chikurinshō kochū*. Kadokawa Shoten, 1978.
Zōho Rengetsu zenshū. Murakami Sodō, ed. 2 vols. Shibunkaku, 2006.
Zoku sarumino—SNKBT 70.
Zoku Sōanshū—SKKT 4.

SELECTED BIBLIOGRAPHY

ABBREVIATIONS

HJAS *Harvard Journal of Asiatic Studies*
MN   *Monumenta Nipponica*

TRANSLATIONS

General
Bownas, Geoffrey, and Anthony Thwaite, trans. and eds. *The Penguin Book of Japanese Verse.* London: Penguin, 1964.
———. *The Penguin Book of Japanese Verse.* Rev. ed. London: Penguin, 2009.
Carter, Steven D., trans. *Traditional Japanese Poetry: An Anthology.* Stanford, Calif.: Stanford University Press, 1991.
Keene, Donald, ed. *Anthology of Japanese Literature: Earliest Era to Mid-Nineteenth Century.* New York: Grove Press, 1955.
Kern, Adam L., trans. *The Penguin Book of Haiku.* London: Penguin, 2018.
Miner, Earl, trans. *Japanese Poetic Diaries.* Berkeley: University of California Press, 1969.
Ōoka Makoto. *A Poet's Anthology: The Range of Japanese Poetry*, trans. Janine Beichman. Santa Fe, N.M.: Katydid Books, 2006.
Pekarik, Andrew J., trans. *The Thirty-six Immortal Women Poets.* New York: Braziller, 1991.
Rexroth, Kenneth, trans. *Love Poems from the Japanese*, ed. Sam Hamill. Boston: Shambhala, 1994.
———, trans. *One Hundred More Poems from the Japanese.* New York: New Directions, 1976.
———, trans. *One Hundred Poems from the Japanese.* New York: New Directions, 1964.
Rexroth, Kenneth, and Atsumi Ikuko, trans. *The Burning Heart: Women Poets of Japan.* New York: Seabury Press, 1977.
Sato, Hiroaki, trans. *Japanese Women Poets: An Anthology.* London: Routledge, 2008.
Sato, Hiroaki, and Burton Watson, trans. *From the Country of Eight Islands: An Anthology of Japanese Poetry.* Seattle: University of Washington Press, 1981.
Shirane, Haruo. *Traditional Japanese Literature: An Anthology, Beginnings to 1600.* New York: Columbia University Press, 2007.
Waley, Arthur, trans. *Japanese Poetry: The "Uta."* Honolulu: University Press of Hawaii, 1919.
Watson, Burton, trans. *Japanese Literature in Chinese.* 2 vols. New York: Columbia University Press, 1975, 1976.

The Ancient Age

Aston, W. G., trans. *Nihongi: Chronicles of Japan from the Earliest Times to A.D. 697*. Tokyo: Tuttle, 1972.
Brannen, Noah, and William Elliot, trans. *Festive Wine: Ancient Japanese Poems from the Kinkafu*. New York: Weatherhill, 1969.
Cranston, Edwin, trans. *A Waka Anthology: Volume 1, The Gem-Glistening Cup*. Stanford, Calif.: Stanford University Press, 1993.
Heldt, Gustav, trans. *Kojiki: An Account of Ancient Matters*. New York: Columbia University Press, 2014.
Kojima, Takashi, trans. *Written on Water: Five Hundred Poems from the Man'yōshū*. Tokyo: Tuttle, 2011.
Levy, Ian Hideo, trans. *Love Songs from the Man'yōshū: Selections from a Japanese Classic*. Tokyo: Kodansha International, 2000.
———. *The Ten Thousand Leaves: A Translation of the "Man'yōshū," Japan's Premier Anthology of Classical Poetry; Volume One*. Princeton, N.J.: Princeton University Press, 1981.
Miller, Roy Andrew, trans. *The Footprints of the Buddha: An Eighth-Century Old Japanese Poetic Sequence*. New Haven, Conn.: American Oriental Society, 1975.
———. "The Lost Poetic Sequence of the Priest Manzei." *MN* 36, no. 2 (1981): 133–72.
Nippon Gakujutsu Shinkōkai, ed. *The Man'yōshū: One Thousand Poems*. New York: Columbia University Press, 1965.
Philippi, Donald L., trans. *Kojiki*. Tokyo: University of Tokyo Press, 1968.
———, trans. *This Wine of Peace, This Wine of Laughter: A Complete Anthology of Japan's Earliest Songs*. New York: Grossman, 1968.
Wright, Harold, trans. *Ten Thousand Leaves: Love Poems from the Man'yōshū*. Woodstock, N.Y.: Overlook Press, 1986.
Yasuda, Kenneth. *Land of the Reed Plains: Ancient Japanese Lyrics from the Man'yōshū*. Rutland, Vt.: Tuttle, 1960.

The Classical Age

Arntzen, Sonja, trans. *The Kagero Diary*. Ann Arbor: University of Michigan Press, 1997.
———. *The Sarashina Diary: A Woman's Life in Eleventh-Century Japan*. New York: Columbia University Press, 2014.
Bowring, Richard, trans. *The Diary of Murasaki Shikibu*. London: Penguin, 1996.
———. *Murasaki Shikibu: Her Diary and Poetic Memoirs*. Princeton, N.J.: Princeton University Press, 1982.
Bradstock, Timothy R., and Judith R. Rabinovitch, trans. *Dance of the Butterflies: Chinese Poetry from the Japanese Court Tradition*. Ithaca, N.Y.: East Asia Program, Cornell University, 2010.
Cranston, Edwin A., trans. *The Izumi Shikibu Diary: A Romance of the Heian Court*. Cambridge, Mass.: Harvard University Press, 1969.
———, trans. *A Waka Anthology: Volume 2, Grasses of Remembrance*. 2 vols. Stanford, Calif.: Stanford University Press, 2006.
Dalby, Liza, and Rae Grant, trans. *Ariake: Poems of Love and Longing by Women Courtiers of Ancient Japan*. San Francisco: Chronicle Books, 2000.
Harries, Phillip Tudor, trans. *The Poetic Memoirs of Lady Daibu*. Stanford, Calif.: Stanford University Press, 1980.
Harris, H. Jay, trans. *The Tales of Ise*. Tokyo: Tuttle, 1972.
Hirshfield, Jane, and Mariko Aratani, trans. *The Ink Dark Moon: Love Poems by Ono no Komachi and Izumi Shikibu, Women of the Ancient Court of Japan*. New York: Scribner, 1988.
MacMillan, Peter, trans. *The Tales of Ise*. London: Penguin, 2016.
McCullough, Helen Craig, trans. *Kokin Wakashū: The First Imperial Anthology of Japanese Poetry, with "Tosa Nikki" and "Shinsen Waka."* Stanford, Calif.: Stanford University Press, 1985.
———. *Tales of Ise: Lyrical Episodes from Tenth-Century Japan*. Stanford, Calif.: Stanford University Press, 1968.

McCullough, William H., and Helen Craig McCullough, trans. *A Tale of Flowering Fortunes: Annals of Japanese Aristocratic Life in the Heian Period*. 2 vols. Stanford, Calif.: Stanford University Press, 1980.
Moriguchi, Yasuhiko, and David Jenkins, trans. *The Dance of the Dust on the Rafters: Selections from "Ryōjin-hishō."* Seattle: Broken Moon Press, 1990.
Morris, Ivan, trans. *As I Crossed a Bridge of Dreams: Recollections of a Woman in Eleventh-Century Japan*. New York: Dial Press, 1971.
Mostow, Joshua S., trans. *At the House of Gathered Leaves: Shorter Biographical and Autobiographical Narratives from Japanese Court Literature*. Honolulu: University of Hawai'i Press, 2004.
Mostow, Joshua S., and Royall Tyler, trans. *The Ise Stories*. Honolulu: University of Hawai'i Press, 2010.
Rimer, J. Thomas, and Jonathan Chaves, eds. and trans. *Japanese and Chinese Poems to Sing*. New York: Columbia University Press, 1997.
Rodd, Laura Rasplica, and Mary Catherine Henkenius, trans. *Kokinshū: A Collection of Poems Ancient and Modern*. Princeton, N.J.: Princeton University Press, 1984.
Seidensticker, Edward G., trans. *The Gossamer Years: The Diary of a Noblewoman of Heian Japan*. Rutland, Vt.: Tuttle, 1964.
——, trans. *The Tale of Genji*. New York: Knopf, 1981.
Tahara, Mildred, trans. *Tales of Yamato: A Tenth-Century Poem-Tale*. Honolulu: University of Hawai'i Press, 1980.
Teele, Nicholas J., trans. "Rules of Poetic Elegance: Fujiwara no Kintō's *Shinsen Zuinō* and *Waka Kuhon*." *MN* 31, no. 2 (Summer 1976): 145-64.
Tyler, Royall, trans. *The Tale of Genji*. New York: Viking, 2001.
Videen, Susan Downing, trans. *Tales of Heichū*. Cambridge, Mass.: Harvard University Press, 1989.
Vos, Frits. *A Study of the Ise-monogatari*. 2 vols. The Hague: Mouton, 1957.
Watson, Burton. *Japanese Literature in Chinese: Volume 1, Poetry and Prose in Chinese by Japanese Writers of the Early Period*. New York: Columbia University Press, 1975.

The Early Medieval Age

Brazell, Karen W., trans. *The Confessions of Lady Nijō*. Stanford, Calif.: Stanford University Press, 1976.
Brower, Robert H., trans. "'Ex-Emperor Go-Toba's Secret Teachings': *Go Toba no In Gokuden*." *HJAS* 32 (1972): 3-70.
——, trans. "The Foremost Style of Poetic Composition: Fujiwara Tameie's *Eiga no Ittei*." *MN* 42, no. 4 (Winter 1987): 391-429.
——, trans. *Fujiwara Teika's "Hundred-Poem Sequence of the Shōji Era," 1200*. Tokyo: Sophia University, 1978.
——, trans. "Fujiwara Teika's *Maigetsushō*." *MN* 40, no. 4 (Winter 1985): 399-425.
Brower, Robert H., and Earl Miner, trans. *Fujiwara Teika's "Superior Poems of Our Time": A Thirteenth-Century Poetic Treatise and Sequence*. Stanford, Calif.: Stanford University Press, 1967.
Bundy, Roselee. "Poetic Apprenticeship: Fujiwara Teika's *Shogaku Hyakushu*." *MN* 45, no. 2 (Summer 1990): 157-88.
——. "*Santai waka*: Six Poems in Three Modes." *MN* 49, nos. 2-3 (1994): 197-227, 261-86.
——. "Solo Poetry Contest as Poetic Self-Portrait: The One-Hundred-Round Contest of Lord Teika's Own Poems; Part Two." *MN* 61, nos. 1-2 (Spring and Summer 2006): 1-58, 131-92.
Fujiwara, Yoshitsune. *The Complete Poetry Collection of Fujiwara Yoshitsune (1169–1206)*. Yokohama: Warm-Soft Village Branch K-L, 1986.
Galt, Tom, trans. *The Little Treasury of One Hundred People, One Poem Each*. Princeton, N.J.: Princeton University Press, 1982.
Heine, Steven. *A Blade of Grass: Japanese Poetry and Aesthetics in Dōgen Zen*. New York: Lang, 1989.
——. *The Zen Poetry of Dōgen: Verses from the Mountain of Eternal Peace*. Rutland, Vt.: Tuttle, 1997.

Heldt, Gustav. "Saigyō's Traveling Tale: A Translation of *Saigyō Monogatari*." *MN* 52, no. 4 (Winter 1997): 467-521.
Huey, Robert N., trans. "Fushimi-in Nijūban Uta-awase." *MN* 48, no. 2 (1993): 167-203.
——. "The Kingyoku Poetry Contest." *MN* 42, no. 3 (1987): 299-330.
Huey, Robert N., and Susan Matisoff, trans. "Lord Tamekane's Notes on Poetry: *Tamekane-kyō Wakashō*." *MN* 40, no. 2 (Summer 1985): 127-46.
Katō, Hilda. "The *Mumyōshō* of Kamo no Chōmei and Its Significance in Japanese Literature." *MN* 23, no. 3 (1968): 321-430.
Kim, Yung-Hee, trans. *Songs to Make the Dust Dance: The "Ryōjin hishō" of Twelfth-Century Japan*. Berkeley: University of California Press, 1994.
LaFleur, William R., trans. *Mirror for the Moon: A Selection of Poems by Saigyō (1118–1190)*. New York: New Directions, 1978.
MacMillan, Peter, trans. *One Hundred Poets, One Poem Each: A Treasury of Classical Japanese Verse*. London: Penguin, 2017.
Marra, Michele, trans. "*Mumyōzōshi*, Introduction and Translation" [3 parts]. *MN* 39, no. 2 (Summer 1984): 115-45; no. 3 (Autumn 1984): 281-305; no. 4 (Winter 1984): 409-34.
McKinney, Meredith, trans. *The Tale of Saigyō*. Ann Arbor: Center for Japanese Studies, University of Michigan, 1998.
Messer, Sarah, and Kidder Smith, trans. *Having Once Paused: Poems of Zen Master Ikkyu (1394–1481)*. Ann Arbor: University of Michigan Press, 2015.
Miyata, Haruo, trans. *The Ogura Anthology of Japanese Waka: A Hundred Pieces from a Hundred Poets*. Osaka: Osaka Kyoiku Tosho, 1981.
Morrell, Robert E. "The *Shinkokinshū*: 'Poems on Sakyamuni's Teachings (*Shakkyōka*).'" In *The Distant Isle: Studies and Translations in Honor of Robert H. Brower*, ed. Thomas B. Hare, Robert Borgen, and Sharalyn Orbaugh, 281-320. Ann Arbor: Center for Japanese Studies, University of Michigan, 1996.
Mostow, Joshua S. *Pictures of the Heart: The "Hyakunin Isshu" in Word and Image*. Honolulu: University of Hawai'i Press, 1996.
Perkins, George, trans. *The Clear Mirror: A Chronicle of Japan During the Kamakura Period (1185–1333)*. Stanford, Calif.: Stanford University Press, 1998.
Rodd, Laurel Rasplica, trans. *Shinkokinshū: New Collection of Poems, Ancient and Modern*. Boston: Brill, 2015.
Sato, Hiroaki, trans. *String of Beads: Complete Poems of Princess Shikishi*. Honolulu: University of Hawaii Press, 1993.
Tanahashi, Kazuaki, ed. *Moon in a Dewdrop: Writings of Zen Master Dōgen*. New York: North Point Press, 1985.
Watson, Burton, trans. *Saigyō: Poems of a Mountain Home*. New York: Columbia University Press, 1991.
Watson, Frank, trans. *One Hundred Leaves: A New Annotated Translation of the "Hyakunin Isshu."* Plum White Press, 2012-2013.
Whitehouse, Wilfred, and Eizo Yanagisawa, trans. *Lady Nijō's Own Story: "Towazu-Gatari"; The Candid Diary of a Thirteenth-Century Japanese Imperial Concubine*. Rutland, Vt.: Tuttle, 1974.

The Late Medieval Age

Arntzen, Sonja. *Ikkyū and the Crazy Cloud Anthology*. Tokyo: University of Tokyo Press, 1986.
Berg, Stephen. *Crow with No Mouth: Ikkyū, Fifteenth-Century Zen Master*. Port Townsend, Wash.: Copper Canyon Press, 2000.
Brazell, Karen. "'Blossoms': A Medieval Song." *Journal of Japanese Studies* 6, no. 2 (Summer 1980): 243-66.
Brower, Robert H., and Steven D. Carter, trans. *Conversations with Shōtetsu*. Ann Arbor: Center for Japanese Studies, University of Michigan, 1992.

Carter, Steven D., trans. "Chats with the Master: Selections from *Kensai Zōdan*." *MN* 56, no. 3 (Autumn 2001): 295-347.
—, trans. *Just Living: Poems and Prose by the Japanese Monk Tonna*. New York: Columbia University Press, 2003.
—, trans. "Sōgi in the East Country, *Shirakawa Kikō*." *MN* 42, no. 2 (Summer 1987): 167-209.
—, trans. *Three Poets at Yuyama*. Berkeley: Institute of East Asian Studies, 1983.
—. "A Translation of Sōgi's *Oi no Susami*" [2 parts]. *MN* 71, nos. 1-2 (2017): 1-42, 296-369.
—, trans. *Unforgotten Dreams: Poems by the Zen Monk Shōtetsu*. New York: Columbia University Press, 1997.
—, trans. *Waiting for the Wind: Thirty-six Poets of Japan's Late Medieval Age*. New York: Columbia University Press, 1989.
Cranston, Edwin A. "Shinkei's 1467 *Dokugin Hyakuin*." *HJAS* 54, no. 2 (December 1994): 461-507.
Ebersole, Gary L. "The Buddhist Ritual Use of Linked Poetry in Medieval Japan." *Eastern Buddhist* 16, no. 2 (1983): 50-71.
Hare, Thomas B. "Linked Verse at Imashinmei Shrine: *Anegakōji Imashinmei Hyakuin*, 1447." *MN* 34, no. 2 (Summer 1979): 169-208.
Hirota, Dennis, trans. "In Practice of the Way: *Sasamegoto*, an Instruction Book in Linked Verse." *Chanoyu Quarterly* 19 (1977): 23-46.
Horton, H. Mack, trans. *The Journal of Sōchō*. Stanford, Calif.: Stanford University Press, 1999.
—. "Renga Unbound: Performative Aspects of Japanese Linked Verse." *HJAS* 53, no. 2 (1993): 443-512.
Merwin, W. S., and Soiku Shigematsu, trans. *Sun at Midnight: Poems and Letters*. San Francisco: North Point Press, 1989.
Pollack, David, trans. *Zen Poems of the Five Mountains*. New York: Crossroad; Decatur, Ga.: Scholars' Press, 1985.
Ramirez-Christensen, Esperanza, trans. *Murmured Conversations: A Treatise on Poetry and Buddhism by the Poet-Monk Shinkei*. Stanford, Calif.: Stanford University Press, 2008.
Ury, Marian, trans. *Poems of the Five Mountains: An Introduction to the Literature of the Zen Monasteries*. Tokyo: Mushinsha, 1977.

The Early Modern Age

Abé, Ryūichi, and Peter Haskel, trans. *Great Fool: Zen Master Ryōkan; Poems, Letters, and Other Writings*. Honolulu: University of Hawai'i Press, 1996.
Addiss, Stephen, trans. *The Art of Haiku: Its History through Poems and Paintings by Japanese Masters*. Boston: Shambhala, 2012.
—. *Haiku Humor: Wit and Folly in Japanese Poems and Prints*. New York: Weatherhill, 2007.
Barnhill, David Landis, trans. *Bashō's Haiku: Selected Poems by Matsuo Bashō*. Albany: SUNY Press, 2005.
Blyth, R. H. *Haiku*. 4 vols. Tokyo: Hokuseido Press, 1949-1952.
—. *Japanese Life and Character in Senryu*. Tokyo: Hokuseido Press, 1960.
—, trans. *Senryu: Japanese Satirical Verses*. Tokyo: Hokuseido Press, 1949.
Bowers, Faubion, trans. *The Classic Tradition of Haiku: An Anthology*. New York: Dover, 2012.
Bradstock, Timothy, and Judith Rabinovitch, eds. and trans. *An Anthology of Kanshi (Chinese Verse) by Japanese Poets of the Edo Period (1603–1868)*. Lewiston, Maine: Mellen Press, 1997.
—. *The Kanshi Poems of the Ozasa Tanzaku Collection: Late Edo Life through the Eyes of Kyoto Townsmen*. Kyoto: International Research Center for Japanese Studies, 2002.
Britton, Dorothy, trans. *A Haiku Journey: Bashō's "Narrow Road to a Far Province."* Tokyo: Kodansha International, 1980.
Carter, Steven D., trans. *Haiku before Haiku: From the Renga Masters to Bashō*. New York: Columbia University Press, 2011.

Corman, Cid, and Kamaike Susumu, trans. *Back Roads to Far Towns: Bashō's "Oku-no-Hosomichi."* New York: Mushinsha / Grossman, 1968.
—, trans. *Back Roads to Far Towns: Bashō's Travel Journal.* Buffalo, N.Y.: White Pine Press, 2004.
Donegan, Patricia, and Yoshie Ishibashi, trans. *Chiyo-ni: Woman Haiku Master.* Tokyo: Tuttle, 1998.
Hamill, Sam, trans. *The Essential Bashō.* Boston: Shambhala, 1999.
—, trans. *The Sound of Water: Haiku by Bashō, Buson, Issa, and other Poets.* Boston: Shambhala, 1995.
—, trans. *"The Spring of My Life" and Selected Haiku.* Boston: Shambhala, 1997.
Hass, Robert, ed. and trans. *The Essential Haiku: Versions of Basho, Buson and Issa.* Hopewell, N.J.: Ecco Press, 1994.
Henderson, Harold G, ed. and trans. *An Introduction to Haiku: An Anthology of Poems and Poets from Bashō to Shiki.* Garden City, N.Y.: Doubleday Anchor Books, 1958.
Huey, Robert N., trans. "Journal of My Father's Last Days: Issa's *Chichi no Shūen Nikki.*" *MN* 39, no. 1 (Spring 1984): 25-54.
Keene, Donald, trans. "Bashō's Diaries." *Japan Quarterly* 32 (1985): 374-83.
—, trans. "Bashō's Journal of 1684." In *Landscapes and Portraits: Appreciations of Japanese Culture,* ed. Donald Keene, 94-108. Tokyo: Kodansha International, 1971.
—, trans. "Bashō's Journey to Sarashina." In *Landscapes and Portraits: Appreciations of Japanese Culture,* ed. Donald Keene, 109-30. Tokyo: Kodansha International, 1971.
—, trans. *The Narrow Road to Oku.* New York: Kodansha International, 1996.
Kodama, Misao, and Hikosaku Yanagishima, trans. *The Zen Fool Ryōkan.* Tokyo: Tuttle, 1999.
Mackenzie, Lewis, trans. *The Autumn Wind: A Selection from the Poems of Issa.* Tokyo: Kodansha International, 1957.
Maeda, Cana, trans. *Monkey's Raincoat.* New York: Grossman, 1973.
Mayhew, Lenore, trans. *Monkey's Raincoat (Sarumino): Linked Poetry of the Bashō School with Haiku Selections.* Rutland, Vt.: Tuttle, 1985.
McCullough, Helen Craig, trans. "The Journey of 1684." In *Classical Japanese Prose: An Anthology,* ed. Helen Craig McCullough, 513-22. Stanford, Calif.: Stanford University Press, 1990.
—, trans. "The Narrow Road of the Interior." In *Classical Japanese Prose: An Anthology,* ed. Helen Craig McCullough, 522-51. Stanford, Calif.: Stanford University Press, 1990.
Mei Hui Liu Huang and Larry Smith, trans. *The Kanshi Poems of Taigu Ryōkan.* Huron, Ohio: Bottom Dog Press, 2009.
Merwin, W. S., and Takako Lento, trans. *Collected Haiku of Yosa Buson.* Port Townsend, Wash.: Copper Canyon Press, 2013.
Miner, Earl, and Hiroko Odagiri, trans. *The Monkey's Straw Raincoat and Other Poetry of the Bashō School.* Princeton, N.J.: Princeton University Press, 1981.
Nippon Gakujutsu Shinkōkai, ed. *Haikai and Haiku.* Tokyo: Nippon Gakujutsu Shinkōkai, 1958.
Reichhold, Jane, trans. *Basho: The Complete Haiku.* Tokyo: Kodansha International, 2008.
Rogers, Lawrence, trans. "Rags and Tatters: The *Uzuragoromo* of Yokoi Yayū." *MN* 34, no. 3 (Autumn 1979): 279-91.
Sato, Hiroaki, trans. *Bashō's Narrow Road: Spring and Autumn Passages.* Berkeley: Stone Bridge Press, 1996.
—, trans. *Breeze Through Bamboo: Kanshi of Ema Saikō.* New York: Columbia University Press, 1997.
—. *One Hundred Frogs: From Renga to Haiku to English.* New York: Weatherhill, 1983.
—, trans. "Record of an Autumn Wind: The Travel Diary of Arii Shokyū." *MN* 55, no. 1 (Spring 2000): 1-43.
Sawa, Yuki, and Edith M. Shiffert, trans. *Haiku Master Buson.* San Francisco: Heian International, 1978.
Shirane, Haruo, ed. *Early Modern Japanese Literature: An Anthology, 1600-1900.* New York: Columbia University Press, 2002.

Stevens, John, trans. *Dewdrops on a Lotus Leaf: Zen Poems of Ryōkan*. Boston: Shambhala, 2004.
——, trans. *Lotus Moon: The Poetry of the Buddhist Nun Rengetsu*. New York: Weatherhill, 1994.
——, trans. *One Robe, One Bowl: The Zen Poetry of Ryōkan*. New York: Weatherhill, 2016.
——, trans. *Rengetsu: Life and Poetry of Lotus Moon*. Brattleboro, Vt.: Echo Point Books, 2014.
Stryk, Lucien, trans. *On Love and Barley: Haiku of Bashō*. New York: Penguin Books, 1985.
Tanahashi, Kazuaki, trans. *Sky Above, Great Wind: The Life and Poetry of Zen Master Ryōkan*. Boston: Shambhala, 2012.
Terasaki, Etsuko, trans. "*Hatsushigure*: A Linked Verse Series by Bashō and His Disciples." *HJAS* 36 (January 1976): 204–39.
——, trans. "The Saga Diary." *Literature East and West* 16 (1971–1972): 701–18.
Ueda, Makoto, ed. and trans. *Light Verse from the Floating World: An Anthology of Premodern Japanese Senryu*. New York: Columbia University Press, 1999.
Watson, Burton, trans. *Grass Hill: Poems and Prose by the Japanese Monk Gensei*. New York: Columbia University Press, 1983.
——, trans. *Kanshi: The Poetry of Ishikawa Jōzan and Other Edo-Period Poets*. San Francisco: North Point Press, 1990.
——, trans. *Ryōkan: Zen Monk-Poet of Japan*. New York: Columbia University Press, 1977.
Young, David, trans. *Moon Woke Me Up Nine Times: Selected Haiku of Basho*. New York: Knopf, 2013.
Yuasa, Nobuyuki, trans. *The Narrow Road to the Deep North and Other Travel Sketches*. London: Penguin Books, 1968.
——, trans. *The Year of My Life: A Translation of Issa's "Oraga Haru."* Berkeley: University of California Press, 1960.
——, trans. *The Zen Poems of Ryōkan*. Princeton, N.J.: Princeton University Press, 1981.

The Modern Age

Beichman-Yamamoto, Janine, trans. "Masaoka Shiki's *A Drop of Ink*." *MN* 30, no. 3 (Autumn 1975): 291–315.
Heinrich, Amy Vladeck, trans. "'My Mother Is Dying': Saitō Mokichi's '*Shinitamau Haha*.'" *MN* 33, no. 4 (Winter 1978): 407–39.
Ishikawa, Takuboku. *Poems to Eat*, trans. Carl Sesar. Tokyo: Kodansha International, 1966.
——. *Sad Toys*, trans. Sanford Goldstein and Seishi Shinoda. West Lafayette, Ind.: Purdue University Press, 1977.
Shigematsu, Sōiku, trans. *Zen Haiku: Poems and Letters of Natsume Sōseki*. New York: Weatherhill, 1994.
Ueda, Makoto, ed. and trans. *Haiku by Modern Japanese Women: Far Beyond the Field*. New York: Columbia University Press, 2003.
——, ed. and trans. *Modern Japanese Haiku: An Anthology*. Tokyo: Tokyo University Press, 1976.
——, ed. and trans. *Modern Japanese Tanka*. New York: Columbia University Press, 1996.
Watson, Burton, trans. *Masaoka Shiki: Selected Poems*. New York: Columbia University Press, 1998.
Yosano, Akiko. *Tangled Hair: Selected Tanka from "Midaregami,"* trans. Sanford Goldstein and Shinoda Seishi. West Lafayette, Ind.: Purdue University Press, 1971.

STUDIES

General

Asada, Tōru. "The Discourse of Poetic Theory: 'Japanese Poetry Takes the Human Heart as Seed.'" In *Waka Opening Up to the World*, ed. Haruo Shirane et al., 331–39. Tokyo: Benseisha, 2012.
Brower, Robert H. "Japanese." In *Versification: Major Language Types*, ed. W. K. Wimsatt, 38–51. New York: New York University Press, 1972.

—. "Waka." In *Kodansha Encyclopedia of Japan*, 8:201-17. Tokyo: Kodansha International, 1983.
Brower, Robert H., and Earl Roy Miner. "Formative Elements in the Japanese Poetic Tradition." *Journal of Asian Studies* 16, no. 4 (August 1957): 503-27.
—. *Japanese Court Poetry*. Stanford, Calif.: Stanford University Press, 1961.
Carter, Steven D. *Householders: The Reizei Family in Japanese History*. Cambridge, Mass.: Harvard University Asia Center, 2007.
Cranston, Edwin A. "The Dark Path: Images of Longing in Japanese Love Poetry." *HJAS* 35 (1975): 60-100.
Denecke, Wiebke. "Japan's Vernacular and Sino-Japanese Poetry: A Bird's Eye View from Ancient Rome." In *Waka Opening Up to the World*, ed. Haruo Shirane et al., 203-15. Tokyo: Benseisha, 2012.
Harries, Phillip. "*Fūryū*: A Concept of Elegance in Premodern Literature." In *Europe Interprets Japan*, ed. Gordon Daniels, 137-44. Tenterden, Kent, Engl.: Norbury, 1984.
Ito, Setsuko. "The Muse in Competition: *Uta-awase* Through the Ages." *MN* 37, no. 2 (Summer 1982): 201-22.
Kamens, Edward. *Utamakura, Allusion, and Intertextuality in Traditional Japanese Poetry*. New Haven, Conn.: Yale University Press, 1997.
—. *Waka and Things, Waka as Things*. New Haven, Conn.: Yale University Press, 2018.
Kanechiku, Nobuyuki. "Waka and Media: *Kohitsu-gire*, *Kaishi*, and *Tanzaku*." In *Waka Opening Up to the World*, ed. Haruo Shirane et al., 378-89. Tokyo: Benseisha, 2012.
Keene, Donald. *Japanese Literature: An Introduction for Western Readers*. New York: Grove Press, 1955.
—. *The Pleasures of Japanese Literature*. New York: Columbia University Press, 1988.
—. *Seeds in the Heart: Japanese Literature from Earliest Times to the Late Sixteenth Century*. New York: Holt, 1993.
Kobayashi, Kazuhiko. "Reizei and the Power of the Poetic House." In *Waka Opening Up to the World*, ed. Haruo Shirane et al., 298-306. Tokyo: Benseisha, 2012.
Konishi, Jin'ichi. "Association and Progression: Principles of Integration in Anthologies and Sequences of Japanese Court Poetry, A.D. 900-1350," trans. Robert H. Brower and Earl Miner, *HJAS* 21 (1958): 67-127.
—. *A History of Japanese Literature*. 3 vols. Princeton, N.J.: Princeton University Press, 1984-1991.
LaFleur, William R. *The Karma of Words: Buddhism and the Literary Arts in Medieval Japan*. Berkeley: University of California Press, 1983.
Marra, Michele. *The Aesthetics of Discontent: Politics and Reclusion in Medieval Japanese Literature*. Honolulu: University of Hawai'i Press, 1991.
—. *Representations of Power: The Literary Politics of Medieval Japan*. Honolulu: University of Hawai'i Press, 1993.
—. *Seasons and Landscapes in Japanese Poetry: An Introduction to Haiku and Waka*. Lewiston, N.Y.: Mellen Press, 2009.
Miner, Earl. *Comparative Poetics: An Intercultural Essay on Theories of Literature*. Princeton, N.J.: Princeton University Press, 1990.
—. *An Introduction to Japanese Court Poetry*. Stanford, Calif.: Stanford University Press, 1968.
—. *Japanese Poetic Diaries*. Berkeley: University of California Press, 1969.
—. "Japanese Poetry." In *Princeton Encyclopedia of Poetry and Poetics*, ed. Alex Preminger, 423-31. Princeton, N.J.: Princeton University Press, 1965.
—. "Japanese and Western Images of Courtly Love." *Yearbook of Comparative and General Literature* 15 (1966): 174-79.
—. "Toward a New Conception of Classical Japanese Poetics." In *Studies on Japanese Culture*, ed. Japan P.E.N. Club, 1:99-113. Tokyo: Japan P.E.N. Club, 1973.
Miner, Earl, Hiroko Odagiri, and Robert Morrell. *The Princeton Companion to Classical Japanese Literature*. Princeton, N.J.: Princeton University Press, 1985.

Morris, Mark. "Waka and Form, Waka and History." *HJAS* 46, no. 2 (December 1986): 551–610.
Naitō, Akira. "Waka, Tanka, and Community." In *Waka Opening Up to the World*, ed. Haruo Shirane et al., 307–18. Tokyo: Benseisha, 2012.
Ōoka, Makoto. *The Colors of Poetry: Essays in Classic Japanese Verse*. Santa Fe, N.M.: Katydid Books, 1991.
Pollack, David. *The Fracture of Meaning: Japan's Synthesis of China from the Eighth Through the Eighteenth Centuries*. Princeton, N.J.: Princeton University Press, 1986.
Shirane, Haruo. *Japan and the Culture of the Seasons*. New York: Columbia University Press, 2012.
———. "Waka: Language, Community, and Gender." In *Waka Opening Up to the World*, ed. Haruo Shirane et al., 185–200. Tokyo: Benseisha, 2012.
Shirane, Haruo, and Tomi Suzuki, with David Lurie, eds. *The Cambridge History of Japanese Literature*. Cambridge: Cambridge University Press, 2016.
Tani, Tomoko. "Imperial Waka: Sacred Matrimony, War, and *Riseibumin*." In *Waka Opening Up to the World*, ed. Haruo Shirane et al., 271–77. Tokyo: Benseisha, 2012.
Ueda, Makoto. *Literary and Art Theories in Japan*. Cleveland: Press of Case Western Reserve University, 1967.
Walker, Janet A. "Conventions of Love Poetry in Japan and the West." *Journal of the Association of Teachers of Japanese* 14, no. 1 (1980): 31–65.
Wang, Sook Young. "Waka and Korean Poetry." In *Waka Opening Up to the World*, ed. Haruo Shirane et al., 216–30. Tokyo: Benseisha, 2012.
Watanabe, Yasuaki. "The Rhetoric of Waka." In *Waka Opening Up to the World*, ed. Haruo Shirane et al., 321–30. Tokyo: Benseisha, 2012.

The Ancient Age

Commons, Anne. *Hitomaro: The Poet as God*. Boston: Brill, 2009.
Cranston, Edwin A. "Man'yōshū." In *Kodansha Encyclopedia of Japan*, 5:103–11. Tokyo: Kodansha International, 1983.
———. "The River Valley as *Locus Amoenus* in Man'yō Poetry." In *Studies in Japanese Culture*, ed. Saburo Ota and Rikutaro Fukuda, 1:14–37. Tokyo: Japan P.E.N. Club, 1973.
———. "Water-Plant Imagery in the *Man'yōshū*." *HJAS* 31 (1971): 137–78.
Denecke, Wiebke. "Anthologization and Sino-Japanese Literature: *Kaifūsō* and the Three Imperial Anthologies." In *The Cambridge History of Japanese Literature*, ed. Haruo Shirane and Tomi Suzuki, with David Lurie, 86–91. Cambridge: Cambridge University Press, 2016.
Doe, Paula. *A Warbler's Song in the Dusk: The Life and Work of Ōtomo Yakamochi (718–785)*. Berkeley: University of California Press, 1982.
Duthie, Torquil. *"Man'yōshū" and the Imperial Imagination in Early Japan*. Leiden: Brill, 2014.
———. "Songs of the Records and Chronicles." In *The Cambridge History of Japanese Literature*, ed. Haruo Shirane and Tomi Suzuki, with David Lurie, 40–44. Cambridge: Cambridge University Press, 2016.
Ebersole, Gary L. *Ritual Poetry and the Politics of Death in Early Japan*. Princeton, N.J.: Princeton University Press, 1989.
Horton, H. Mack. "*Man'yōshū*." In *The Cambridge History of Japanese Literature*, ed. Haruo Shirane and Tomi Suzuki, with David Lurie, 50–85. Cambridge: Cambridge University Press, 2016.
———. *Traversing the Frontier: The "Man'yōshū" Account of a Japanese Mission to Silla in 736–737*. Cambridge, Mass.: Harvard University Asia Center, 2012.
Levy, Ian Hideo. *Hitomaro and the Birth of Japanese Lyricism*. Princeton, N.J.: Princeton University Press, 1984.
Takamatsu, Hisao. "Establishment of the Functions of Waka." In *Waka Opening Up to the World*, ed. Haruo Shirane et al., 278–8. Tokyo: Benseisha, 2012.

Yu, Angela. "The Category of Metaphorical Poems (*Hiyuka*) in the *Man'yōshū*: Its Characteristics and Chinese Origins." *Journal of the Association of Teachers of Japanese* 24, no. 1 (April 1990): 7-33.

The Classical Age

Arntzen, Sonja. "The *Wakan rōeishū*: Cannibalization or Singing in Harmony?" *Proceedings of "Acts of Writing" Association of Japanese Literary Studies Annual Conference 2000* (2001): 155-71.

Borgen, Robert. *Sugawara no Michizane and the Early Heian Court*. Harvard East Asian Monographs, no. 120. Cambridge, Mass.: Harvard University Press, 1986.

Bowring, Richard. "The *Ise monogatari*: A Short Cultural History." *HJAS* 52, no. 2 (December 1992): 401-80.

Bundy, Rose. "Court Women in Poetry Contests: The *Tentoku Yonen Dairi Utaawase* (Poetry Contest Held at Court in 960)." *U.S.-Japan Women's Journal* 33 (2007): 33-57.

———. "Siting the Court Woman Poet: *Waka no kai* (Poetry Gatherings) in Rokujō Kiyosuke's *Fukuro zōshi*," *U.S.-Japan Women's Journal* 37 (2009): 3-32.

Ceadel, E. B. "The Ōi River Poems and Preface." *Asia Major* 3 (1952): 65-106.

———. "Tadamine's Preface to the Ōi River Poems." *Bulletin of the School of Oriental and African Studies* 18 (1956): 331-43.

———. "The Two Prefaces of the *Kokinshū*." *Asia Major*, n.s., 7, pts. 1-2 (1968): 40-51.

Commons, A. E. "Japanese Poetic Thought, from Earliest Times to the Thirteenth Century." In *The Cambridge History of Japanese Literature*, ed. Haruo Shirane and Tomi Suzuki, with David Lurie, 218-29. Cambridge: Cambridge University Press, 2016.

Cranston, Edwin A. "The Dark Path: Images of Longing in Japanese Poetry." *HJAS* 35 (1975): 60-100.

———. "The Poetry of Izumi Shikibu." *MN* 25, no. 1 (Spring 1970): 1-11.

Denecke, Wiebke. "'Topic Poetry Is All Ours': Poetic Composition on Chinese Lines in Early Heian Japan." *HJAS* 67, no. 1 (June 2007): 1-49.

Forrest, Stephen M. "Strangers Within: *Noin shū* and the Canonical Status of Private Poetry Collections." *Proceedings of the Association for Japanese Literary Studies* 1 (Summer 2000): 431-46.

Harries, Phillip T. "Personal Poetry Collections: The Origin and Development Through the Heian Period." *MN* 35, no. 3 (Autumn 1980): 297-317.

Heinrich, Amy Vladeck. "*Blown in Flurries*: The Role of the Poetry in *Ukifune*." In *Ukifune: Love in the Tale of Genji*, ed. Andrew Pekarik, 153-71. New York: Columbia University Press, 1982.

Heldt, Gustav. "*Kokinshū* and Heian Court Poetry." In *The Cambridge History of Japanese Literature*, ed. Haruo Shirane and Tomi Suzuki, with David Lurie, 110-20. Cambridge: Cambridge University Press, 2016.

———. *The Pursuit of Harmony: Poetry and Power in Early Heian Japan*. Ithaca, N.Y.: East Asia Program, Cornell University, 2008.

Jinno, Hidenori. "Waka in *The Tale of Genji*: Characters Who Do Not Compose Waka." In *Waka Opening Up to the World*, ed. Haruo Shirane et al., 289-97. Tokyo: Benseisha, 2012.

Kamens, Edward. *The Buddhist Poetry of the Great Kamo Priestess: Daisaiin Senshi and Hosshin Wakashū*. Ann Arbor: Center for Japanese Studies, University of Michigan, 1990.

———. "Dragon-Girl, Maidenflower, Buddha: The Transformation of a Waka Topos, 'The Five Obstructions.'" *HJAS* 53, no. 2 (December 1993): 389-442.

———. "Terrains of Text in Mid-Heian Court Culture." In *Heian Japan: Centers and Peripheries*, ed. Mikael Adolphson et al., 129-52. Honolulu: University of Hawai'i Press, 2007.

Kimbrough, Keller. *Preachers, Poets, Women, and the Way: Izumi Shikibu and the Buddhist Literature of Medieval Japan*. Ann Arbor: Center for Japanese Studies, University of Michigan, 2008.

Kondō, Miyuki. "Waka Expression and Gender." In *Waka Opening Up to the World*, ed. Haruo Shirane et al., 243-52. Tokyo: Benseisha, 2012.

Konishi Jin'ichi. "The Genesis of the *Kokinshū* Style." Trans. Helen C. McCullough. *HJAS* 38 (1978): 61-170.
Kwon, Yung-Hee. "The Emperor's Songs: Emperor Go-Shirakawa and *Ryōjin Hishō Kudenshū*." *MN* 41, no. 3 (Autumn 1986): 261-98.
——. "Voices from the Periphery: Love Songs in *Ryōjin Hishō*." *MN* 41, no. 1 (Spring 1986): 1-20.
LaMarre, Thomas. *Uncovering Heian Japan: An Archaeology of Sensation and Inscription*. Durham, N.C.: Duke University Press, 2000.
——. "Writing Doubled Over, Broken: Provisional Names, Acrostic Poems, and the Perpetual Contest of Doubles in Heian Japan." *positions* 2, no. 2 (Fall 1994): 250-73.
McCullough, Helen Craig. *Brocade by Night: "Kokin Wakashū" and the Court Style in Japanese Classical Poetry*. Stanford, Calif.: Stanford University Press, 1985.
Miller, Marilyn Jeanne. *The Poetics of Nikki Bungaku*. New York: Garland, 1985.
Miner Earl. "*Waka*: Features of Its Constitution and Development." *HJAS* 50, no. 2 (December 1990): 669-706.
Morrell, Robert E. "The Buddhist Poetry in the *Goshūishū*." *MN* 28, no. 1 (Spring 1973): 87-100.
Morris, Mark. "Sei Shōnagon's Poetic Catalogues." *HJAS* 40, no. 1 (June 1980): 5-54.
Persiani, Gian Piero. "China as Self, China as Other: On Ki no Tsurayuki's Use of the *wa-kan* Dichotomy." *Sino-Japanese Studies* 23 (2016): 31-58.
——. "Whether Birds or Monkeys: Indefinite Reference and Pragmatic Presupposition in Reading Waka." *Proceedings of the Association for Japanese Literary Studies* 5 (Summer 2004): 280-96.
Ramirez-Christensen, Esperanza. "The Operation of the Lyrical Mode in the *Genji Monogatari*." In *Ukifune: Love in the Tale of Genji*, ed. Andrew Pekarik, 21-61. New York: Columbia University Press, 1982.
Rouzer, Paul. "Early Buddhist *Kanshi*: Court, Country, and Kūkai." *MN* 59, no. 4 (Winter 2004): 431-61.
Sarra, Edith. *Fictions of Femininity: Literary Conventions of Gender in Japanese Court Women's Memoirs*. Stanford, Calif.: Stanford University Press, 1999.
Shirane, Haruo. *The Bridge of Dreams: A Poetics of the Tale of Genji*. Stanford, Calif.: Stanford University Press, 1987.
——. "Gendering the Seasons in the *Kokinshū*." *Proceedings of the Association for Japanese Literary Studies* 6 (Summer 2005): 47-55.
Smits, Ivo. "Heian Canons of Chinese Poetry: *Wakan rōeishū* and Bai Juyi." In *The Cambridge History of Japanese Literature*, ed. Haruo Shirane and Tomi Suzuki, with David Lurie, 184-87. Cambridge: Cambridge University Press, 2016.
——. "Heian Popular Songs: *Imayō* and *Ryōjin hishō*." In *The Cambridge History of Japanese Literature*, ed. Haruo Shirane and Tomi Suzuki, with David Lurie, 206-8. Cambridge: Cambridge University Press, 2016.
——. "Pictured Landscapes: Kawara no In, Heian Gardens and Poetic Imagination." *Proceedings of the Association for Japanese Literary Studies* 5 (Summer 2004): 159-65.
——. "The Poem as a Painting: Landscape Poetry in Late Heian Japan." *Transactions of the Asiatic Society of Japan*, 4th ser., 6 (1991): 61-86.
——. "Song as Cultural History: Reading *Wakan rōeishū* (Interpretations)." *MN* 55, no. 3 (2000): 399-427.
——. "Song as Cultural History: Reading *Wakan rōeishū* (Texts)." *MN* 55, no. 2 (2000): 225-56.
——. "The Way of the Literati: Chinese Learning and Literary Practice in Mid-Heian Japan." In *Heian Japan: Centers and Peripheries*, ed. Mikael Adolphson et al., 105-28. Honolulu: University of Hawai'i Press, 2007.
Sorensen, Joseph T. "Poetic Landscapes and Landscape Poetry in Heian Japan." *Proceedings of the Association for Japanese Literary Studies* 6 (Summer 2005): 87-98.

Teele, Roy E., Nicholas J. Teele, and Rebecca Teele. *Ono no Komachi: Poems, Stories, Nō Plays*. New York: Garland, 1993.
Tuck, Robert. "Poets, Paragons, and Literary Politics: Sugawara no Michizane in Medieval Japan." *HJAS* 74, no. 1 (June 2014): 43-99.
Walker, Janet A. "Poetic Ideal and Fictional Reality in the *Izumi Shikibu nikki*." *HJAS* 37, no. 1 (June 1977): 135-82.
Wallace, John R. "Reading the Rhetoric of Seduction in *Izumi Shikibu nikki*." *HJAS* 58, no. 2 (December 1998): 481-512.
Webb, Jason. "Beyond *Wa-kan*: Narrating *Kanshi*, Reception, and Literary Infrastructure." *Proceedings of the Association for Japanese Literary Studies* 5 (Summer 2004): XXX-XXX.
Wixted, John Timothy. "The *Kokinshū* Prefaces: Another Perspective." *HJAS* 43, no. 1 (June 1983): 215-38.

The Early Medieval Age
Atkins, Paul. "Fabricating Teika: The *Usagi* Forgeries and Their Authentic Influence." *Proceedings of the Association for Japanese Literary Studies* 1 (Summer 2000): 249-58.
——. "*Shinkokin wakashū*: The New Anthology of Ancient and Modern Japanese Poetry." In *The Cambridge History of Japanese Literature*, ed. Haruo Shirane and Tomi Suzuki, with David Lurie, 230-37. Cambridge: Cambridge University Press, 2016.
——. *Teika: The Life and Works of a Medieval Japanese Poet*. Honolulu: University of Hawai'i Press, 2017.
Bialock, David. "Voice, Text, and the Question of Poetic Borrowing in Late Classical Japanese Poetry." *HJAS* 54, no. 1 (June 1994): 181-231.
Carter, Steven D. "*Waka* in the Medieval Period: Patterns of Practice and Patronage." In *The Cambridge History of Japanese Literature*, ed. Haruo Shirane and Tomi Suzuki, with David Lurie, 238-55. Cambridge: Cambridge University Press, 2016.
Cranston, Edwin A. "'Mystery and Depth' in Japanese Court Poetry." In *The Distant Isle: Studies and Translations in Honor of Robert H. Brower*, ed. Thomas B. Hare, Robert Borgen, and Sharalyn Orbaugh, 65-104. Ann Arbor: Center for Japanese Studies, University of Michigan, 1996.
Gotō, Shōko. "Men's Poems by Women Poets: One Perspective on a Poem by Princess Shikishi." In *Waka Opening Up to the World*, ed. Haruo Shirane et al., 253-67. Tokyo: Benseisha, 2012.
Hisamatsu, Sen'ichi. "Fujiwara Shunzei and Literary Theories of the Middle Ages." *Acta Asiatica* 1 (1960): 29-42.
Huey, Robert N. *The Making of "Shinkokinshū."* Cambridge, Mass.: Harvard University Asia Center, 2002.
Kamens, Edward. "The Past in the Present: Fujiwara Teika and the Traditions of Japanese Poetry." In *Word in Flower: The Visualization of Classical Literature in Seventeenth Century Japan*, ed. Carolyn Wheelwright, 16-28. New Haven, Conn.: Yale University Art Gallery, 1989.
Kimbrough, Keller. "*Nomori no kagami* and the Perils of Poetic Heresy." *Proceedings of the Association for Japanese Literary Studies* 4 (Summer 2003): 99-114.
——. "Reading the Miraculous Powers of Japanese Poetry: Spells, Truth Acts, and a Medieval Buddhist Poetics of the Supernatural." *Japanese Journal of Religious Studies* 32, no. 1 (2005): 1-33.
Klein, Susan Blakeley. "Allegories of Desire: Poetry and Eroticism in *Ise Monogatari Zuinō*." *MN* 52, no. 4 (Winter 1997): 441-65; 53, no. 1 (Spring 1998): 13-43.
Konishi Jin'ichi. "Michi and Medieval Writing." In *Principles of Classical Japanese Literature*, ed. Earl Miner, 181-208. Princeton, N.J.: Princeton University Press, 1985.
Kubota, Jun. "Allegory and Thought in Medieval *Waka*: Concentrating on Jien's Works Prior to the Jōkyū Disturbance." *Acta Asiatica* 37 (1979): 1-28.

Laffin, Christina. *Rewriting Medieval Japanese Women: Politics, Personality, and Literary Production in the Life of Nun Abutsu.* Honolulu: University of Hawai'i Press, 2013.

——. "The Road Well Traveled: Poetry and Politics in *Diary of the Sixteenth Night Moon.*" *Proceedings of the Association for Japanese Literary Studies* 8 (Summer 2007): 95–103.

——. "Travel as Sacrifice: Abutsu's Poetic Journey in *Diary of the Sixteenth Night Moon.*" *Review of Japanese Culture and Society* 19 (December 2007): 71–86.

LaFleur, William R. *Awesome Nightfall: The Life, Times, and Poetry of Saigyō.* Somerville, Mass.: Wisdom Publications, 2003.

Miyake, Lynne K. "The *Tosa* Diary: In the Interstices of Gender and Criticism." In *The Woman's Hand: Gender and Theory in Japanese Women's Writing,* ed. Paul Gordon Schalow and Janet A. Walker, 41–73. Stanford, Calif.: Stanford University Press, 1966.

Naito Mariko. "Poetic Imagination and Place Names: Women Travelers and the Creation of the *Utamakura* Shiga no Yamagoe." *Proceedings of the Association for Japanese Literary Studies* 8 (Summer 2007): 82–95.

Plutschow, Herbert Eugen. "Two Conversations of Saigyō and Their Significance in the History of Medieval Japanese Poetry." *Asiatische Studien / Études Asiatiques,* 33, no. 1 (1979): 1–8.

Ratcliff, Christian. "The Traveling Poet as Witness: Established Poets Face New Realities in the Kamakura Period." *Proceedings of the Association for Japanese Literary Studies* 6 (Summer 2005): 99–112.

Raud, Rein. "Narrative and Poetic Progression: The Logic of Associativity." *Proceedings of the Association for Japanese Literary Studies* 4 (Summer 2003): 54–65.

Royston, Clifton. "*Utaawase* Judgments as Poetry Criticism." *Journal of Asian Studies* 34, no. 1 (November 1974): 99–108.

Shirane, Haruo. "Lyricism and Intertextuality: An Approach to Shunzei's Poetics." *HJAS* 50, no. 1 (June 1990): 71–85.

——. "Poetic Essence (*Hon'i*) as Japanese Literary Canon." *Proceedings of the Association for Japanese Literary Studies* 1 (Summer 2000): 153–64.

Smits, Ivo. "The Poet and the Politician: Teika and the Compilation of the *Shinchokusenshū.*" *MN* 53, no. 4 (1998): 427–72.

——. *The Pursuit of Loneliness: Chinese and Japanese Nature Poetry in Medieval Japan, ca. 1050–1150.* Stuttgart: Steiner, 1995.

——. "Unusual Expressions: Minamoto no Toshiyori and Poetic Innovation in Medieval Japan." *Transactions of the Asiatic Society of Japan,* 4th ser., 8 (1993): 85–106.

Stoneman, Jack. "Medieval Recluse Literature: Saigyō, Chōmei, and Kenkō." In *The Cambridge History of Japanese Literature,* ed. Haruo Shirane and Tomi Suzuki, with David Lurie, 259–67. Cambridge: Cambridge University Press, 2016.

——. "So Deep in the Mountains: Saigyō's *Yama fukami* Poems and Reclusion in Medieval Japanese Poetry." *HJAS* 68, no. 2 (December 2008): 33–75.

Tabuchi, Kumiko. "Women Poets in Court Poetry Salons." In *Waka Opening Up to the World,* ed. Haruo Shirane et al., 233–42. Tokyo: Benseisha, 2012.

Yoshino, Tomomi. "*Hyakunin isshu* and the Popularization of Classical Poetry." In *The Cambridge History of Japanese Literature,* ed. Haruo Shirane and Tomi Suzuki, with David Lurie, 256–58. Cambridge: Cambridge University Press, 2016.

The Late Medieval Age

Arntzen, Sonja. *Ikkyū and The Crazy Cloud Anthology.* Tokyo: Tokyo University Press, 1986.

——. "Literature of Medieval Zen Temples: Gozan (Five Mountains) and Ikkyū." In *The Cambridge History of Japanese Literature,* ed. Haruo Shirane and Tomi Suzuki, with David Lurie, 311–16. Cambridge: Cambridge University Press, 2016.

Carter, Steven D. "A Lesson in Failure: Linked Verse Contests in Medieval Japan." *Journal of the American Oriental Society* 104, no. 4 (October-December 1984): 727-37.

———. "Mixing Memories: Linked Verse and the Fragmentation of the Court Heritage." *HJAS* 48, no. 1 (June 1988): 5-45.

———. "Readings from the Bamboo Grove: A Translation of Sōgi's *Oi no susami*" [2 parts]. *MN* 71, no. 1 (2016): 1-42; no. 2:295-369.

———. "*Renga*." In *The Cambridge History of Japanese Literature*, ed. Haruo Shirane and Tomi Suzuki, with David Lurie, 317-27. Cambridge: Cambridge University Press, 2016.

———. *The Road to Komatsubara: A Classical Reading of the Renga Hyakuin*. Cambridge, Mass.: Harvard University Press, 1987.

———. "'Seeking What the Masters Sought': Masters, Disciples, and Poetic Enlightenment in Medieval Japan." In *The Distant Isle: Studies and Translations in Honor of Robert H. Brower*, ed. Thomas B. Hare, Robert Borgen, and Sharalyn Orbaugh, 35-58. Ann Arbor: Center for Japanese Studies, University of Michigan, 1996.

———. *Three Poets at Yuyama*. Berkeley: Institute of East Asian Studies, 1983.

Cook, Lewis. "Waka and Commentary." In *Waka Opening Up to the World*, ed. Haruo Shirane et al., 350-64. Tokyo: Benseisha, 2012.

Ebersole, Gary L. "The Buddhist Ritual Use of Linked Poetry in Medieval Japan." *Eastern Buddhist* 16, no. 2 (Autumn 1983): 50-71.

Flueckiger, Peter. "The Discourse of 'Makoto' and the Canonization of Tokugawa Waka." *Proceedings of the Association for Japanese Literary Studies* 1 (Summer 2000): 165-76.

Horton, H. Mack. *Song in an Age of Discord: "The Journal of Sōchō" and Poetic Life in Late Medieval Japan*. Stanford, Calif.: Stanford University Press, 1999.

Huey, Robert N. *Kyōgoku Tamekane: Poetry and Politics in Late Kamakura Japan*. Stanford, Calif.: Stanford University Press, 1989.

———. "The Medievalization of Poetic Practice." *HJAS* 50, no. 2 (December 1990): 651-68.

———. "Warrior Control over the Imperial Anthology." In *The Origins of Japan's Medieval World: Courtiers, Clerics, Warriors, and Peasants in the Fourteenth Century*, ed. Jeffrey P. Mass, 170-91. Stanford, Calif.: Stanford University Press, 1997.

Keene, Donald. "The Comic Tradition in *Renga*." In *Japan in the Muromachi Age*, ed. John W. Hall and Toyoda Takeshi, 241-77. Berkeley: University of California Press, 1977.

———. "Jōha, a Sixteenth-Century Poet of Linked Verse." In *Warlords, Artists, and Commoners: Japan in the Sixteenth Century*, ed. George Elison and Bardwell L. Smith, 113-31. Honolulu: University Press of Hawaii, 1981.

Konishi, Jin'ichi. "The Art of Renga," trans. Karen Brazell and Lewis Cook. *Journal of Japanese Studies* 2, no. 1 (Autumn 1975): 29-61.

Miner, Earl. *Japanese Linked Poetry: An Account with Translations of Renga and Haikai Sequences*. Princeton, N.J.: Princeton University Press, 1979.

———. "Some Theoretical Implications of Japanese Linked Poetry." *Comparative Literature Studies* 18, no. 3 (1981): 368-78.

Okuda, Isao. "*Renga* in the Medieval Period." *Acta Asiatica* 37 (1979): 29-46.

Parker, Joseph D. "Attaining Landscapes in the Mind: Nature Poetry and Painting in Gozan Zen." *MN* 52, no. 2 (Summer 1997): 235-58.

Pollack, David. "Gidō Shūshin and Nijō Yoshimoto: *Wakan* and *Renga* Theory in Late Fourteenth Century Japan." *HJAS* 45, no. 1 (June 1985): 129-56.

Ramirez-Christensen, Esperanza. *Emptiness and Temporality: Buddhism and Medieval Japanese Poetics*. Stanford, Calif.: Stanford University Press, 2008.

———. "The Essential Parameters of Linked Poetry." *HJAS* 41, no. 2 (December 1981): 555-95.

———. *Heart's Flower: The Life and Poetry of Shinkei*. Stanford, Calif.: Stanford University Press, 1994.

Raud, Rein. "*Waka* and *renga* Theory: Shifts in the Conceptual Ground." *Oriens Extremus* 39, no. 1 (January 1996): 96–118.
Sasaki, Takahiro. "Waka and the Scroll Format." In *Waka Opening Up to the World*, ed. Haruo Shirane et al., 367–77. Tokyo: Benseisha, 2012.
Sakomura, Tomoko. *Poetry as Image: The Visual Culture of Waka in Sixteenth-Century Japan*. Boston: Brill, 2015.
Tamamura, Takeji, and Gaynor Sekimori. "Literature from the Gozan Zen Temples: A Historical Overview." Trans. Gaynor Sekimori. *Chanoyu Quarterly* 43 (1985): 14–29.
Ueda, Makoto. "Verse-Writing as a Game: Yoshimoto on the Art of Linked Verse." In *Literary and Art Theories in Japan*, ed. Makoto Ueda, 37–54. Cleveland: Press of Case Western Reserve University, 1967.
Unno, Keisuke. "A History of Reading: Medieval Interpretations of *Kokin wakashū*." In *Waka Opening Up to the World*, ed. Haruo Shirane et al., 340–49. Tokyo: Benseisha, 2012.
Wang, Sook Young. "Journey of Sōgi: Utamakura/Beyond Visits to Scenic Spots." *Proceedings of the Association for Japanese Literary Studies* 8 (Summer 2007): 47–55.

The Early Modern Age

Addiss, Stephen, and J. Thomas Rimer, trans. *Shisendo: Hall of the Poetry Immortals*. New York: Weatherhill, 1991.
Blyth, Reginald H. *A History of Haiku*. Vol. 1, *From the Beginnings up to Issa*. Tokyo: Hokuseido Press, 1963.
——. *A History of Haiku*. Vol. 2, *From Issa up to the Present*. Tokyo: Hokuseido Press, 1964.
Carter, Steven D. "Bashō and the Haikai Profession." *Journal of the American Oriental Society* 117, no. 1 (January–March 1997): 57–69.
——. "Bashō and the Mastery of Poetic Space in *Oku no Hosomichi*." *Journal of the American Oriental Society* 120, no. 2 (April–June 2000): 190–98.
Crowley, Cheryl. "Haikai Poet Shokyū-ni (1714–81) and the Economics of Literary 'Families.'" *U.S.-Japan Women's Journal* 39 (2010): 63–79.
——. *Haiku Poet Buson and the Bashō Revival*. Boston: Brill, 2006.
——. "Women in *Haikai*: The *Tamamoshū* (Jeweled water-grass anthology, 1774) of Yosa Buson." *U.S.-Japan Women's Journal* 26 (2004): 55–74.
——. "Yosa Buson's Imagined Landscapes." *Proceedings of the Association for Japanese Literary Studies* 6 (Summer 2005): 113–22.
Flueckiger, Peter. *Imagining Harmony: Poetry, Empathy, and Community in Mid-Tokugawa Confucianism and Nativism*. Stanford, Calif.: Stanford University Press, 2011.
Fujikawa, Fumiko. "The Influence of Tu Fu on Bashō." *MN* 20, nos. 3–4 (1965): 374–88.
Henderson, Harold G., ed. and trans. *An Introduction to Haiku: An Anthology of Poems and Poets from Bashō to Shiki*. Garden City, N.Y.: Doubleday Anchor Books, 1958.
Hibbett, Howard S. "The Japanese Comic Linked-Verse Tradition." *HJAS* 23 (1960–1961): 76–92.
Kawamoto, Kōji. "Modern Japanese Poetry to the 1910s." In *The Cambridge History of Japanese Literature*, ed. Haruo Shirane and Tomi Suzuki, with David Lurie, 613–22. Cambridge: Cambridge University Press, 2016.
——. *The Poetics of Japanese Verse: Imagery, Structure, Meter*. Tokyo: University of Tokyo Press, 2000.
Keene, Donald. *World within Walls: Japanese Literature of the Pre-Modern Era, 1600–1868*. New York: Holt, Rinehart and Winston, 1976.
Markus, Andrew. "Dōmyaku Sensei and 'The Housemaid's Ballad' (1769)." *HJAS* 58, no. 1 (June 1998): 5–58.
Ogata, Tsutomu. "Five Methods for Appreciating Bashō's Haiku." *Acta Asiatica* 28 (1975): 42–61.
Nishimura, Sey. "First Steps into the Mountains: Motoori Norinaga's *Uiyamabumi*." *MN* 42, no. 4 (Winter 1987): 449–93.

Pollack, David. "Kyōshi: Japanese 'Wild Poetry.'" *Journal of Asian Studies* 38, no. 3 (May 1979): 499-517.

Rabinovitch, Judith N., and Timothy R. Bradstock. "Early to Mid-Edo *Kanshi*." In *The Cambridge History of Japanese Literature*, ed. Haruo Shirane and Tomi Suzuki, with David Lurie, 457-64. Cambridge: Cambridge University Press, 2016.

Sawa, Yuki, and Edith M. Shiffert. *Haiku Master Buson*. San Francisco: Heian International, 1978.

Shirane, Haruo. "*Aisatsu*: The Poet as Guest." In *New Leaves: Studies and Translations of Japanese Literature in Honor of Edward Seidensticker*, ed. Aileen Gatten and Anthony H. Chambers, 89-113. Ann Arbor: Center for Japanese Studies, University of Michigan, 1993.

——. "Matsuo Bashō and the Poetics of Scent." *HJAS* 52, no. 1 (June 1991): 77-110.

——. "Matsuo Bashō's *Oku no hosomichi* and the Anxiety of Influence." In *Currents in Japanese Culture: Translations and Transformations*, ed. Amy Vladeck Heinrich, 171-83. New York: Columbia University Press, 1997.

——. "The Rise of Haikai: Matsuo Bashō, Yosa Buson, and Kobayashi Issa." In *The Cambridge History of Japanese Literature*, ed. Haruo Shirane and Tomi Suzuki, with David Lurie, 403-14. Cambridge: Cambridge University Press, 2016.

——. "Satiric Poetry: *Kyōshi*, *Kyōka*, and *Senryū*." In *The Cambridge History of Japanese Literature*, ed. Haruo Shirane and Tomi Suzuki, with David Lurie, 503-9. Cambridge: Cambridge University Press, 2016.

——. *Traces of Dreams: Landscape, Cultural Memory, and the Poetry of Bashō*. Stanford, Calif.: Stanford University Press, 1997.

Suzuki, Ken'ichi. "Material Culture and Waka in the Edo Period." In *Waka Opening Up to the World*, ed. Haruo Shirane et al., 390-99. Tokyo: Benseisha, 2012.

Takahashi, Sayumi. "Beyond Our Grasp? Materiality, Meta-genre, and Meaning in the Po(e)ttery of Rengetsu-ni." *Proceedings of the Association for Japanese Literary Studies* 5 (Summer 2004): 261-78.

Thomas, Roger K. "In His Footsteps: Shokyū-ni and the Canonization of Bashō." *Proceedings of the Association for Japanese Literary Studies* 1 (Summer 2000): 287-304.

——. "Macroscopic vs. Microscopic: Spatial Sensibilities in Waka of the Bakumatsu Period." *HJAS* 58, no. 2 (December 1998): 513-42.

——. "Ōkuma Kotomichi and the Re-Visioning of *Kokinshū* Elegance." *Proceedings of the Midwest Association for Japanese Literary Studies* 3 (1997): 160-81.

——. "Poetry Fit to Sing: Tachibana Moribe and the Chōka Revival." *Proceedings of the Association for Japanese Literary Studies* 4 (Summer 2003): 151-65.

——. "A Voice of the Tenpō Era: The Poetics of Ōkuma Kotomichi." *MN* 59, no. 3 (Autumn 2004): 321-58.

——. "*Waka* Practice and Poetics in the Edo Period." In *The Cambridge History of Japanese Literature*, ed. Haruo Shirane and Tomi Suzuki, with David Lurie, 471-78. Cambridge: Cambridge University Press, 2016.

Ueda, Makoto, trans. *Bashō and His Interpreters: Selected Hokku with Commentary*. Stanford, Calif.: Stanford University Press, 1992.

——. *Dew on the Grass: The Life and Poetry of Kobayashi Issa*. Boston: Brill, 2004.

——. *Matsuo Bashō: The Master Haiku Poet*. Tokyo: Kodansha International, 1982.

——. *The Path of Flowering Thorn: The Life and Poetry of Yosa Buson*. Stanford, Calif.: Stanford University Press, 1998.

Yasuda, Kenneth. *The Japanese Haiku: Its Essential Nature, History, and Possibilities in English, with Selected Examples*. Rutland, Vt.: Tuttle, 1957.

Zolbrod, Leon M. "Buson's Poetic Ideals: The Theory and Practice of Haikai in the Age of Revival, 1771-1784." *Journal of the Association of Teachers of Japanese* 9, no. 1 (January 1974): 1-20.

——. "Talking Poetry: Buson's View of the Art of Haiku." *Literature East and West* 15-16 (1971-1972): 719-34.

The Modern Age

Beichman, Janine. *Masaoka Shiki*. New York: Twayne, 1982.
——. *Masaoka Shiki: His Life and Works*. New York: Columbia University Press, 2013.
Brower, Robert H. "Masaoka Shiki and Tanka Reform." In *Tradition and Modernization in Japanese Culture*, ed. Donald H. Shively, 379-418. Princeton, N.J.: Princeton University Press, 1971.
Keene, Donald. *Dawn to the West: Japanese Literature in the Modern Era*. Vol. 2, *Poetry, Drama, Criticism*. New York: Holt, Rinehart and Winston, 1984.
——. *The First Modern Japanese: The Life of Ishikawa Takuboku*. New York: Columbia University Press, 2016.
——. *The Winter Sun Shines In: A Life of Masaoka Shiki*. New York: Columbia University Press, 2013.
Morris, Mark. "Buson and Shiki" [2 parts]. *HJAS* 44, no. 2 (December 1984): 381-425; 45, no. 1 (June 1985): 256-319.

INDEX OF JAPANESE NAMES, TITLES, AND TERMS

Italicized numbers indicate illustrations. A lowercase p after a page number indicates that a poem by the author in question appears on that page.

Abutsu, 63, 64-65p, *insert 4*
ageku (last verse of a linked-verse sequence), 139, 203
aishōka (lament), 203
Akashi, Lady. *See* Murasaki Shikibu
Akechi Mitsuhide, 132
Akera Kankō, 183
Aki no yo hyōgo, 237
akikaze no ki, 153-54
allusive variation. *See honkadori*
Amaterasu, 52
Ana ureshi, 157
Arano, 140, 144, 231, 249
Archbishop Henjō, 73p, 256p
Ari no mama, 226
ari no mama, 65, 67, 142, 215-18, 249
Arii Shokyūni, 153-54p
Arima ryōgin kochū, 120-21
Ariwara no Narihira, 181-82p
Asai Masasuke, 133
Asaji, 127
Asayama Bontō, 240, 242p; on *ari no mama*, 217; on *hon'i*, 228; on *jimon*, 234; on *keiki*, 237; on *kotowari*, 208; on *taketakashi*, 255; on *za*, 213
Ashida Rokuzaemon. *See* Kao
Ashikaga Yoshihisa, 123-24, 176
Ashikaga Yoshimasa, 123-24
Asō Jirō, 186-87p
asobi, 98
Asukai Masatsune, 274n17

Atago hyakuin, 131-32
atarashi, 121
aware (moving, touching), 122, 126, 142, 219-20, 224, 231, 244-45, 256, 263
Azuma mondō, 270
azumauta (eastern song), 208

background. *See jimon*
Bai Juyi, 41-42p, 51, 183, 191, 194, 230
Baizan, 154-55p
Ban Kōkei, 240
banka (lament), 20-21, 203
Bashō. *See* Matsuo Bashō
Bashōmon kojin shinseki, 146-47
Betsuzashikijo, 234
Biwa'en zuihitsu, 271
Bodhidharma, 145
Bontō. *See* Asayama Bontō
Book of Songs, 146, 197
Buddhist poems. *See shakkyōka*
bunjin, 198
Buson. *See* Yosa Buson
Buson kushū, 150-51
byōbu uta (screen poem), 41, 203

"Chang hen ge," 41-42
chanoyu (tea ceremony), 75-76
charming. *See en*
Chichi no shūen nikki, 162
Chief Abbot Jien. *See* Jien
Chikubun, 235, 246

Chikurinshō, 10, 112–13, 113–14, 117–18, 191, 227, 235, 239, 246, 248, 257, 266
Chirenshō, 259
Chiun. *See* Ninagawa Chiun
chōka (long poem), 20–35 passim, 42–43, 46, 71–73, 78, 81–83, 83–84, 92, 96, 99, 203; definitions of, 1–3
chokusenshū (imperial anthology), 3, 107, 203, 210
Chōmu, 146
Chōrokubumi, 250–51, 258
Chōtanshō, 208, 213, 217, 228, 234
Chūka jakuboku shishō, 194–95
close linking. *See shinku soku*
Comments on the First Sequence of the New Year. *See Hatsukaishi hyōchū*
courtly elegance. *See miyabi*
Crown Prince Katsuhito. *See* Emperor Go-Kashiwabara

dai (prescribed topic), 7, 9, 43, 45, 50, 53, 55, 56, 57, 59, 61, 64, 66, 68, 69, 70, 74, 78, 79, 88, 102, 126, 155, 164, 179, 180, 183, 204, 207, 209, 212, 230; definitions of, 14–15, 204, 220–24
daiei (composing on topics), 68, 204, 220–24
daisan (third verse of a linked-verse sequence), 128, 204, 212
Danrin toppyakuin, 136–37
Dassai shōoku haiku chō shō, 249
deep feeling. *See ushin*
Deki Shōkyū, 136–37p
design. *See jimon*
distant linking. *See shinku soku*
Dokuraku gin, 86–87
dōri. *See kotowari*
double entendre. *See kakekobota*
Du Fu, 241

Earl Miner, 11, 215
Ehon yamato hiji, 106
Eiga no ittei, 68, 144, 205, 206, 234, 242
Eiga taigai, 142
elegant and refined. *See yū*
elegy. *See banka*
Emperor Fushimi, 65, 65–66p
Emperor Go-Daigo, 192
Emperor Go-Hanazono, 262p
Emperor Go-Kashiwabara, 127–28

Emperor Go-Murakami, 257p
Emperor Go-Saga, 107
Emperor Go-Shirakawa, 98–99
Emperor Go-Toba, 55, 59, 125, 220; and *dai*, 57; and *en*, 224; and *heikai*, 226; and *hosoku karabitaru*, 261; and *jukkai*, 207; and *karabitaru*, 248; on *yasashi*, 260
Emperor Go-Tsuchimikado, 119, 123, 127–28
Emperor Hanazono, 216–17p
Emperor Jinmu, 17
Emperor Jomei, 61, 78p
Emperor Juntoku, 54, 215, 226
Emperor Kiritsubo, 42
Emperor Ninmyō, 190
Emperor Saga, 189–90
Emperor Tenchi, 21–22, 24, 61–62p
Emperor Tenmu, 24, 61
Emperor Uda, 41
Emperor Xuanzong, 41–42
Emperor Yuryaku, 95–96p
Empress Eifuku, 66
Empress Jingū, 52
Empress Suiko, 20
en (charming, lovely), 58, 62, 122, 224–25, 270
engo (associated words), 213
Enokoshū, 7, 135–36
envoy. *See hanka*
essence. *See hon'i*
ethereal beauty. *See yōen*
Etsujin, 140p

famous places. *See nadokoro*
final verse. *See ageku*
first verse. *See hokku*
foundation poem. *See honkadori*
fu (rhapsody or rhyme prose), 189, 204
fudōki, 208
fueki ryūkō, 240
fūga (courtly elegance), 240, 225–26, 297
Fujiwara Munechika. *See* Uejima Onitsura
Fujiwara no Akisue, 242, 266
Fujiwara no Ietaka, 60–61p
Fujiwara no Kintō, 48–50p, 94
Fujiwara no Kiyosuke, 51–52p, 60–61p, 241–42p, 263
Fujiwara no Mitsumoto, 274n34
Fujiwara no Mototoshi, 205
Fujiwara no Sanekata, 46–47p

Fujiwara no Sanesada, 219p
Fujiwara no Shunzei: 205p, 242p; and *aware*, 244; contest judgments of, 56-57, 212, 266; and *en*, 58, 224, 226, 242; and *heikaitei*, 54, 226; on *Man'yōshū* poets, 22; and *sabi*, 247; and *yōen*, 261; and *yū*, 53, 266; and *yūgen*, 268
Fujiwara no Takasuke, 220p
Fujiwara no Tameie, 63, 64, 107-8p, 144; and *daiei*, 68; and *hare no uta*, 205; on *jimon*, 234; and *makoto*, 240; on *nadaraka*, 242
Fujiwara no Tameuji, 62-63, 64
Fujiwara no Teika, 14, 55, 57-58p, 106, 107, 122, 155, 207-8p, 211, 226, 229-30p, 241p, 250p, 265p; and *daiei*, 220-21; and *honkadori*, 229-30; and *ke no uta*, 207-8; and *keikyoku*, 236; and *Ogura hyakunin isshu*, 51, 61-62; and *shinku/soku*, 250; and *taketakaki yō*, 55; and *ushin*, 52, 58, 61, 62, 219, 256; and *uta-awase*, 212, 220; and *yōen*, 58; and *yōen* and *yojō*, 261-64; and *yūgen*, 45-46, 62, 110, 268
Fujiwara no Yoshitsune, 245p, 261p, 266-67p
Furu no nakamichi, 254
furyū, 204, 225. See also *fūga*
fusei, 200, 225
Fusen, 144p
Fushimatsu no Kaka, 182-83p
Fushimiin gyoshū, 65-66
fuzei (artistic atmosphere), 63, 204, 234

Ganryū, 133
ganzen. See *ari no mama*
Gekimōshō, 232
Gendai haiku, 218
Genji monogatari, 42, 47-48, 56, 67, 113-14, 138, 213, 216, 219, 220, 230, 232, 262
Genjūan no ki, 164
Gidō Shūshin, 9
Gion Nankai, 198-99p
Gishūmon'in no Tango, 260p
Go-Toba no in gokuden, app. 1, 207, 224, 226, 260
gojisshu-uta, 59, 206
Gojō Tametaka, insert 3
Gojūshichigajō, 212
Gosenshū, 62, 256
Goshūishū, 46, 73
goun (skandhas), 192

Grand Consort, the, 21-22p
Guhishō, 236, 250
Gukenshō, 236
Guku wakuraba, 251, 121
Gumon kenchū, 234
Gyōjo, 114-15, 246-47p
Gyōkō, 146
Gyoku sanjin kashū, 162-63
Gyokuyōshū, 65-67, 240, 253, 254
Gyōyū, 131

haikai, 135-72 passim, 176, 178, 179, 181, 184-86, 203-71; definitions of, 4-5, 204
haikai dai, 155, 164, 223
Haikai nishi kasen ato, 159
haikai no uta (comic or unorthodox *waka*), 46, 47, 204
haikai renga (comic or unorthodox linked verse), 204
haikai renku (*haikai* linked verse), 4, 235, 238
Haikai sabishiori, 138, 203, 223, 249
Haikai Shirao yawa, 143-44
haiku, 6, 164-70, 204, 206
Hamada Chinseki, 243
Hana no magaki, 236, 242, 253-54
hana no moto renga (*renga* beneath the blossoms), 110, 122, 123
Hanabinokoji Ichion, 152
hanka (envoy), 17, 23, 28, 30, 32, 34, 72, 82, 84, 91, 203, 204; definitions of, 3, 203-4
hanshi, han no kotoba (contest judgments), 44, 53, 54, 56-57, 129, 204, 212, 220
hare no uta (formal or public poem), 62, 205, 207
Haru no hi, 138-39, 232
Harusame monogatari, 78
Haseba no Kuromasa, 36p
Hatsukaishi hyōchū, 141-42, 236, 141-42, 238-39
Hattori Tohō, 237, 243-44
headnote. See *kotobagaki*
heikai, heikaitei (ordinary or plain style), 54-55, 226-27
Heike monogatari. See *Tales of the Heike*
heitanbi, 242
Hekidōsai, 218
Hekirenshō, 120, 238, 264
Henjō. See Archbishop Henjō
hibiki, hibikizuke, 139, 244, 265. See also *nioizuke*
hie. See *hieyase*

hiekōritaru. See hieyase
hiesabi. See hieyase
hieyase (cold and spare), 225, 227-28, 261
Higuchi Ichiyō, 88-89p
Hino Suketomo, 192
Hino Tomiko, 123-24
Hino Toshimoto, 191-92
Hirota no yashiro no uta-awase, 52-53, 245, 247
Hisago, 243
Hitomaro. See Kakinomoto no Hitomaro
Hitorigoto (by Shinkei), 225, 227, 228
Hitorigoto (by Uejima Onitsura), 145
Hōjōki. See The Ten-Foot-Square Hut
hokku (first verse of a linked-verse sequence), 4-8, 11, 12, 108, 111-12, 122-26 passim, 130-31, 135-38 passim, 143-51 passim, 153-55, 157-70 passim, 204, 205-6, 212-13; definitions of, 4, 205-6
hokku-awase (*hokku* contest), 212
Hokkuchō, 11, 125
Hokusō sadan, 80-81
hon'i (essence), 68, 206, 220, 228-29, 229-32
honbun, 232. See also *honzetsu*
Honchō ichinin isshu, 189-92
honkadori (allusive variation), 60-61, 73, 138, 206, 190, 215, 229-32
honku, 164. See *honkadori*
honzetsu (allusion to tales or other writings), 230, 232
hōraku renga, 125
Hosokawa Yūsai, 130-31p
hosoku karabitaru, 249, 261. See also *hieyase*; *sabi*
hosomi (spare, slender), 232-33
Hōtoku ninen jūichigatsu sentō uta-awase, 262
Hototogisu, 170
Housman, A. E., 1
hundred-poem sequence. See *hyakushu uta*
Hyakuban renga-awase, 116-17
hyakuin (hundred-verse *renga* sequence), 4, 5, 107, 108, 114-15, 126, 128, 131, 206, 207
Hyakunin isshu. See Ogura hyakunin isshu
Hyakunin isshu ōeishō, 226, 274n34
hyakushu waka (hundred-poem sequence of *uta*), 55, 58, 61, 206, 233

Ichijō Kaneyoshi, 262
Ichiyō kashū, 88-89
iisute, 128, 206
Ikkyū Sōjun, 175-76p

Imawaga Ryōshun, 216-17, 264
imayō (modern song), 4, 99-102, 206
imperial anthologies. See *chokusenshū*
Inaka no ku-awase, 256, 261
Inawashiro Kenzai, 14, 71-73p, 83, 113-14, 122-23p, 228, 233p, 236, 248p, 259p, 266; on *hieyase*, 227; and *kotobazuke*, 239; and *sabi*, 248; on *shinku soku*, 251-52; and *yariku*, 259
Inbunmon'in Chūnagon, 244-45p
Inoue Seigetsu, 163-64
Inu tsukubashū, 177
Iozakura, 229
Ippontei Fuyōka, 179-80p
Iseshū, 41-42
Ishida Hakyō, 169-70p
Ishikawa Jōzan, 195-96
Ishikawa Takuboku, 92
Ishiwara Masaakira, 265
Isonokami Otomaro, 28
Issa. See Kobayashi Issa
Issa Suikei ryōgin hyakuin, 155-56
Itchō. See Toyoshima Itchō
Itō Shintoku, 256p
Iwashimizu wakamiya no uta-awase, 262
Izayoi nikki, 64
Izumi Shikibu, 53

Jakunen, 247p
ji. See jimon
Jichin. See Jien
Jien, 59-60p, 224p
jikkei, 218
jimon (background and design), 111, 121, 116-17, 118, 122-23, 129, 206, 209, 233-34, 237, 252
jimon no renga. See jimon
jimon no uta. See jimon
Jinmu. See Emperor Jinmu
jisei no uta, kanshi, or *ku* (death poem), 176-77, 192, 206
jitsujō, 79, 222
Jiun, 79, 222
jo, jokotoba (metaphorical preface), 26, 39, 43, 55, 76, 89, 206-7
Jōha. See Satomura Jōha
johakyū (prelude, breakaway, presto), 115, 206
jōruri, 6
judgments. See *hanshi*
jueju, 6, 194-96, 207
Jūhachi-ban hokku-awase, 231

jukkai (expressing feelings), 74, 207
Juntokuin onhyakushu, 58
Jūronibenshō, 265

Kabekusachū, 219
Kaen rensho kikigaki, 217, 250, 276n101
kaeshi uta. See hanka
Kafū haikushū, 168-69
Kaga no Kogimi, 33
Kagaku teiyō, 219
Kagami Shikō, 148p, 265
Kagawa Kageki, 85-86p, 210, 218p, 231-32p
Kagetsu ichiyaron, 149
kagurauta (sacred song), 3, 96-97, 118, 207, 208
Kaka. See Fushimatsu no Kaka
Kakanshū, 13
kakekotoba (pivot word), 1, 2, 3, 26, 57, 73, 76, 97, 124, 178, 180, 207, 262
Kakinomoto no Hitomaro, 3, 16, 22-24p, 26, 43, 63, 236p
kami asobi uta, 96. See also kagura
Kamo no Chōmei: on dai, 204; on sugata, 210-11; on keikyokutei, 236; on shūitsu, 252-53; on yūgen, 268, 269-70
Kamo no Mabuchi, 77-78p, 82
Kamo okina kashū, 77-78
Kamuri sen, 184-85
kamurizuke, 184-85
Kan Chazan, 199-200p, 201
Kanginshū, 102-4
Kankō. See Akera Kankō
kansei (affecting), 142
kanshi, 189-201; definitions of, 5-6, 207. See also jueju; lushi; shi
Kanshō hyakushu, 226-27
Kao, 152-53p
karabitaru (sere, dessicated), 248. See also hieyase; sabi
Karagoromo Kisshū, 180-81p
Karai Senryū, 185
Karasumaru Mitsuo, 240
karauta. See kanshi
karumi (lightness), 141, 148, 149, 227, 234-35, 252
Kasa no Kanamura, 27-29p
kasen (thirty-six-verse haikai sequence), 5, 139, 159, 170-72, 207
katami, 38
Katō Chikage, 82

Katsukawa Shunshō, 10, 16, 40, 94
Kawai Kenpū, 149p
Kawai Sora, 153
Kaya Shirao, 138, 157, 223, 249
kayō (popular song), 17-19, 95-104 passim; definitions of, 3-4, 207
ke no uta (informal waka), 207
Kei Kiitsu, 185-86
Keien isshi, 85-86, 218, 231-32
Keikandō, 113-14, 239, 248, 266
keiki (scene or scenery), 207, 236, 241
keikizuke, 139, 156, 235-36, 241
keiko (practice), 133
keikyokutei, 207, 236-38. See also keiki
ken'yō. See miru tei
kendai, kenjitsu no dai, 204, 207, 211
kenjitsu no kai, 207
Kenkō, 221p
Kenkō hōshi shū, 221
Kenzai. See Inawashiro Kenzai
Kenzai zōdan, 61, 123
keshiki, 235, 236. See also keiki; keikizuke; keikyokutei
Ki no Tsurayuki, 43-44p, 64, 125, 252p
Kifū, 238p
kigo (season word), 135, 152, 167, 168, 169, 171, 209, 223, 228
Kijō. See Murakami Kijō
Kikaku. See Enomoto Kikaku
Kikusha. See Tagami Kikusha
Kindai shūka, 262, 268
King Hsiang, Uchiko, 189
Kinkafu, 95-96
Kinkaishū, 255
Kinoshita Chōshōshi, 7p, 76-77p, 195
Kinshi, 154p
kinuginu no uta (morning-after poem), 45, 48
Kirihioke, 56
Kisei Reigen. See Son'an Reigen
Kitamura Kigin, 142
Kitō. See Takai Kitō
Kiyūkyoku, 170-72
kōan (Zen meditation exercise), 193
Kobayashi Issa, 155-56p, 158, 162p
Kochiku, 129, 218, 230, 264
kodai kayō (ancient song), 2-3, 17-19, 208
Kojijū, 265p
Kojiki, 2, 17-18, 18-19
Kojima Kaneyuki. See Karagoromo Kisshū

Kokinshū, 38, 44, 45, 46, 73, 84, 85, 97, 117–18, 203; poems from, 42–43, 45, 46, 96, 178, 182, 204, 222, 230–31, 236, 259, 263
Kokinshū preface, 125–26, 150, 253
Kokon ikyoku shū, 176, 177–78
kokoro (heart, feeling), 57, 194, 208, 238, 239
kokoro ari. See *ushin*
kokoro no amari. See *yojō*
kokorobososhi (desolate, forlorn), 233
kokorozuke, 238–40, 244, 258
kokugaku, 77, 78
Komo jishi shū, 146
konashi, 227
Korai fūteishō, 22, 62
kotoba (diction, vocabulary), 57, 208, 239–40
kotobagaki (headnote), 14, 208
kotobazuke, 208, 239–40. See also *yoriaizuke*
Kotojirishū, 81–82, 136
kotowari (principle, logic), 129, 208
Kōun, 226; on *daiei*, 222; and *heikaitei*, 226; and *omoshiroki tei*, 245, and *yūgen*, 269
Kōun kuden, 222, 245, 269
kouta (little song), 4, 102–4, 209
Kōyō sekiyō sonjashi, Chazan, 199, 200
Kubo Shunman, 3–4, 14
kudai kanshi, 194–95
kudai waka, 194–95, 209
Kūge. See Ōshima Kanrai
Kūgeshū, 9, 160
kugutsu, 98
Kuhyō, 220, 245
Kume Masao, 167
kunimi, 78
Kunizane-kyō no ie no uta-awase, 244
kuraizuke, 143
Kusakabe Kyohaku, 225p
Kyōgen ōashū, 180
Kyōgoku school, 63–66, 217, 218, 240, 241, 250, 253–54
Kyōgoku Tamekane, 218, 240p, 241, 253; and *makoto*, 66, 240
Kyōgoku Tameko, 66–67p, 253p
Kyōgoku Tamenori, 63
Kyohaku, 238p
Kyohakushinhyō, 76
Kyohakushū, 7, 76
kyōka (comic *waka*), 47, 86, 175–84 passim, 47, 86; definitions of, 5, 209
Kyōka godaishū, 179

Kyōka kanshō jiten, 176, 178
kyōku, 185, 209. See also *kyōka*
Kyomyōshi Gitō, 145
Kyoraishō, 142, 147, 232, 235, 248, 252, 265
Kyūshu no michi no ki, 130–31
Kyūso, 152p
Kyūzei, 14, 110, 111, 116, 253p, 255p, 264p

Lady Horikawa, 164
Lady Ise, 40, 141–42p
Lady Kasa, 38–39p
Lady Kenreimon'in, 144
Lady Kunaikyō, 56–57p
Lady Sakuheimon'in, 65–66p
laments. See *banka*
landscape trays (*suhama*), 44
Li Bai, 198
lightness. See *karumi*
link. See *tsukeku*
linked verse. See *renga*
lofty style. See *taketakaki yō*
lovely. See *en*
lushi, 6, 189–90, 190–91, 193–94, 197, 199–200, 209

ma no atari. See *ari no mama*
Maeda Toshitsune, 132
maeku, 110, 116, 126–27, 131, 133, 140, 142, 143, 233–34, 238, 239, 247, 251, 252, 254, 255, 259, 261, 264
maekuzuke, 5
Maigetsushō, 256
makoto (truth, sincerity), 66, 85, 145, 210, 217, 240–41, 249
Makura no sōshi. See *The Pillow Book*
makurakotoba (pillow word), 3, 18, 21, 22, 24, 30, 73, 83, 84, 92, 96–97, 209, 212
manku (ten-thousand-verse *renga* sequence), 206, 222
Man'yōshū, 2, 3, 20, 26–27, 29, 30, 34, 35–36, 37, 61–62, 64, 73, 77, 86, 88, 89, 203, 204, 208, 220; poems from, 19–20, 21, 22–23, 25, 26, 27–28, 30, 31–32, 33–34, 35, 36, 37, 38, 39, 63, 73, 78
Masaoka Shiki, Shiki, 24, 163, 164–65p, 166, 169, 238, 249p
Masara. See Prince Masara
Mashita Mitsuhiro, 227p
Matsue Shigeyori, 135–36p

Matsumura Gekkei, 134
Matsunaga Teitoku, 8, 139
Matsuo Bashō, 5, 14, 132, 137-38p, 139, 140, 144, 147-48; 154-55, 159, 162p, 164p, 166, 172, 177, 186p, 203, 223, 226, 227, 231p, 232p, 234, 235p, 243p, 244p, 249p, 256, 267p, insert 11; and *en*, 225; on *hosomi*, 232; on *karumi*, 141-42; and *kasen*, 207; on *keiki*, 237; and *kokorozuke* and *nioizuke*, 238; and *makoto*, 240; and *miyabi*, 197; and *nioizuke*, 243-44; and *sabi*, 248; and *soku*, 251; and *shiori*, 252; on *taketakashi*, 256; and *yasashi*, 261; and *yojō*, 265
Matsuoka Shisen, 220p
me no mae. See *ari no mama*
meisho. See *nadokoro*
metaphorical preface. See *jo*
Mibu no Tadamine, 45-46p, 58, 211
michi (way), 160
Mikata no Sami, 33-34p
Mimosusogawa uta-awase, 54, 226, 247
Minamoto no Kanemasa, 266p
Minamoto no Kunizane, 244p
Minamoto no Michitomo, 216p
Minamoto no Sanetomo, 255p
Minamoto no Shunrai, 205
Minamoto no Sukekata, 99
Minamoto no Tomochika, 220-21p
Minamoto no Toshiyori, 242, 244, 268
Minase sangin hyakuin, 125
Minasedono koi jūgoshu uta-awase, 56-57
Minishū, 60-61
mirutei, miruyōtei (the style of visual description), 236, 241-42
Miura Chora, 258p
miyabi (courtly taste), 6, 225
Miyako no Yoshika, 50-51p
Mizuta Saigin, 229p
Mokudō, 237p
mon. See *jimon*
mondō, 231
mono no aware tei. See *aware*
monthly meeting. See *tsukinamikai*
Mori Ōgai, 89-92p, insert 13
Morikawa Kyoriku, 252p, 271
morning-after poem. See *kinuginu no uta*
Moto no shimizu, 267-68
Motoori Norinaga, 220
mujō (impermanence), 11, 13, 119, 137

Mukai Kyorai, 142-43p, 147, 248p, 265
Mumyōshō, 204, 211, 236, 253, 268, 273n1
Murakami Kijō, 170p
Murasaki Shikibu, 47-48p, 49, 216p, 269p. See also *The Tale of Genji*
Murata Harumi, 81-83p, 136
Mushanokōji Sanekage, 79, 222
musubidai (compound topics), 209
Mutamagawa, 185-86
mystery and depth. See *yūgen*

nadaraka (smooth, gentle), 242-43
nadokoro (famous places), 30, 55, 64, 130, 209, 212
"Nagai hei," 187
Nagai Kafū, 168-69p, insert 14
Nagai Tatsuo, 167
nagauta. See *chōka*
Naidaijin-ke uta-awase, 266
Naitō Jōsō, 143-44p
Nakajima Shichirō, 186
Nakao Kaishi, 203
Nanimichi hyakuin, 114
Nankai Sensei shibunshū, 198-99
Nankai. See Gion Nankai
nari, 236. See also *keikyokutei*
national studies. See *kokugaku*
Natsume Seibi, 158-59p, 162p
Natsume Sōseki, 165-66p
Natsume Sōseki nikki, 165-66
nenbutsu, 161
Nennen zuihitsu, 265
Nichisei, 117p
Nihon no chizu, 93
Nihon shoki, 17, 20, 208
Nijō school, 217, 241, 242, 250, 253, 256, 276
Nijō Tameyo, 269p
Nijō Yoshimoto, 111-12p, 206, 213, 216; on *ari no mama*, 216; on *fūga*, 225; and *honzetsu*, 232; and *keikyokutei*, 236; on *kokorozuke*, 238; on *waki*, 120; on *yariku*, 259; on *yojō*, 264
nikki, 166
Ninagawa Chiun, 2, 14, 112-13p, 175-76p, 248p, 266p
nioi (scent), 157
nioizuke, 156, 243-44, 251, 265
Nishiyama Sōin, 137, 145

Nisui, 144
Nōa, 118-19, 257p
Noguchi Zaishiki, 136-37p
Nōin, 68p, 212
Nōjun, 132-33
Notes from My Backpack. See *Oi no kobumi*
Nozarashi kikō, 162, 267
Nozawa Bonchō, 12, 146p, 147-48p
Nun Abutsu. See Abutsu

Ochi Etsujin, 140-41p
Oda Nobunaga, 74, 132
Ōe no Chisato, 229-30p
Ogura hyakunin isshu, 16, 45, 51, 52, 58, 61-62, 226
Oguri Shiyū, 143
Ogyū Sorai, Sorai, 196-97
Oi nikki, 166, 186
Oi no chiri, 160-61
Oi no kobumi, 138, 164, 225
Oi no kurigoto, 240, 251
Oi no susami, 118, 258
Okada Yasui, 140-41p
Okai Takashi, 171-72p
okashi (witty, novel), 244-45, 256
Oku no hosomichi, 132, 153, 161
Okun, 78-79p
Okunshū, 78-79
Omoidasu koto nado, 166
omokagezuke, 244. See also *nioizuke*
omomi (heaviness), 234-35. See also *karumi*
omoshiroshi, 142, 208, 263, 270. See also *omoshirotei*
omoshirotei, *omoshiroyō* (the style of cleverness), 57, 110, 234, 245-47. See also *omoshiroshi*
One Hundred Poems by One Hundred Poets. See *Ogura hyakunin isshu*
Onitsura. See Uejima Onitsura
Onitsura haiku hyakusen, 241
Ōshikōchi no Mitsune, 42-43p, 43-44p, 82, 84
Ōshima Kanrai, 159-60
Ōshima Ryōta, 159
Ōta Nanpo. See Yomo no Akara
Ōtabon Shunmusōchū. See *Shunmusōchū*
Ōtagaki Rengetsu, 87-88p
Ōtomo no Yakamochi, 26, 34, 37-38p, 38-39
overtones. See *yojō*

Ozawa Bokuseki, 136-37p
Ozawa Roan, 80-81p, 85, 145, 254p

personal anthology. See *shikashū*
Pillow Book of Sei Shōnaogon, The, 6, 102, 169, 219, 242
pillow word. See *makurakotoba*
pivots, pivot word. See *kakekotoba*
poem contest. See *uta-awase*
poems by guards of the capes. See *sakimori no uta*
Poetry Contest at Hirota Shrine. See *Hirota no yashiro no uta-awase*
Prince Katsuhito. See Go-Kashiwabara
Prince Masara, 190p
Prince Munenaga, 69-70p
Prince Shōtoku, 19-20p
Prince Sukehito, 190-91p
Princess Senseimon'in, 269
Princess Shikishi, 55-56p, 255p
Princess Uchishi, 189-90

Rai San'yō, 200-201p
Rakusho roken, 246, 250, 264
Ranpa, 118-19p
Ranshitsu, 154p
refined feeling. See *ushin*
Reizei school, 64, 217, 250, 254
Reizeike waka hihikuden, 217
renga (linked verse), 107-33 passim 2, 6, 10, 75, 82, 106-33 passim, 137, 163, 175, 203-71 passim; definitions of, 4-5, 209
Renga entokushō, 252, 227
renga kaishi, 131
Renga shotai hidenshō, 234, 255
renga-awase (renga contest), 116-17
Renri hishō, 236
Retired Emperor Fushimi. See Emperor Fushimi
Retired Emperor Go-Saga. See Emperor Go-Saga
Retired Emperor Go-Toba. See Emperor Go-Toba
Retired Emperor Juntoku. See Emperor Juntoku
reverberation. See *hibiki*
Reverend Kūdō, 241
Reverend Prince Shukaku, 229p, 263
Rika, 235p

Rikashū, 69-70
rikka, 117
Rikyū hyakushu, 75-76
rinne (repetition), 209
Rokujō Arifusa, 276n101
Rokujō eisō, 80-81, 254
Rōnyaku gojisshu uta-awase, 59-60
Roppyaku-ban uta-awase, 224, 266
ryōgin, 120, 156
Ryōjin hishō, 97-103
Ryōkan kashū, 83-84
Ryōkan, 83-84p
Ryūsui, 152-53p

sabi (lonely, forlorn), 71, 146, 149, 153, 247-49, 263, 268
Sabi shiori, 152
sabishi. See *sabi*
sabishiori. See *shiori*
sabitaru. See *sabi*
sabu. See *sabi*
sacred song. See *kagurauta*
saguridai (drawing topics), 204
saibara, 3, 208, 209
Saigō Takamori, 88
Saigyō, 54-55p, 195, 203, 211p, 212, 225, 221, 225, 226p, 247p, inserts 1 and 12
Saigyō shōnin danshō, 54, 226
Sairyūshō, 216, 273n2
Saishōsō, 243, 275n83
Sakanoue Kōshun, 142
Sakanoue ōiratsume, 37-38
sakimori no uta, 36, 209
Sakuheimon'in, 65-66p
sama (poetic style or effect), 209, 220
samuku yasetaru. See *hieyase*
sandaishū, 204
Sanetaka-kō ki, 127-28
Sangoki, 219, 250
Sanjōnishi Kin'eda, 109
Sanjōnishi Sanetaka, 75, 122-23, 127-28, 219-20, 224, 243p; and *aware*, 219-20; and *shinku/soku*, 250; and *yūgen*, 270
Sankashū, 54-55
Santai waka, 248, 261
San'yō shishō, 200-201
Sanzōshi, 147, 225, 243, 244
sarikirai (clashing), 115, 209
Sarumino, 12, 232

Sasamegoto, 60, 110, 120, 250, 270, 276nn103,104
Sassa Narimasa, 73-74p
sata (decree), 129
Satomi Ton, 167
Satomura Jōha, 109p, 131-32p, 228
scenery link. See *keikizuke*
Sei Shōnagon, 102, 242. See also *The Pillow Book of Sei Shōnagon*
Seiashō, 240, 256, 257
Seibi hokku shū, 162
Seibyō senku chū, 233, 248, 259, 275nn94,95
Seigetsu kushū, 163-64
Seihakudō Kōfū, 177-78p
Seikatsu o utau, 92-93
Sen no Rikyū, 75-76p, 225
Sen'ya, 152-53p
Senjun, 114-15p, 117-18p, 121
Senka, 141-42p
senku (thousand-verse *renga* sequence), 206, 222
senryū (comic *haikai*), 2, 5, 185-87, 209; definitions of, 5, 209, 184-87
Senryū nyūmon, 186-87
Senseimon'in. See Princess Senseimon'in
Senzaishū, 48-49, 182, 226, 242
Sesshu Tōyō, *fuga*, 128, 193, 225
Sesson Yūbai, insert 2
Setchū'an the Fourth. See ōshima Kanrai
Sha'en, 155p
shakkyōka (Buddhist poem), 48-49, 210
Sharakudō no ki, 177
shasei (sketching from life), 163, 170, 217, 249
shi (Chinese poem), 5, 192, 210. See also *kanshi*
Shibakusa, 10
Shichinin tsukeku hanshi, 126
Shihōshō, 228
shikashū (personal anthology), 210
Shikashū, 53
Shiki zenshū, 164-65
shikimoku (rules of linked verse), 4, 109, 115, 122, 128, 135, 137, 171, 206, 209, 210, 225
Shikishi Naishinnō. See Princess Shikishi
Shimada Shūji, 170-72p
Shimizu Ippyō, 162-63p
Shimomura Shunpa, 223p
Shin kokinshū, 60, 62, 125, 203, 204, 208, 212, 220, 264; poems from, 51, 54, 55, 56, 57-58, 59, 68, 73, 195, 205, 207, 211, 216, 219, 229, 241-42, 245, 250, 260, 265, 266-67, 268, 269

Shin zōdanshū, 223, 256
Shin'yōshū, 257
Shinkei hōin teikin, 260
Shinkei, 10p, 111, 114-15p, 116-17p, 119-21p, 122, 191, 226-27p, 227-28p, 236, 239p, 250-51p, 270; on *en*, 225, 227; and *heikaitei*, 226-27; on *hiekōritaru*, *hieyase*, 117, 225, 227, 228, 261; and *keiki*, 236; and *kotobazuke* and *kokorozuke*, 239-40; and *omoshiroki tei*, 110; on *shinku soku*, 250-52; on *soku*, 60; on *waki*, 120; on *yasashi*, 260; and *yasetaru tei*, 261; and *yūgen*, 270
shinkeikō, 186
shinku. *See shinku soku*
shinku soku (close and distant linking), 60, 112, 115, 120, 129, 133, 238, 249-52. *See also kokorozuke, kotobazuke*
Shinonome, 250-51
Shinpen fushōshū-a, 195-96
Shinpen fushōshū-b, 196
Shinsen kyōkashū, 177
Shinsen Tsukubashū, 122-24, 126-27
Shinsen zuinō, 208
Shinshō, 109-10
shiori (withered, bent), 252
shirabe ("tuning"), 85, 210
Shirai Chōsui, 138
Shirin shūyō, 79, 222
shisenshū, 210
Shitakusachū, 267
Shitoribe no Karamaro, 35-36p
Shogaku yōshashō, 115, 205, 226, 228
Shōhaku, 125-26p, 128, 224, 237p, *insert 5*; and *en*, 224
Shōji ninen jūgatsu tsuitachi uta-awase, 220
Shōkenkō, 193
Shoku gosenshū, 62-63
Shoku goshūishū, 269
Shokusan hyakushu, 182
Shōkyū. *See* Deki Shōkyū
Shokyūni. *See* Arii Shokyūni
Shōmyōin tsuizen senku, 109
Shōrin'an naniki hyakuin, 259
Shoshin kyūeishū, 237, 255
Shoshinshō, 205
Shōshō no Naishi, 107-8p
Shōsō, 144p
Shōtetsu, 1, 61, 70-71p, 117, 146p, 197, 250, 254, 270p; and *yojō*, 265; on *yūgen*, 270

Shōtetsu monogatari, 265, 270
Shōwa shika haiku shi, 170
shū (collection, anthology), 1, 3, 210
Shūa, 116, 217p
Shūchūka, 169
Shugen, 141-42p
shugihan, 205, 220
Shūi gusō, 241, 263
Shūi gusō shōshutsu kikigaki, 241
Shūishū, 44, 60-61, 246, 252
shūitsu (superb verse), 118, 143, 252-53. *See also jimon*
shūka, 252-53. *See also shūitsu*
Shūkei, 11p
shūku (tour de force), 252. *See also shūitsu*
Shunmusōchū, 125-26, 237
Shunpa. *See* Shimomura Shunpa
Shunzei. *See* Fujiwara no Shunzei
Shunzei's Daughter, 262p
Sino-Japanese linked verse. *See wakan renku*
Sōanshū, 12
Sōboku. *See* Tani Sōboku
Sōchō, 72, 103, 121, 122, 126-27, 177, 219-20p, 267, 224-25p, 267, *insert 5*
Sōchō hyakuban renga-awase, 219, 224
Sodō. *See* Yamaguchi Sodō
Sōgi, 71-73, 106, 113, 115, 117, 121-22p, 122p, 125, 126-27, 128, 129p, 160, 177, 193, 225, 238p, 251p, 267p, *insert 5*; on *ari no mama*, 216; on *hiesabitaru*, 228; and *hokku*, 120-21; on *jimon*, 234; on *kokorozuke*, 238; on *soku*, 250-51; and *taketakashi*, 118; and *ushin*, 118, 257-58; and *yariku*, 259; and *yūgen*, 118, 270
Sōgi jisankachū, 216
Sōgi shūenki, 71-73
Sōi. *See* Sugihara Sōi
Sōjinbon wakuraba. *See Wakuraba*
Sōjun, 118-19
Sōkan. *See* Yamazaki Sōkan
Sōkonshū, 70-71, 269-70
soku. *See shinku/soku*
Son'an Reigen, 194-95
"Song of Everlasting Sorrow, The." *See* "Chang hen ge"
Song Yu, 189
Soraishū, 196-97p
Sōsaku nōto, 169. *See also* Nagai Kafū
Sosei, 46p

Sōseki. *See* Natsume Sōseki
sōshō, 171
Sōzei. *See* Takayama Sōzei
stylized epithet. *See makurakotoba*
Suganami Tokinori. *See* Kan Chazan
sugata (total effect or configuration), 54, 210, 242, 244. *See also sama*
Sugawara no Michizane, 132
Sugihara Katamori. *See* Sugihara Sōi
Sugihara Sōi, 120-21
Sugino Suikei, 156p
Sugita Tankō, 138-39p
Sugiyama Sanpū, 141-42p
Sujū. *See* Takano Sujū
Sukehito Shinnō. *See* Prince Sukehito
Suketomo. *See* Hino Suketomo
Sumika o utsusu kotoba, 158

Tachibana Akemi, 86-87p, 224, 240
Tachibana Nankei, 80
tadagotouta (poems in colloquial style), 253-54
tadakotoba (everyday language), 81, 253
Tagami Kikusha, 160-61p
tai. *See tei*
taigendome, 58
Taigi kusen, 8
Taikenmon'in Horikawa, 164-65p
Taikenmon'in Horikawa shū, 164
Taikōki, 73-74
Taira no Kanemori, 246p
Taira no Narifusa, 99
Takahama Kyoshi, 170, 217-18p
Takahashi no Mushimaro, 31-33p
Takahashi Riichi, 267
Takai Kitō, 154, 223p, 256, 258
Takano Kimihiko, 170-72p
Takano Sujū, 170p
Takarai Kikaku, 256p, 261p
Takasunagoshū, 241
Takayama Sōzei, 113-14p, 114-15p, 118, 121, 235; and *keiki,* 236; and *miru tei,* 242; and *tadakoba,* 253-54p
Takeno Jōō, 75
taketakashi, taketakakiyō (the grand or lofty style), 55, 60, 118, 142, 211, 215, 254-56, 263, 270
Tale of Genji, The. *See Genji monogatari*
Tales of the Heike, 18
Tamatsukuribe no Hirome, 36p

Tamekane-kyō wakashō, 240
Tamekane. *See* Kyōgoku Tamekane
Tamenori. *See* Kyōgoku Tamenori
Tan Taigi, 8p
tandai. *See saguridai*
Tanganshi. *See* Tōdō Sengin
Tani Sōboku, 128-29p, 218p, 230p, 231, 264p, 264
tanka, 3, 92-93, 170, 211
Tanka kenkyū, 171
Tanzaku (poem strip), 87
Tao Yuanming, 145
Taorigiku, 161
Taueuta (rice-planting songs), 3, 208
tei (style or mood), 211
Teijiin Emperor. *See* Emperor Uda
Teijiin uta-awase, 44-45
Teika. *See* Fujiwara no Teika
Teika jittei, 45-46, 52, 55, 62, 219, 241
Ten-Foot-Square Hut, The, 10
tenchi ninjō, 139
tendō, 126
Teramura Hyakuchi, 245p
Tō no Tsuneyori, 146
Tōbun, 139p
Tōdō Sengin, 138
Tokodokoro hentō, 111, 227
Tokoyoda Chōsui, 157-58p
Tokugawa Muneharu, 79
Tokuwaka gomanzaishū, 182-83
Tomotsune, 52-53p
Tonna, 63, 67-68p, 79p, 160, 222p, 246p, 270p; and *dai,* 11-12, 221-22; and *heikaitei,* 226; on *jimon,* 234; and *makoto,* 240; and *ushin,* 256-57
Tonna hōshi ei, 67-68, 79, 222
topic. *See dai*
torimonouta (presentation song), 96
Tosa nikki, 64-65
Tōsei. *See* Matsuo Bashō
Tōyashū kikigaki, 146, 226
Toyoshima Itchō, 136-37p
Toyotomi Hideyoshi, 74, 130
tōza, 68, 212. *See tōza no uta*
tōza no dai, 207. *See tōza no uta*
tōza no uta (extemporaneous *waka*), 68, 204, 211
Tsuboi Tokoku, 249
Tsuginohara, 225

Tsukamoto Kunio, 171
tsukeai (link, linking), 112, 211
Tsukeai tebikizuru, 258–59
tsukeku (link or linked couplet), 4–5, 10, 107–10 passim, 112–22 passim, 131–33, 136–43 passim, 170–72
tsukeyō. See tsukeai
tsukinamikai (monthly meeting), 70, 154, 211
Tsukuba mondō, 225
Tsukubashū, 107, 108, 109, 111, 255
tsuraneuta (linked verses), 4. *See also renga*
Tsurezuregusa, 221

Uchida Hyakken, 186–87p
uchikoshi o kirau, 209
Uchishi. *See* Princess Uchishi
Uda no hōshi, 234, 237, 252
Ueda Akinari, 78
Uejima Onitsura, 144–45p, 241p, 260; and *makoto*, 240–41; on *yariku*, 259–60
ukiuta, 95–96
umon no tei. See jimon
Unaimatsu, 7, 76–77p
Unsui Seigetsu. *See* Inoue Seigetsu
uruwashi (beautiful), 54
ushin, ushintei (the style of deep feeling), 52, 58, 69, 80, 118, 122, 211, 215, 256–59, 263
uta: definitions of, 2–4, 212; and *waka*, 2
uta dai (*waka* topics), 223
Uta nikki, 89–92. *See also* Mori Ōgai
uta-awase (poem contest), 43–45, 52–53, 129, 212, 262
Utagawa Hiroshige, 174
utamakura ("pillows for poems"), 30, 212, 234
utsurizuke, 244. *See also nioizuke*

Vimalakirti Sutra, 49

waka (short poem), 5, 19–93 passim, 203–13 passim; and *uta*, 2; definitions of, 1–6, 204
Waka kuhon, 263
Waka teikin, 63
Wakamiya senka-awase han no kotoba, 57
wakan renku (Sino-Japanese linked verse), 118–19
Wakan rōeishū, 50–51, 121, 183, 188, 194, 263–64

Wakayamatobe no Mimaro, 36p
waki (second verse of a linked-verse sequence), 120, 128, 212
Wakuraba, 121–22, 129
Wasuregusa, 258
Watanabe Junzō, 92–93p
Wife of Yoshimasa, 13

Yahantei. *See* Takai Kitō
Yahantei tsukinami hokku awase, 155, 223
Yakumo mishō, 215
Yamabe no Akahito, 3
Yamaguchi Sodō, 140–41
yamai (poetic fault), 45, 205, 213
Yamamoto Kakei, 138, 139p
Yamanoue no Okura, 25–26p
Yamato Takeru, 18–19
yamatoe, 41
yamatouta (Japanese poem), 2, 213. *See also uta, waka*
Yamazaki Sōkan, 176–77p
Yanagidaru, 185–86
Yang Guifei, 41–42
yariku, 140, 156, 213, 259–60
yasashi (gentle, graceful), 208, 260–61
yasetarutei (the spare or sere style), 261. *See also hieyase*
Yashima Shōrin'an naniki hyakuin, 259
Yasomura Rotsū, 232p
yasuraka, 141
yasushi, 157
yō, 211. *See also tei*
Yodo no watari, 125, 238, 259
yōen, yōenbi (ethereal charm), 58, 261–63
yojō (overtones), 63, 129, 142, 155, 204, 230, 238, 255, 263–66
Yomo no Akara, 181–82p, 183
yoriai (conventional associations), 115, 118, 211, 213
yoriai no bungei, 213
yoriaizuke, 266
Yosa Buson, 134, 150p, 151p, 152, 154, 163, 199, 238, insert 9; and *aware*, 220; and *okashi*, 245
yosei. See yojō
Yoshiya Nobuko, 167–68p
Yoshiya Nobuku nikki, 166–68
Yōsui, 239p
yū, yūbi (polished, refined), 53, 225, 256, 266–68

Yuan Zhen, 121p
yūen, 155
yūgen, yūgentei (the style of mystery and depth), 46, 62, 110, 118, 142, 155, 182, 211, 247, 249, 255, 263, 268-71
Yuki no keburi, 112

za (poetry venue), 126, 143, 154, 210, 213, 260
zadankai (roundtable discussion), 171-72
Zaishiki. *See* Noguchi Zaishiki

zappai (parodic *haikai*), 185-86, 209. *See also senryū*
Zekkai Chūshin, 193-94
Zhang Du, 263-64p
Zhuangzi, 119, 194
Zōho Rengetsu zenshū, 87-88
Zōki, 47p
Zoku Sarumino, 148, 252
Zoku Sōanshū, 270
Zōshun, 118-19p
zōtōka (poem exchange), 48, 213

CPSIA information can be obtained
at www.ICGtesting.com
Printed in the USA
LVHW110714110320
649645LV00006B/8